The Manufacture of Consent

RHETORIC AND PUBLIC AFFAIRS SERIES

- *Eisenhower's War of Words: Rhetoric and Leadership*, Martin J. Medhurst, editor
- *The Nuclear Freeze Campaign: Rhetoric and Foreign Policy in the Telepolitical Age*, J. Michael Hogan
- *Mansfield and Vietnam: A Study in Rhetorical Adaptation*, Gregory A. Olson
- *Truman and the Hiroshima Cult*, Robert P. Newman
- *Post-Realism: The Rhetorical Turn in International Relations*, Francis A. Beer and Robert Hariman, editors
- *Rhetoric and Political Culture in Nineteenth-Century America*, Thomas W. Benson, editor
- *Frederick Douglass: Freedom's Voice, 1818–1845*, Gregory P. Lampe
- *Angelina Grimké: Rhetoric, Identity, and the Radical Imagination*, Stephen Howard Browne
- *Strategic Deception: Rhetoric, Science, and Politics in Missile Defense Advocacy*, Gordon R. Mitchell
- *Rostow, Kennedy, and the Rhetoric of Foreign Aid*, Kimber Charles Pearce
- *Visions of Poverty: Welfare Policy and Political Imagination*, Robert Asen
- *General Eisenhower: Ideology and Discourse*, Ira Chernus
- *The Reconstruction Desegregation Debate: The Politics of Equality and the Rhetoric of Place, 1870–1875*, Kirt H. Wilson
- *Shared Land/Conflicting Identity: Trajectories of Israeli and Palestinian Symbol Use*, Robert C. Rowland and David A. Frank
- *Darwinism, Design, and Public Education*, John Angus Campbell and Stephen C. Meyer, editors
- *Religious Expression and the American Constitution*, Franklyn S. Haiman
- *Christianity and the Mass Media in America: Toward a Democratic Accommodation*, Quentin J. Schultze
- *Bending Spines: The Propagandas of Nazi Germany and the German Democratic Republic*, Randall L. Bytwerk
- *Malcolm X: Inventing Radical Judgment*, Robert E. Terrill
- *Metaphorical World Politics*, Francis A. Beer and Christ'l De Landtsheer, editors
- *The Lyceum and Public Culture in the Nineteenth-Century United States*, Angela G. Ray
- *The Political Style of Conspiracy: Chase, Sumner, and Lincoln*, Michael William Pfau
- *The Character of Justice: Rhetoric, Law, and Politics in the Supreme Court Confirmation Process*, Trevor Parry-Giles
- *Rhetorical Vectors of Memory in National and International Holocaust Trials*, Marouf A. Hasian Jr.
- *Judging the Supreme Court: Constructions of Motives in* Bush v. Gore, Clarke Rountree
- *Everyday Subversion: From Joking to Revolting in the German Democratic Republic*, Kerry Kathleen Riley
- *In the Wake of Violence: Image and Social Reform*, Cheryl R. Jorgensen-Earp
- *Rhetoric and Democracy: Pedagogical and Political Practices*, Todd F. McDorman and David M. Timmerman, editors
- *Invoking the Invisible Hand: Social Security and the Privatization Debates*, Robert Asen
- *With Faith in the Works of Words: The Beginnings of Reconciliation in South Africa, 1985–1995*, Erik Doxtader
- *Public Address and Moral Judgment: Critical Studies in Ethical Tensions*, Shawn J. Parry-Giles and Trevor Parry-Giles, editors
- *Executing Democracy: Capital Punishment and the Making of America, 1683–1807*, Stephen John Hartnett
- *Enemyship: Democracy and Counter-Revolution in the Early Republic*, Jeremy Engels
- *Spirits of the Cold War: Contesting Worldviews in the Classical Age of American Security Strategy*, Ned O'Gorman
- *Making the Case: Advocacy and Judgment in Public Argument*, Kathryn M. Olson, Michael William Pfau, Benjamin Ponder, and Kirt H. Wilson, editors
- *Executing Democracy: Capital Punishment and the Making of America, 1835–1843*, Stephen John Hartnett
- *William James and the Art of Popular Statement*, Paul Stob
- *On the Frontier of Science: An American Rhetoric of Exploration and Exploitation*, Leah Ceccarelli
- *The Good Neighbor: Franklin D. Roosevelt and the Rhetoric of American Power*, Mary E. Stuckey
- *Creating Conservatism: Postwar Words That Made an American Movement*, Michael J. Lee
- *Intertextuality and the 24-Hour News Cycle: A Day in the Rhetorical Life of Colin Powell's U.N. Address*, John Oddo
- *Superchurch: The Rhetoric and Politics of American Fundamentalism*, Jonathan J. Edwards
- *Rethinking Rhetorical Theory, Criticism, and Pedagogy: The Living Art of Michael C. Leff*, Antonio de Velasco, John Angus Campbell, and David Henry, editors
- *Imagining China: Rhetorics of Nationalism in an Age of Globalization*, Stephen J. Hartnett, Lisa B. Keränen, and Donovan Conley, editors
- *Political Vocabularies: FDR, the Clergy Letters, and the Elements of Political Argument*, Mary E. Stuckey
- *To Become an American: Immigrants and Americanization Campaigns of the Early Twentieth Century*, Leslie A. Hahner
- *The Rhetorical Invention of Diversity: Supreme Court Opinions, Public Argument, and Affirmative Action*, M. Kelly Carr
- *Michael Osborn on Metaphor and Style*, Michael Osborn
- *Debating Women: Gender, Education, and Spaces for Argument, 1835–1945*, Carly S. Woods
- *Strains of Dissent: Popular Music and Everyday Resistance in WWII France, 1940–1945*, Kelly Jakes
- *John F. Kennedy and the Liberal Persuasion*, John M. Murphy
- *National Rhetorics in the Syrian Immigration Crisis: Victims, Frauds, and Floods*, Clarke Rountree and Jouni Tilli, editors
- *The Manufacture of Consent: J. Edgar Hoover and the Rhetorical Rise of the FBI*, Stephen M. Underhill

The Manufacture of Consent

J. Edgar Hoover and the Rhetorical Rise of the FBI

Stephen M. Underhill

Michigan State University Press | *East Lansing*

Michigan State University Press
East Lansing, Michigan 48823-5245

Printed and bound in the United States of America.

29 28 27 26 25 24 23 22 21 20 1 2 3 4 5 6 7 8 9 10

LIBRARY OF CONGRESS CATALOGING-IN-PUBLICATION DATA
Names: Underhill, Stephen M., author.
Title: The manufacture of consent : J. Edgar Hoover and the rhetorical rise of the FBI / Stephen M. Underhill.
Description: East Lansing : Michigan State University Press, [2020]
| Series: Rhetoric and public affairs series | Includes bibliographical references and index.
Identifiers: LCCN 2019012805| ISBN 9781611863468 (pbk. : alk. paper) | ISBN 9781609176211 (pdf)
| ISBN 9781628953831 (epub) | ISBN 9781628963847 (mobi/prc)
Subjects: LCSH: United States. Federal Bureau of Investigation—History. | Hoover, J. Edgar (John Edgar), 1895–1972—Language. | Rhetoric—Political aspects—United States.
| United States—Politics and government—1933–1945.
Classification: LCC HV8144.F43 U53 2020
| DDC 363.250973—dc23 LC record available at https://lccn.loc.gov/2019012805

Book design by Charlie Sharp, Sharp DesIgns, East Lansing, MI
Cover design by Erin Kirk New
Cover photo: J. Edgar Hoover delivers a message during "This is Your FBI," at Station WMAL, Washington, D.C., April 6, 1945. National Archives and Records Administration.

"The degree of civilization in a society is revealed by entering its prisons."
—FYODOR DOSTOYEVSKY

This book is dedicated to victims of police violence, prison abuse, and judicial indifference.

Contents

Preface

The Manufacture of Consent: J. Edgar Hoover and the Rhetorical Rise of the FBI explores the Federal Bureau of Investigation (FBI) director's domestic propaganda as well as the institution that he scripted. Accordingly, I examine the following five sets of considerations in this book. First, drawing upon Hoover's use of Anglo-American nationalism to promote the FBI, I investigate how he constituted his leadership and public life in terms of the urban-crime film genre before the New Deal challenged Jim Crow in Franklin D. Roosevelt's second term, and then in the rhetoric of film noir afterward. I focus on how the FBI used the frontier myth to transfer the logic of G-man films to the wartime then Cold War landscapes. Nascent neoliberal critique of the New Deal was mimicked and embedded in Hoover's discourse and the cultural reflex to appraise the present in terms of the past. The move to resuscitate "old" liberalism with a new philosophy on individualism and the state had implications for American law enforcement, an institution underpinned by the same confluence of ideology that was expressed by the rhetorics of political idealism and realism. Anticommunists exploited interpretations of nascent neoliberal texts in ways that both elevated and exploited them, brewing a toxic philosophy for the Cold War era. Conniving critics of the New Deal saw in neoliberalism a disinterested, scientific disguise that masked their intent to roll back FDR's liberal agenda and his workforce.

Second, the move to refashion reality to the contours of the past constrained Hoover's identity and limited the type of leader he could be. While he and Associate Director Clyde Tolson attempted to hide their romantic love from public view, Hoover billed himself as a straight white Anglo-Saxon Protestant man who was intolerant of gays and all proclivities deemed sinful by fundamentalist standards. I examine how his team reinvented him as a heterosexual, red-blooded folk hero, grounded in the rhetoric of Americanism. In particular, I focus on how the FBI's public relations team identified Hoover, the FBI, the nation, the American citizen, and the cosmos. These emphases point towards an attempt by the FBI to remake the social world so that more Americans would continually embrace his coercive practices. The leader that Hoover ultimately became, I argue, was a product of the rhetoric he chose to engage, which cemented him as a hard-line warrior with no room for flexibility, a plight that made him radical and subversive, locked in a paranoid closet of his own design.

Third, Hoover's rhetorical leadership was situated in a historical complex of problems that faced the New Deal. The U.S. president and the FBI director needed the citizenry to support new and expanded federal powers, and stories that heroically situated the government in Hollywood storylines was a boon for both leaders. As the New Deal increasingly threatened the ideals of Anglo-American nationalism, however, the president and the director were increasingly divided by ideology. Their dynamic relationship raises questions about the rhetorical presidency. For instance, I explore how FDR mistakenly used FBI rhetoric on urban crime to justify expanded federal powers, and how Hoover grounded his own protracted authority in Roosevelt's discourse to present himself as an agent of the president. While the rhetoric of Americanism did constrain Hoover between his public and private personae, it was also a deft resource to simultaneously signify loyalty to the presidency and realign the FBI with Roosevelt's and then Harry S. Truman's opponents. More than Hoover, Americanism first and foremost constrained the rhetoric of these presidents.

Fourth, nascent American neoliberalism was contemporaneous with the advent of the "red fascism" analogy. The timing was helpful for conservatives who appreciated the neoliberal critique of the New Deal as well as a means to blend different visions of centralized government into a more unified image of totalitarianism. While Friedrich Hayek's *The Road to Serfdom* (1944) was already realist with its missives against political idealism, I examine how anticommunists shaded how Americans interpreted it, and how the FBI exploited continuity between those interpretations and Hoover's brand of realism in ways that Adolf Hitler's Nazism and Joseph Stalin's Communism could be equated to Roosevelt's social democracy. I focus on how the FBI's culture work in issues of race, religion, sex, class, and gender helped embolden a perspective that equated civil rights with tyranny.

Fifth, the textual dimensions of the FBI's institutionality reveals a government agency that broke from the constitutional order that justified its existence—a move that traded cultural hierarchy for democratic legitimacy as the basis of its power. FBI propagandists substituted frames of governance between New Deal Keynesian social democracy and Cold War political realism, and remodeled the FBI with help from Nazi police officials in secret and in defiance of the Roosevelt administration. At stake for Hoover was the New Dealers' vision for federal law enforcement that had little room for him or the FBI, versus his preferred vision that located the bureau at the center of public life with him in charge for decades to come. Hoover shared his frame with anti-Semitic members of Congress—Republicans and Southern Democrats—who viewed the New Deal as a Jewish takeover of the government. Together, they conspired against the New Deal presidents in ways that left lasting imprints on the Republican Party. I focus on how Hoover and his team manipulated federal authority with rhetorical realism and legitimized hard-line anticommunist practices in all levels and branches of government. I investigate him as a representative of his institution and examine how he created and sustained a culture suited for his leadership style, persona, and practices. I therefore engage an institutional critique and map Hoover's containment rhetoric—rhetoric rich with boundaries and divided spaces good for structuring public life.

I turn to archival research to address these considerations. This public-address study relies upon primary documents to better understand the relationship between discourse and power in institutions. I read through J. Edgar Hoover's childhood diaries as well as his public papers to inform a broader perspective of the motives and collusions of power that were instrumental to his rhetorical agency. Ronald H. Carpenter suggests that such archival research helps "explain what happened as a prelude to discourse [and] choices during rhetors' creative processes."[1] Davis W. Houck notes that it grounds "probable claims about rhetorical strategies and tactics . . . in more certain evidences."[2] James J. Kimble adds that an "archival investigation into the behind-the-scenes creation of a propaganda message is a potent means of producing useful insights about that message and its ultimate public appearance." He concludes that "rhetorical and public address scholars have much to bring to the critical table. As researchers trained to investigate the interplay of both text and context, such scholars are equipped far better than many in other disciplines to grapple with propaganda in action."[3] Accordingly, I turn to speeches, films, radio programs, books, and comic books as well as scholarly journal, newspaper, and magazine articles written by FBI personnel to inform the cultural and institutional contexts in which the director and his FBI operated. Further, I use internal memoranda and other records created by the White House, Department of Justice, and FBI to better explicate Hoover's varied texts. In moving between texts and contexts, this research also engages the director's rhetorical biography. It pulls from his private life to inform his public leadership of the FBI. Therefore, I attend to the behind-the-scenes strategies that accompanied the public discourses of Director Hoover and Presidents

Roosevelt and Truman, as well as to the rhetoric that Hoover imported from his childhood in the Progressive Era. A critic's ability to make sense of anachronistic symbolism is enhanced, I contend, by such stratified contexts.

Moreover, I make sense of how he navigated these contexts with rhetorical theories on myth. Leroy G. Dorsey and Rachel M. Harlow observe that a "myth captures its audience's attention and influences its thinking with three basic elements: the universe, the protagonist, and the narrative." The universe is the backdrop for the story and is culturally encoded with motivations for action. The protagonist is an archetypal character that has been represented many times in many different stories across genres and thereby signifies the values and beliefs of a particular culture. The history of her conflicts in the universe suggest the type of agency required for a culture's survival in the real world. And, the narrative "describes the relationship between the protagonist and the universe, establishing the 'laws of cause and effect, of natural process, and of morality' within which the protagonist acts." Combined, myths "constitute a powerful epistemological rhetoric that offers compelling explanations for the community's development of fundamental concepts such as identity, morality, religion and law."[4] The persuasive power of myth resides in metaphor and analogy. After many retellings, story elements become abstracted and are eventually reduced to icons, keywords, symbols, or clichés. As such, they circulate in public discourse as metaphors in which historical situations are constructed in mythic terms. Audiences are invited to infer similarities in relationships between speaker/protagonist and situation/universe through how the narrative is told, which transfers the rules, logics, and morality of make-believe into history.[5]

The frontier myth, I argue, helped order the rise of neoliberalism, rhetorical realism, and Americanism. Studying Hoover's rhetoric, therefore, is a way for critics to examine a cultural current that misleadingly presents itself as uninterrupted from the Puritan arrival through the Cold War. It is a discourse that naturalizes a political reality that insists that it is natural and historically stable. This illusion was made possible by how deeply saturated the myth had become in U.S. culture, and by how Hoover and other FBI executives used their control over mass media to remake him in the image of the Western hero to discredit other cultural traditions that they displaced.

I argue that rhetorical realism helped the FBI conflate nationalism and national security. Though he sounded scientifically disinterested and appropriately loyal to the president, more particular meanings were activated in conservative audiences that shared what he presumed about racial, religious, sexual, gender, and class hierarchies, structures that were supposed to be violently enforced. Liberals had their own meanings of both "science" and "Americanism." What passed as neutral and patriotic discourse to them bolstered the president's critics. This discursive strategy helps explain how and why FDR could trust and empower a confidant who conspired against him, who subverted the New Deal, and executed what is arguably the most culturally significant, documented political conspiracy in U.S. history, a wholesale domestic propaganda program that incited the Second Red Scare, brainwashed Americans, and manufactured their consent to tyranny.

Acknowledgments

This book was published with generous support from many people and institutions. First, Shawn J. Parry-Giles taught a seminar on the Cold War rhetorical presidency when I arrived in the Department of Communication at the University of Maryland, College Park as a PhD student in fall 2005, in part because I mentioned an interest in the subject area when I applied to the Rhetoric and Political Culture program. From before I was even her student, therefore, Shawn opened a world of possibilities to me and ignited my interest in public address, especially as it relates to the Cold War. As a teacher, mentor, and scholar, Dr. Parry-Giles taught me to think critically about discourse and how to map its origins and significance. Her course sent me to the National Archives and Records Administration (NARA) in College Park, which happened to have J. Edgar Hoover's Official and Confidential files on display. I used those records to write a term paper that evolved into this book. She worked indefatigably on my research and writing practices, and I hope this book does her investment justice.

The fieldtrip to NARA led me to student employment there, where I worked in the reference section and was responsible for declassified FBI and DOJ textual records from 2007 to 2012. I was working in these related capacities—between the rhetorical presidency and Hoover's records—when Classification 94 arrived from the FBI, "Research Matters," a vast trove of records that document his domestic propaganda and betrayal of the New Deal. Therefore, I will forever be grateful for the research assistance I received at NARA. Steven Tilley, James Mathis, Rick Peuser, Tim Nenninger, David Langbart, Tab Lewis, David Pfeiffer, Joe Schwartz, Christine Jones, Gene Morris, and Elizabeth Gray taught me the federal bureaucracy's history through its primary documents and trained me to think like an archivist. Their assistance was further amplified by help from the U.S. Government Information, Maps, and GIS Services in the University of Maryland Libraries. The staff spent countless hours searching the *Congressional Record* and teaching me its arrangement. Still further, I was helped by university librarians who retrieved hundreds of texts that proved central to the project. And, the University of Maryland's Summer Research Fellowship helped underwrite the out-of-pocket expenses. Thank you all for the access, expertise, and generous support you lent an eager student. College Park was a dynamic place to study rhetoric, and its institutions structured how this book developed.

The Department of Communication introduced me to faculty and peers who modeled productivity and excellence. Thank you to James F. Klumpp, Trevor Parry-Giles, and Kathleen E. Kendall who also provided direction on the project. They pressed me to consider the fuller implications of Hoover's figurative language and to imagine the book in terms of a rhetorical biography. Both suggestions proved fruitful and matured the project. Likewise, my peers at UMD were generous with both their time and knowledge. I appreciate the feedback and support I received through the years. Thank you especially to Timothy Barney and Tiffany Lewis for your feedback on the project. Also, I will always value my friendship with Fr. Kyle Ingels of the Catholic Student Center at UMD, who generously shared his wealth of knowledge on Church history in Washington, DC. I had rich times with all of you.

The book project was carried forward at Marshall University. Thank you to Dean R.B. Bookwalter of the College of Liberal Arts and to chair Cam Brammer of the Department of Communication Studies, who generously supported research and conference travel. Additionally, thank you to the staff of Marshall University Libraries who searched for and retrieved many more texts, and the staff of the Government Documents department who helped me search and digitize the *Congressional Record*—a repository of J. Edgar Hoover's many speeches. I also appreciate my opportunity to work with outstanding graduate students who helped in a variety of ways: Nicholas Prephan, Victoria Ledford, Zach Bailey, Gates Campbell, and Erin Jorden. And thank you to Mark Smith for listening and giving me feedback.

Further, a special thank you to the intellectual community that lent its time and resources to this project. As the communication discipline grapples with issues of race, class, gender, sex, and sexuality in society and within its own institutions, I thank the many scholars who challenge the Anglo-American mold, whose contributions made this work possible, and who frequently go unrecognized. Thank you to Mary Stuckey, Charles E. Morris III, and Ned O'Gorman for help with the cover. And again to Morris, thank you for your seminal work on Hoover's passing performance in the *Quarterly Journal of Speech*, "Pink Herring and the Fourth Persona: J. Edgar Hoover's Sex Crime Panic." If not for that article, my work would have suffered. In 2008, he and Stuckey also lent their generous feedback to this research at the National Communication Association's Doctoral Honors Seminar. Martin J. Medhurst and the anonymous reviewers at *Rhetoric & Public Affairs* elevated the quality of the book manuscript and its precursor, the article "Prisoner of Context: The Truman Doctrine Speech and J. Edgar Hoover's Rhetorical Realism." Thank you also to Anastasia Wraight, Elise Jajuga, Catherine Cocks, and Julie Reaume at MSU Press, who packaged and promoted the project. Moreover, as a former reference specialist, I want to acknowledge the many archivists, librarians, and records managers who hunted and duplicated documents near and far, sometimes with vague descriptions. I appreciate the help I received from staffs at the Library of Congress, National Archives at College Park, Center for Legislative Archives, Franklin D. Roosevelt Presidential Library, Harry S. Truman Presidential Library, Richard M. Nixon Presidential Library, FBI Office of Public Affairs, FBI Information Management Division, National Law Enforcement Museum, Scottish Rite of Freemasonry House of the Temple in Washington, DC, Indiana State Library, Johns Hopkins Sheridan Libraries, Maryland Historical Society, Special Collections at the University of Maryland, University of Minnesota Archives, and the Albert and Shirley Small Special Collections Library at the University of Virginia. Without their help, this project would have stalled.

When I look back, I see clearly that this book is also the product of personal relationships that span my lifetime. I will forever be grateful to my in-laws for their generous patience and support. Steve, Julie, and David Cornelius—thank you for the many ways you helped me through the journey. I am grateful for my parents, Ron and Phyllis, for teaching me to chase dreams and mysteries wherever they lead, and the encouragement of my brothers, Mark, Greg, Brian, and Joey, who chased them with me. Our years of debate compelled me to find what I was looking for in research, to find answers to questions we spent years asking each other. Some of these questions were rooted in our family history. My great aunt was blacklisted in the 1950s for traveling to Moscow. Born to Central European immigrants, she visited the USSR at a time when she encouraged nieces and nephews to learn Russian. She soon lost her job as a nurse and became unemployable for over a decade. I long wondered what she did to warrant such trouble. I got my answer in 2017 after waiting five years for her FBI file, my longest Freedom of Information Act (FOIA) request by far. The FBI informed the CIA and the State Department in August 1957 that no "subversive or derogatory information" was contained in her file. She was merely a ruggedly independent Catholic woman with immigrant parents who seemed foreign to her investigators. For this offense, she was punished. Her story captured my imagination and my interest in public life. So, I am very thankful to my family, who fostered my interest in power and authority.

Different phases of the project came with unique resources and challenges, and the final leg was exhausting. My son's arrival in 2013 pressed me forward when I was tired. Riley kept me company and listened and listened and listened to me talk out the project at its most difficult juncture. My time with him over those years was a respite from the busy world around that too frequently stole my attention. Thank you, Riley, for your patience, brilliance, laughter, invention, motivation, and boundless love and energy; I needed all of it. And, to Riley's teachers at Bright Futures Learning Services who became family—Jill Scarbro-McLaury, Teri Leffler, Michael Leffler, Cindy LeGrand, Sara Parker, Taylor Wade, Emily Bock, and Shanna Tucker—you were vital; thank you.

My deepest gratitude goes to Jill C. Underhill, a friend from UMD whom I married. She was there at the beginning in fall 2005 and helped me weigh the value of studying domestic propaganda, always a risky venture. She joined me as a student employee at NARA, where she wandered the stacks, looking for records that might be of help. (She claims to have come across the X-Files, but I could never find them.) In spring 2008, Jill traveled to New York with me to visit the FDR Library. This trip stands out because it was there that the complexity and sheer labor of the project became clear, and Jill formulated a way to manage it. And, it was Jill who kept watch over new literature that might inform the project while I juggled older works and archival documents. She brought to my attention Ira Katznelson's *Fear Itself: The New Deal and the Origins of Our Time* (2013) and John McCumber's *The Philosophy Scare: The Politics of Reason in the Early Cold War* (2016), two works that made this book possible. Every link, every idea, every argument was bounced off of Jill, who also taught extra classes to help finance research expenses. She filed FOIA requests, located and retrieved remote FBI files on microfilm, edited previous drafts of the text, and helped with layout. Thank you for your strategic planning, encouragement, patience, and overall support. You enabled and coauthored this book; you carried me across the finish line. My gratitude is ineffable. As J. Edgar Hoover once wrote to Clyde

Tolson, "Words are mere man-given symbols for thoughts and feelings, and they are grossly insufficient to express the thoughts in my mind and the feelings in my heart that I have for you. But I did want you to know that I realize and appreciate full well the decided influence you have exerted over the [project] during the past fifteen years," which consumed my time and attention. I shared this memo with her hours after I found it. Jill thought it would make for a good book.

Introduction

In March 1947, President Harry S. Truman and Federal Bureau of Investigation (FBI) Director J. Edgar Hoover both delivered the most significant foreign-policy speeches of their careers. The president delivered the Truman Doctrine speech before both houses of Congress. He warned of such threats facing Greece and Turkey as "subjugation by armed minorities" and "such subterfuges as political infiltration," and thereby built support for their defense. Hoover also appeared before Congress. He reported only two weeks later to the House Un-American Activities Committee (HUAC) that Soviet belligerence had spread to the United States. Not only did their warnings share proximity in time and place, but they also shared a style that relied upon biological imagery. Truman professed that the "seeds of totalitarian regimes are nurtured by misery and want. They spread and grow in the evil soil of poverty and strife. They reach their full growth when the hopes of a people for a better life has died."[1] Hoover's speech was similarly ornamental. He observed to HUAC that Soviet Communism was a "way of life—an evil and malignant way of life. It reveals a condition akin to disease that spreads like an epidemic." Truman's and Hoover's speeches, however, diverged where they proposed solutions. Whereas Truman requested congressional approval to aid the beleaguered nations, Hoover called upon jingoism to forestall Soviet influence in American public life. He proclaimed that the "best anecdote to Communism is vigorous, intelligent, old-fashioned Americanism with eternal vigilance."[2] The president did not coordinate his discourse with his FBI director. What unified their style was a rhetorical tradition invented by Anglo-American Protestants in the Progressive Era to help imagine the problems of, and solutions to, mass urbanization, industrialization, and immigration. Unlike Truman, Hoover intentionally deployed the style in an effort to restructure American ideology in terms of the past, and from that build influence.

Rhetoricians can look to Hoover's years with the FBI as a case study on power. Toward the end of his career, the *New York Times* estimated that he "wielded more power longer than any man in American history."[3] The source of his strength has been associated with his covert and illegal spy system that allowed him to accumulate files on many Americans and blackmail them. As *Time* magazine suggested in 1975, Hoover's ability to "acquire and keep that kind of power raises disturbing questions not merely about the role of a national police in a democracy, but also about the political system that tolerated him for so long."[4] Indeed, his authority rested on the values that he shared with millions of other Americans. While some loathed how Hoover maintained law and order, many more identified with his firm commitment to an idealized past that he forcefully defended. The systems that endured him for so long must, therefore, be studied along with the political leader to understand how he could be both tyrant and hero.

Biographers and historians have worked to define Hoover's power. Curt Gentry observes, for example, that Hoover made himself believe that his files were the "source of his power," which was a "myth he'd personally fostered over the years." Even Hoover, Gentry contends, "knew quite well that they were only one of its sources, and quite possibly not even the most important."[5] Richard Gid Powers takes a linguistic turn and suggests that "public identification with the FBI had been the source of Hoover's political and cultural power" in the 1930s.[6] He expands upon this argument in other projects and claims that Hoover learned the political realities of twentieth-century life before he became FBI director in 1924. In particular, he learned that his "survival depended ultimately on public support, which could be translated into political protection in the administration and on the Hill." Hoover's rhetorical rise, therefore, was rooted in his ability to promote his own prestige, and to protect his reputation and that of the institution that he built up. Hoover discovered that an intelligence chief could stock the premises that influenced the national debate over judicial matters. That by "furnishing facts and letting others draw their own conclusions," he could play to win ideological battles, and also be prepared to lose if his luck went bad.[7] The use of language, therefore, was an important source of Hoover's power.

In this book, I explore how Hoover rhetorically managed the FBI during the Franklin D. Roosevelt and Harry S. Truman administrations (1933–1953). I focus more specifically on his influence over the rhetorical presidency as well as the press and film industries, which helped him elevate the FBI in the national security hierarchy. Matthew Cecil views Hoover's media work as a cautionary tale on how the FBI can "influence news and entertainment portrayals of its work; in effect, it can create a mythical version of itself that has the potential to obscure from public view abuses of civil liberties."[8] In examining his public messages and private documents, I demonstrate that his political successes were rooted in three rhetorical strategies. First, he used myth and metaphors from literary realism to activate entrenched cultural traditions. Specifically, Hoover borrowed frontier and scientific symbolism from the Progressive Era (1890–1914) that rationalized race, gender, religious, and class hierarchies. Second, the director learned to dominate mass media. He adapted communication techniques pioneered by the Committee on Public Information during World War I to benefit the FBI. Hoover turned propaganda strategies against his institutional rivals in the federal government and his cultural adversaries across the nation. The FBI's media campaigns helped Hoover cultivate a coalition of conservative organizations, including the American Legion and the Daughters of the American Revolution as well as Christian and Jewish groups. Lastly, Hoover exploited FDR's reliance upon rhetorical surrogates inside the administration and ultimately expanded the FBI at the New Deal's expense. In so doing, he co-opted the rhetorical presidency, a practice that he aggressively ramped up during Truman's presidency when he worked with congressional conservatives to incite the Second Red Scare.

Language and Power

The director's private papers and public statements reveal a public figure whose rhetoric drew heavily on Progressive Era themes. By World War II, Powers suggests, Hoover's discourse reflected the "right-thinking majority's impatience with constitutional limitations on its power." Hoover grounded his public campaigns in diatribes against immorality that reflected the progressive spirit. He transformed legal cases into moral dramas that focused on the survival of nineteenth-century cultural norms. In speeches, films, books, articles, and radio programs, the FBI turned criminal law into a branch of ethics that treated crime as evil incarnate. Americans who were troubled by how social-democratic New Dealers protected organized labor and challenged Jim Crow enthusiastically supported Hoover's guardianship of Anglo-American nationalism.[9] Many Republicans and Southern Democrats viewed the New Deal as an attack on moral, economic, and racial boundaries. Hoover used this sentiment to raise fears of foreign subversives while reformers increasingly challenged the South during Roosevelt's second and third terms in office. This rhetorical history set the Truman Doctrine speech in a context ripe for exploitation by anticommunists like Richard M. Nixon (R-CA) on HUAC, Joseph R. McCarthy (R-WI) in the Senate, his aide Roy Cohn, and Ronald Reagan, president of the Screen Actors Guild.[10]

For the director, liberty depended upon Progressive Era values. He asserted that it was therefore inappropriate for the FBI to support laws or other cultural change that challenged what he called traditional Americanism.

RHETORIC OF PROGRESSIVISM

Hoover's speech to HUAC was steeped in a vision of Americanism that mimicked discourses from the Progressive Era. This doctrine was supposed to stop alleged threats against American manhood as well as those against what he imagined to be an American race. Such language helped Hoover establish the democratic legitimacy of coercive law enforcers who only purportedly balanced concerns for both civil liberties and national security. FBI rhetoric informs us of his ability to make new meanings from previously entrenched, but seemingly antiquated, cultural ideas. It also reveals the cultural tradition of Anglo-American nationalism from which he drew and indulged his excesses.

The rhetoric of Americanism provided a helpful context to expand the FBI. Theodore Roosevelt, novelists, and early film directors helped constitute American reality with notions of the frontier. Leroy G. Dorsey explains that Roosevelt grounded Americanism in the frontier myth to articulate a vision of American national identity. The myth was a centuries-old archetypal narrative that remembered America's history of racial violence with sacred respect. Roosevelt traced the rise of a supposed American race back to the admixture of European bloodlines that comingled out in the frontier where settlers pushed westward, but also envisioned a pathway by which others could encapsulate American ideals. First, he gendered notions of national identity and made hardihood a requisite for Americanism. In practice, manhood was illustrated through the ability to survive chaotic terrains. Second, he lauded Protestant moral norms that echoed the Christian reformist tone of the Progressive Era. And third, Roosevelt equated national identity with themes of equality, which made room for racial and ethnic minorities who fit the first two requirements of Americanism. But Roosevelt still made the equality of others dependent on their acceptance by Anglo-Americans.[11] Moreover, the frontier myth was an outgrowth of American exceptionalism, a myth invented by colonial Puritans that suggested they were on a sacred errand into the wilderness to be an exemplar to the world, which justified aggressive interventions into worldly affairs. The myths operated interdependently, Joseph M. Valenzano and Erika Engstrom add, wherein the frontier myth emphasized the "importance of the hero, personified in the character of the cowboy who erases those vestiges of cultures that do not conform to the American way of life through individual acts of aggression on behalf of the community he protects." The cowboy persona signified the interventionist emphasis of American exceptionalism, which took the doctrinal form of manifest destiny in politics.[12]

Roosevelt used the American frontier as a scene to base a theory of race, class, and progress. He deployed frontier mythology to suggest that the civilized world developed through race and class conflict in which the inferior gave way to the dominant. He coordinated his vision of the frontier around social Darwinian notions of race. Anglo-Americans and Protestant immigrant groups, he suggested, evolved to a point in which they had no choice but to exterminate the "red" race because it was unevolved and therefore stood against progress. Since the terrain of the frontier was difficult, Americans had to adapt to their environment and learn how to fight savages, like savages. These heroic pioneers, Roosevelt observed, knew better than to mix their civilized blood with mongrelized blood, and so they had no choice but to exterminate or remove, to kill or contain, the savage natives. He used this historiography to argue that American vitality was regenerated by the conquest of uncivilized peoples in new territories.[13] Richard Slotkin concludes that Roosevelt told the myth to rationalize class rule by a new aristocracy and to assimilate Protestant European immigrant groups to Anglo-American norms.[14] Reformers like Roosevelt made conquest and race purity the scaffolding of progress. Similar ideas were also evident in the work of novelists.

Literary naturalists invented a style in the 1890s that would remain popular into the 1930s. They used a rich array of metaphors to imagine marginal groups in terms of animals and disease. Writers grounded their discourses in scientific theories of race and eugenics that helped communicate pessimistic determinism about the human condition.[15] Their scientific rhetoric evoked a posture of disinterested neutrality. Anglophile protagonists were compelled to react against antagonists. The latter came from minority communities and were imagined to be cognitively undeveloped and prone to violence if not properly controlled. Heroes, therefore, were required to patrol strict racial boundaries for the good of the human race.[16]

The novelists turned their backs on the first generation of realistic writers who paved the way for their own work. Naturalists sometimes referred to the fiction of their forebears as "teacup tragedies" and thereby ridiculed a previous focus on domestic life. Naturalists failed to appreciate the way that the first generation of realists distinguished themselves from their own predecessors along similarly gendered lines.[17] Literary realism was pioneered by male writers soon after the Civil War, when they needed a response to the feminine gender role assigned to novelists before the war. Novel writing became a respectable profession for men at a time when America suffered from the posttraumatic stresses of war. These realists denigrated the work of women novelists to justify their own. They jeered at the work of women, calling it mere sentimentalism when it invoked idealistic Christian virtues like peace, joy, grace, hope, mercy, and charity. Such literary idealism was flawed, they argued, because it presupposed the possibility of universal truth as well as harmony between different types of peoples.[18] Instead, realists imagined a world marked by agony and conflict. They raided the language of biological science, especially Charles Darwin's *The Descent of Man* (1872), to imagine public life in terms of a competition for survival.[19] Mike Hawkins observes that Darwinism produced a "whole range of equivalencies, analogies, images and metaphors" that compared societies to biological organisms, races to biological species, individuals to cells, war to the struggle for existence, and women and children to savages. Social hierarchy was cast as a food chain in the animal kingdom.[20] The Darwinian framework spoke to the Protestant heart. The Puritan tradition taught Victorians that God rewarded white men who were entrepreneurial, dutiful, and sober.[21] Naturalists incorporated such ideas and infused the genre of literary realism with the frontier myth in the 1890s to create what was then called "red-blooded realism."[22] They located their stories at sea, in deserts, on mountaintops, among other frontier settings, and even imagined urban centers as a new frontier that needed to be reclaimed from foreign, non-Anglo, working-class inhabitants.[23]

The genre also swelled with theories of scientific racism that glorified Anglo-Saxon culture.[24] They feared that their group's genetic dominance might have become too refined, that it had degenerated to a state of feminine decadence after the frontier closed in 1890. In contrast to stuffy blue bloods, naturalist writers like Frank Norris called for heroes who were "strong, brutal men with red-hot blood in 'em, with unleashed passions rampant in 'em, blood and bones and viscera in 'em." These characters knew how to "love and hate." Heroes were American xenophobes whose perspectives were unbiased by foreign influence. These character types were supposed to radiate a kind of individuality that hailed from the more isolated regions of the country.[25] The emphasis on individualism bespoke the Victorian values of self-reliance and self-restraint.[26] Masculine heroes were expected to use violence to uphold such values and keep the Anglo-Saxon race unpolluted by minority bloodlines.[27]

Novelists worked to evolve male gender norms in response to the new realities of the Progressive Era. The rise of monopolistic industrial capitalism replaced the long-standing national credo of self-reliant individualism with economic dependency. Owners and executive officers of large corporations made middle-class men their subordinates in elaborate bureaucracies, a process that many experienced as feminization.[28] This perceived threat to manhood was compounded by the emergence of homosexuality as a known category of identity. The visibility of Oscar Wilde's sexuality and urbane lifestyle caused many cosmopolitan men to fear that they were perceived as gay.[29] Moreover, middle-class Protestant male control over public life was further destabilized by anarchists, by labor groups, by the New Woman, and by political machines that served Catholic immigrants.[30] Writers cynically wrote about the alienation of Anglo-American men and the cultural decline of the Anglo-American nation in a broken country that was contaminated by hordes of immigrants.[31]

In response, naturalists closely related visions of what it meant to be Anglo-American and what it meant to be a man in this new world. They invented a confidently heterosexual superman who was individualistic, selfish, and amoral.[32] Writers encouraged middle-class men to trade the mid-century ideals of manliness, which connoted high-mindedness and honor, for a new vision of masculinity that embraced pugnacity as well as sexual and physical prowess.[33] They heavily invoked insect, animal, parasite, and contagion metaphors to tell stories of primordial survival in a biological competition where brute force prevailed.[34] Such language and logic helped distinguish a literary genre that was purportedly based in scientific facts of daily life.[35]

Roosevelt and the red-blooded novelists soon saw their frontier storylines grafted onto film in the form of the Western. The genre was identified as realistic in style. Landscapes were rugged, cityscapes looked mean, and characters looked gritty. The universe was hard-boiled and dominated by evil. Protagonists were Anglo-American Protestant men, and villains were racially mixed with Mexican blood (and thus Catholic) or violated sexual norms of white racial purity. The hero was a violent masculine avenger who brutally enforced religious credo against cultural outsiders.[36]

The Western genre dominated the film industry throughout the 1920s but was overcome by the urban-crime genre during the next decade. Filmmakers borrowed conventions from naturalism to make movies about G-men and gangsters. FBI agents were presented as Anglo-American heroes who violently illustrated Protestant morality and were redeemed by white women. Antagonists were usually poor aliens from Catholic European nations. And, like the Western, urban-crime films were typified by climactic shootouts, but in speakeasies instead of saloons.[37] FBI administrators helped write and produce G-man movies, which marked J. Edgar Hoover's entrance into the film industry. The urban-crime genre set the foundation for the film noir of spy versus spy that accompanied the wartime era, which was a hotbed of invention for Hoover to use in his portrait of the FBI, his leadership, and political reality.

The language of naturalism informed the rhetorical context of the

New Deal. Ira Katznelson bookends the federal program between the presidencies of FDR and Truman, and defines it in a manner that accounts for the interrelationship of their domestic and international agendas.[38] The FBI particularly benefited from the program as measured by the institution's skyrocketing appropriations, manpower, and jurisdiction. For example, the bureau was annually appropriated only $2.77 million and employed 353 agents in fiscal year 1933, but was appropriated $91 million with 6,451 agents in 1952.[39] Hoover's time as FBI director began in 1924 and lasted until his death in 1972, but it was under the social-democratic presidencies of Roosevelt and Truman that the FBI enjoyed its most dramatic growth. How, then, did Hoover so successfully expand his executive department throughout the Great Depression and beyond, and under presidents who seemingly were adversarial to his worldview?

I look into the spaces between the rhetorical presidency and the rhetorical surrogacy that modern presidents expect of their department directors to answer this question. Powers suggests that Hoover transferred his loyalty from the presidency to Congress when he appeared before HUAC in March 1947.[40] To the contrary, I argue he made the switch years before. Roosevelt's critics adopted the red-blooded rhetoric of Americanism when the New Deal increasingly challenged the primacy of Jim Crow. Southern Democrats sometimes divided the party to keep the South segregated, which limited the New Deal during FDR's first term in office (March 1933–January 1937). The president lost support in the South when organized labor crossed the southern color line during his second term.[41] By mid-1937, a bipartisan conservative coalition emerged in response to strikers, to the National Labor Relations Act, to anti-lynching laws, and to what was seen by conservatives as an ideological move to the left. Some conservatives then referred to fascism, Nazism, Bolshevism, and the New Deal as equally totalitarian. The FBI director was a reliable spokesman for the president before New Dealers challenged Jim Crow, but Hoover used the symbolic authority of his office to begin building a coalition of Southern Democrats and Republicans afterward.[42] Together, FBI executive personnel and congressional conservatives mimicked the rhetoric of Anglo-American nationalism from the Progressive Era to imagine the New Deal as a foreign conspiracy and social-democratic New Dealers as traitors.[43]

Conservatives also enjoyed the rhetorical support of early neoliberal theorists who warned that the New Deal would gradually drift into collectivism, from Walter Lippmann's *The Good Society* (1937) to Friedrich Hayek's *The Road to Serfdom* (1944).[44] Inderpal Grewal observes that neoliberalism "produces its own geopolitics in terms of how market logics could be linked to social concerns for differently located, gendered, and racialized populations."[45] As such, neoliberalisms are situated in a transnational world where they take more distinct forms in localized national settings. Dieter Plehwe traces the American national experience with neoliberalism to dynamic institutional forces linked together by Hayek, who founded the Chicago School of neoliberalism when he arrived at the University of Chicago in the fall of 1946 and founded the Mont Pelerin Society in April 1947. Hayek used his roles in both to cross-pollinate each other. Plehwe concludes that the society was an evangelical epistemic community that worked to "integrate various types of specialized knowledge within and across the confines of philosophy, academic research in economics, history, sociology, and applied policy knowledge in its various forms."[46] Trade and financial liberalization, privatization, and deregulation were at its center, and these were goals shared by Hayek's anticommunist bankrollers and publicists. These benefactors, Rob Van Horn and Philip Mirowski conclude, "pushed for a reformulation of classical liberalism in the American context to conform to its Cold War antisocialist agenda" and the creation of a powerful Cold War state.[47] To the chagrin of nascent neoliberal philosophers, anticommunists exploited their language and arguments in ways that made neoliberalism and anticommunism indistinguishable when the New Deal ceded to the Cold War.[48]

Meanwhile, Hoover rhetorically aligned the FBI with the presidency, but subtly provided the nation with an anticommunist alternative to Roosevelt's and Truman's national security leadership. Kenneth O'Reilly notes that when FDR "looked at the FBI he did not often see a bureaucracy whose agents looked for subversives even in the White House" or that "broke into the offices of the left-wing American Youth Congress to photograph the correspondence of his own wife." Instead, he only "saw a bureaucracy that appeared to be under control."[49] Roosevelt, he contends, "never fully appreciated the nature of the FBI's opposition or the fact that the FBI was not *his* FBI—a supportive, pliable, apolitical agency to be modified and used."[50] FBI rhetoric masked its betrayal of the presidency, which began in FDR's second term (January 1937–January 1941) and lasted until Truman left office in January 1953. This timeline of events underlies a broader intellectual move in the nation that substituted Cold War political realism and neoliberalism for the New Deal's social-democratic idealist philosophy.

IDEALISM, REALISM, AND NEOLIBERALISM

Federal administrators betrayed the cultural tenets of Anglo-American nationalism soon after the Progressive Era. President Woodrow Wilson challenged cultural norms in the wake of World War I when he commissioned a group of premier intellectuals to explore how world peace might be maintained.[51] This esteemed study group, known as The Inquiry, helped found the framework for his Fourteen Points, which became the blueprint for the idealist perspective of international relations. The group's prestige was perhaps most noticeable at the Paris Peace Conference in 1919. Members like Walter Lippmann helped draft the Treaty of Versailles and formulate the League of Nations. Amid Communist revolutions across Eastern Europe, they highlighted international democracy as a preferred alternative to Vladimir Lenin's international communism. They promoted cultural pluralism in a manner that outpaced President Wilson or America writ large.[52] These political idealists placed their faith in the rationality and basic goodness of peoples, in the belief in a harmony of interests between nations, and in the possibility of an absolute form of justice.[53] These ideas became the cornerstone of internationalism during the interwar era.

Idealists quested for harmony and justice. They were optimistic about the human condition. All white peoples were believed to have a rational and common interest that could form a peaceful world community, if it were properly organized.[54] Idealists even conceptualized notions of political crime as noncriminal acts. They reframed law enforcement and prison as a means to reform the criminal and viewed oppositional ideology and its activities as removed from the criminal justice system.[55] To be certain, nonwhites and non-Protestants were excluded from this universalistic vision of ideological tolerance, but the emphasis on harmony and goodness lent a helpful political value to racial and religious minorities interested in social equality, and helped underpin the social-democratic framework of the New Deal. Such ideology was diametrically opposed to J. Edgar Hoover's vision for the FBI and the nation. Wilson promoted a democratic world order, open diplomacy, free trade, labor safeguards, disarmament, and national autonomy, and he sought to form a "general association of nations" to draw "covenants for the purpose of affording mutual guarantees of political independence and territorial integrity to great and small states alike."[56] He, however, did not emphasize how such an international arrangement could be enforced to ensure international stability, and the rise of fascism soon eclipsed that of idealism.

The general failure of political idealism to maintain order raised skepticism about its feasibility. E. H. Carr suggested in 1939, for example, that "wishing prevailed over thinking" in idealism and that the outbreak of war "revealed the inadequacy of pure aspiration" as the framework of politics and scholarship. Instead, he argued that the international-relations community should analyze "political reality" to correct the "wish-dreams" of political idealism. As an alternative, he argued that a more realistic perspective should emphasize the irresistible strength of force.[57]

Such critique led to a different set of values and assumptions about state power and state identity. Realists presumed that nation-states sought power as a means to other ends or as an end in itself, and treated the federal government as the key unit of action.[58] Like idealists, realists presumed that the international scene was marked by anarchy. At the same time, however, realists concluded that order could only be maintained through balanced international powers. Political realists echoed literary realists when they presumed that human nature was evil or self-destructive, and thus needed to be controlled.[59] They argued that the attempt to prevent the world from falling into chaos was the highest moral purpose of power.[60] Like naturalists, they proclaimed that force and violence were amoral phenomena that were justified by intent.[61] These ideas influenced domestic law enforcement. Hard power was then used to insulate the nation's government bodies from ethnic and economic citizen groups, and from spies and traitors who might work on behalf of foreign governments.[62] Cold War political realism was persuasive in that it "supplied modern political thought with its epistemology and, most importantly, its dominant style for describing the world," observe Robert Hariman and Francis A. Beer. "The key to political success was to see through all the distractions of culture in order to assess the material conditions of state power" regardless of what any audience might want them to be.[63] In this context, the infrastructure of national security was geared to resist cultural change by social activists.

The rise of political realism was continuous with the rise of neoliberalism—unsurprising because Hayek, in part, built his arguments on the work of political realists like E. H. Carr.[64] David Harvey notes that like realists, neoliberal theorists rose to prominence in the early Cold War era. They were suspicious of democracy and the problems that majority rule posed to economic elites. At Hayek's urging, neoliberal theorists from philosophy, history, and economics departments of select universities began to circulate a perspective in the late 1940s that echoed Theodore Roosevelt's theories of race and class conflict. They proposed that civilization was advanced by "liberating individual entrepreneurial freedoms and skills within an institutional framework characterized by strong private property rights, free markets, and free trade." The role of the state, they argued, was to maintain frameworks appropriate for such practices with military, defense, police, and legal structures. But once markets were established, the state was supposed to remain neutral, to not intervene into such domains as civil rights or human rights, and let markets resolve disputes. Neoliberal theorists crafted the ideology in response to the rise of centralized state apparatuses evident in Soviet Communism, German Nazism, and the Keynesian social-democratic structure of the New Deal; all were said to stifle the potential of entrepreneurialism. As with realism, neoliberalism sought to insulate powerbrokers from the stresses of dissent by minority groups who protested economic conditions. These theorists were bankrolled by wealthy individuals and corporate leaders after the war who embraced "anything from McCarthyism to neoliberal think-tanks to protect and enhance their power."[65] Wendy Brown adds that neoliberalism located capitalism at the center of American governance and eroded more radical expressions of democratic participation. It replaced commitments to popular sovereignty with proofs of legitimacy grounded in the strength of the economy. She concludes that neoliberalism and twentieth-century fascism converged where they both devalued "politics, publics, intellectuals, educated citizenship, and all collective purposes apart from economy and security."[66]

Combined, political realism and neoliberalism helped to discursively reframe the role of federal police forces and prisons in U.S. public life, institutions that became committed to order through force, often with disregard for the constitutional rights of those in their charge. With such abandonment of due process, the FBI took responsibility to monitor civil-rights and civil-liberties activists, religious groups, labor organizers, and literary modernists, as well as more liberal scholars of criminology, sociology, anthropology, history, and law. Hoover and his colleagues championed a rhetoric of Americanism that helped promote democratic exclusion and second-class citizenship. As dominant ideological patterns changed, so too did the institutions that expressed their tenets, like the Department of Justice (DOJ). "Americanism" became shorthand for moves in politics and economics.

Political realists imagined the nation-state as a container, which framed issues of national security in containment rhetoric.[67] So central was this language feature that scholars identify "containment" as the root metaphor of American politics and culture in the Cold War. Some scholars even argue that Cold War culture, in total, was containment culture.[68] In the Cold War, conformity was insisted upon in issues of race, religion, class, sexuality, and gender because of the fear that Communists would exploit differences in U.S. multicultural life to destabilize order. Realists argued that their insistence upon dominant cultural hierarchies was a matter of national security.[69] FBI counterintelligence officials even wrote in literary blackface to culturally police racialized issues of sex, morality, and political control.[70] Popular culture replicated such themes and placed narratives of containment in Hollywood films, books, and magazines. By virtue of repetition, containment tropes like "cancer" and other biological maladies were naturalized and Cold War culture was normalized.[71] What appeared as natural or real was thus closely tied to the language used to make such judgments.

The move from political idealism to realism represented an epistemic transformation of public life. The Cold War was accompanied by an epistemology that was corrosive to the New Deal. Writing about realism, Pam Morris observes that an "epistemic order of reality is produced and sustained by an interconnected network of discursive practices: religious, political, literary, scientific, and everyday."[72] Hoover's emphasis on public relations placed the FBI in these disparate fields of meaning and more, where he was both propagandist and censor. In a nod to his rhetorical agency, Cecil notes it is "significant that Hoover, director of the FBI for forty-eight years, had no training in PR, yet his bureau practiced, at an early stage in the development of the field, sophisticated public relations techniques on a nationwide scale to build and maintain a myth that sustained public support for the organization for decades." The myth was a public relations template for disparate communities of meaning that reduced the FBI to images of science, responsibility, and Hoover's paternal leadership. Cecil concludes that the "impetus that led Hoover to create an alternative reality through public relations was a basic question of the legitimacy of federal law enforcement" in the wake and crest of scandal.[73] Creating and maintaining an alternative reality insulated the FBI from criticism. Its public relations practices were used to "create and maintain an iconic public facade that for decades hid the true nature of the Bureau's work from the public."[74] But this PR work was more than just a defensive strategy, for as Claire Bond Potter explains, FBI crime-control rhetoric also helped transform the American nation-state to be more centralized, administrative, interventionist, and in some ways, jaded.[75]

Scholars have begun to map where and how Hoover intervened in different communities of meaning. For example, Mike Forrest Keen summarizes that the FBI's COINTELPRO (Counter-Intelligence Program) was instituted to surveil and undermine the legally protected activities of the Communist Party, Socialist Workers Party, Puerto Rican Independence Movement, American Indian Movement, and the New Left and Black Liberation movements. These campaigns were extended to "encompass black America and its most prominent leaders (Martin Luther King Jr. and Malcolm X), America's most well-known authors, many churches and church leaders, academics, and virtually any others who might be construed as liberal, 'un-American,' or critical of the FBI." It is in this context that Keen examines the targeting of sociologists and its effects on the discipline.[76] Similarly, Fred Jerome examines how Hoover's FBI monitored Albert Einstein's political ideas and activities to "undermine his credibility and influence," a scientist who was an "ardent democrat, believing in the equality of all men (to a lesser extent, women) and the right and duty of each person to question authority and resist tyranny."[77] In his review of the FBI's outreach program to, and through, the Catholic Church, Steve Rosswurm adds that Hoover and the Church shared values, language, and sexual and gender politics that brought them together to defend the sex/gender system of their day, "rooted in the subordination of women, the normalization of heterosexuality, and the patriarchal family." They both championed "antimodernism, perceiving virtually every manifestation of change as a sign of decline."[78] Writing about the American religious landscape more generally, Sylvester A. Johnson and Steven Weitzman agree, noting that Hoover's FBI "infiltrated religious life in the United States (both literally and metaphorically) and that American religion . . . infiltrated the culture of government."[79] Moreover, John Sbardellati examines the FBI's investigation of Hollywood from 1942 to 1958, wherein Hoover, HUAC, and their Hollywood allies "sought to induce the motion picture industry to spread 'American' ideas while simultaneously pressuring it to contain suspect ideas."[80] Claire A. Culleton traces Hoover's "persistent intervention in one of the most important critical constructs of his time: literary modernism, a movement rife with diverse, inconsistent, even over-determined approaches, practices, and responses to early twentieth-century cultural, aesthetic, and political events and attitudes."[81] William J. Maxwell adds that the FBI was a dedicated foe of the African American literary intelligentsia who "worked to modernize racial representation beginning with the Harlem Renaissance." As such, the FBI was among their most avid readers, "convinced by the focal thesis of these intellectuals, the still-enticing proposition 'that black cultural production is necessarily central to black politics.'"[82] William Beverly points toward the end goal of this work in his examination of New Deal era narratives of flight. He notes an institutional effort to remap disparate regions and jurisdictions into a more singular national whole, under the control of new surveillance technologies with unfettered police power.[83]

I examine in this book how Hoover's FBI intervened in these realms and more to create a political reality receptive to his leadership and hard-line anticommunism. Writing about Hans J. Morgenthau's political realism, Hartmut Behr observes that realists claimed that idealists fabricated reality with a priori moral principles, and failed to collect immediate facts about the world. He notes that their critique can be summarized in the argument that idealist epistemology failed to account for the "concepts of 'power' and 'interest,'" which overlooked an alleged tragic essence of reality within the human condition. Like literary realists, political realists instead grounded their philosophy in a belief that knowledge depended on common sense and self-evident principles. Behr observes, however, that they were strikingly unreflective about their own a priori vision of the world.[84] Hoover ensured that the rise of realism and neoliberalism in domestic politics was, in part, cultural and that it would run along the fault lines of race, religion, class, gender, and sexuality in U.S. public life.

Rhetorical critics have already examined how the Truman Doctrine speech helped to displace political idealism with realism. Denise M. Bostdorff observes that Truman attempted to balance his own entrenched commitments to lofty ideals with the apparent necessity to adopt a more realistic interpretation of Soviet actions. She contends that the administration's perceptions were constrained by a "rhetoric of the past—and the reality that it generated."[85] Moreover, Martin J. Medhurst suggests that the speech shattered the president's reticence about how American-Soviet relations had soured after the war. His previous silence created a vacuum of presidential rhetoric about international relations that was filled by opponents who set the agenda with xenophobic anticommunism. Medhurst concludes that Truman had trapped himself with his "prior commitment to an idealistic world and the rhetorical reticence entailed by that vision," and so he entered the debate on Communism, subversion, and loyalty too late and "found himself a prisoner of historical events."[86]

The Truman Doctrine speech has also been examined in terms of how it fit a naturalist language pattern. Bostdorff and Robert L. Ivie illustrate how White House speechwriters embedded metaphors of natural phenomena like fire, flood, and fever within the text, which borrowed from an anticommunist stockpile of imagery that highlighted imagery of health and disease.[87] Similarly, Paul A. Chilton suggests that the finalized text was structured according to preliminary drafts that featured infectious-disease metaphors and container images. He links containment rhetoric to a container schema in security logic, which entails an interior, a boundary surface, and an exterior. National borders figuratively separate insiders from outsiders and maintain order by limiting movement.[88] The boundary surface is frequently personified in terms of the human immune system, and foreign influence as something that infiltrates the cardiovascular or respiratory systems to attack and disrupt internal organs. The language adopted by the administration, the linguist concludes, created the "impression of a naturally based description," which influenced how policy was drafted.[89] Whereas biological imagery placed humans in a Darwinian contest for survival, container discourse suggested how the spread of a biosocial problem could be stopped. I illustrate in one of my earlier studies that the Truman Doctrine speech was interpreted in the context of Hoover's rhetorical realism, which reinforced his claims about internal security and the natural order of humanity. His discourse helped consolidate the postwar realist consensus in ways that encouraged Cold War containment culture, with its insistence on conformity in issues of race, religion, class, sexuality, and gender. It helped to normalize an alternative reality wherein people could not "talk about racial, economic, and religious equality without raising suspicions about disloyalty or foreign loyalties."[90]

Hoover had long prepared for this moment. He turned to propaganda in the early years of the New Deal to cast himself as a masculine war hero in combat against corrupt politicians.[91] Writing about Hoover's early propaganda work, Charles E. Morris notes that the director's "sexual identity was significant to FBI policy in the years prior to Hoover's Cold War dominance," evident in its work to portray him as indisputably masculine and heterosexual in the 1930s.[92] Potter agrees, and asks scholars to consider how to "read the queer evidence left behind by this influential political figure." She suggests that queer studies' perspectives from "dissonance, repression, stigma, perversion, and inversion might represent an important intervention in political history."[93] Hoover operated in a sex/gender system that sometimes made his sexuality visible to critics. Historically, these systems have been male-dominated, observes Nancy J. Chodorow, and have "organized society around two and only two genders, a sexual division of labor that always includes women's mothering, and heterosexual marriage."[94] The drive to stabilize gender norms inside and outside the FBI was foundational to its rhetorical rise. Jessica R. Pliley observes that policing sexuality was central to the development of the FBI and its capacity for political surveillance, and the history of such informs the "gender conservatism" that animated it, always working to defend against cultural shifts that challenged the status of gender roles, sexual norms, and marriage.[95]

Critics identify how a stockpile of anticommunist imagery was built up before the Cold War and infused the Truman Doctrine with meaning. Lynn Boyd Hinds and Theodore Otto Windt Jr. describe a "rhetorical prism through which Americans viewed the Soviets" that was "refracted by the American self-image, a blending of the political and the religious that portrayed America as a people with a special relationship to God," and placed American and Soviet manifest destinies in rhetorical competition with each other. The scholars cite figurative language grounded in the natural environment that was deployed against organized labor during the First Red Scare (1919–1920) and then again against the New Deal, which helped link alien doctrines and domestic radicals.[96] Accordingly, this project focuses on how Hoover's rhetorical realism undermined the social-democratic agenda of the New Deal, and thereby made way for the rise of political realism and neoliberalism as an alternative epistemological paradigm for public life.

THE RHETORICAL PRESIDENCY AND DOMESTIC PROPAGANDA

The FBI popularized rhetorical realism through discourses on Americanism, which were contextualized by the rhetorical presidency and broadcast by mass communication technologies. Shawn J. Parry-Giles suggests that "America's commitment to government-sponsored propaganda programs not surprisingly parallels the rise of the rhetorical presidency," both of which are "traceable to the Wilson presidency."[97] William McKinley was an early adopter of mass communication technology and used it in his 1896 campaign.[98] This maneuver broke a presidential tradition to maintain an appearance of political disinterest.[99] McKinley's successors went even further. Whereas Theodore Roosevelt broke new ground when he manipulated the national press corps to build public support for his initiatives, Wilson used oratory to pressure Congress for support of his programs. His interest in presidential persuasion was also evident in the purposes to which he put mass communication.

What many Americans presumed about democracy was challenged by the rumbles of war. Wilson invited his academic colleagues to prepare the nation for battle and commissioned the Committee on Public Information (CPI). This agency produced wholesale propaganda and used all available channels of communication to secure the citizenry's enthusiastic support to intervene in Europe. Wilson recognized the rhetorical opportunities made available through the spread of mass media and the nascent field of public relations. Chaired by newspaperman George Creel, the committee was the federal government's first propaganda bureau and invented a style that American and Nazi propagandists would replicate in World War II. Thomas Hollihan summarizes how Creel's rhetorical strategy presented a world in which the forces of good were pitted against the forces of evil.[100] Propagandists like Hitler and Hoover studied and mimicked the CPI's work. James J. Kimble concludes that agonism has always defined domestic propaganda, wherein antagonists were either demonized or dehumanized; granted little or no rationality, agency, or subjectivity; and constructed as pests, animals, savages, and monsters.[101] After the Great War, intellectuals rethought the contours of government in a political environment susceptible to organized persuasion.[102]

Walter Lippmann helped lead the discussion with his work on the nature of propaganda and democracy in *Liberty and the News* (1920). He argued that leaders had learned to manipulate symbols to deliberately misrepresent the social world through mass communication, which placed a "premium upon the manufacture of what is usually called consent." He discussed the failure of the press to protect the nation from government propaganda during the war and noted that this collapse of the fourth estate was a part of the executive's new form of rhetorical power. Lippmann identified the enhanced power of the presidency early and noted that democratic life had become controlled by how the executive manipulated public opinion.[103] His warnings did not diminish the executive's interests in persuasion, but were used as a theoretical rationale for the presidency to communicate even more with its publics.

The Oval Office increasingly valued the assistance of public relations counselors throughout the 1920s and 1930s. President Herbert Hoover instituted the Office of White House Press Secretary in 1929. Soon after, FDR established press offices in each of his executive agencies. These offices propelled the growth of the federal government. They advertised FDR's leadership to targeted audiences. CPI veterans were hired to promote the DOJ.[104] Roosevelt's move to publicize the executive branch created dilemmas for democratic leadership. DOJ publicist Henry Suydam would become both an ally and competitor of FBI Assistant Director

Louis B. Nichols. Whereas Suydam was hired to promote the DOJ more broadly, Nichols was directed by Hoover to advertise the FBI more singularly. Roosevelt's interest in securing support for the expanded federal bureaucracy led one scholar to warn in 1939 that the move for publicity offered bureau heads the opportunity to enhance their own prestige at the expense of democratic legitimacy. Petty bureaucrats, he correctly predicted, would use covert practices to control their own media coverage, which would help them secure the consent of the American people on both domestic and international issues.[105] J. Edgar Hoover's leadership of the FBI fully realized this problem.

Scholarship on presidential rhetoric focuses on discourse and the channels employed for its delivery. Accordingly, Parry-Giles wants to expand the traditional notions of the rhetorical presidency to include covert "discourse controlled by the executive branch" and disseminated by surrogates. She ultimately concludes that to divorce "covert messages from the rhetorical presidency is naïve and misreads the practice of presidential communication in this 'age of secondary orality.'"[106] I take such concerns seriously and examine how Hoover's rhetorical decisions and institutional leadership informed Roosevelt's and Truman's rhetorical presidencies.

Rhetorical Agency and Institutions

The FBI operated in overlapping rhetorical, institutional, and historical contexts. Critics must appreciate how such constraints interacted with each other to comprehend Hoover's rhetorical agency. As Karlyn Kohrs Campbell observes, such "agency refers to the capacity to act . . . to have the competence to speak or write in a way that will be recognized or heeded by others in one's community." She suggests that agency is communally constructed and learned by performers; it is demonstrated when a speaker illustrates the ability to appropriately respond to historically situated circumstances. As such, agency is constrained by identities rooted in issues of race, class, ability, gender, sex, and sexual orientation.

She explains that these issues exist before human action and are enforced by laws, institutions, and norms. Constraints create positionalities that present both obstacles to and opportunities for how performers may temporally invent their personae. Rhetorical agents are thus inventors who link the past to the present and find ways to "connect the psyche, society, and world." Agency is also located in the embodied artistry that is evident in how a speaker or writer mimics culturally appreciated stylistic forms to fit her or his own rhetorical situation. Finally, artistry also embeds agency inside texts. Formal features produce signals that help audience members categorize and "understand how a symbolic act is to be framed. This kind of agency is related to generic conventions, to allusion, to the pleasures of alliteration and assonance, to the transformations effected by tropes."[107]

I extend Campbell's perspective that agency is rooted in subject positions. Although she does observe that such locations are temporary, shift, and are not fixed, she seems to suggest something different than the ability of a performer to migrate and pass into an incongruous social coordinate, and from there leverage power. Louis A. Montrose argues that representations "of the world in written discourse are engaged in constructing the world, in shaping the modalities of social reality, and in accommodating their writers, performers, readers, and audiences to multiple and shifting subject positions within the world they both constitute and inhabit."[108] From this tradition, I argue that the force of Hoover's rhetoric was related to a particular positionality that he purposefully invented for himself. Specifically, his passing strategy to rebut whispers of a hidden gay identity helped empower his discourses on Americanism, wherein exaggerated performances of heterosexuality were read as Anglo-American nationalist orthodoxy. Jack Babuscio argues that the style of passing-for-straight is marked by exaggerated performances, which moves an emphasis from "what a thing or a person is to what it *looks* like; from what is being done to *how* it is being done."[109] For Hoover, exaggerated style is evident in incongruities between the rhetoric he used on stage to address mass audiences and how he wrote private memoranda to Associate Director Clyde Tolson, his lifetime partner.

Exaggerations of gender transformed into exaggerations of control that legitimated coercive and undemocratic police practices. As Hoover told it, he was a rugged gangbuster and spy chaser, not the femme gay man that the rumors suggested. His tough talk in support of tough law-enforcement policies and practices enacted a red-blooded persona that signified heterosexuality. Hoover's artistry made sense to his audiences precisely because he did present himself from a position that was contradictory to that of the "sissy," a derogatory identity that haunted his career. Agency, I argue, is also located in balances between the artistry of self-reinvention, communal norms, exigency, and text to produce ethos. James S. Baumlin defines ethos as the "inner harmony among language, character, and truth . . . the space where language and truth meet or are made incarnate with the individual."[110] Perceptions of authenticity in character are created by acts of imitation whereby speakers successfully mimic performances appropriate for the persona they seek to emulate, defined by audience expectations.[111] In a multimodal campaign, Hoover grounded his performance in truths from an interconnected network of discursive practices and thereby produced an image that was read by audiences to be authentic and credible.[112]

Even more, he communicated in a manner that was supported and followed by mutually exclusive audiences and ideological sectors of the national community, some of which he actively organized against. This ability raises further questions about the boundaries of what Campbell refers to as "one's community." Hoover and his public relations staff presented his vision of public safety, national security, and patriotic gender norms in ways that conservatives and (more impressively) liberals could recognize and heed. He deployed discourses that iterated language from the New Deal, but did so in a manner that resisted its ideological underpinnings. The sexual-gendered identity that Hoover encouraged the nation to accept was one that helped FDR expand the federal government, but one that also helped drive the hard-boiled, homophobic, racist, xenophobic, conspiratorial political vision that marked his career. His charade aligns in provocative ways with Bonnie J. Dow's observation that the "performance of masculinity often is synonymous with the exercise of rhetorical power."[113] The relationship between masculinity and authority informs Gentry's argument that Hoover's files were not the most important source of his power, but were merely one source that worked in conjunction with his linguistic strategies of control.

I locate Hoover's power where his public identity and the stories he told about public life intersected. John Louis Lucaites and Celeste Condit observe that the ability of narrative to frame an interpretation of evidence and to move audiences to action is "functionally contingent upon the speakers' credibility. . . . This contingency manifests itself in rhetorical narrative as an inherent, formal unity of narrator, author, and speaker." These interrelated components of personae work together to create, sustain, and enhance credibility of both speaker and text. Credible authors/speakers lend credibility to the stories they tell, and credible stories lend credibility to the authors/speakers who invent and tell them.[114] Ann Chisholm adds that first-person narratives that appeal to the national identity of its audience can "confirm or enhance credibility by negotiating their narrator's public persona, their narrator's narrative personae, and the narratives themselves," and can also "encourage audience identification and participation by constructing a role for its audience and by endowing that role with mythic, historic, and legendary significance."[115] This function of narrative was foundational to Hoover's rise in power. I have observed elsewhere that the rhetorical structure of press conferences allowed him to be an "onstage narrator of events in which he was also the leading protagonist and all others were supporting characters." From the spotlight, he constructed a "personal struggle against offstage villains" and enlisted the "support of citizens from across the country" in national campaigns against his critics.[116] I contend that Hoover made himself and the FBI credible among diverse audiences with voluminous narratives about the FBI, spoken in a voice continuous with his public persona, which belonged to a character type continuous with literary naturalism. Such voice constituted his narrative persona and the institution that he made synonymous with himself. He used the naturalist voice to spin narratives that encouraged audience identification and participation with appeals to Americanism.

The director's rhetorical strategy neatly aligns with Kimble's definition of domestic propaganda. He argues that propaganda takes an agonistic form because of its two metaphoric tasks, to construct an internal protagonist and an external antagonist. Propagandists find "ways to use propaganda to construct themselves as powerful and formidable faces" of the national body politic and thereby create a "positive persona onto which its recipients can map themselves cognitively" and identify with the mass protagonist, namely, J. Edgar Hoover. Conversely, propagandists reconstruct antagonists into "some form of a threatening entity. Audiences come to understand what initially appeared to be human through the lens of another domain, one assigned by the propagandist." In this manner, antagonists are constructed as the antithesis of the protagonist. Such arrangement defines boundaries of humanity and acceptable action. Kimble concludes that domestic propaganda is the ultimate example of the masculine style of rhetoric, defined as "discourse that establishes and exploits hierarchies in an attempt to dominate others." It is an institutional rhetoric that operates top down, rather than bottom up. Institutional sources disseminate propaganda to mass audiences, and it takes the "form of multiple messages or even a campaign. Institutional sources typically have the sort of resources that can support a series of messages, including the use of strategists who orchestrate the mechanics of a propaganda campaign over time."[117] The objective of propaganda is to amass power for the propagandists who control the institution that creates it. This project, therefore, explores intersections between the FBI as an institution of the presidency and the messages it created.

Institutional critique presses scholars to focus on interactions between discursive and material structures. I have observed elsewhere that institutions are "constituted by interactions between communally written texts, material artifacts specified by those texts, and personnel who manage the artifacts by translating and implementing the texts in to verbal and nonverbal practices before different audiences."[118] Accordingly, critics can investigate discursive frames used by federal employees to direct and legitimize the actions of city- and state-level personnel in their daily work practices. As much as institutions are the buildings that house action, institutions are also the language that scripts policy, ceremony, and official statements. Language, after all, guides which material structures are built, purchased, or appropriated; how such will be accomplished; and for what purposes.[119] Organizational scholars already concluded that frontier mythology left deep cultural imprints on American institutions in pervasive ways and to the detriment of women, racial minorities, and gays.[120] Institutional critique may therefore focus upon the rhetorical agency of leaders who use propaganda to guide how their organizations operate internally and interdependently.

The FBI's mythic appeals to Americanism helped Hoover realign ideology in undemocratic ways that imagined a more restrictive image of American citizenship and a more robust role for law enforcement in public life. Rhetorical realism helped him discursively support the liberal drive for more government in the realm of law enforcement and also support conservatives who objected to how the New Deal protected organized labor and racial minorities. And, generic conventions helped him cut and mend conservative ideology to make room for anticommunist Catholics and Jews, even though they had been previously excluded. He seemed to rise above, reinvent, and deploy ideology in contradictory manners that consistently supported a more robust and autonomous FBI. His often-repeated stories justified an imbalance between the federal machinery of control and the tools needed to protect civil rights and civil liberties, which was a hallmark of his vision for anticommunism.

The FBI borrowed language and logic from literary naturalists that presupposed the world imagined by progressives. Specifically, Hoover's team of writers projected an evil universe in which the common person was embattled by determined antagonists and, therefore, needed to be protected by violent protagonists. The scene was divided between an upperworld where citizens and heroes resided, and an underworld where all evildoers operated in a concerted network to seduce, rape, assault, rob, kill, dupe, and/or brainwash American citizens. The underworld invisibly surrounded the upperworld and could infiltrate it at any moment, which made the universe more evil than good. Red-blooded FBI agents were remade in the image of Hoover's gendered identity and were said to stand in the way of gangster "vermin," Nazi and Communist "fifth columnists," and Communist "red fascists." Hoover deployed ancillary animal, environmental, and contagion metaphors that suggested these threats needed to be quarantined and exterminated to keep Americans safe, or ideologically pure. The director placed these metaphors in stories of Anglo-American nationalism that taught again and again and again that safety required unhampered violence, unregulated law enforcement, and virulent notions of law and order.

CHAPTER 1

The Life and Times of J. Edgar Hoover, 1895–1932

The Woodrow Wilson administration took a hard line against radicalism during J. Edgar Hoover's formative years in government. In December 1919, Attorney General A. Mitchell Palmer declared "unflinching, persistent, aggressive warfare against" Bolshevik sympathizers in America, whom he characterized as "criminals, mistaken idealists, social bigots" and stricken with "hyperesthesia," a syndrome that made people overly sensitive. Palmer recounted that the "dictatorship of the proletariat" in Russia had "degenerated into a military dictatorship," and that the same problem almost spread to America with its own "Red movement."[1] He elaborated in a 1920 issue of *Forum* magazine that, like "a prairie-fire, the blaze of revolution was sweeping over every American institution of law and order a year ago," marriage, home, church, and school, "burning up the foundations of society."[2] In January, the *New York Times* reported that "Hoover, special assistant to Attorney general Palmer, in charge of prosecutions" announced that "3,000 of the 3,600 aliens taken into custody during the recent nationwide round-ups of radicals are 'perfect' cases for deportation."[3] Hoover and Palmer had the broader support of the cabinet. Vice President Thomas R. Marshall declared in March, for example, that "Americanism" meant that "America belonged" to only those citizens who comported themselves in "orderly and constitutional ways" and that all others "should be taught, peacefully" if possible, and forcibly if necessary, that America was "not an international boarding house nor an anarchist cafe."[4] The association of disease with idealism, Marxist ideology, and sensitivity, which should be counteracted with violence in the name of Americanism, was invented in the Progressive Era, would become a mainstay of Hoover's lexicon, and would be foundational to the domestic front of the Cold War.

Palmer, Hoover, and Marshall deployed the xenophobic language and logic that typified their political moment. Palmer imagined public life in terms of a culture war wherein criminals were morally subversive people, whom he described with the scientific rhetoric of disease and degeneration. Hoover sought to deport immigrants to contain the threat of radicalism. And, Marshall suggested that force was a legitimate resource for the federal government to use against marginal groups with unpopular opinions. The administrators used rhetorical patterns invented or popularized by novelists in the late nineteenth century to culturally contain the influences of racial and ethnic minorities and thereby preserve dominant Anglo-Saxon norms.

Hoover was socialized into a political world that he later referenced in his official capacities as FBI director in the New Deal era and beyond. His later discourses on crime and Communism continually deployed language that was distinct to the time around the Progressive Era. Hoover imagined masculinity, patriotism, citizenship, science, professionalism, heroes, and villains, as well as problems and solutions in public life in ways that stemmed from the early years of his career and mimicked the progressives who taught him how to be a reformer. Whereas scientific reformers modeled disinterested bureaucratic professionalism in the federal government, Christian reformers modeled a nationalist zest that referenced and revered the nation's white Anglo-Saxon Protestant cultural

John Edgar Hoover as a child with his parents, ca. 1900.

history. Hoover's public persona emerged from the way he blended these alternative frames of progressivism in ways in which the former concealed and justified the latter.

A Cold War Origin Story

J. Edgar Hoover was born on January 1, 1895, in Washington, DC, where he was raised in a quiet Southern town at the turn of the century. It was a setting before modernity, a time when popular writers and political reformers referred to black people, immigrants, and laborers as disease. Throughout his long career, Hoover perpetually referenced such imagery when he called out for "Americanism."

Hoover joined the Department of Justice (DOJ) during World War I and was quickly promoted into its administrative level.[5] The DOJ's *Appointment Letter Books* indicate that he abbreviated his name and was appointed to the dual titles of "special employee" and "clerk" of the DOJ in July 1917. Both of these positions were "payable from the appropriation for 'National Security & Defense.'"[6] In his early career, he reported to the department's War Emergency Division and was assigned to work with the Department of Labor and the Bureau of Immigration.[7] He helped administer the Espionage (1917), Sedition (1918), and Immigration (1918) Acts during and after the war, which charged him with the duty to help coordinate how the federal government combated American radicalism. His work soon included the move to silence dissent and champion coercive methods of law enforcement.

Together, these acts militarized the DOJ and coordinated it with the Office of Military Intelligence (OMI) to protect industry from labor.[8] Palmer then added the General Intelligence Division (GID) to the DOJ in 1919, which Hoover was selected to direct as the attorney general's "special assistant" in July, at the age of twenty-four.[9] Hoover reported to Congress that the work of the GID was "at first confined solely to the investigations of the ultraradical movement," but he expanded it to include "the study of matters of an international nature, as well as economic and industrial disturbances incident thereto."[10] Hoover's GID was thus an early precursor to the FBI, which conceived of organized labor as a subversive form of international threat. He coordinated the government's move against the 3,600 strikes that occurred between 1919 and 1920 that interfered with defense plans and challenged the principle of private property.[11] He and Palmer helped create an atmosphere that was toxic to reformers. Industry colluded with the DOJ to break strikes and discredit proponents of organized labor and business regulation.[12] The Bureau of Investigation was indistinct as a military or civilian department, or as a public or private security apparatus.

Moreover, the attorney general warned of an imminent revolutionary uprising when he declared war on radicalism after his house was bombed.[13] More than thirty bombs were mailed by anarchists to the homes and offices of business and government leaders in the spring of 1919, which sparked the First Red Scare.[14] The DOJ then cast a nationwide dragnet to round up immigrant laborers, beat them, arrested them, deported them, and also established local, state, and federal police apparatuses that investigated, identified, and punished radicals of all stripes.[15] Unsure of where the anarchists' bombs came from, the Justice Department blamed the newly formed Communist Party of the United States of America (CPUSA).

The Palmer Raids targeted immigrant and labor organizations in November 1919 and January 1920.[16] The first raids rounded up at least 465 alleged radicals. The attorney general directed Hoover to prepare these cases for trial. Three hundred of these detainees were deported to Russia in December, including Emma Goldman and Alexander Berkman.[17] The speed of the government in deciding these cases was a testament to the momentum against immigrants and Communists in America after the war.

Hoover could join the DOJ at twenty-two as a clerk and rise in just two years to direct its counterespionage unit, in part, because he was already fluent in the department's voice and vision. He graduated from George Washington University in 1917 with a master of laws degree, where he took courses from influential legal minds who took hostile stances against immigrants in the wartime era. Andrew Simpson argues that Professors Charles Noble Gregory and William Cabell Van Vleck imparted to Hoover a "legal principle that immigrant aliens relinquished their rights to be within the United States once they advocated violent revolution."[18] Before law school, he attended a prestigious Washington, DC, high school where he was a decorated debater, captain of the cadet corps, and graduated valedictorian in 1913, while he taught Sunday school. Debate helped foster combativeness and shrewdness in progressive politics, and taught him how to use language to persuade audiences with appeals to the Anglo-American Protestant tradition. Moreover, Steve Rosswurm observes that it is "virtually impossible, especially in light of Hoover's latter years, to overestimate the importance of his cadet experience." The corps taught him leadership, regimentation, self-control, group identity, and cohesion, which were important ingredients in "his social bonding with men at the very time when many of his peers were becoming heterosexually oriented."[19] Even more, his Sunday school mentor was an influential progressive organizer who was well spoken in the language of reform politics. Hoover recorded in a 1910 diary entry that he joined the First Presbyterian Church and took his first communion from Dr. D. C. MacLeod.[20] Hoover taught Sunday school under MacLeod's supervision and then served him as an assistant superintendent.[21] The pastor was a president and chairman of the Anti-Saloon League (ASL) of the District of Columbia.[22] As such, he worked with President Wilson to organize the lobby's successful campaign against liquor licenses in Washington, DC.[23]

The ASL, in part, treated prohibition as a response to immigrants. It printed in a 1916 *American Issue* article, for example, that the "future of America" depended on the "Americanization movement." Either the republic would "perish as a conglomeration of racial colonies," or America would become "one nation united by common ideals against enemies without and within."[24] The Eighteenth Amendment was passed three years later, which marked the zenith of the temperance movement's success. The Constitution then prohibited the "manufacture, sale, or transportation of intoxicating liquors" and enforced these rules with the Volstead Act.[25] Also passed in 1919, this law was drafted by the ASL and empowered federal agents to investigate liquor violations in the states under the supervision of the attorney general.[26] Like Hoover, MacLeod helped create a centralized policing apparatus that placed federal agents across the country to police Protestant norms. The Bureau of Prohibition would become steeped in scandal before it finally collapsed in 1933 at the dawn of the New Deal.

Hoover's first attempt to coordinate a national police force failed almost immediately. His early career as a Communist hunter ended abruptly when the cases that he prosecuted were reversed on appeal and the DOJ's methods were ruled unconstitutional.[27] Stories quickly circulated about how the GID routinely violated civil liberties, which implicated the department and Hoover's unit in illegal activities.[28]

Hoover and Palmer argued that the Immigration Act made Communist Party membership a deportable offense. Consequently, they rounded up suspected Communists wherever and however they could find them.[29] The law enforcers were directly challenged by the assistant secretary of labor and powerbrokers within the legal community.[30] For example, future Supreme Court justice Felix Frankfurter, among others, reported in 1920 that federal agents worked with magazines and editors to create propaganda that resembled an "advertising campaign in favor of repression."[31] This machinery was indicative of Hoover's early interest in public relations and propaganda. William J. Maxwell observes that it was under Palmer and against the backdrop of the Harlem Renaissance that Hoover transformed the bureau into the "head office of lit.-cop federalism, part library, part editorial board, part authors guild, part literary-critical tendency, all parts committed to sowing state authority in the print public sphere." Maxwell identifies the GID's *Radicalism and Sedition among the Negroes as Reflected in Their Publications* (1919) as the "American states' earliest acknowledgement of the Harlem Renaissance and as a seminal document of African Americanist criticism produced from any quarter."[32] All of it was ruled unconstitutional. Hoover's propaganda work with the GID foreshadowed what would come with the Cold War.

Palmer and anticommunist collaborators discovered that such intelligence work and roundups were politically safer during times of war and hysteria. Labor Department officials and federal judges reversed thousands of Justice Department deportation rulings.[33] Additionally, Congress acted against the executive branch when the House and Senate investigated the Justice Department for misconduct. The legislature ruled that the bureau did not have the authority to engage in intelligence work without congressional approval.[34] This backlash revealed the power of civil liberties claims to challenge unmonitored domestic counterintelligence programs. Palmer charged that his opponents were Communist sympathizers and liars who wanted to help the alleged Communist revolution in America.[35] His redbaiting tactics failed when a federal judge ruled in June 1920 that the attorney general's procedures violated civil liberties statutes and that Communist Party membership did not qualify aliens to be deported.[36] The revolution never materialized, and Palmer spent the rest of his term under congressional investigation.

Hoover kept control of the GID after Palmer left the DOJ. His unit networked with the newly formed American Legion to promote what Richard Gid Powers calls countersubversive anticommunism. This perspective was prone to conspiracy theories and conflated attempts made by Moscow to co-opt American reform movements through the CPUSA as evidence of actual Soviet control. Accordingly, Hoover and his colleagues sought to prove that the Soviet Union held influence over labor organizations, pacifist groups, universities, women's clubs, churches, and schools. Hoover and the Legion chased make-believe conspiracies and construed political activities outside of Anglo-American culture as foreign and menacing. Hoover also helped produce literature that supported his worldview.[37] For example, reactionaries published books like Blair Coan's *The Red Web* (1925), which warned of Soviet intrigue in public life.[38] R. M. Whitney even thanked "Mr. John Edgar Hoover" of the "Bureau of Investigation of the Department of Justice" for his "advice and friendly criticism" of *Reds in America* (1924), a book that Whitney dedicated to abiding "loyalty to American institutions" amidst the "trackless sea of 'liberalism' as now defined."[39] Even before the New Deal and the neoliberal response to it, therefore, anticommunists like Hoover and Whitney griped that multiculturalism made liberalism unworkable.

Hoover promoted conspiracy theories at a time when the DOJ was entangled in some of its most notorious political conflicts. Attorney General Harry M. Daugherty (1921–1924) attempted to use his power to protect the Republican interior secretary from an investigation of Teapot Dome by Democratic senators Burton K. Wheeler and Thomas J. Walsh. The bureau tapped the senators' phones, read their mail, and burglarized their homes and offices. Agents even attempted to lure Wheeler into a sexual liaison and manufactured evidence to discredit him.[40] He was indicted by a grand jury but won acquittal when witnesses admitted that they had perjured their testimony. The Teapot Dome scandal was possibly more offensive than others because it occurred at a time of government reform, and the attorney general was counted as a reformer. According to the Administrative Orders, Circulars, and Memorandums of the DOJ, for example, he ordered executive officers to refrain from displaying "such obtrusive partisanship as to cause public scandal" in 1922.[41]

Daugherty's hypocrisy helped usher in an era of organizational reform. Attorney General Harlan F. Stone (1924–1925) limited bureau investigations "exclusively to violations of the Federal Laws" and ordered the discontinuance of "unnecessary investigations."[42] And, Attorney General John G. Sargent (1925–1929) stipulated that "all publicity" about "cases pending in this Department or . . . the ordinary administrative business of the Department" must be "authorized and given to the press through the Office of the Attorney General only, and not otherwise." He prohibited the "imparting of confidential information to newspaper representatives and others outside the Department" by penalty of "disciplinary action."[43] He further forbade executive officers from using their "official authority or influence for the purpose of interfering with an election or affecting the result thereof."[44] In December 1924, Stone appointed Hoover as director of the Bureau of Investigation in this context of reform and restraint.[45] The attorney general ordered him to dismantle the GID and reduce the size of the bureau.[46] On the surface, Hoover carried out his orders. In practice, however, the bureau quietly continued to monitor American socialists and Communists, organized laborers, and reformers who challenged the racial boundaries established by Jim Crow.[47] Stone also gave Hoover complete authority over bureau personnel, and the ability to hire and fire agents without the oversight of the Civil Service Commission. Hoover would use this authority over the span of decades to staff the FBI with agents who shared his proclivities for Anglo-American nationalism. The middle and late 1920s were relatively quiet years for the bureau, yet foundational for the rise of Hoover's public and narrative personae.

SCIENCE IN LAW ENFORCEMENT

When Attorney General Palmer claimed that the DOJ rounded up people afflicted with "hyperesthesia," he couched his language in scientific draping that suggested professionalism to progressives. In the spirit of clean government, scientific reformers attempted to elevate federal departments above the stresses of partisanship. For example, the Bureau of Efficiency developed a rating system to ascertain the Justice Department's and the Bureau of Investigation's productivity and wastefulness.[48] It also systematized how they requested funds and made them account for how funds were spent.[49] Justice Department officials limited telegraphs, telephones, and other office equipment to official use only.[50] Hoover joined the ranks of scientific managers who studied public-opinion management, used scientific strategies to solve problems, and relied on statistics to demonstrate results. Every year the director reported record accomplishments to the House Appropriations Committee, which usually approved his budgetary requests. The director pressured special agents in charge of field offices (SACs) to annually increase their caseloads and then used those numbers as evidence of his successful leadership. This move pushed agents to pursue quantity-over-quality cases, to misreport their work, and to focus on low-level infractions rather than on white-collar crime, which President Theodore Roosevelt had intended for the bureau when he formed it in 1908.[51]

The rise of scientific administrators in the federal government guided the ways in which Hoover reshaped the bureau. Reformers envisioned impartial administrative systems that could be managed scientifically and apart from politics and special interests. Notions of public efficiency became the central component of a political program that sought to remove sectarianism from government organizations. Managers tried to apply scientific methods to the political problems of public administration, and thereby safeguard government work from corrupt practices, religious-political factions, and waste.[52] Police Chief August Vollmer of Berkeley, California, established a model for how clean law enforcement would later be judged. In the Progressive Era, he created the nation's first police school that offered courses in fingerprinting, law, photography, and criminology. Vollmer pressed police officials to keep records to solve crimes. He was the first to make college degrees a prerequisite for police employment and was the first to place a bacteriologist and pharmacologist in charge of a crime lab. He was also the first to equip police cars with radios. And, he opposed politicians who interfered in the selection of police personnel.[53] Such innovations became the hallmark of scientific police administration.

Hoover rhetorically reinvented the bureau and his public persona in ways that mimicked Vollmer's reforms. The International Association of Chiefs of Police (IACP) successfully lobbied Congress on behalf of the Bureau of Investigation for a Division of Identification and Information in 1924.[54] Like Vollmer, Hoover would later report to Congress in the 1930s that he had developed a "training school for appointees," created a "system of uniform crime reporting based on police records," opened a "technical-research laboratory and the single-fingerprint section," and launched a "National Police Academy."[55] He also mimicked Vollmer when he spoke of the "intensive training courses in the training school of the Division at Washington."[56] Hoover boasted that trainees were taught to scrutinize "all reports" to "insure the employment of the latest, most scientifically comprehensive methods."[57] He claimed that like Vollmer's crime lab, the "Bureau's Technical Laboratory" scientifically administered "chemical analytical methods" and "spectrographic" exams.[58] And, he reported that like Vollmer's college cops, "all special agents coming within the jurisdiction of this Bureau must either be lawyers or graduate accountants with experience in investigative work."[59] Hoover thus deployed a rhetoric of science to imagine an organization and a personal identity that was safely above ideological reproach. Walter Lippmann captured the ploy in *The Good Society* (1937) when he quipped that citizens had become "more credulous in their opinions and more anxiously compulsive in their actions. Only the scientists seemed to know what they were doing. Only governments seemed to have the power to act. . . . In science there was knowledge. In government there was power."[60]

CRIME RECORDS SECTION

Hoover used standards of scientific professionalism as a pretense to hire a staff of propagandists who would transform the bureau. According to Powers, crime data offered the director "an excuse to put together a staff of researchers and writers that gave the bureau a potential public relations capability," a move for public-opinion management that was characteristic for scientific administrators.[61] Hoover staffed the bureau with personnel who were talented administrators and public communicators, like Clyde Tolson and Louis Nichols. Tolson joined the bureau in 1928 as a clerk in the Washington, DC, field office and rose to the rank of inspector, working in FBI headquarters, in 1929. He was promoted to assistant director in 1930, assistant to the director in 1936, and associate director in 1947. He organized and executed FBI protocol. Matthew Cecil observes that it is "clear that to Tolson, Hoover and the FBI were one and the same, and both were internalized as part of his own identity."[62] The lovers would forever claim to be red-blooded heterosexual men, but would together perform the practices of marriage in public life: exclusively eating, driving, and vacationing together, photographing intimate glances of each other, willing property to each other, wearing wedding rings, and choosing to be buried adjacent to each other for eternity with Hoover's family. Powers identifies their partnership as a "spousal relationship," with "bonds that grew stronger and more exclusive with passing years. . . . The relationship was so close, so enduring, and so affectionate that it took the place of marriage for both bachelors."[63] Together, they used each other to pass for straight in public life while secretly intimate in private, a perplexing and closeted relationship that carried grave consequences for U.S. culture.

Professionally, Tolson functioned as an administrative supervisor, who was joined on the FBI Executive Committee by an assistant director who oversaw investigative work, and Nichols, who supervised the Crime Records Section (CRS) for decades.[64] Nichols joined the bureau in 1934, was transferred to the Publications Section in 1935, was promoted to inspector in 1939, and became an assistant to Tolson. He was promoted to assistant director of the Administrative Division in 1941, which placed

National Archives and Records Administration.

J. Edgar Hoover and Clyde Tolson in Director's Office, May 6, 1937.

National Archives and Records Administration.

J. Edgar Hoover and Clyde Tolson at the Louis-Sharkey fight, Madison Square Garden, August 18, 1936.

National Archives and Records Administration.

Photo album, ca. 1935–1938: J. Edgar Hoover and Clyde Tolson on vacation in Miami, Florida.

National Archives and Records Administration.

Photo album, ca. 1935–1938: J. Edgar Hoover and Clyde Tolson in matching clothing, Miami, Florida.

him in charge of the CRS. He was appointed assistant to the director in 1951, and retired in 1957 for a lucrative position in Schenley Industries.[65] Nichols earned his law degree in 1934 from George Washington University, while he worked in public relations for the YMCA as an associate business secretary.[66] He was evaluated by peers in 1937 as a "devout and capable Bureau salesman" when it was noted that "Nichols' enthusiasm and salesmanship are his greatest assets."[67] Nichols explained in an April 1936 memo that he segmented the director's publics by demographics (e.g., sex, age, and religious affiliation) and spheres of influence.[68] He targeted "civic organizations," business groups, "police training classes," "church groups," "educational groups," "teacher groups," "high school [and] grammar school students," "peace officers," "accountants," "college faculty," and many others.[69]

Nichols did not build the FBI's public relations empire from scratch. He was recommended to the director by *Washington Evening Star* reporter Rex Collier, who teamed up with Hoover in 1929 in a relationship that traded access to bureau files for favorable coverage. Collier was joined by pulp crime writer and circus promoter Courtney Ryley Cooper in 1933, and together they invented a narrative formula to promote the FBI. Powers suggests that Cooper "convinced Hoover that public relations" was "the bureau's most important job" and used Crime Records as the director's "face to the world."[70] Cecil adds that with the combined labor of Tolson, Nichols, Cooper, Collier, and an army of invisible staff writers, no other organization "could match the cultural capital of Hoover's FBI" with the thousands of FBI stories that "appeared in newspapers, magazines, comic strips, radio programs, and motion pictures, and ultimately on television."[71] The mass culture invented by the CRS situated Hoover's public speeches in strategic contexts, which was a top priority for the FBI. The section wrote speeches in a systematic process wherein assistant directors would shop for speaking invitations among audiences and forums that promised to be friendly. Hoover would then convene the Executive Committee to discuss what content to include, and it would draft a manuscript. According to Powers, "Hoover would edit these speeches minutely, so that the final speech reflected not only his ideas, but his feelings and style," sometimes ending with completely new manuscripts.[72] Prior to this system, Collier and Cooper ghostwrote manuscripts for the director, which he edited. What they invented, the Cooper-Collier narrative formula, extended a frame already outlined by Hoover. He proclaimed in a 1925 speech to the IACP, for example, that the Division of Identification represented a "development of science" that would aid their "endless war against crime," language that bespoke scientific neutrality and was continuous with the narrative voice that marked his later speech patterns.[73] Hoover ended his partnership with Cooper in early 1940.[74] After that point, propaganda strategizing was a strictly in-house job. It was at this time that the CRS began to more overtly cajole Hoover's superiors in the DOJ, Congress, and the White House.

The FBI's first publications included Uniform Crime Reports and the Law Enforcement Bulletin. Paid for by the appropriation to collect crime statistics in 1930, the Bulletin showcased criminals wanted by the FBI, their fingerprints, and other identification information.[75] Hoover told Congress in 1936 that it also included articles that were "of special interest to law-enforcement officials which would usually not otherwise be available to them."[76] The pieces included messages from the director and articles about scientific police work, crime prevention, foreign police systems, federal-local police cooperation, political corruption, juvenile delinquency, sex crime, and bank robbery.[77] The Bulletin was mailed to subscribers for free and circulated widely around the nation. The director explained in the 1937 Annual Report of the Attorney General that the "circulation of the bulletin is approximately 14,000 and is sent monthly to more than 10,400 law-enforcement agencies in the United States and 81 foreign countries and territorial possessions."[78] Members of the press and popular entertainment received the other copies.[79] By 1938, CRS publications also included an annual pamphlet titled The Federal Bureau of Investigation, and another annual publication titled Criminal Identification and the Functions of the Identification Division.[80]

Moreover, the CRS also cultivated relationships with members of local and national media. SACs were in charge of local public relations.

They aggressively networked with corporate executives, church officials, and other opinion leaders in print, radio, and film. Field agents were expected to promote the FBI's official perspectives at police headquarters, city hall, civic events, and at local schools.[81] In the 1930s alone, Hoover worked with Cooper and Collier to script twenty-four articles in nationally syndicated magazines, four movies, three books, and a nationally syndicated radio program and comic strip.[82] These were all commercial ventures. The CRS closely shaped their storylines and many other commercial storylines in an attempt to enhance the bureau's crafted image.

The director's behind-the-scenes relationships with members of the print media created mutually beneficial arrangements. The CRS traded access to bureau files in return for secret information and favorable coverage from journalists, columnists, editors, and cartoonists. Because stories of cops and robbers increased readership in newspapers, magazines, books, and journals, access to bureau files was a commodity. Likewise, the bureau blacklisted publications that provided more adversarial coverage. This system allowed the CRS to cultivate a pool of friendly public-opinion leaders and to insulate the FBI from those who were less cooperative. The former were added to the "special correspondents list," while the latter were relegated to the "do not contact list."[83] Many newspaper reporters eventually became FBI surrogates. This symbiotic relationship was created during the New Deal and lasted at least until Hoover's death in 1972.

The CRS's public discourse perpetually referenced a symbolic universe in which scientific administrators were heroes of professionalism. Cecil summarizes that the section represented the FBI as a "responsible and careful law enforcement agency, frequently shown as being reluctant to intervene in local investigations." The bureau's constructed image "emphasized clinical, scientific law enforcement as an antidote to concerns that such a powerful, nationwide law enforcement agency might abuse its authority. Hoover himself was portrayed" as a "tough but fair, avuncular American protector, a thoughtful leader as concerned about preserving civil liberties as he was about catching criminals."[84] With this public persona, social pariahs could safely be cast in naturalist terms, akin to Palmer's description of a "prairie-fire" that spread the "blaze of revolution."[85] The containment culture that would later dominate Cold War America was the product of a literary style that was widely broadcast through mass media to shape mass culture—culture that presumed public life was reserved for white Anglo-Saxon Protestant men.

Americanism: Contagion and Quarantine

When Vice President Marshall defined "Americanism" in nationalist terms, he referenced an ideological system that was born in the Progressive Era from the same frustrations that animated naturalism. While Attorney General Palmer equated idealism and Marxism with a social disease, Marshall referenced "Americanism" as a system of quarantine to isolate the threat, which Hoover enacted with mass deportations. The term signified an exclusionary worldview steeped in eugenics that equated patriotism with xenophobia. Americanism and naturalism belonged to the same realistic system of meaning and projected a universe where Anglo-Americans needed to organize against biosocial threats to the civilized order. Whereas scientific discourse helped Hoover establish his public persona, his narrative persona spoke in a realistic voice. Over a span of decades, the two personae would lend credibility to each other, between what was said and how it was said.

Theodore Roosevelt fired shots in a culture war when he published an article titled "What 'Americanism' Means" (1894) that addressed the state of popular fiction. He lamented how literature was then dominated by cosmopolitan writers. He wrote that "over-civilized, over-sensitive, over-refined . . . weaklings" may "write graceful and pretty verses, essays, novels," but "lost the hardihood and manly courage" that was kept by those "Americans" who were "strong enough to stand" on their "own feet." He further described the "undersized man of letters" as the one who fled his "country because he, with his delicate, effeminate sensitiveness," found the "conditions of life on this side of the water crude" and thus took "abode in Europe." His words targeted the "leaders of the so-called social world" from the "northeastern cities" who harbored "colonial habit of thought" and "provincial spirit of admiration for things foreign." He wanted, instead, an "American literature" that encouraged "waging relentless war on rank-growing evils of all kind."[86] Roosevelt was not alone in his criticism. Reviewers would soon celebrate "fiction" that was "infused with red blood—the red blood that stimulates men to vigorous exercise of body and mind" and that was the stuff of "Americanism." Reviewers praised the work of authors who would go on to write the canon of literary naturalism, such as Hamlin Garland, Frank Norris, and Jack London, as well as the work of Roosevelt's friend Owen Wister, inventor of the American Western.[87]

The future president registered his concerns about popular culture at a pivotal moment in literature. The *Atlantic Monthly* printed in 1897 that a "Feminine Principle" in "American letters" had been replaced by a "Masculine Principle," and that the "faith of the nation" stood "ready to be transferred to it." The principles served as binaries to encourage "Virility as opposed to Refinement, Strength as opposed to Delicacy, Massiveness as opposed to Grace." The magazine observed that the "state of American fiction" was "peculiar" because it had passed "through one of those intervals which separate the departing supremacy of one principle from the approaching supremacy of the other." This sense of supremacy was related to the "Anglo-Saxon race" and its quest to "win the entire earth for the measure of its strength."[88] Literary naturalism emerged from such gendered binaries and white supremacy.[89]

Naturalism did more than just reflect the ideas of the Progressive Era in literary form; it in some ways anticipated the politics to come. Writers did not argue for political programs in their fiction to address the social problems that they described. They did, however, cast themselves as scientific reformers and invented a universe that supposedly referred to some extratextual world that existed in their time. June Howard observes that the naturalist "claim to represent reality accurately" entailed "not only a descriptive but a prescriptive power," that their "account of what *is*" exerted "considerable influence over what . . . *ought* to be done." She thus treats the work of naturalists as a form of immanent ideology that was used to teach their middle-class readers how to imagine the world and themselves in it. Naturalists borrowed ideas from criminal anthropologists about social boundaries, and both imparted them to political progressives.[90]

Naturalism was marked by middle-class fears of social descent down the socioeconomic scale, and by fears that others might ascend it. Either way, many native-born white Americans perceived a threat to their own status in disaffected workers and proponents of racial equality.[91] Such concerns, in part, motivated reform politics. Progressives passed legislation that responded to the belief that members of the middle class wanted to protect themselves from unruly laborers and from challengers of white supremacy. Reformers from different quarters of public life extensively deployed hygiene rhetoric and established boundaries between their own imagined purity and the contaminated masses whom they feared. This discourse complemented a rhetoric of Americanism that prescribed the methods and attitudes requisite to purify the nation. Hoover spent his career referencing this world from the position of a disinterested, scientific professional reformer, which empowered his ethos as a storyteller and helped make a world of mythic make-believe come to life.

HYGIENE RHETORIC AND THE UNCLEAN

The Progressive Era was a time of reform in U.S. public life. Americans built government institutions to resolve problems created by industrial and legislative practices. Progressives passed laws that regulated drugs, food, alcohol, child labor, and industry. The executive branch was expanded then to include the Food and Drug Administration, Federal Trade Commission, and the Federal Reserve. Progressives subsidized education and public projects to build highways, and created national forests and parks. They established the eight-hour workday for railroad workers in 1916 and exempted organized labor from antitrust laws. Progressives also passed four amendments in seven years that allowed Congress to collect income tax, allowed citizens to directly elect their U.S. senators, allowed women to vote, and prohibited all U.S. citizens from producing and consuming alcohol.[92] J. Michael Hogan observes that progressives made these changes with discourse that reveals "an implicit faith in the power of words to change the world for the better."[93] In these ways and more, the Progressive Era was a time of democracy when many Americans worked together to build a more perfect union as they saw fit.

There was no singular politics of progressivism, however, but politics of progressivisms that informed and constrained each other. Richard L. Watson identifies progressivism as a "pluralistic" movement of changing coalitions that united in different ways to address different problems.[94] Leroy G. Dorsey concurs, arguing that there was "not one but many Progressive movements, each with its own agenda. While some stressed the role of professionalism or scientific management in solving social problems, others emphasized the moral foundations of reform."[95] Robin E. Jensen adds that there was "irony inherent in much Progressive Era communication that included sexist, racist, classist, and xenophobic appeals. Often reformers' rhetorical appeals did garner support for much-needed social programs. However, their words . . . were thick with discriminatory language that reiterated social hierarchies."[96] Some reforms and reformers would later be remembered as forward-thinking and visionary, therefore, while others as backward-thinking and reactionary.

Progressives passed a series of laws that illustrated a reactionary current in their politics, a reaction against a seeming deterioration of public life and culture.[97] Southerners worked with Northerners, and liberals with conservatives to pass the Immigration Act (1891), Anarchist Exclusion Act (1903), White-Slave Traffic Act (1910), and Harrison Narcotics Tax Act (1914).[98] The Immigration Act excluded destitute immigrants and people with contagious disease from naturalization. The act established the Bureau of Immigration and a system to deport aliens.[99] The Anarchist Act prohibited immigrants who opposed government from naturalization, and thereby created a criterion of thought for citizenship.[100] The white-slavery act, in part, was codified in response to how immigrants and African Americans were seen as sex traffickers of Anglo-American girls from the countryside.[101] And, the Harrison Act was passed out of particular fears of black men who were said to become resistant even to bullets and nearly impossible to constrain when under the influence of cocaine.[102] Reformers pushed for these laws to control what a more urbanized, industrialized, and ethnically diversified America might become. Freed blacks, Catholics, workers, and immigrants filled industrial centers where they were portrayed as captivated by hedonistic desires and to blame for commercial vice. Many progressives saw the city as a place where Anglo-American women would be forced into sexual slavery and upon degenerate men of different ethnicities, where black men were violent dope fiends, and where society became a drunken wasteland. Accordingly, moral reformers like Vice President Marshall wanted federal agents to deploy violence and maintain order where they perceived only sinful chaos.[103]

Naturalism helped to encourage such visions and to ideologically underpin the rise of scientific professionalism in the federal government. The world imagined by scientific managers resembled naturalism's realm of force. Government administrators and their advisers cultivated fantasies of abnormalities in criminal minds, diseased bodies, political conspiracies, and threats to national security. The world that many scientific progressives imagined was amoral and in a constant state of crisis. Their professionalism, Howard contends, was particularly conservative in the way it cast experts as disinterested agents of a neutral state and thereby concealed how elite powerbrokers served their own group interests, but in the name of everybody. The middle-class writers and readers of naturalism were creatures of place who lived in a world that was built upon standards that separated them from others.[104] If professionals were disproven, the entire middle class could lose what separated and made it different from the lower classes. The middle class thus invested in secretive elites who guarded the mantle of knowledge and knew why democratic life must be organized in sometimes peculiar ways.

Naturalists incorporated ideas from criminal anthropologists that portrayed criminality as the product of racial inferiority. Novelists and anthropologists alike theorized that criminals belonged to a biological human subspecies and were degenerated life-forms. They believed that drugs and alcohol could trigger a process that caused racial minorities to revert to an earlier stage of human development. The deviant races were thought to produce children who were physically or mentally disabled, or criminals who were strong, huge, stupid, and crude. They were slow and dull until roused by anger or sexual desire, at which time a primitive beast from within was released upon the world to steal, rape, and kill.[105] Naturalists rationalized how immigrants and African Americans would be destroyed by their own inherent contagion and suggested that such disease was commutable to Anglo-America.[106] Criminologist Henry M. Boies, for example, concluded in *Prisoners and Paupers* (1893) that "criminality" was a "disease," it was "contagious, and sometimes epidemic." Accordingly, he wrote that the "'unfit,' the abnormals, the sharks, the devil-fish, and other monsters" should be "confined and secluded until they are exterminated," and not free to "multiply."[107] Decades later, such scientific ideas would, in part, also underpin Nazi ideology.[108]

Contagion imagery helped writers invent strategies of containment. Fredric Jameson observes that naturalists relied on a narrative system that imagined how the wholeness of American culture affected its parts. This model presupposed that a totality of culture could be reduced to an inner essence that expressed "some unified inner truth—a worldview or a period style or a set of structural categories." Writers totalized cultural life in what he calls a "strategy of containment" that relocated what was considered unthinkable outside the borders of respectable discourse. In practice, naturalists isolated and privileged some kinds of thought, belief, and political structures over others, and treated them as master codes that informed the displaced elements. Writers drove home the "ultimate message for the lower class: stay in your place!" They portrayed political discontents from marginal groups as people with personal failures who were thus motivated to complain.[109] Contagion rhetoric communicated that an essence of America needed to be isolated from people and ideas that could somehow infect it in ways that corrupted the cultural whole.

Progressive Era quarantine logic crystallized with segregation. Reformers suggested that blacks had regressed outside the beneficent confines of chattel slavery. Prudential Life Insurance Company published a widely influential study that linked the black "race" with contagion two months after the Supreme Court decided *Plessy v. Ferguson* (1896). The report concluded that African Americans were diseased and would soon die out. Scientists and politicians worried that the race was susceptible to new diseases in this weakened state that might spread to Anglo-America. The medical community grounded claims made by Southerners that imagined blacks in terms of cancer and parasite. A precursor to Palmer, Marshall, and Hoover, they "supplied medicoscientific support for the white Southern backlash that followed Reconstruction by characterizing the region's black population as a physical, moral, and sexual contagion" and described "segregation as a quarantine to protect whites from infection," observes Melissa Stein. The South's "negro problem" was seen as a national problem because blacks had immigrated to Northern cities and urban centers. By 1913, however, scientists agreed that the black population had grown. They adjusted their language to then suggest that black people needed to be removed or contained to protect the social body. African Americans who organized and agitated for political equality were considered the most dangerous among the group because their efforts struck against the barrier that was said to protect society.[110]

The emergence of hygiene rhetoric coincided with a debate over the type of equality that blacks should enjoy. After the Civil War, Southern conservatives fought to regain the racial order that had once characterized their public life. Whites in the South professed that social and political equality were different matters, and developed what Kirt H. Wilson calls a rhetoric of place that determined the social spaces that whites and blacks should occupy, and how they should interact with each other in public and private settings. They asserted that issues of equality should be determined by a person's role in society, and civil rights should be apportioned from their responsibilities. Moreover, since whites were considered more socially advanced, the natural order predicated that they should be treated as overseers of servile blacks, which necessitated that they receive a greater portion of civil rights.[111] This perspective laid the groundwork for the doctrine of separate but equal that *Plessy* later substantiated. Most of all, Southerners wanted a system that separated the races, but one that also provided whites with more rights than blacks when contact was unavoidable. They hoped to prevent cultural convergence and preserve some framework of antebellum life.[112] Contagion rhetoric helped articulate a perspective that was too radical to state more explicitly, and one that racist Northerners could also embrace.

Ultimately, naturalism and its use of hygiene rhetoric communicated pessimistic determinism. Writers invented asymmetrical roles for heroes and villains that gestured for social control. Antagonists were imagined to be incurably sick and irrational. Protagonists had to use force to protect society from the chaos that would otherwise prevail if brutal disease carriers were allowed to run amok.[113] Such contagion discourse justified a rhetoric of Americanism that suggested what white America ought to be and how it should accomplish this goal.

AMERICANISM AND AMERICANIZATION

While hygiene rhetoric helped define marginalized groups, Americanism structured the middle class to be militaristic, intolerant, and exclusive. To be white was not enough. Allegedly patriotic whites knew to keep away from the unclean, while naively idealistic whites attempted to reconcile differences and supported the rights of minorities. This arrangement was at the core of a program that was commonly called "Americanism" by reformers like Marshall. It did much to shape public policy in particular ways. Capital was to be redistributed upward and not downward. Blacks were supposed to serve whites. Protestant cultural norms were supposed to reign supreme. And, violence was supposed to be the key method to accomplish these goals.

President William McKinley promoted Henry Clay's "American system" when he advanced the interests of industrial capitalists. Aligned with Alexander Hamilton, Clay spent his long career in public life (1806–1852) as an advocate for a strong central bank to ensure capital for investment to develop American industries. The role of government under this system was to encourage industrial growth.[114] This mission was consistent with Hamilton's "Report on Manufacturers" (1791), which recommended "leaving Industry to its own direction" but also encouraged the "incitement and patronage of government."[115] McKinley's era was accented by monopolies and court rulings that offered more civil rights to corporations than to women, African Americans, or marginal immigrant groups.[116] For example, the president announced in his 1897 Inaugural that Congress should give "ample protection and encouragement" to industries because no "portion of our population" was more entitled to the federal government's "wide and liberal care" than the owners of industry. In his successful attempt to further subsidize corporations, McKinley concluded that "friendly legislation" for producers in the "American name" was "beneficial to all."[117] The president, thus, derived the nation's identity from the welfare of elite economic interests. This belief was further refined by his vice president.

Theodore Roosevelt bolstered notions of Americanism through Christian benevolence and militarism. He declared in his "Strenuous Life" address (1899), for example, that which was "most American in the American character" was a "life of toil and effort, of labor and strife" whereby the "highest form of success" went to "the man who does not shrink from danger." He encouraged "every self-respecting American" who was "manly and adventurous" to engage in wars for wealth in "Hawaii, Cuba, Porto Rico [*sic*], and the Philippines." Pointing to religious differences, he advocated belligerence against "warlike Moslems, and wild pagans" who were "utterly unfit for self-government" and who showed "no signs of becoming fit."[118] Roosevelt's Americanism used issues of race and religion to discern which types of people were intellectually equipped or ill-suited for democratic governance.[119] His internationalism elevated the spread of Christianity above liberalism. He suggested, for example, that real "men" were uninterested in notions of "'liberty' and the 'consent of the governed'" if Christian "salvation" could be achieved through force.[120] Roosevelt campaigned extensively on "Americanism" and made it a force of public culture.

Some of Roosevelt's ideas were further championed by Woodrow

Wilson. Having articulated various pronouncements of Americanism since at least 1894, Roosevelt popularized "100% Americanism" to denounce what he called "hyphenated Americans" (e.g., German-Americans) during his 1916 bid for the Republican nomination. Wilson then embraced "100% Americanism" when he was reelected president in 1916 as part of his program to intervene in World War I. Wilson's endorsement made the "Americanization" of immigrants a nationwide effort sponsored by the federal government.[121] The American flag was a symbol of conformity, the president suggested, and was an emblem of "our unity, our power, our thought and purpose as a nation."[122] Such cohesion was a goal of his administration while it built support for a monolithic perspective that worked to drown out dissenters.

The Wilson administration's campaign for unity coerced Marxist immigrant groups to accept Clay's system in the name of Americanism. The Bureau of Education launched an Americanization program that was financed by the National Americanization Committee (NAC). Supported by Christian organizations like the Anti-Saloon League , the NAC was a business group that viewed Americanization as an effort to Americanize the immigrant workforce for industrialists during an era punctuated by labor radicalism. Its leadership overlapped with the Immigration Committee of the Chamber of Commerce. The Education Bureau became a subsidiary of the NAC, which coordinated Americanization programs across the country. The committee transformed from a business lobby into a federal agency when it became the War Work Extension of the Bureau of Education.[123] The NAC developed curriculum to teach the "American Way" for the Treasury, War, and Navy Departments; the Bureaus of Education and Naturalization; the Committee on Public Information; and the Council of National Defense, as well as for education, business, publishing, and labor organizations. Attorney General Palmer, the DOJ, and the Bureau of Investigation used this momentum to press for the Espionage and Sedition Acts. The Americanization campaign consummately heightened tensions in a period marked by red scare. Numerous civic associations formed their own Americanism campaigns during the interwar period.[124]

The discourses of Christian and scientific progressive reformers provided a rich tapestry for Hoover to mimic. The Protestant zest of the Anti-Saloon League and its zeal for reform illustrated a pattern in U.S. government practices that supported suppression of marginal groups for Christian reform causes. Hoover would spend his career threading continuity between a public persona that bespoke disinterested scientific professionalism and a narrative persona that voiced scientific racisms embedded in naturalist code words. The identity that existed at this intersection belonged to the epistemic order of the Progressive Era. For the identity to be "real" in the New Deal era and beyond, the dated ideologies that stabilized it would need to be revitalized as well. This system of meaning was signified by notions of Americanism, which Hoover would also advocate throughout his career. Reformers like Palmer, Marshall, and Hoover invented a pattern of speaking that combined these threads. It was a delicate pattern because it required a public persona that was above reproach lest it be guilty of hypocrisy and be discredited. But when perceived as credible, the persona was trusted to narrate the values of American public life in a voice that rang with alarm.

Americanism: A Rhetoric of Reform

The rhetoric of Vice President Marshall, Attorney General Palmer, and special assistant J. Edgar Hoover illustrated the rhetorical world occupied by Anglo-American nationalists who wanted to contain cultural changes brought about by mass immigration, industrialization, and urbanization. Hard-line reformers performed strategies of containment that used middle-class culture to identify what was allegedly "American" in essence and to define the experience of others as un-American. What such groups had to say about their own American experience mattered little; what scientific professionals had to say about outsiders officially constituted their character and experience in the eyes of the law.

Nationalists used the rhetoric of Americanism to communicate boundaries. The frontier myth cast a racialized historiography that justified violence in an order that placed white Anglo-Saxon Protestant men at the center of public life, a police-state order culturally policed along divisions of race, nation, class, religion, gender, sex, and sexuality. America was not a place where people of different races or ethnicities were supposed to mix their genetic traits; it was a place where Anglo-American bloodlines were imagined to be superior and privileged by law. America was not a place where people of different national origins were supposed to celebrate their diversity; it was a place where such people were supposed to imagine themselves in terms of the Anglo-American experience. America was not a place where workers were supposed to constrain how owners managed their property; it was a place where the middle classes and upper classes were supposed to have almost unchecked liberty. America was not a place where immigrants should campaign for class equality; it was a place where such protesters should be deported. America was not a place where drugs should be used recreationally; it was a place where such activity should be violently repressed. Finally, America was not a place where real men were supposed to apply transcendent or idealistic values to public life; it was a place where men were supposed to unreflectively achieve success in war and business with forcefulness. Anglo-American nationalists used these differences to help separate what was American from what was un-American and, ultimately, to expand the federal government in the Progressive Era and beyond.

Such nationalism was a staple of J. Edgar Hoover's discourse in the New Deal era and became increasingly explicit as the nation prepared for war. In the meantime, his language borrowed from another quarter of public life that believed science was a solution to partisanship. He located his identity and that of the FBI between these two currents of meaning, using the rhetoric of scientific administrators to illustrate that his leadership style was sufficiently nonpartisan. When international threat became apparent once again, he would pair such linguistic neutrality with the rhetoric of Americanism in racialized containment discourses, rich with naturalist imagery steeped in the frontier myth. This language structure masked ideological motives behind a pretense of professionalism. Hoover solved multiple rhetorical problems with this strategy, from public readings of his sexual orientation by critics to professional challenges to his leadership by bureaucratic rivals.

CHAPTER 2

The War on Crime, 1933–1938

In May 1935, Warner Brothers released a film that marked J. Edgar Hoover's entrance into Hollywood. *'G' Men* opened with a scene where a "crook" from a different "ward" told James Cagney, "You'll never get anywhere playing shyster for that rat." His claim referenced a crime boss and his network of corrupt lawyers and politicians. Later in the film, a fictional FBI director proclaimed before a group of congressmen: "Gentlemen, give us national laws with teeth in them, covering the whole field of interstate crime. . . . Arm governmental agents, and not just with revolvers. If these gangsters want to use machine guns—give the special agents machine guns, shotguns, tear gas, and everything else! This is war!"[1] Audiences were familiar with such realism. *Scarface* (1932), for example, climaxed when the hero told the villain, "I told you you'd show up this way. Get you in a jam without a gun and you squeal like a yellow rat." The film's antagonist was a homicidal maniac and the "detective chief" complained of gangsters that were freed from police custody by "the red tape, the crooked lawyers," and corrupt "politicians." In one scene, the publisher of the local newspaper told a group of concerned citizens: "Don't blame the police!" Rather, they should push the government to "pass a federal law that puts guns in the same class as drugs and white slavery. Put teeth in the deportation act. These gangsters don't belong in our country. Half of them aren't even citizens."[2] Indeed, the linguistic patterns of Attorney General A. Mitchell Palmer and Vice President Thomas R. Marshall that equated immigrants with biosocial threats that needed to be violently contained survived in cinema.

More than just fictional stories of urban crime, this scheme also ordered crime news and the voice of Hoover's narrative persona. When he staged the arrest of Alvin Karpis in May 1936, the New Orleans *Times-Picayune* subtitled one of its articles "GANGSTER 'YELLOW RAT,' Says Hoover"; the Pittsburgh *Sun-Telegraph* headlined a story "Karpis Quit 'Like Rat,' Says Chief of G-Men"; and the *Milwaukee Journal* ran the title "'Respectable' Citizens Who Shield 'Rats' the Real Public Enemies."[3] While this language was popular, it was far different from what framed the dominant worldview of federal law-enforcement professionals at the time.

The reputation of law enforcement was diminished in the 1920s by a series of embarrassments, from Palmer's false flags, to the Teapot Dome scandal, to stories that linked police to bootleggers. In response, President Herbert Hoover appointed former attorney general George W. Wickersham (1909–1913) to chair the National Commission on Law Observance and Enforcement. Wickersham was trusted with this responsibility, in part, because he was the president of the American Bar Association's (ABA) American Law Institute. President Hoover used his 1929 State of the Union address to announce the "widest inquiry into the shortcomings of the administration of justice and into the causes and remedies for them."[4] The commission released a fourteen-volume report in 1931 that championed the greater inclusion of marginalized groups and blamed American culture for its failings during the Prohibition era.

OPPOSITE: *You Can't Get Away with It.* Universal documentary on the Federal Bureau of Investigation, 1936. J. Edgar Hoover top right.

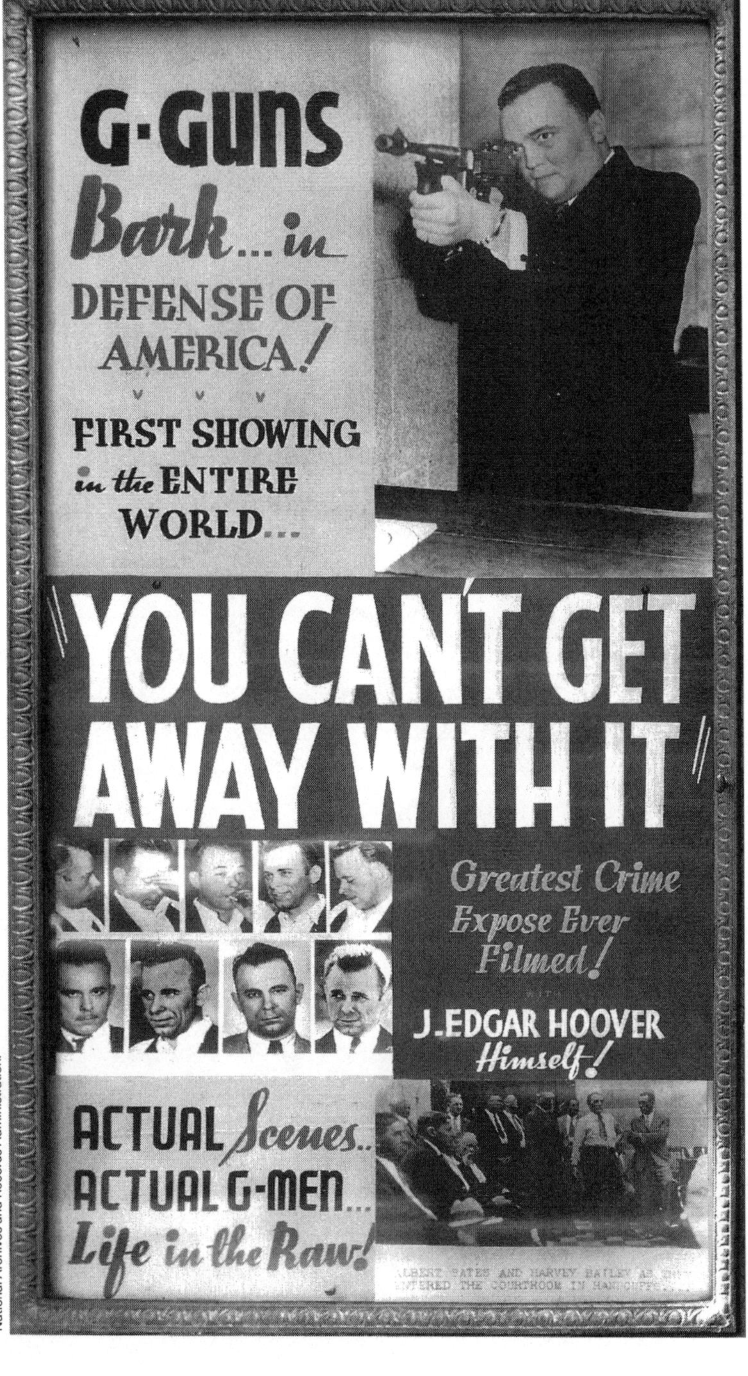

National Archives and Records Administration.

Wickersham lambasted a "clamorous group" in America who emphasized "only the difficulties connected with immigration" and "lost sight of all its beneficial effects." His commission argued that this xenophobic group advanced the "easy theory that our social difficulties are not to be charged to our own mistakes and failures. It is easy to shift the responsibly for what is wrong by charging it upon the nationals of other countries."[5] The commission condemned unconstitutional deportation laws and the use of torture by police against marginal groups.[6]

Instead of such practices, President Hoover encouraged a much more idealistic program. He proclaimed that the country needed "new federal prisons and a reorganization of our probation and parole systems" to "prepare [prisoners] for return to duties of citizenship." He suggested that there "should be established in the Department of Justice a Bureau of Prisons [BOP] with a sufficient force to deal adequately with the growing activities of our prison institutions"—a force that would emphasize criminal rehabilitation over deterrence.[7] By 1933, the BOP's annual appropriation was $12.3 million, which was more than a quarter of the DOJ's total appropriation and more than quadruple what was appropriated to the Bureau of Investigation.[8] In little time, the nascent BOP overshadowed the twenty-five-year-old investigative unit.

President Hoover instituted a move that stocked the DOJ with a generation of academic and lawyerly reformers who were further empowered by the social-democratic idealism of the New Deal. For example, the dean of Duke University's Law School became the special executive assistant to the attorney general in 1934. He acknowledged in September 1933 that Wickersham's bar association had come to "play an increasingly important part in the life of this country . . . in providing leadership for the further guidance of those who are charged with the duties of government and the administration of justice."[9] Members of the DOJ investigated the relationship between poverty and crime in line with how President Franklin D. Roosevelt championed vulnerable populations.

Rather than violence, the lawyerly group backed a wide-scale prison-reform program that emphasized probation and parole as means to protect society. Congress passed several laws that drove up the appropriations of the BOP and expanded its jurisdiction. The legislature created the Federal Parole Board, granted the Public Health Service access to federal prisoners, commissioned building projects, diversified prison employment to train prisoners for the trades, and amended the Probation Act of 1925 to enlarge the probation system.[10] Persons subject to probation remained in the custody of the court. Though not confined, they were required to report to probation officers.[11] These investigators counseled juvenile offenders, which further diminished Hoover's bureau. No one represented this idealistic emphasis more than Sanford Bates, the first director of the BOP and the only other bureau director in the DOJ.

Moreover, Director Hoover faced other challenges to his authority of a much more personal nature. Charles Morris links Hoover's leadership style in the 1930s to a passing performance.[12] Stories began to appear in the press that raised questions about Hoover's sexuality. *Collier's* printed in September 1933, for example, that Hoover "walks with mincing step" and "dresses fastidiously, with Eleanor blue as the favorite color for the matched shades of tie, handkerchief and socks," in a critical article that described the bureau as a "secret federal police" and Hoover as an operator of a "personal and political machine."[13] *Time* observed in 1935 that he had a "strong streak of sentimentality," lived with his mother, and had no time for other women.[14] The *New Yorker* added one year later that "certain things marked Hoover apart" from his peers. He "dressed better than most, a bit on the dandyish side."[15] Morris observes that this scrutiny coincided with a homosexual panic that undermined the nation's manhood when Hoover and others "could not escape the homophobic fear that accompanied turbulence in gender and sexual norms."[16] Such language threatened Hoover's career. In *Degeneration* (1895), influential criminal anthropologist Max Nordau linked homosexuality to cross-dressing, sadism, bestiality, necrophilia, and murder—a work that influenced attitudes about criminality, sexuality, and realistic fiction.[17] Innuendos about Hoover's sexual orientation, therefore, were scandalous and could have destabilized his public stature as well as his control over the Bureau of Investigation.

Amid these challenges, a rhetorical opportunity opened for Hoover to reinvent his public persona. In June 1933, Attorney General Homer S. Cummings unveiled a New Deal campaign against "the racketeers of high finance and the racketeers of violence and bloodshed," which would be an "unrelenting and persistent effort continued over a long period of time."[18] One week later, "Pretty Boy" Floyd murdered a group of lawmen in the Kansas City Massacre. This event helped crystallize the attorney general's vision, which was rhetorically and institutionally backed by FDR. In September, Cummings declared a war on crime (1933–1938), which was allegedly a "real war which confronts us all—a war that must be successfully fought if life and property are to be secure in our country."[19] In this context, Hoover instituted the Crime Records Section (CRS) in 1935 when he rebranded his bureau as the Federal Bureau of Investigation (FBI), and used the war metaphor to recast the bureau in militaristic terms and himself as a general. FDR used Hoover's status as celebrity crime fighter to represent the power of federal-state cooperation. The campaign elevated the director in the political-cultural hierarchy over critical congressional overseers whom he aligned with criminals.[20] Moreover, Morris notes that Hoover used the crime war to incite a "moral panic about sex crime to alleviate his homosexual panic, thus diverting attention from his sexuality and silencing those who might question it."[21] Hoover's militarized persona was central to his passing performance and aligned his persona with red-blooded masculinity and the realistic policies and performances it prescribed. While this persona offered safe cover, the struggle to keep up appearances also constrained the leader he would become, ultimately setting him on the path of subversion.

Hoover enhanced his credibility by making his public persona, narrative persona, and the narratives he told continuous with the urban-crime film genre, which encouraged audience participation by constructing a role for it endowed with mythic significance. In particular, writers in the CRS offered an alternative paradigm for action in federal law enforcement that was designed to counter and replace Wickersham's idealistic framework. Hoover used the cultural frame popularized by the public relations unit to raise doubts about the motivations and practices of prison reformers, and laid seeds that precipitated the rise of the Second Red Scare, Cold War political realism, and a toxic neoliberalism. His red-blooded performance deflected unwanted attention from his sexuality and built support for criminal deterrence over rehabilitation. He was helped by Clyde Tolson, Louis Nichols, and writers inside and outside the bureau who worked to align the FBI with FDR's rhetorical presidency and ultimately gain the support of congressional New Dealers, which further legitimized Hoover's personae and realist framework.

The New Deal and the War on Crime

The war on crime extended a militarized frame used by FDR that communicated his desire for expanded federal authority. In his first Inaugural, the president requested "broad Executive power to wage war against the emergency, as great as the power that would be given" to him if the nation were "invaded by a foreign foe."[22] Cummings used the war metaphor to address problems brought on by technological changes that threatened public order. Bank robbers with faster cars, faster communication, and faster guns could more easily outrun local police when they crossed state lines and so escaped their jurisdiction. High-profile, high-powered bank robberies were spectacles that revealed the inability of government to maintain order in daily life. The special assistant to the attorney general wrote in an August 1933 *New York Times* editorial that "vast changes have taken place in the vital affairs of life" that had sped up travel and communication, and that gave rise to "immense problems in law enforcement as well as economics." What was needed, he offered, was a new sense of cooperation among the states, which came in the form of expanded federal jurisdictions and appropriations for various agencies that would serve all "citizens of the United States."[23] The war on crime symbolized the power of the federal government to resolve problems that the states could not solve on their own.

The scope of the campaign materialized in December 1934 at the Attorney General's Conference on Crime. In his closing remarks,

Cummings described the keynote of the conference as "cooperation, with all that it implies, and a permanent structure" for the "marshalling of the forces that affect and sustain public interest."[24] The principle of cooperation drove his perspective on law enforcement. Cummings previously stated in an August 1933 speech to the ABA, for example, that "conditions and public opinion change from one era to another; and so does judicial interpretation." He suggested that "rugged individualism . . . no longer appeared to be adapted to a highly relational society," and pointed to a "steady drift from the competitive to the co-operative ideal."[25] How the war on crime would be waged, however, was unclear and open for debate. Conference speakers ranged the ideological spectrum from FDR to the directors of the FBI and BOP, to the commissioner of narcotics, the president of the International Association of Chiefs of Police (IACP), the former secretaries of war and state, the chairman of the Senate Judiciary Committee, presidents of the ABA, criminologists from Harvard University and the University of Pennsylvania, the deans of Duke and Yale law schools, the president of the Federation of Women's Clubs, the president of the American Society of Newspaper Editors, the secretary of the Motion Picture Producers and Distributors of America, and leaders from state probation and parole systems. Whereas new and expanded federal authority was certain, how it would take shape was not yet so clear.

The debate on how to wage the war on crime was influenced by crime news spectacles. By May 1934, the FBI had captured George "Machine Gun" Kelly and had killed John Hamilton, Eddie Green, Bonnie and Clyde, and Kate "Ma" Barker and her son, Fred, in shootouts that were dramatized in the press. That month, political economist Raymond Moley reported to FDR and Cummings that the "gravity of the crime problem, and recent successes of the federal government in dealing with it, have produced a considerable opinion in favor of enlargements in federal criminal jurisdiction." He recommended that the number of Hoover's field agents be more than doubled and his clerical staff and equipment be proportionally increased. Moley reassured the president that there was "no danger of autocracy" in the New Deal if such increases of federal power were accompanied by a development "on the part of the citizen [of] an increasing participation in public affairs."[26] Moley would prove to be mistaken. National audiences were receptive to the highly visible strategies of crime deterrence—strategies that offered visibility to the New Deal and FDR's leadership. One of my earlier studies illustrates how Hoover mythically narrated the war on crime in ways that "enlisted the support of spectators to help insulate the FBI from its senatorial oversight," evident in volumes of letters sent to local newspaper editors from across the country.[27] By the time of the crime conference in December, the FBI had arrested Bruno Hauptman for the kidnap and murder of Charles Lindbergh Jr. and had killed John Dillinger, "Pretty Boy" Floyd, and "Baby Face" Nelson. Matthew Cecil observes that these outlaws "became useful props in a publicity campaign FDR and Cummings envisioned as a powerful prompt for congressional action."[28]

Scholars of the rhetorical presidency have traditionally separated the institutional and rhetorical presidencies in ways that confound relationships between them. Jeffrey Tulis, for example, suggests that the core structures of the executive "established in 1789 remain essentially unchanged," but the rise of the bully pulpit in the nineteenth century changed the "understanding of the character of the constitutional system and the president's place in it." Writing about the New Deal, he observes that FDR's more robust speechwriting staff only continued and developed a precedent begun by Alexander Hamilton for institution building.[29] But, I argue, FDR created unprecedented tensions between the Oval Office and its discourse that changed both forever in a move to defend the presidency from congressional conservatives who wanted to restrain his power. The war on crime represented a return to the experiment launched by Woodrow Wilson with the Committee on Public Information, but in a much more permanent and unrestrained way. FDR symbolized his leadership with crime spectacles that represented the power of the New Deal. His strategy was simple: give the mass audience what it wanted in terms of crime control to satisfy its thirst for retributive justice. Herbert Hoover's administration was ridiculed for its procedural response to organized crime; this was accentuated by Al Capone's 1931 conviction for income tax evasion. Richard Gid Powers observes that the press taught "the public to see crime as a test of the government's ability to meet violent challenges with violent force." Instead of action, "President Hoover gave the country lectures about cooperation, states' rights, and constitutional limits on federal jurisdiction"—this after the Lindbergh baby was kidnapped and murdered.[30] When FDR requested broad executive power in his Inaugural, he announced that he planned to change the institutional presidency in ways that moved its power into the states, and his response to the crime problem was a means to represent what could be accomplished. Director Hoover was a tool that conservatives could not resist, for he was quick to align his detractors with the criminal underworld across the nation's local presses. The rhetorical and institutional presidencies transformed in how they converged with each other to extend executive power to a class of professional surrogates. New or rebranded bureaus with their own publicity units moved the locus of executive authority into the pressrooms of the bureaucracy, which diffused the power of the Oval Office to a bench of unelected surrogates.

Public excitement for crime drama aside, the DOJ, with its preference for academic professionalism, favored the idealistic philosophy of criminal rehabilitation over the FBI's realism. The *Washington Herald* reported in October 1935 that a "feud long standing in the Department of Justice" had surfaced "between Hoover and Sanford Bates, director of the Bureau of Prisons and Paroles." The newspaper explained that "Hoover's outspoken attack on parole abuses furthered the strife," and that DOJ personnel generally "sided with Bates."[31] The rivalry posed by the BOP to the FBI was significant for several reasons. As the only other DOJ bureau, the BOP served as the FBI's foremost competitor for appropriations. This juxtaposition created clashes where their jurisdiction overlapped. With his own statistical division, Bates could check Hoover's expertise with his own. Both men used aggregated data as evidence for claims that constituted epistemologically different realities. Hoover realistically located truth in Anglo-American culture. Bates idealistically located truth in sociological experimentation. Whereas Hoover recommended that society must "preserve itself" with the "Machine Gun School of Criminology," Bates recommended that society could be protected through rehabilitation programs as suggested by the Wickersham Commission.[32] In Bates's vision, most prisoners were persons who would better themselves if they had such opportunity. In this reality, the militarized law-enforcement apparatus that Hoover promoted, and FDR desired to symbolize the power of the New Deal, was not necessary or justified.

Moreover, Hoover's machine-gun school of criminology did more than just stop gangsters; it also diverted attention away from his sexuality and was a means to discredit critics who saw through his gendered performance. Whereas toughness on crime was enough to deceive sexual "dupes" who "'knew' a homosexual when they saw one," Morris argues, Hoover was paranoid and feared even more those gay "clairvoyants in his midst" who could see through his passing performance. The clairvoyant belongs to an "invisible audience for whom the pass is legible; who in turn collaborates in preserving by silence the perilous secret kept from unsuspecting dupes. Every act of passing is enacted, in other words, by means of the *fourth persona*: a collusive audience constituted by the textual wink." The scholar concludes that "Hoover's passing performance placed him in the spotlight but, ironically and strategically, beyond the pale of speculation" when he performed straightness by accusing and condemning criminals and critics of being gay to muddy the waters about his own sexuality. Morris identifies this tactic as the "pink herring." Unlike its conventional "counterpart of deflection that protects a silent subject avoiding exposure," the pink herring "must always deflect and signify at the same time," making obfuscation and intimidation the "twin acts of every pass."[33] This rhetorical strategy was a mainstay of Hoover's discourse; it was a part of a "pattern of claiming limited jurisdiction, denying charges outright, and ascribing subversive motives to accusers," observes Cecil.[34] Claims of limited jurisdiction reframed policy matters. Denials of malfeasance made claims upon reality. And, ascribing subversive motives to his accusers reframed his need for a secretive private life.

Toughness, denial, and accusation constrained Hoover's narrative persona between acts of police violence and the voice he used to justify such practices. Northwestern University law professor Newman F. Baker captured Hoover's voice in a February 1938 *Journal of Criminal Law and Criminology* article. In a series of quotes he borrowed from the director, Baker wrote:

> Criminals are not just criminals. They are: "Scum from the boiling pot of the underworld," "public rats," "lowest dregs of society," "scuttling rats in the ship of politics," "vermin in human form," "the slimy crew who feed upon crime," "desperados," "vermin spewed out of prison cells to continue their slaughter," "the octopus of the underworld." These "post graduates of outlawry" and "professors of crime" thrive "in the great fog of crime," and the "swamp and morasses of suffering," amid the "appalling scourge of perjury" and the "oleaginous connivings of venal politicians," aided and abetted by "sentimental yammerheads," "moronic adults" of "asinine behavior," "maudlin sentiment," and "inherent criminal worship." Away with these "moo-cow sentimentalists" with their "hashish dreams," "crime coddlers," "convict indulging theorists" with "their idiotic idolatry of cowardly outlaws"; "these sentimental theorists who dominate present day child guidance" with their "mealy mouthings" and their "whining pleas for sympathy"; these "hoity-toity professors."

Baker offered this mosaic from Hoover's speeches, and highlighted the melodramatic world to which Hoover's character belonged. He sarcastically added that the director "announced a hearty contempt for the 'cream-puff school of criminology whose daily efforts turn loose upon us the robber, the burglar, the arsonist, the killer, and the sex-degenerate.'" Written in the final months of the war on crime, Baker framed Hoover's rhetorical realism and the implications it had for public policy. He noted that Hoover's language encouraged a "'Catch 'Em and Hang 'Em' method of dealing with criminals" in what appeared to be a successful attempt to "get a handsome appropriation from Congress for his department."[35] Baker could confidently link Hoover's rhetoric, philosophy, and practices because, as Donald Pizer observes, theories from criminal anthropology of genetic degeneration were embedded into the style of literary realism, which suggested criminals were in a Darwinian struggle for survival against society and needed to be violently contained—a eugenicist perspective that also linked homosexuality with criminality.[36]

With FDR's help, the FBI director and his assistants in the CRS popularized a realistic rhetoric for crime discourse that resuscitated the work of Palmer and Marshall, and presented it as representative of New Deal philosophy. This discourse constituted an alternative frame to what Wickersham prescribed. Hoover's realism aligned with Cummings's war rhetoric, but diverged where he blamed crime on cultural changes that were also responsible for the New Deal, such as its embrace of academic experimentation. Instead, FBI rhetoric encouraged a worldview that preceded modernity. CRS discourse was persuasive, epistemologically, because it established continuity between public address, popular entertainment, and a range of discursive practice in the 1930s—political, economic, literary, scientific, and everyday life, and then religion in the 1940s. Realist logic interconnected political culture and popular entertainment in fiction and nonfiction texts that drew from the same types of evidence, relied on the same types of assumptions, and offered the same types of conclusions about crime, order, and human nature. The continuity spread simultaneously into different quarters of public life, such as the White House, Congress, and the press. With the spread of the FBI's rhetorical influence in so many different places, prison reformers in the ABA, universities, and the DOJ were increasingly isolated. Values that underpinned the New Deal were increasingly maligned in favor of an allegedly new worldview of law and order that was glamorized in a multimodal propaganda campaign. The worldview favored Hoover's insatiable appetite for appropriations and a political-cultural paradigm of government control. Contrary to what Moley advised, public participation in government initiated a slow drift toward citizen obedience to the state.

Crime News and Institutional Rhetoric

Pulp crime writer and circus promoter Courtney Ryley Cooper was instrumental in Hoover's makeover. Employed by the *American Magazine*, Cooper pitched the FBI a story idea in October 1933 that reprimanded the prison reform program and blamed reformers for coddling criminals.[37] Cooper would work closely with the CRS to highlight the perils of bank robbers, kidnappers, and sex offenders whose motives were often conflated and made to be the antithesis of Hoover in a domestic propaganda campaign. Additionally, the CRS operated as a liaison office between the director, the press, and Congress.[38] The publicity work was visible on the House floor. When Hoover entered Hollywood in 1935, he then also became a staple of the *Congressional Record* as Republicans and Democrats raced to show their support of his work, which he leveraged against his many rivals.

Cooper's inventive resources complemented Nichols's institutional mechanics within the CRS. The unit operated as a public relations office that traded access to crime reports for partnerships with many reporters, broadcasters, and editors through a letter-writing mill that carried Hoover's signature. Cecil observes that Hoover used his "iconic cultural status and the popular appeal of FBI crime stories" to build relationships with friendly members of the press and thereby "converted his fame and authority into a powerful public relations tool by creating the illusion of personal relationships with individual reporters and editors, members of Congress, local officials, and others." The partnership between Nichols and Cooper illustrates the institutionality of the FBI's power. Whereas Cooper invented a core message, Nichols promoted it across different communities of meaning and thereby undermined various systems depended upon for the separation of powers in government and culture.

Cooper turned to crime news after stints as a circus clown, publicist, manager, and press agent for the frontier spectacle of Buffalo Bill Cody's Wild West Show. As a journalist, he worked at the *Kansas City Star*, *New York World*, *Denver Post*, and *Chicago Tribune* before he was hired by the *American Magazine* to write about the prison reform program.[39]

Cooper ingratiated himself with Hoover and helped reinvent the FBI in terms of urban-crime storylines that cast Hoover as a red-blooded hero set against degenerates who made containment the only possible police strategy. Hoover worked with Cooper and Rex Collier to develop a formula for law-enforcement propaganda. Powers observes that it unified "all aspects of the FBI's operations into one coherent image" and it "became the model for all future publicity."[40] The narrative promoted containment rhetoric. In films, books, newspapers, magazines, journals, radio programs, and comic books, Cooper used this framework to lump criminals, lawyers, and politicians as well as police and prison reformers together in a foreign conspiracy against Anglo-America.

The formula was structured by popular Hollywood schema. Hoover recorded in a September 1934 memo that Cooper wanted to prove that a setup existed in practically every town where the gangster had "naturally assumed the place whereby he can control bonds, paroles," and the like through political affiliations, and to "'lick' the crime problem all this must be uprooted." Hoover told Cooper that this generic underworld conspiracy theory was absolutely sound.[41] Although Hoover admitted to Cooper that FBI files contained no information along these lines, Hoover still encouraged him to write a story about "political affiliations in gangster activities."[42] Cooper's theory did not emanate from historical records, but instead from realistic fiction. The urban-crime film genre witnessed a quick succession of "mouthpiece" films between 1931 and 1934 in which shyster lawyers with political affiliations successfully defended gangsters in the legal system. This film cycle was inspired by Gene Fowler's *The Great Mouthpiece* (1931), a biography about mafia defense attorney Bill Fallon, who died before the prison reform movement began.[43]

Cooper helped to circulate archetypal characters that insisted upon forms of containment. In October 1933, he proposed a story to the FBI on an "insidious creeping process" invented by the "convicts themselves and persons who perhaps meant well but who have brought about a serious condition in this country." In the wake of the Wickersham Commission's report and President Hoover's drive for criminal rehabilitation, Cooper wanted to write about prisons and how they had been turned into "country clubs." Cooper's editor sought a focus on how various convict organizations were behind the prison reform program, and how the convicts accomplished their goals by threat, force, and bribery. Cooper suggested that this would "arouse the country to such a point that something could be done about it" if the story indicted "the SYSTEM and the people of the United States who have permitted convict coddlers to get the upper hand." The charge of softness mimicked the first generation of realist writers who scoffed at the female novelists who preceded them, as well as the naturalists who later ridiculed the older realists for their own domesticity. The charge also preceded how political realists would dismiss idealists as somehow utopian, moralistic, legalistic, or emotional. Cooper suggested that his storylines should tell of "meddling women" and how they had "freed guilty man after guilty man."[44] This finer point of Cooper's conspiracy theory was also the subject of urban crime plotlines; female defense attorneys were repeatedly portrayed as conflicted by the love they felt for the men they defended.[45] The character logics circulated by Hollywood, therefore, interacted with the Cooper-Collier formula and set the bureau against soft or sentimental dupes, a condition that Palmer identified as "hyperesthesia" in 1919.[46]

Beyond his missives, the narrative formula also laid a path to stabilize Hoover's sexual identity. In the 1930s, a popular dichotomy existed in the public mind between gay and straight personality types.[47] The image of the gay man was informed by language coined in the Progressive Era to outline different types of men in public life after Oscar Wilde became the popular representation of homosexuality. G. Lowes Dickinson wrote in *Appearances* (1914), for example, that we have "divided men into Red-bloods and Mollycoddles. 'A Red-blood man' is a phrase which explains itself, 'Mollycoddle' is its opposite. We have adopted it from a famous speech of Mr. Roosevelt, and redeemed it—perverted it, if you will—to other uses." Dickinson described the red-blood man as the man of action, as the businessman and the soldier, as physically marked by muscularity, and who required a wife "for the instinct to propagate" who was estranged from him because he could not know "any point of view but his own." Conversely, the "Mollycoddle in action is the Crank; it is he who accomplishes reforms; who abolished slavery, for example, and revolutionized prisons and lunatic asylums." Dickinson described the Mollycoddle as the critic, as the intellectual, as the smug weakling who questioned everything, as isolated, alone, and without companions.[48] Kevin P. Murphy argues that the term "Mollycoddle" was used to ridicule "patrician, highly educated white men with literary associations" who were blamed for idealistic and sentimental literature, which was treated as a "feminizing influence on American culture." The invective, he concludes, "functioned as a precursor to the modern figure of the 'homosexual'" and was used by reformers like Roosevelt to stigmatize anti-imperialists and socialists.[49] Cooper's focus on "convict coddlers" and "meddling women," therefore, gendered prison reformers in ways that aligned the reform movement with homosexuality and aligned Hoover with the red-blooded man of action. As much as this gendered alignment would empower the FBI, its rich hypocrisy also locked it in a trajectory that ended in tyranny and eroded the very system it was sworn to protect.

The Cooper-Collier formula was significant for the manner in which it created the dichotomy and thereby offered Hoover a means to rebut whispers that he was gay and enact a more strategic persona. Equally as significant was the infrastructure built by Nichols in the CRS to amplify Hoover's cultural presence and authority. Through its network of contacts in the press, the unit saturated the media landscape and congressional spaces with rhetorical realism. The infrastructure not only supported continuity between popular entertainment and the FBI's claims on reality, it also drafted a bench of congressional surrogates who placed their rhetorical support behind the FBI and its propaganda. Below, I first examine how the FBI enlisted the help of Congress and then turn to the rhetorical world it constituted between the underworld and the middle-class home in everyday life.

CONGRESS, CRIME, AND THE NEW DEAL

Members of Congress responded to Professor Baker's article on the House floor with language that justified the CRS's narrative framework.

In March 1938, Representative Fred L. Crawford (R-MI), for example, declared that whatever "can be accomplished by publicly castigating the chief G-man for so ably labeling criminals is not plain in the editorial, but a person needs to be struck but once with the fangs of one of these serpents of Satan to have his own vocabulary of bolder and more stinging indictments against the criminal." He reassured his audience in gendered terms that there was no need to adopt "soft-toned phraseology in discussing" criminal activity, and that it was "no time for mollycoddling" or to "revert to a lavender-and-lace role in dealing with criminals, irrespective of what Mr. Baker and his experts in criminology might believe should be said."[50] Hoover could expect such rhetorical support because the CRS wrote speeches for members of Congress and built alliances with local and national media outlets across the country, which cast the FBI's political opponents as public enemies and built political support for members of Congress who publicly aligned themselves with the director.[51]

Additionally, for Democrats, the rhetoric of the CRS belonged to the New Deal. Quick to symbolize his rhetorical presidency with the war on crime, FDR announced at the crime conference that the "constant struggle to safeguard ourselves against the attacks of the lawless and the criminal elements" was a component part of his larger objective to release and direct the "vital forces that make for a healthy national life." Therefore, the president concluded, "law enforcement officers" were to be cured of "inadequate organization, unscientific administration and lack of public support and understanding."[52] These statements expanded upon his May 1934 "Statement on Signing Bill to Help the Federal Government Wage War on Crime and Gangsters." One day before Moley endorsed Hoover, FDR proclaimed that the spread of "fear in the underworld" was an "event of the first importance." He then suggested that "gangster extermination" would not be "completely effective so long" as the "public looks with tolerance upon known criminals, permits public officers to become corrupted," or "applauds efforts to romanticize crime." The president's rhetorical selection of "underworld" and "extermination" highlighted the frame used by the FBI to discuss criminals as rats, termites, and other pests to be eradicated. Roosevelt promised to arouse "public opinion" and equip the FBI with "new facilities, men and funds" to make it as "effective an instrumentality of crime detection and punishment as any of the similar agencies of the world."[53] FDR, therefore, aligned his presidency with FBI rhetoric, which also enjoyed bipartisan support in its feud with the BOP.

Three weeks after Crawford spoke to the House, Representative Lawrence J. Connery (D-MA) reprinted a letter in the *Congressional Record*, written by Tolson and addressed to the *Journal of Criminal Law and Criminology*, that reaffirmed Hoover's narrative persona. The associate director wrote, for example, "I believe Mr. Hoover needs no defense against the appropriate designation of habitual criminals in his speeches. Perhaps 'agricultural implement' is a more euphonious appellation for a spade, but it hardly seems to improve the accuracy of the designation," and he suggested that Baker had an "ostrich-like attitude in confronting the crime situation."[54] The FBI continually used a pattern of metaphors that imagined the social world in terms of the animal kingdom. This naturalist strategy cast public life as a Darwinian contest and offered Hoover a persona fit for mass culture.

The style dissociated the red-blooded from the mollycoddle persona, and thereby helped stabilize Hoover's sexual identity. Baker observed that Hoover insisted "one must belong to the machine-gun school of criminology or the cream-puff school" with "no middle ground."[55] Such language exemplified Hoover's longtime pattern of reframing arguments, denial, and accusing critics of what he might be accused of, to muddy the waters of public debate. The strategy placed Hoover on the side of straight men of action and advanced his support of deterrence over rehabilitation. Tolson responded in his letter that "Hoover would be extremely proud to be registered as one of those who are members of the machine-gun school of criminology for the reason that society is protected by machine guns and it has not been definitely determined that cream puffs are a marked deterrent to the desperado type of criminal." With the distinction drawn between Hoover and prison reformers, Tolson worked to impugn the motivations of critics and explain their difference of perspective.

He argued that there was something "radically wrong" with the "proponents of any system who are not only unable or unwilling to reform their organization, but resent efforts on the part of others to point out and remedy those evils." Academics like Baker were resentful and out of touch, Tolson argued, because they mistakenly prioritized their own authority in the "protected cloisters of the classroom." Here, Tolson again grounded Hoover's professional authority in a red-blooded persona and falsely claimed that Hoover risked "his life in the actual personal apprehension of these desperados."[56] This claim referenced the spectacle of the May 1936 Alvin Karpis arrest. Hoover fraudulently cast himself as the arresting officer in a narrative that impugned the motivations of the chairman of the Senate Judiciary Committee, Kenneth McKellar (D-TN), and elevated himself in the political-cultural hierarchy, a narrative that also helped silence whispers about his sexual orientation.[57]

The CRS used the dispute with Baker to attack BOP Director Bates by implication. Nichols's predecessor, Assistant Director W. H. D. Lester, observed in a January 1935 memorandum to Tolson, for example, that his unit's rhetorical campaign made "considerable criticism, directly and by innuendo, of local police departments as well as of the Bureau of Prisons of the Department of Justice."[58] Hoover preferred this strategy because, as he explained to Cooper in November 1933, it protected him from potential objections made by the BOP against him for using his "position in the Department" to make sensitive information available to the press.[59] Tolson argued that if Hoover "had advocated that every criminal should have a radio in his cell; that recreational features for confirmed, habitual criminals should be such as to render their incarceration a thing of pleasure rather than a punishment," or if he had "spent his life catering to the wants and desires of habitual criminals," then "he would have merited the approval of Mr. Baker," who was marred by "sentimentality and even ignorance." This perspective echoed Cooper's own description of prisons as "country clubs" and caricatured the system promoted by Bates. Tolson made a finer point of the matter and referred to American prisons as a "combination of sieve and ladies' seminary with the accompaniment of 'swing' bands, which seems to characterize our modern prisons."[60] Tolson's gendered language, therefore, reframed the controversy over the FBI's rhetorical style, denied that it embellished the crime situation, and accused its critics of sentimentality (which was code for gay), all of which helped constitute a heterosexual identity for Hoover and defamed his critics.

Moreover, the image of the soft or comfortable prison was a realistic attack on Bates, his idealism, and the public policy that empowered him. For example, the Act to Reorganize the Administration of Federal Prisons (1930) "established in the Department of Justice a Bureau of Prisons, to be in charge of a director who . . . shall be appointed by and serve directly under the Attorney General." This act charged the BOP director with "the management and regulation of all Federal penal and correctional institutions" and the responsibility for the "safe-keeping, care, protection, instruction, and discipline" of all prisoners. In the event of overcrowding, the attorney general was given authority to build more facilities with the consent of Congress.[61] The BOP had nineteen institutions by January 1934, including penitentiaries, federal jails, reformatories, drug addiction centers, hospitals, and prison work camps.[62] These facilities were marked by decorative architecture, expansive libraries, quality furniture and food, sanitary living conditions, landscaped grounds, and staffs of social workers.[63] Idealist fervor in the DOJ threatened the FBI's potential for growth. It did not make moral sense to spend large sums of money on a department that would kill criminals if another department could use that appropriation to reform them—a difference of moral sense that epistemologically divided idealists and realists, and the worlds in which they operated.

The difference in perspective limited Hoover's control of reality. Tolson, for example, queried if Baker would "still cry 'peace where there is no peace,' and pretend, in approved Pollyanna-ish terms, that all is well with the country, that crime is not a serious menace as has been stated recently by one of Mr. Baker's associates"—namely, Bates—or would Baker "point to the figures which reveal" that crime was always on the rise.[64] This argument underscored the tension between the bureau directors. As the FBI arrested more and more individuals, its suspects were eventually transferred to Bates's custody. This flow of bodies filled BOP facilities at an accelerated rate, which threatened FBI appropriations and room for institutional growth. Bates explained to the House Appropriations Committee in 1936 that the prison population had ballooned at an unforeseen rate, in part, because of the "general increased activity of the Department of Justice in the old lines of crime."[65] Of course, he also wrote in the *New York Times* that America had "more crime" than other nations because it had "more crimes. We have attempted to lift people to a higher standard of morality" by the "doubtful method of punishing them into conformity," and thereby signaled the origins of containment culture.[66] The FBI's realism and the BOP's idealism, therefore, intersected and clashed where the institutions overlapped, and Hoover's gendered response was a wholesale universe that deflected attention away from his own motives and impugned those who might obstruct his ascendant power.

THE CRS IN MASS CULTURE

Members of Congress could so comfortably take sides in the DOJ feud and claim the FBI's rhetorical style as their own because, from the CRS's inception in 1935, Nichols's unit worked tirelessly to make rhetorical realism dominant in popular culture through a multimodal campaign that spanned fiction and nonfiction formats. This media content offered Hoover a red-blooded persona from which to narrate the story of the FBI with realism, an option otherwise not available. Ann Chisholm observes that the first-person narrative must be "consistent with the narrator's manifold personae. If a narrator's account is to be believed, if it is to present a feasible guide for action, the story must contain a narrator whose personae are harmonious with the choices within, and with the trajectory of, the story in its entirety."[67] This rule of harmony suggests that Hoover's narratives could only be credible if he were perceived to be confidently heterosexual, because red-blooded realism was thought to be a product of heterosexuality. Conversely, the credibility of Hoover's heterosexual public persona required him to tell realistic stories, lest an inconsistency between narrative and persona lead to an unfavorable read

National Archives and Records Administration.

Shirley Temple with J. Edgar Hoover in Hollywood, wearing wedding ring, September 1937.

of his private life. Accordingly, he routinely lent the assistance of his department to film producers in return for various levels of influence over their scripts. The CRS first collaborated with Hollywood to make Warner Brothers' *'G' Men* (1935), MGM's *Whipsaw* (1935), United Artists' *Let 'Em Have It* (1935), Twentieth Century Fox's *Show Them No Mercy!* (1935), and Paramount Pictures' *Mary Burns, Fugitive* (1935).[68] In these films, the FBI represented gangsters as human vermin and thus reproduced the naturalist language schema of earlier gangster films.[69] The success of these films led to more G-man movies that ran through the war on crime, like Warner Brothers' *Public Enemy's Wife* (1936), RKO Radio Pictures' *Special Investigator* (1936), RKO Radio Pictures' *Smashing the Rackets* (1938), Universal Pictures' *Missing Evidence* (1939), Paramount Pictures' *Persons in Hiding* (1939), and Paramount Pictures' *Queen of the Mob* (1940).[70]

The films switched the central character of the gangster with the G-man in urban-crime plotlines that extended from the Prohibition era. Thomas Shatz explains that the popular story formulas maintained "coherent, value-laden narrative systems" that celebrated ideological precepts and affirmed American values. Specifically, urban-crime films reified cultural threats in the form of antagonists who were irrationally brutal and opposed law and order. Gangsters represented the "perverse alter ego of the ambitious, profit-minded American male" in an alienated urban environment with class distinctions. Because antagonists were denied legitimate routes to power and success, they turned to depersonalized "technology—guns, cars, phones, etc." Conflict was "translated into violence" and resolved through the elimination of the character.[71] The use of deadly force by antagonists justified its use by protagonists, which led the urban-crime genre to treat the punishment of cultural offenders in a hard-boiled, unsentimental manner.[72]

Beyond film, the CRS also turned to radio and print media, and exploited perceptions of a free and independent press. Cecil argues that the story of Hoover's public relations is also a "story of the alleged watchdog of the Fourth Estate—molders of public opinion—who, because of some combination of personal politics and ambition, chose to close their eyes to the Bureau's excesses, toe the FBI public relations line, and uncritically amplify Hoover's FBI myth, thus enabling the Bureau's transgressions of civil liberties."[73] The CRS helped script commercial radio programs like CBS's *Gang Busters* (1936–1957). In 1935, Phillips H. Lord proposed a program that would emphasize "the scientific angle in which the Department attacks crime." He offered to "work in close harmony" with the bureau and to "have the scripts checked by some member of the Department."[74] The emphasis on scientific administration reaffirmed Hoover's public persona and offered a counterpoint to the professional stature of prison reformers like Baker, who reminded readers that Hoover's career began as a redbaiter under Palmer, a mode of politics out of step with the New Deal.[75] The CRS also developed content for comic strips like Ledger Syndicate's *War on Crime*.[76] Pulps, comic strips, movie serials, cereal boxes, Big Little Books, and bubblegum cards all provided a framework suitable to advance realist notions of a world steeped in chaos and on the verge of collapse, and therefore in need of state control by the FBI. Storylines reinforced isolationism and xenophobia through contrasts between heroic Anglo-Saxon men who were motivated to do good for the sake of justice and antagonists who were motivated by evil to threaten cultural values and social stability.[77] Wilbur R. Miller notes that protagonists held pessimistic views of city life and perpetually revealed underworld conspiracies wherein upper-class villains hired street hoodlums to commit crimes against society. He adds that the genre "expressed the fears and values" of middle-class American society toward a new and uncertain city life, filled with strange peoples and ideas.[78]

Cooper placed Hoover in this scripted world and, with the help of Nichols's networking, won the rhetorical support of Congress for the persona they invented. Representative Otha Wearin (D-IA) encouraged his colleagues in March 1937, for example, to "read some of the authoritative writings on crime by Courtney Riley Cooper, who knows more about the manner in which that rotten disease of the body politic, and the people themselves, has spread over this land than any other man in America, and is rendering a profound public service by exposing it." He added that the FBI deserved praise for how it had established a new "psychology of law enforcement."[79] In August 1933, near the zenith of Hoover's sexual vulnerability and his turf war with Bates, Cooper described Hoover's persona in terms that mimicked the pulps. He wrote that Hoover was a "master detective who simply does not conform to any picture of the average crime chaser." A student of French, English, and Canadian law-enforcement methods, the director was accepted as an "expert all over the country" and knew "all the scientific short cuts devised for the unraveling of crime."[80] That same month, *Newsweek* added that Hoover's "build resembles a light heavy-weight's."[81] Soon afterward, the *New York Herald Tribune* commended him as "one of the world's great criminologists" and for his "faultless breeding."[82] Hoover was lionized in such fashion throughout the war on crime. In the introduction to *Person in Hiding* (1938), for example, Cooper praised the director for having "machine-gun" speech delivery, with a "sixth sense" that could find a "flaw in seeming perfection."[83] Hoover's public persona was thus built in large measure by third parties who prepackaged a public identity that would likely appeal to national audiences, balanced somewhere between verisimilitude and suspended disbelief.

True-crime storylines bridged the world of pulp fiction into reality with sensational crime news stories that offered the FBI a coherent narrative to discredit its critics. Ron Goulart observes that content for pulp-fiction characters like ace detective Nick Carter was largely drawn from "newspaper crime reporting and other contemporary accounts," which allowed comic strip detectives to travel to "real locales" and challenge "the real criminals of the day."[84] Conversely, a mediated Hoover existed in true-crime texts with superhuman crime-fighting powers and fought fictitious villains. The press largely adopted the CRS's generic frames, which allowed the director to traverse these interconnected worlds. Publishers celebrated the rise of J. Edgar Hoover and his G-men as a new breed of action detective heroes.[85] This genre was well suited for Hoover to demonstrate his leadership and interpretations of the war on crime.

The urban-crime genre interplayed realist notions of power and technocratic control. George Orwell observes in "Boys' Weeklies" (1939) that detective stories oriented readers to identify with an "all-powerful character who dominates everyone" through the threat of violence. The protagonist is a superman whose power emanates from physical strength and whose usual method for problem solving is a "sock on the jaw."[86] Goulart adds that heroes could "box, fence, swim, and operate whatever new mechanism came along—automobile, airplane, etc."[87] Poetic justice was privileged before law. Villains were routinely punished by death in gun battles, mob lynching, and suicide; courts were nonexistent. Similarly, public enemies were rarely imprisoned or executed by the state.[88] In this manner, notions of law and justice were squarely separated. The genre dictated that deterrence—not rehabilitation—was the natural response to criminals who challenged American value sets.

Members of Congress almost uniformly offered their support to the FBI in the rhetorical context invented by the CRS. Representative John

McCormack (D-MA) rose on the House floor in June 1936 to "refute certain unfair and improper criticism recently made against the Federal Bureau of Investigation, and to let the American people know that those few criticisms do not represent the viewpoint of Members of Congress."[89] This defense came after Representative Marion Zioncheck (D-WA) referred to Hoover as a "dictator" and scoffed at "real American justice" when he described the "illusion that has been deliberately created and built up by the master of fiction, J. Edgar Hoover, the great 'G-man'" as one of the "most popular illusions that the American people are suffering from today." In particular, Zioncheck condemned Hoover for the FBI's use of violence and noted that "four 'G-men' have been killed and eight gangsters, and we cannot find out how many innocent people were killed in the process."[90] Nevertheless, McCormack shielded Hoover and warned of "unfair and unwarranted" criticism that had been "directed against him," that a "silent whispering campaign has been undertaken from some known sources, but the unanimous press of America have editorially commented upon the unfair criticism and have supported Mr. Hoover." For the congressman, the support of the press was evidence of Hoover's virtue. He noted that the "press of America have unanimously expressed appreciative sentiments of the American people for Director Hoover and the men of his bureau for purging America of organized crime."[91] Senator Henry Ashurst (D-AZ) shared such sentiments. Without mention of Sanford Bates or the BOP, he proclaimed in May that "Attorney General Cummings and Mr. J. Edgar Hoover have nobly striven to provide . . . protection and security," and that their work justified the senator's use of superlatives in "describing the activities of the Department of Justice in its efforts to detect crime [and] prosecute law violators."[92] For most members of Congress, the style of realism justified the violence it invoked.

Such rhetorical support helped the FBI in disputes with the Bureau of the Budget over its expansive appropriation, a strategy observed by Baker. Representative McCormack directed his comments toward the 1937 budget when he told his colleagues that "we cannot be lulled into a feeling of security which will result in the Congress reducing [the FBI's] appropriation."[93] In negotiations for the 1938 budget, Representative Virginia Jenckes (D-IN) appealed to "American womanhood" when she pleaded on the House floor in March 1937 that "Congress give Attorney General Cummings and Mr. J. Edgar Hoover all the money and all the men that they deem necessary" to end "kidnaping, white slavery, extortion, bank robbery, and other crimes." She encouraged her colleagues to "give the Federal Bureau of Investigation this money and let them put on duty the G-men they think are necessary, not the number of men the Budget Bureau thinks are necessary." After the Budget Bureau reduced the FBI's requested amount, she reassured Congress that "your constituents, parents, women, churches, women's organizations, and business organizations, will applaud and praise you if you will heed my plea and place back in the appropriation the full amount requested by Mr. Hoover."[94] Similarly, Crawford justified the FBI's request one year later, explaining that the "Bureau of the Budget is fully aware that the Federal Bureau of Investigation is a growing institution. Burdens automatically placed upon it increase each year. . . . Despite the fact the G-men broke the backbone of the 'snatch' racket, other crimes have increased."[95] With such rhetorical backing in Congress, the FBI's appropriation grew from $2.75 million for fiscal year 1933 with 353 special agents to $6.2 million for fiscal year 1938 with 658 agents, amid the economic constraints of the Great Depression.[96]

FDR's linguistic framework and what it entailed for matters of law enforcement was adopted by New Dealers in Congress in speeches that celebrated the forcefulness of the FBI. The combined support of Congress and the presidency lent official credibility to a fantasy of law and order that blurred the boundaries of fact and fiction in ways that made Hoover a celebrity in popular and political culture. He was used by anxious New Dealers to signify what federal-state cooperation could accomplish at a time when expanded federal power was still subject to critique by Republicans. They were seemingly naive about the power of language and the philosophical baggage it carried. Prison reformers understood the problem more acutely because they experienced how it maligned their motives and image, and how it displaced the influence of the Wickersham Commission. What congressional New Dealers did not appreciate was how a staunch anti–New Deal message was embedded into the style of the FBI's rhetorical realism.

Repetition, Amplification, and Cultural Authority

The language used by Hoover's boosters in Congress belonged to the narrative formula developed by Cooper and Collier, which was soon amplified by a circulation strategy. "Nichols's value to Hoover and the Bureau," Cecil observes, "extended beyond his work with the news and entertainment media. It extended as well to government relations, where Nichols was similarly successful as the Bureau's primary liaison to members of Congress and other government officials."[97] When Nichols arrived in the CRS in 1935, the unit began to systematically request that Democratic members of Congress insert Hoover's speeches into the *Congressional Record.* Between 1935 and 1938, Representatives William P. Connery Jr. (D-MA), Thomas S. McMillan (D-SC), F. Ryan Duffy (D-WI), Wright Patman (D-TX), Jennings Randolph (D-WV), Virginia Jenckes (D-IN), and William Gibbs McAdoo (D-CA) added the FBI director's speeches to the *Congressional Record.* These speeches were addressed to the New York Chamber of Commerce, IACP, Peace Officers Association of Oklahoma, Round Table Forum of the *New York Herald Tribune*, Daughters of the American Revolution (DAR), Boys' Club of America, American Newspaper Publishers Association (ANPA), Association of Life Insurance Presidents, FBI National Police Academy, General Federation of Women's Clubs, and Oklahoma Baptist University.[98]

The CRS's practice of inserting speeches into the *Congressional Record* was only one part of a larger publicity program to extend the reach and influence of its rhetoric. The section forged relationships with the press under Hoover's signature to amplify his cultural presence and authority. Former assistant director William C. Sullivan later revealed that the network of field offices allowed Hoover to "place 'news' stories—invented and written in the bureau, really nothing more than press releases, puff pieces for the FBI—in newspapers around the country." The FBI's strength "was in the small dailies and weeklies; and with hundreds of these papers behind him, Hoover didn't give a damn about papers like the *New York Times* or the *Washington Post.*" However, Sullivan noted that "scores of Washington-based reporters printed stories we gave them too, and they usually printed them under their own bylines."[71] This system of dissemination generated thousands of news articles and editorials published in local newspapers, credited to local newsmen, and written in the naturalist style. Frequently, periodicals reprinted FBI speeches in full or reported on them, which granted his rhetoric still further reach. With this infrastructure in place, publications like *Vital Speeches of the Day*, *Dicta*, *New York Herald Tribune*, *New York Times*, and *The Quill* reprinted speeches that were added to the *Congressional Record.*[99] The CRS transformed the American media landscape into an FBI echo chamber.

The context in which the FBI could expand so quickly, amid the Great Depression no less, was infused with the rhetoric and ideology of the Progressive Era, another moment in time marked by large-scale federal institution building. Then, reformers were driven by the stresses of urbanization, industrialization, and immigration—stresses communicated by orators like Theodore Roosevelt and a generation of novelists with a style that Hoover mimicked in the war on crime. The world that he narrated was divided between two spaces of action in which Anglo-America was forever on the verge of invasion by an underworld. These spaces were animated by Protestant mores of good and evil wherein criminals from the underworld attempted to invade, creep, or spread into the moral geography of the middle-class home. The process of movement was characterized by imagery of animals, disease, and natural disaster that could be stopped if properly contained. The soul of the New Deal was likewise divided. Whereas expanded government power was a tool that could be used to fight against evil and the underworld, the reform spirit of national cooperation and social uplift was aligned with forces that worked against Anglo-American culture. The loyalty of prison reformers was maligned for how they wanted to rehabilitate criminals, which sharply contrasted with red-blooded masculinity. In his many speeches, Hoover and his ghostwriters invented narratives and an appropriate voice for the director that constituted his narrative persona, which lent him credibility. For now, New Dealers in Congress from across the country could stand united and proud of the resources they brought to the fight. Below, I examine speeches inserted into the *Congressional Record* during the war on crime, which were sometimes also reprinted elsewhere. These texts represent a small sample of discourse from a propaganda mill that circulated an immense volume of rhetoric that was designed to immerse diverse audiences in the FBI's rhetorical realism.

CRIME AND THE UNDERWORLD

Consistent with Cooper's 1933 memo about "country club" prisons, the FBI cast facilities operated by the BOP as controlled by criminals. Hoover told the DAR in April 1936, for example, that "convict lovers" had brought about the "system of traveling bands for convicts, football games for convicts, tennis courts for convicts, radios in the prison blocks, and newspapers in every cell," for the "sneering vermin of gangdom" and the "foul offspring of our national filth." The FBI director equated such comforts to probation and parole, which he argued allowed criminals to "walk sneeringly through prison doors [and] again seize their instruments of depredation."[100] The problem, as outlined by Cooper, was systemic. Hoover lamented to the Boys' Club of America in May 1936 that the "community institution has fallen into the grasping hands of the renegades of our political system." He described such people as "the traitor, the vile enemy in our political family which seeks to disrupt our institutions of government; who knifes from within; who has only selfish purposes; who is the antagonist of everything that is honorable in our present-day form of government." Hoover implied that the BOP director and his employees were suspects in this conspiracy. This kind of reformer, he argued, "sneaks into our reformatories, into our probation system, into our prisons, always with one foul purpose—the realization of personal gain at the expense of the common wealth."[101] In Hoover's realistic perspective, reform was a façade used to empower criminals and advance their lives of crime. Because the realistic purpose for prison was punishment, it was supposed to be cruel and uncomfortable to achieve a deterrent effect.

The ideology behind literary naturalism was at the core of the FBI's attack on prison reformers, which surfaced as political realism when he spoke on degeneracy. In his December 1937 speech to the Association of Life Insurance Presidents, for example, Hoover argued that "crime is as malignant as any cancer, and it is as distinct a subject of health as tuberculosis." In a reference to homosexuality, he informed his audience that many "crimes are those of degeneracy, often committed by persons afflicted with diseases which only recently have been discussed in public." He elaborated that "the surprising increase of degenerate sex crimes within the last few years has revealed an urgent necessity for corrective action" by way of a "program of suppression and prevention" that would remove gay men from the "communion of daily life." He traced, like other problems, the invasion of homosexuality to the BOP and argued that "degenerates" were "improperly incarcerated" in "many of our jails and some of our reformatories and penitentiaries" where they "can spread their degeneracy to others and thus increase their menace."[102] Morris is therefore right to see in Hoover's discourse a strategy to divert attention away from his own sexuality. But, Hoover's discourse on sex crime also needs to be placed in the context of the war on crime, where it was used in the realist tradition for other political purposes as well.

Discourses on degeneracy functioned as containment rhetoric that attempted to separate Anglo-America from people marked as sexually, culturally, and racially different. Naturalists scripted plotlines in which drugs mixed with heredity caused people who were not purebred Anglo-American to become wild beasts. For example, Frank Norris wrote in "A Case for Lombroso" (1897) that a Spanish woman's "race was almost exhausted, its vitality low, and its temperament refined to the evaporation point," and she could thus be "called a degenerate."[103] Drug use was said to trigger a biological process that undid evolution and thus reduced the user to a less evolved and civilized state.[104] This perspective was informed by Progressive Era criminology. In *Criminal Man* (1889), for example, Cesare Lombroso observed that alcohol caused animals to become "irritable and savage like their wild ancestors" and suggested the same for criminals, whom he identified as trapped in "reversion to a former state" of evolution. His colonialist perspective was racialized. He noted that in "Africa, the explorer Stanley found a species of bandit called Ruga-Ruga, an indigenous people who made use of cannabis," which led them to "crime, suicide, or insanity" as well as mental and physiological "degeneration." He sometimes described criminals as people with "dark skin, thick and curly head hair" who resembled "savages and the colored races," and other times as "atavistic reproductions of not only savage men but also the most ferocious carnivores and rodents."[105] Notions of degeneracy were thus steeped in racialized terms that communicated determinism, so no amount of investment could reform or uplift the criminal and any attempt was foolhardy. Crime prevention, therefore, required force and violence to eliminate the lawbreaker who violated human law and the laws of nature.

The rhetoric of degeneracy limited policy solutions to more red-blooded responses, which aligned Hoover with the realist ideal of the confident heterosexual fighter. Theodore Roosevelt constructed what he called "impractical idealists," Murphy observes, in ways that transformed the "familiar figure of the effete and effeminate reformer" into the "degenerated and mentally diseased homosexual." Roosevelt's language conflated political and sexual crime along the lines of criminal anthropological theories, which classified anarchists and other criminal types as homosexuals.[106] In "How Not to Help Our Poor Brother" (1897), for example, Roosevelt condemned the "maudlin sentimentalist" for his attempt to "bring down the work and reward of the thrifty and intelligent to the level of the capacity of the weak, the shiftless, and the idle."[107] Likewise, in Hoover's speech to the Boys' Club of America, he proclaimed that the FBI's "first problem" was to eliminate the "maudlin sentiment" of the "cocktail bar" and "sentimental yammerheads."[108] He further elaborated in his speech to the DAR that "patriotic organizations" must quash the "sob sisters," the "theorists, pseudo criminologists, hypersentimentalists, criminal coddlers, convict lovers, and fiddle-faced reformers," the "medical quacks, the parole panderers, and the misguided sympathizers."[109] In the Progressive Era, critics of reform counterpoised modern ideas for prison in ways that linked sentimentalism, idealism, and homosexuality.[110] Hoover mimicked this strategy to refute a philosophy that ran counter to his interests as well as to prove his own heterosexual confidence.

Realist presumptions about human nature ordered an entire cast of public enemies in ways that lumped together gangsters, defense attorneys, prison reformers, and legislators who passed laws in support of the BOP. In July 1935, for example, Hoover enumerated before the IACP that law enforcement was up against the "human rat" with a "gun in his hand and murder in his heart" who was not a "victim of environment or circumstances or inhibitions or malformed consciousness, to be reformed by a few kind words, a pat on the cheek and freedom at the earliest possible moment." He elaborated that their "enemies" were the "criminals themselves and their friends and allies," such as "shyster lawyers and other legal vermin who consort with criminals," the "criminal jackal" or "legal shyster in law-making who, in meetings of bar associations and legislatures, cries out against every statute which aids the law-enforcement officer and works with fanatical zeal for laws which will hamper him." This enemy was "backed by the politician, crooked and otherwise, who is willing to trade the property, the well-being, the security, and even the lives of law-abiding persons for ballots spawned in prison cells, and the support of gutter scum." Hoover charged that all these characters were "enemies to our cause and enemies to society," so therefore belonged to the "underworld."[111] Because criminals were allegedly unredeemable, the FBI cast aspersions on the motivations of all who attempted their social uplift, a principle of the New Deal and a harbinger of things to come.

He projected an invasive vision of threat, one based in naturalist imagery of the Western frontier, which required containment. In his January 1936 speech to the Peace Officers Association of Oklahoma, for example, he compared the spread of crime to that of wildfire. Similar to how Palmer compared Communism to a "prairie fire," the FBI director suggested that like "the prairie fires that once swept this region, starting from a tiny blaze and raging with the first sweep of the wind into instruments of major disaster, crime of today may begin with a petty infraction and, within [a] seemingly insignificant space of time, encompass every form of outlawry."[112] In this way, crime was also like a cancerous growth, or in Hoover's words, "malignant." The influence of "crime," Hoover argued, "creeps into the courts, it creeps through the bars of the penitentiaries, it makes its insidious way into the meetings of pardon and parole boards, and it practically places a medal of honor upon the man who can defeat the law and get away with it." Even small infractions, therefore, were worthy of great concern because the "spark and tiny flame" of "local crime violations" often led to the "sweeping destruction of the prairie fire." His analogy cast reformers as the oxygen that fueled combustion. He referred to "prisons" as a "springboard toward major criminality" under the watch of "sentimental or otherwise expedient boards" that gave "freedom for a new assault upon the peace and dignity of our citizens."[113] In the FBI's imagination, therefore, crime could not be left undisciplined because it invaded or multiplied when left unpunished. This rationale justified the expansion of repressive power, given to people who illustrated moral authority and a willingness to fight on behalf of the community against those who showed a lack of moral self-restraint.

MORAL GEOGRAPHY OF THE MIDDLE-CLASS HOME

Hoover worked to make the crime problem seem local and immediate in everyday life to his audiences, where he placed it against the middle-class home, his second and idealized space of action. As David B. Danbom explains, the Progressive generation matured in the Victorian Era, which linked Victorianism and Progressivism in ways that informed the modern age. The Victorian world was structured by white, native-born, middle-class, Protestant theories of human nature and behavior that hypocritically stressed the principle of self-restraint, which in religion and politics was said to be a requisite to advance civilization. Whereas self-restraint in sobriety, hard work, and thrift was strictly adhered to, its advocates frequently failed to regulate their own ambition, avarice, aggression, materialism, or gluttony. Because drunkenness was frequently blamed for poverty, advocates of individualism frequently argued that poverty could only be addressed when the poor replaced their self-indulgence with self-restraint.[114] Moreover, Nancy Tomes observes that affluent Victorians were "house-proud people" who operated in a cult of domesticity and worked to offer moral uplift with their homes. They invested "family life, particularly child rearing, with enormous moral and social significance," which was frequently framed in terms of cleanliness, hygiene, and sanitation.[115] Such ideas helped the FBI transform the crime war into a culture war, and to transform evidence of cultural drift into that of moral corruption.

The FBI's appeals to tradition were continuous with more liberal criticisms of the New Deal, which were also grounded in the frontier myth. Walter Lippmann observed in *The Good Society* (1937), for example, that political "progressivism in countries like England and the United States" was merely the "increasing ascendency of the state: always the cry is for more officials with more power over more and more of the activities of men." He described the drift as a "great schism in the human outlook," and noted that the "essential difference between the faith that our generation has embraced and the faith that it has forsaken" was located in the belief that "some men can . . . manage the destiny of other men." Like Hoover, he castigated social democracy as a "gigantic heresy of an apostate generation" and a betrayal of nineteenth-century "pioneers of liberalism." He drew analogies between political systems in Russia, Germany, Italy, and America to argue that all used "unremitting government propaganda" from a "government bureau" to remake public opinion among the citizenry. Lippmann anchored the analog in the naturalist tradition, arguing that there were "important differences between lions and tigers, even between African and Indian lions. But from the point of view of . . . a goat or a lamb, the common characteristics of all the great carnivores are more significant than their differences."

In America, Lippmann called this process the "gradual collectivism" of the "New Deal," and a "rebellion against the moral heritage of western society" that threatened a "relapse into barbarism."[116] The text was significant in its critique of the New Deal, Dieter Plehwe observes, in that its publication "marked the beginning of a new dawn in the history of neoliberalism. . . . The book was brimming with insights that would later constitute the conventional wisdom in neoliberal circles."[117] Even more, it rebutted New Deal practice and philosophy with a liberal rhetoric of the past, draped in a realistic language scheme that emphasized the frontier myth. All of which was significant, adds Angus Burgin, because Lippmann, through "his column 'Today and Tomorrow,' syndicated in more than 100 newspapers and read by more than ten million Americans," played a role in public life "that garnered his opinions an extraordinary breadth of influence."[118] Lippmann's criticisms of the New Deal offered fodder to FBI propagandists who sought to turn New Dealers against themselves. Hoover's culture war was thus bolstered by liberal appeals to government restraint, even those that implicated the FBI.

The director worked to infuse the symbolic value of the war on crime with Victorian theories of self-restraint and individualism in ways that synced with liberal calls for a more restrained New Deal. Hoover told the DAR in March 1936, for example, "We can never make peace with the underworld. It constantly threatens an invasion of our homes, our happiness, and our civil and public rights." The collapse of the middle-class home and Victorian mores, Hoover argued, was the cause of the crime problem. He observed that the nation required "good old-fashioned American housecleaning" to restore the "old-fashioned influence of the old-fashioned home." This space was central to order, he argued, because it was there that the "strong men, good men, honest men" of the past were "reared in homespun surroundings, upon homespun philosophies." He contended that, historically, "America grew and prospered by unswerving loyalty to high ideals, by unfaltering respect and reverence for the law and by the kindly but unfailing vigilance of the home. Until that vigilance is restored we cannot hope for a lessening of the terrible toll of crime upon the youth of America."[119] In Hoover's vision, the middle-class home was central to law and order because it taught discipline and moral order. Hoover professed before the General Federation of Women's Clubs in May 1938, for example, that "discipline is something definitely inculcated in other days, and there were ideals and principles taught in other days that we may well teach again before America and the world forget the qualities that created and sustained it." Chief among these values was repression, a core value of both Victorianism and realism. He explained that the "field of the home preeminently belongs to the women." It was in this space that "lessons in constructive discipline" should be taught, "which seems so sadly lacking in these modern times" when "expressionism has run riot." He lamented that "children" were too often encouraged to "express the viler phases of their individual nature which should be definitely and eternally repressed. We can have no future expression of our higher qualifications unless the lower conflicting elements are repressed by discipline," as represented by the "dens of vice and debauchery."[120] What was strong, good, honest, and "real," said Hoover, was gained by discipline, not desire, and could be achieved through repression.

While the FBI praised self-restraint or individualism as a prominent value of the national character, it still also expected cooperation from affiliated institutions that reported crime news. Hoover told the ANPA in April 1937, for example, that he "preferred the term 'public rat,' rather than 'public enemy'" because it better captured the "craven stealthiness" of criminals. The FBI director suggested that John Dillinger should have been framed as the "filthy type of vermin that he was, crawling through the holes of our law enforcement" rather than a "Robin Hood."[121] William Beverly notes that Dillinger "understood public relations" and enjoyed "popular media representations that aestheticized him and repressed the danger he posed" so much that "he briefly became more popular than his G-man pursuers."[122] For example, *Time* magazine exclaimed in May 1934 that "to be plentifully loved and diligently hunted is the lot of desperadoes." *Time* also referred to Dillinger as "Robin Hood"—a metaphor that equated Hoover with the villainous Sheriff of Nottingham.[123] Such frames obviously threatened the director's stature, which in turn jeopardized the FBI's jurisdiction and appropriations. Hoover stressed the importance of conformity among the media in order to eclipse other representations. He announced at the March 1936 Round Table Forum of the *New York Herald Tribune* that America was "supposed to be one nation, one people," yet diversity in thought required a "heavy reconstruction of the American viewpoint toward better parental discipline and a greater sense of law abiding beginning in the home."[124] Hoover thus identified individualism as a philosophy of thought control and repression to advance Anglo-American culture.

Like the naturalists, Hoover cast the worldview that the CRS popularized in terms of the frontier myth. Richard Slotkin observes that "mythology is a complex of narratives that dramatizes the world vision and historical sense of a people or culture, reducing centuries of experience into a constellation of compelling metaphors." He concludes that the "narrative action of the myth-tale recapitulates that people's experience in their land, rehearses their visions of that experience in its relation to their gods and the cosmos, and reduces both experience and vision to a paradigm."[125] When members of Congress praised the FBI for the new "psychology of law enforcement," they identified the depth of his public program but not the power it represented. Hoover sought to remake the American mind. Mimicking Lippmann's "pioneers of liberalism," Hoover suggested as much when he told police officers at the FBI National Police Academy in April 1938 that they were in a "new profession. I have said that you are pioneers. That is actually true. You are pioneers, carrying forth new ideas and new standards, and those ideas and standards should be upon a very high plane."[126] This new plane was philosophical and harbored realist epistemology, grounded in the frontier myth. In his May 1938 speech at Oklahoma Baptist University, Hoover argued that "America and Americans" had "new frontiers to face" and suggested that the "pioneering spirit which conquered the frontiers of the Southwest has its modern counterpart in the present-day attitude which is beginning to form against the underworld and its criminal army." He elaborated that from the "turbulent frontier spirit" came a "new era, a new outlook" of a "new and better order" that took the form of a "crystallization of nation-wide public opinion against crime," which was necessary because "without the right kind of public opinion nothing good can be accomplished."[127] The FBI superimposed the frontier myth over the foundations of culture to rationalize a new and unstated system of government that would empower Hoover and the groups he represented with appeals to tradition.

In many ways, FBI realism used Victorian values as the benchmark of what was real and proper. Hoover elaborated at Oklahoma Baptist University that the "war on crime" represented a "new frontier" in which there were "forces that can be conquered," like improper "parole" and "shyster lawyers" and "venal politics," and other "subversive forces." He set this frontier against the rise of postwar idealism and the reforms it brought. He condemned the "years of prohibition and prohibition violation," and the "people that had emerged from the post-war era with a lackadaisical attitude toward crime and a perverted sense of civic responsibility, and whose moral conscience had atrophied into a state of deterioration." He identified this past moment as the "black era of toleration of lawlessness." His language suggested a pushback against the creep of cultural change to, instead, spread order into places seen as unorderly. He concluded that it was time to explore the "criminal home" that permitted children to "degenerate into the basest form of life." This move was necessary, Hoover argued, because there had been "little investigation made into the homes from which crime comes—there is no greater subject that can be studied, for crime all too often begins in the home, is part of the home, is nurtured in the home, and grown in the home because of the improper attitude on the part of parents."[128] The spread of cultural change, therefore, was read as a subversive invasion that needed to be contained by an enlarged FBI, which would fight back, in part, with a perspective that supported Hoover's mission.

The new order encouraged Hoover's audiences to participate in his drama in ways that further emboldened the FBI, undermined the BOP, and raised suspicions of legislators who did not back the bureau. He told the New York Chamber of Commerce in February 1935, for example, that it was "the citizen's duty to see to it that the prisoner is not coddled nor allowed to be freed through easy and sometimes, I regret to say, financially reachable persons with powers of clemency."[129] He even made his budget battles a matter of public concern. He told the IACP in July 1935 that when "politics seeks" to stay the hand of law enforcement "by reduced appropriations, by red tape, by enforced appointments, I feel that the official who makes the fight against it will have the support of the public."[130] He drove this point home at Oklahoma Baptist University when he noted that there "remains a tremendous amount of work to be done which naturally is held in check until appropriations can be granted" and "obstacles can be overcome."[131] Unless citizens actively backed the FBI's expansive appropriations and were suspicious of congresspersons who backed prison reformers, Hoover warned, public safety would remain in danger. Those New Dealers who offered Hoover public support in his feud against Bates, therefore, lent their support to a public philosopher who despised what they represented.

The BOP director responded to the CRS's assault against his authority both privately and publicly. He complained directly to FBI Assistant Director Edward A. Tamm about how the FBI released restricted information to the press.[132] Hoover recorded in a March 1935 memo that Bates regularly complained to Cummings in regard to Hoover's speeches "made from time to time concerning the granting of paroles." The memo indicated that an especially long controversy erupted between the two after Hoover delivered a speech to Wickersham's American Bar Association, an organization that Cooper said needed to "clean house."[133] In a May 1936 memorandum to the attorney general, Bates complained of "adverse publicity" that was inspired by the "Bureau of Investigation." He noted that it "was discouraging to feel" that "public opinion" was "being built up in a way which is not justified by the facts and which is damaging to some of the ideals which we are trying to establish."[134] Bates also wrote a letter to Cooper in March 1935 and lamented that the writer had fallen "into the too prevailing habit" of "exaggerating the figures of crime" as he portrayed "intrigue, and conniving, and corruption in prison" as a common occurrence.[135]

The Office of the Attorney General made some attempts to control the FBI director. In 1936, Cummings leaked material to the press in an unsuccessful attempt to embarrass Hoover and expose the CRS. Like other former superiors, Cummings would later regret not replacing Hoover before he became too powerful to control.[136] In August 1937, Cummings issued an order to DOJ employees that again required all publicity to be "authorized and given to the press through the office of the Attorney General and not otherwise. Any matter arising in any Bureau or Division of the Department" that deserved publicity must "be submitted to the office of the Attorney General for such action as may be deemed appropriate." The order stated that this policy was meant to prevent an "imparting of information" to press members that could lead to "charges of favoritism from press representatives. In addition, the failure to clear press information through the office of the Attorney General results occasionally in confusion as to what the policy of the Department may be on a particular matter."[137] The feud turned the DOJ against itself.

Concluding the War on Crime: Forecasting a Realist Future

In August 1938, the *Washington Star* published a short article titled "G-Men See Era of Gangsters Gone" and quietly announced that the FBI would soon turn its attention to other matters.[138] FDR and Hoover had gained what they wanted from the campaign. Five months later, the Gallup Poll reported that whereas 81 percent of respondents supported Hoover as "head of the G Men," 37 percent said the same about Cummings, and nothing was asked about Bates, who had already resigned his post.[139] With Roosevelt's interest in crime spectacles, the prison director could not keep pace with Hoover to interpret the crime problem and propose solutions. Hoover had become the nation's top authority on law enforcement and would remain so for the rest of his long career.

Hoover used his authority to mold narratives that portrayed him as the essential figure in the war on crime. Powers explains that "one of J. Edgar Hoover's cultural roles after 1935 was to be the 'great detective' of his day, the official narrator of action detective stories to the American public."[140] Hollywood and radio producers disseminated these narratives in Hoover's rhetorical voice, which featured the director as a militarized leader and centered him in Washington, DC, where he coordinated the campaign, but also made him available to lead more local cases when his personal expertise was needed. His service in both capacities was depicted as a heroic response to a criminal army that attacked the nation. Hoover's feud with Director Bates was framed as part of this conflict at the national level in the true-crime universe. In this world, realism associated liberals and criminals through an underworld conspiracy. The CRS's various constructions in fiction and nonfiction formats advanced a continuous logic across different fields of meaning that promoted Hoover's philosophy and leadership over those ideas promoted by Bates and blurred the line between fantasy and reality. This symmetry was reinforced by continuity between his public and narrative personae. Hoover's public persona, narrative persona, and the narratives he told all pointed toward a straight man who told stories straight, who dismissed people who said otherwise because they were probably gay or otherwise evil.

The relationship between CRS discourse and Hoover's institution building reveals that they were both parts of a related strategy to remake the Department of Justice. The utility of the CRS was its capacity to invent and instill an alternative cultural frame from that of the Wickersham Commission, which Hoover and other FBI representatives could use to coordinate and justify their own motives, practices, and language. Hoover embodied the epistemic paradigm with his red-blooded speeches and other performances, and New Dealers in Congress and the White House authorized it with rhetorical support, both of which also helped stabilize Hoover's public persona. Moreover, Hoover's narrative persona suggested the motivations that drove his war on crime. The red-blooded character was a man of action, a soldier or businessman, who found his identity in combat. Because Hoover was sufficiently Protestant and heterosexual, the CRS suggested by innuendo, he was bound to be a crime fighter and bound to vigilantly fight mistaken reformers. Because he was a crime fighter, he was realistic about the agony of the human condition. This rationale operated between the mediated construction of Hoover and his public performances, and located his positionality where they intersected, far away from the whispers of a hidden gay identity. This operation to remake Hoover as a man of action ran counter to Moley's reassurances because it required a backstage arena, closed to public scrutiny. Rather than increase public participation in government to guard against autocracy, the CRS exposed audiences to volumes of propaganda that encouraged loyalty to a government department that worked to substitute a lawful framework of law and order for militarism.

The rise of the G-man action hero paralleled the rise of twentieth-century Christian realist treaties, such as Reinhold Niebuhr's *Moral Man and Immoral Society* (1932) and *An Interpretation of Christian Ethics* (1935), tracts in which he railed against the value of social cooperation. Writing about the FBI's narrative formula, Powers explains that "public interest later shifted from gangsters to Nazi spies and then to Communist subversion."[141] Though the bureau's public campaigns would evolve, its core realist principles of anarchy, power, and Anglo-American nationalism would transcend time and genre, and were echoed by realist writers. The vermin menace turned into the fifth column threat, which, in turn, evolved into the crisis of red fascism. In FBI discourse, these menaces were related in several ways. They implicated New Dealers in subversion, they revealed that cultural changes were "really" disguised threats from culturally "foreign" enemies, and they demonstrated that America needed a militarized FBI. Like Lippmann's nod to neoliberalism and the implications it would have for economics, Christian realism would blossom during the war and open the door for the FBI to remake organized religion.

CHAPTER 3

Fighting the Fifth Column, 1939–1945

The FBI's relationship with Hollywood moved J. Edgar Hoover's rhetorical style in ways the Crime Records Section (CRS) did not always control, but further empowered him nonetheless. Alarmed by German anti-Semitism, executives at Warner Brothers released *Confessions of a Nazi Spy* in April 1939 without Hoover's consent, and rereleased it in June 1940 with updated newsreel footage.[1] The film was loosely based on the 1938 Guenther Rumrich spy case in which the FBI discovered a German espionage network in New York City. Through the cell, Germany successfully collected blueprints for military aircraft and new navy destroyers, military communication devices, classified army maps, reports on tactical military exercises, confidential ship-to-shore communication codes, and contingency plans to fortify the New York metropolitan area.[2] In February, the *Washington Post* described the Rumrich discovery in a front-page story as "one of the biggest spy cases in American history."[3] Warner Brothers used the context to retell the

National Archives and Records Administration.

This billboard in Boston, MA, was in one of the most prominent advertising locations in America. October 1944.

story in the naturalist tradition with metaphors that emphasized notions of invasion. A U.S. attorney in the film announced, for example, that the "invasions of Poland, Norway, and Denmark by Nazi Germany and Russia, and Finland's invasion by Communist Russia" illustrated how "peaceful nations had their entire national structures eaten away by the boring of the enemies within," by the "bacteria of aggressive dictatorships and totalitarian states."[4]

The emphasis on internal subversion held promise for the president. The frame reinforced conspiracy theories that tied isolationists to the German government during the buildup to war, when many members of Congress from both parties opposed intervention. In response, Richard W. Steele explains, "FDR led an education campaign that portrayed his domestic critics" as part of a Nazi conspiracy.[5] Francis MacDonnell notes that the president "played a more influential role in shaping popular attitudes towards" the conspiracy theory "than did any other single individual."[6] His intelligence chiefs, however, were certainly instrumental to his cause.

The president met considerable opposition, and his critics spanned the political spectrum. He was flanked on the far right by foreign propagandists and American media sources that were sympathetic to the military actions of Germany. These groups were joined by isolationist organizations and publishers as well as conservative and liberal members of Congress who sought to deter intervention, all of whom were represented by Charles Lindbergh's influential America First Committee (AFC). The information campaigns launched by these groups were bolstered by the Congress of Industrial Organizations (CIO), which was simultaneously isolationist and radical in its support for neutrality.[7] Such opposition was reinforced by the African American press, which alleged discriminatory practices in the war effort. Civil rights and labor advocates were further supported by liberal academics and jurists who attempted to preserve freedom of speech in the buildup to war. Communists and socialists strengthened the resistance even further and pledged their support to neutrality. These groups were politically divergent. The president, however, treated them as part of a grand conspiracy to undermine national defense. MacDonnell explains that "FDR lumped together actual spies in the employ of Hitler with his isolationist critics" and thus failed to recognize a "distinction between legitimate opposition and treason."[8] Roosevelt reasoned that loyalty in war was expressed through unified political support, which required all factions to rally behind him.[9]

The FBI exploited how FDR used stories of internal subversion to align isolationists with Germany. The director used FDR's rhetorical presidency to sow division among congressional Democrats and the press with a rhetoric of Americanism, and thereby resuscitated the language patterns of progressives like Vice President Thomas R. Marshall during the First Red Scare. The FBI director first deployed the framework before the wartime era, and in ways that encouraged the containment of reformers. He applauded the American Legion as early as September 1938 for how it protected the "principles of Americanism" from "viciously anti-American, alien ideas and ideals, systems and policies" soon after the legion aligned with FDR's congressional critics.[10] In August 1938, the legion's National Americanism Commission reported to Martin Dies's (D-TX) Special Committee on Un-American Activities that the New Deal employed Communists.[11] Ira Katznelson explains that while Dies had once been an ardent New Dealer, when "he discerned no contradiction between his racism and progressive populism," he turned against Roosevelt when the New Deal threatened racial segregation. Dies and other Southern Democrats began to work with Republicans when the Democratic Party moved to federally outlaw lynching and supported the effort to organize black sharecroppers and domestic workers in the South. Ultimately, social-democratic New Dealers challenged the primacy of Jim Crow after the National Labor Relations Act (1935) was passed.[12] In religious and secular terms, the FBI cast these reformers as internal subversives who sought to incite racial and economic unrest. Hoover's religious rhetoric mimicked Christian realism, which emerged in the 1930s to rebut inroads made by Marxism in public life and informed rhetorical realism in the wartime era and beyond.

Roosevelt's campaign to educate the public about subversives coincided with how he, again, changed the institutional presidency and elevated the FBI in the wartime era. With Hoover's help, Roosevelt secretly created an intelligence community that had jurisdiction over the entire federal government and its constituencies but was only responsible to the president.[13] Kenneth O'Reilly explains that in addition to chasing spies, FDR used this new policing apparatus to "*occasionally* exploit the bureau's intelligence functions for partisan purposes, thereby sometimes demonstrating an ambivalent commitment to civil liberties."[14] Frank J. Donner adds that such expansion of "civilian anti-subversive surveillance" institutionally militarized the FBI and allowed the president to circumvent the "austere language of the Constitution limiting the Army's role in civilian affairs."[15] The expansion was strikingly visible in how the FBI grew in terms of personnel and appropriations. Whereas it employed

713 special agents with an appropriation of $6.6 million in 1939, it employed 4,370 agents with an appropriation of $44.2 million in 1945.[16]

With the domestic intelligence apparatus under his control, the FBI director exploited the president's interest in political intelligence. Roosevelt requested information from the director on American fascists in 1934, his critics in 1935, and domestic Communists and Nazis in 1936. These requests began an expansive program throughout the remainder of Roosevelt's presidency whereby the FBI forwarded solicited and unsolicited reports to the White House.[17] This program elevated Hoover's administrative role and made Roosevelt increasingly suspicious of even friendly critics. Douglas M. Charles observes that FBI officials "played to President Roosevelt's political interests" and forwarded "intelligence to the administration that suggested its critics were, indeed, 'subversive.'" Specifically, Hoover more eagerly shared intelligence summaries that portrayed New Dealers who distrusted the FBI as treasonous.[18] The monitoring program carried nascent traces of neoliberalism with its penchant for surveillance, coercive legislation, and police tactics against labor.[19] Hoover explained to Roosevelt in October 1940, for example, that the FBI used its expanded authority to create a "friendly relationship over a period of many years with many banking establishments" and in return received "excellent cooperation" from "financial institutions" in a "monitoring program" to detect "espionage, sabotage and similar activities." He pledged that extraordinary care was "exercised at all times" to avoid "so-called 'labor spying.'"[20] The FBI's social-democratic critics, who sympathized with the Wickersham Commission, clarified the disingenuity of the latter claim.

The rhetorical and institutional strategies that the CRS cultivated during the war on crime to amplify the FBI's cultural presence and authority transformed into wholesale containment culture in the wartime era, with its insistence on conformity in issues of race, class, sexuality, gender, and support for law enforcement. In this chapter, I argue that Hoover adapted and redirected FDR's rhetorical campaign against isolationists and subversives to malign the director's institutional and cultural adversaries, in part, by the continued use of innuendo, with subtle meanings that were clarified across the CRS's vast propaganda program. That is, FBI public discourse read by audiences in the context of film noir and FDR's rhetorical presidency offered an alternative narrative framework for federal law enforcement grounded in Anglo-American nationalism, instead of the more restrained frame offered by FDR to castigate isolationists, both of which broke from the Wickersham Commission. Hoover's language cast the nation in a Darwinian contest for survival, structured by puritanical, covenantal logic that required group conformity to Victorian cultural hierarchies that made room for conservative Catholics and Jews at the expense of their liberal counterparts. While New Dealers rebuked racism and promoted tolerance as part of the war effort, the FBI more narrowly attacked anti-Semitism and aligned multicultural tolerance with Communism. CRS propaganda suggested that cultural drift and challenges to Victorian ideals evidenced internal subversion that required a red-blooded, tough, unsympathetic, or realistic response. This frame normalized Hoover's administrative practices and his pessimistic language about human nature, and would help give rise to neoliberalism in the early Cold War era when the FBI unraveled the New Deal coalition. Moreover, his rhetoric of red-blooded Americanism helped protect his public persona while his partnership with Clyde Tolson became more committed and even celebrated in the associate director's personnel file. Lastly, his move to frame New Dealers as subversive betrayed the presidency and bordered on subversion as the FBI secretly forged links with the Nazi government and draped its ideology in patriotic terms. Indeed, Hoover's sexual charade locked him on a path that became increasingly radical and anathema to the system he swore to protect.

A New Deal for Wartime

The buildup to war helped define how the conflict would be fought at home. Repressive neoliberal policing practices awoke from the slumber that fell after the Palmer Raids and the Teapot Dome scandal, and would operate as anticommunism for decades thereafter.[21] The president's misplaced trust in Hoover only became more apparent over time. Hoover showed increased contempt for New Dealers throughout the war, though it was their vision of expanded federal law enforcement that empowered the framework that he and nascent neoliberal theorists insisted upon. Inside the frame, markets settled issues of civil rights, and the government cracked down on organized labor and other types of market interference. The spirit of centralized control in America changed after FDR died in 1945, and so did the purpose and practice of the U.S. presidency.

FDR's interventionist policies faced strong opposition in Congress since he first attempted to aid the Allied powers. For example, the isolationist bloc used the Neutrality Act of 1935 to limit his power to lend material assistance to friendly nations. Whereas FDR sought authority to selectively embargo countries at war, Congress passed a more general embargo that prohibited arms trade with any nation that the president deemed at war. Isolationists strengthened this position with the Neutrality Act of 1936, which forbade financial assistance to countries at war. After Roosevelt refused to acknowledge belligerency in the Spanish Civil War, Congress passed the Neutrality Act of 1937 to specifically prohibit arms trade with Spain. This legislation also required countries at war that wished to trade with the United States to pay cash and to carry away nonmilitary goods on their own ships.[22] Furthermore, Senate Foreign Relations Committee member Gerald P. Nye (R-ND) called Roosevelt's Destroyers for Bases deal a "direct act of war in violation of our treaties and statutes" when it was ratified in September 1940.[23] Still further, the *New York Times* paraphrased from Senator Burton K. Wheeler (D-MT), chairman of the Interstate Commerce Committee (ICC), that FDR's March 1941 Lend-Lease program was the "beginning of a dictatorship" that "gave blanket authority for the President to commit many and varied acts of war any place in the world."[24] Wheeler was victimized by the Teapot Dome scandal, so FDR and Hoover shared him as a rival. The senator loathed Hoover and how he operated the FBI.

Hoover's critics were embittered by how he manipulated the national security apparatus. Wheeler, for example, proclaimed in March 1940 that

Hoover's "spy systems" and "wire tapping" increased the "power of law-enforcement agencies to oppress" workers who were under investigation "only by reason of their views and activities in regard to labor unions and other economic movements."[25] Such neoliberal police tactics strained FDR's relationship with Congress. Senator George W. Norris (I-NE), for example, warned in February 1940 that the "methods resorted to by the representatives of the Bureau" were abhorrent to "constitutional liberty" and the rights presumably enjoyed by "citizens of the United States under the Constitution."[26] To illustrate his concerns, Norris inserted a *New Republic* article into the *Congressional Record* that observed various similarities between the FBI, the "German Gestapo," and the "Russian OGPU" (predecessor to the KGB), and thus mimicked the analog offered by Lippmann in *The Good Society*. The magazine called on Congress to investigate the "lawlessness of Hoover's bureau, and also the wide scale salesmanship by which Hoover" had made "himself much too powerful to be easily curbed by a superior."[27] In April, the *New Republic* specifically called for a congressional investigation into the FBI's "publicity squad" to reveal its hidden connections with supposedly independent media outlets.[28] Roosevelt's alliance with the director would help end the careers of these congressmen and raised suspicions of the magazine's editors and other public-opinion leaders aligned with the New Deal.

To Hoover's consternation, local presses reported more exact details about the practices of field offices. In May 1940, for example, the *Southern News Almanac* of Birmingham, Alabama, reported on a union's grievance against the FBI. It printed that federal agents had used "Hitler's 'secret police' methods" to break a strike. These tactics included false charges to justify arrests and involved the herding of twenty "strikers into a private concentration camp" where they were "held for six days, questioned and threatened" until some members signed "confessions" under "the use of force."[29] The *People's Voice of Helena*, Montana, further reported that FBI agents had "doped" and "tortured" these strikers to "extort confessions" by making "threats against the men's families, alternate freezing and roasting treatment, and forcing victims to sit straight for hours on high stools."[30] Such news stories widely reported on practices that were derided by the Wickersham Commission.

FDR's education campaign opened a context for Hoover and the CRS to attack the FBI's critics with proxies in Congress. Henry Bridges (R-NH), for example, pledged his support to Hoover on the Senate floor in April 1940 and accused Norris of an "intensive 'smear' campaign," one that compared the bureau to the "secret police of Nazi Germany and Communist Russia." He rhetorically asked, whence "come these charges that the F.B.I. is an Ogpu or a Gestapo?" He argued that the

> radical forces, the false liberals, and the "pinks" throughout the country are up in arms against Mr. Hoover and the F. B. I. Around Washington my colleagues know as well as I there are rumors that prominent New Dealers are using some of these radical elements to "get" J. Edgar Hoover. As I previously said, these rumors are to the effect that they wish to control the entire Department of Justice and pass upon the question of who is to be prosecuted and who is not to be prosecuted without hindrance.

The senator concluded that those who "call themselves the New Deal" had given their "active support, indeed, the encouragement and the coddling" to "subversive elements" who had launched a "steady attack on our institutions, on our very way of living."[31] Such criticism also targeted Representative Vito Marcantonio (American Labor Party–NY). In January, he charged that Hoover had built a "system of terror by index cards" that reflected "Himmler's super secret service in Germany." The congressman correctly warned that Hoover had laid the foundation for "Palmer raids, for a Palmer system, and for a Gestapo system in the United States."[32]

Members of Congress like Wheeler, Norris, and Marcantonio represented a significant threat to Hoover's credibility because their charges were coordinated and backed by research. In May, Assistant Director Louis B. Nichols reported to Hoover that Max Lowenthal was behind the "smear campaign," that he closely "worked with the Wickersham

Committee" and examined a bureau case that had been "reversed by an appellate court because of 'third degree' or other improper treatment of defendants."[33] In 1931, the committee revealed and defined the "third-degree" as a "secret and illegal practice" that inflicted "suffering, physical or mental, upon a person, in order to obtain from that person information about a crime."[34] Lowenthal served as the committee's executive secretary in 1929, where he worked with Alger Hiss, who was then a researcher for the committee's general counsel. Lowenthal and Hiss became friends—a friendship that would have ramifications in the Cold War.[35] In 1935, Wheeler hired Lowenthal to be the ICC's chief counsel, and according to Nichols, Lowenthal became an assistant to Norris by December 1940.[36] That spring, Lowenthal began a large research program to investigate the relationship between Hoover's activities under Palmer and the director's later wartime planning.[37] Norris published Lowenthal's findings in the *Congressional Record* in May 1941, and Lowenthal would go on to publish them in *The Federal Bureau of Investigation* (1950), the first book to critically investigate J. Edgar Hoover and the only one to do so until former FBI agent William W. Turner published *Hoover's FBI: The Men and the Myth* (1970).[38]

The FBI's critics in Congress and the press compared the director to Hitler, which teased an uncomfortable connection between the FBI and the German SS. In May, for example, Norris called Hoover the "furor of adulation and praise" who wanted to direct the "Government by tyrannical force" through his use of "secret police and secret detectives" and by way of "newspaper advertising for adulation."[39] Such rhetoric was poignant because Hoover developed the FBI's centralized police methods in conjunction with foreign police departments that were also anticommunist and interested in racial, religious, and ideological boundaries. He networked with the German Gestapo and members of the Waffen-SS through the International Criminal Police Commission (ICPC) from May 13, 1935, until December 4, 1941, just three days before the attack on Pearl Harbor.[40] In this time period, the FBI collaborated with Chief of the German Security Police Reinhard Heydrich, who the FBI learned in August 1940 had taken control of the ICPC, and who was

Medal presented to J. Edgar Hoover by Premier Benito Mussolini's touring university students before the IACP, September 1934.

later identified as the architect of the Holocaust.[41] With its membership in the commission, the FBI also kept professional relations with Chief of German Police Heinrich Himmler through May 1941.[42] By then, Hoover had already accepted a medal from Benito Mussolini through the International Association of Chiefs of Police (IACP).[43] Assistant to the Director Alan H. Belmont recorded in February 1939 that the FBI had moved to become "permanently connected with the Commission in view of the possible contacts with outstanding law enforcement officials throughout the world and the possibility of learning new scientific developments and methods of interest to the Bureau."[44] For example, the ICPC advertised in January 1939 that it would study and teach "repressive and preventative measures against actions preparatory to crimes and other dangerous conduct showing criminal intentions."[45] Propaganda techniques were also exchanged as the FBI reprinted its speeches in ICPC publications.[46] Whereas the FBI used the vermin metaphor to represent criminals and prison reformers, the Gestapo used the metaphor to represent Jews.[47]

Though they were from different cultures, these anticommunist police forces could intersect in such ways, in part, because they were all informed by the criminal anthropology of Cesare Lombroso and other tracts of eugenics that cross-pollinated between America and Europe in the interwar era. For example, German eugenicist Fritz Lenz wrote in *Human Heredity and Racial Hygiene* (1921), "I am inclined to think that there is even a certain amount of truth in the doctrine formulated a good many years ago by Lombroso, that the 'born criminal' belongs to a special and primitive racial stock."[48] The book was studied by Adolf Hitler and informed his discourse on white supremacy. The third edition was translated into English and published in America by Macmillan as *Human Heredity* (1931), where it was promoted by the Carnegie Institution of Washington, DC.[49] Lombroso condemned racial equality and praised eugenics and segregation.[50] The FBI broke with the ICPC once its headquarters moved from Austria to Berlin in the fall of 1941 out of concerns that continued cooperation could give "foundation for criticism of the Bureau."[51] The potential for criticism was evident because the State Department raised concerns of possible FBI impropriety in 1939 when the ICPC announced that its annual convention would be held in Berlin. At that time, Hoover and Tolson disingenuously pledged that the announcement did not signify that Nazis had taken control of the ICPC, a stain that required the commission to rename itself the International Police Organization (INTERPOL) after the war.[52]

FDR entrusted Hoover and others to speak for the White House in a campaign to discredit isolationist critics as subversive and loyal to the Axis Powers. From Roosevelt's position, Hoover was uniquely qualified because the war on crime helped symbolize, sell, and expand the New Deal. Hoover glamorized federal law enforcement and helped relocate the locus of American power from the states to Washington, DC. Similarly, Hoover offered Roosevelt a means to adapt ideology again, to trade America's historic commitment to isolation for intervention. Roosevelt, however, did not see a propagandist in his midst who had already planted seeds against the New Deal writ large. Hoover would deliver the interventionist frame that FDR desired, but also added suspicions to that frame about the motives of New Dealers to intervene into issues of class, race, and police technique. The director claimed to be victimized by a Communist "smear campaign" as a pretext to deny charges made against him by New Dealers and reframe those charges as evidence of an organized conspiracy against due process, which was continuous with his pattern to reframe, deny, and accuse critics for what he was guilty of, to muddy the waters of debate. Courtney Riley Cooper became persona non grata at the FBI in January 1940, for which he committed suicide in September. Matthew Cecil traces his departure to blowback that Hoover received for a controversial article about crime in motor camps.[53] Be that as it may, Cooper was pushed away at the very moment when the CRS worked to rhetorically align New Dealers in Congress with the Nazis while the FBI had its own hidden institutional links to the Gestapo, an arrangement that was hypocritical, disloyal to the president, and subversive. In his absence, the Cooper-Collier narrative formula was expanded in ways that helped Southern Democrats undermine their social-democratic New Deal counterparts and helped Republicans limit the influence of organized labor. In exchange, these members of Congress purposefully supported Hoover's repressive techniques while most Democrats across the board continued to support him as a loyal member of FDR's administration.

Rhetorical Realism in Wartime

The CRS resorted to practices it developed during the war on crime to enlist the support of Congress for the FBI's wartime mission. The new campaign was more complicated because FDR did not have the same unified support of New Dealers to combat the Axis Powers as he did to fight bank robbers and kidnappers. This rhetorical situation led the CRS to craft a multimodal message that was amenable to isolationists, interventionists, Republicans, New Dealers, and Southern Democrats in ways that rebalanced the New Deal coalition and, in time, limited mainstream public life to Anglo-American nationalists and conservative members of marginal religious groups. CRS writers drafted a narrative that made Hoover's red-blooded public persona continuous with a narrative persona that emphasized his loyalty to a nation that was imperiled by destruction. The script helped realign mainstream religion with apocalyptic language that linked nationalism, anticommunism, and capitalism to patriotism, and liberalism and Communism to atheism.

The president's interest in political intelligence presented an opportunity for Hoover to suggest that an ideologically diverse group of critics was acting in concert to undermine the nation's sovereignty. Charles observes that the America First Committee represented the hub of Roosevelt's most influential opposition and the greatest challenge to his wartime planning.[54] The process of sending reports to the White House on the president's critics was formalized in February 1941 when the president ordered Hoover to investigate the committee's funding.[55] The historian further explains that this request opened a floodgate of misinformation in which Hoover forwarded "political intelligence to either sustain or create the impression" that AFC members had links to subversive individuals who held foreign loyalties.[56] The FBI associated prominent isolationists in Congress with Nazis, Communists, and fascists, and did the same to publishers, academics, and civil rights and labor activists who criticized Hoover.[57]

The FBI's portrait of the AFC as a widespread subversive organization was predicated, in part, on reports that the committee had deeply penetrated the legislative branch to promote an insurgent campaign. The director warned the president in March 1941 that Wheeler worked with the AFC to have senators and congressmen travel throughout the United States to oppose "any plans that the President might have" to bring the "country into war."[58] The FBI continued to sow doubts about its members after war was declared. The Washington, DC, field office suggested in May 1942, for example, that the AFC was the "spearhead" of a larger "totalitarian movement" of "Nazis" and "Fascists" who sought to use the "war and its aftermath as an opportunity for totalitarian-democratic revolution." This report estimated that the AFC had over 15 million members and included "more than one hundred representatives and thirty-one senators" who were "known to be in sympathy openly or clandestinely with the America First movement."[59] The make-believe guerilla army was expansive and well-connected; alleged traitors included Nye,

Wheeler, Senate Committee on Naval Affairs chairman David I. Walsh (D-MA), and Representative Hamilton S. Fish (R-NY).[60]

To undercut Hoover's opponents, Nichols and other institutional mechanics in the CRS worked to maintain the rhetorical support of congressmen divided by party, region, and support for Lend-Lease in a vast propaganda operation.[61] Between 1939 and 1945, Representatives Daniel Reed (R-NY), Charles Leavy (D-WA), Joseph O'Brien (R-NY), Samuel Dickstein (D-NY), George Grant (D-AL), Fred Hartley Jr. (R-NJ), Fred Crawford (R-MI), Samuel Weiss (D-PA), Martin Dies (D-TX), and Charles Plumley (R-VT) entered FBI speeches and news articles into the *Congressional Record*, as did Senators Alben Barkley (D-KY), Henry Ashurst (D-AZ), Robert Reynolds (D-NC), Theodore Green (D-RI), and Alexander Wiley (R-WI), some of which were reprinted in *Vital Speeches of the Day*.[62] These speeches were addressed to the Detroit Economic Club, FBI National Police Academy, National Fifty Years in Business Club, U.S. Junior Chamber of Commerce, Boy Scouts of America, *New York Herald Tribune* Forum, IACP, DAR, New York Federation of Women's Clubs, the Federal-State Conference on Law Enforcement Problems of National Defense, American Legion, Drake University, National Police Academy, Rutgers University, and the Jewish organization B'nai B'rith.[63] The reprinted news articles first appeared in the *New York Herald Tribune*, *Atlanta Constitution*, *Los Angeles Times*, *Baltimore Sun*, *Signs of the Times*, and *American Magazine*.[64] This propaganda was informed by still other speeches to religious and fraternal organizations, such as Father Flanagan's Boys' Town, the Knights of Columbus, Notre Dame University, St. John's University, Holy Cross College, and the Holland Society of New York.[65] These speeches were rich with innuendo that was clarified by their intertextuality with other FBI discourse, and marked a move to target organized religion with government propaganda—propaganda that was reprinted by Catholic and Jewish presses as well as mainstream media outlets.

The work of the congressmen did not go unnoticed. O'Brien (R-NY) rose to the floor in May 1940 with a clipping from the *Rochester Democrat and Chronicle*. He paraphrased that the paper cited Norris in a story about how "Hoover has an organization maintained at public expense to write speeches for him and they are sent to every newspaper throughout the United States," but failed to mention that the CRS also wrote speeches for members of Congress.[66] O'Brien reassured Congress that

> I, on numerous occasions, have had permission to address the House and to extend my own remarks in the RECORD to include speeches given by J. Edgar Hoover, and may I state most emphatically that at no time has J. Edgar Hoover ever asked me to include in my remarks a speech made by him. The contrary is true. I have asked for them, and will continue to do so.[67]

His denial was true only insofar that Nichols made such requests, not Hoover. Six weeks before, Senator Reynolds (D-NC) had already defended Hoover's propaganda tactics when he acknowledged that Hoover did receive an "unusually large amount of beneficial publicity through the magazines and the newspapers of the country, but it is well that he does, and I hope that he will write more articles to be read by the youth of our land, because in every one he cites proofs to them that crime does not pay."[68] Such defenses signaled the nascent arrangement formed between the FBI, Republicans, and Southern Democrats that would eventually topple the New Deal at the dawn of the Cold War.

Rhetorical support did not mean that these congressmen uniformly defended Hoover, or that they wittingly participated in a conspiracy against the presidency. Lowenthal tracked fallout in the Senate when Attorney General Robert H. Jackson (1940–1941) declared in March 1940 that the FBI should stop tapping telephone wires and "conform to the decisions of the Supreme Court in recent cases."[69] Lowenthal observed in his research notes that the "most vigorous defenses of Hoover and the FBI were made by Wiley (R-WI) and Bridges (R-NH), the anti-New Dealers." Their tone was more radical than that of Reynolds (D-NC) and Ashurst (D-AZ), who "joined in defending Hoover" but were "much milder" than Hoover's "anti-Jackson and anti-Roosevelt supporters, and even indicated that they would be willing to go along with the idea of having a Senate investigation of the FBI and Hoover." Wiley so vehemently supported Hoover that he even charged on the Senate floor that Reynolds sided with Hitler for his support of an investigation.[70] While all these congressmen communicated with the CRS, such charges suggest that it is unlikely they coordinated with each other, with Hoover's most ardent support coming from Republicans at that time.

THE FIFTH COLUMN AND THE RHETORICAL PRESIDENCY

Though these congressmen were a mix of isolationists and interventionists, their choice to reprint the FBI's rhetorical realism advanced FDR's interventionist campaign, which was an appreciated asset to the president. The director's speeches unequivocally extended the narrative frame popularized in *Confessions of a Nazi Spy*, which suggested that war had already begun inside America. In the film, a U.S. attorney warned that "Trojan Horses and fifth column Bundists" in Poland, Norway, Denmark, and Finland "threw off their masks and stabbed these countries in the back while the wanton Nazi war machine attacked in the front." Borrowing from Judeo-Christian imagery, German military forces were described as a "plague of locusts" that were helped by "Nazi fifth columnists."[71] General Emilio Mola coined the fifth-column metaphor during the Spanish Civil War when he boasted in 1936 that "four columns of troops" had surrounded the capital city and a "fifth column" of subversives coordinated from within.[72] At their core, the fifth column and Trojan Horse metaphors communicated an unlawful and secret relationship between insiders and outsiders in advance of an external attack. The film ended with the U.S. attorney and an FBI agent celebrating how the jury found the spies guilty of espionage and treason, which they read as a move toward intervention.[73]

The film's framework informed FDR's rhetorical presidency and shaded perceptions of threat in realistic terms. In May 1940, for example, the president publicly announced that Americans had "seen the treacherous use of the 'fifth column' by which persons supposed to be peaceful visitors were actually a part of an enemy unit of occupation."[74] Days later, he privately ordered Attorney General Jackson to disregard the Supreme Court's recent prohibition of wiretapping in "matters involving the defense of the nation" in order to prevent "sabotage, assassinations and 'fifth column' activities." FDR justified this illegal expansion of executive power because national security plans would otherwise be "too late to do anything about it after" such acts were completed.[75] This directive illustrated a preference for crime prevention over criminal prosecutions during the wartime era, especially to forestall sabotage. Because criminal cases could not be built on intelligence illegally gathered, this focus on counterespionage represented a robust departure from the statutory frame of law enforcement favored by the Wickersham Commission. Roosevelt thus used the fifth-column metaphor and fears of a guerrilla army to introduce a new frame for law enforcement that Hoover would stretch and exploit for decades to come.

Furthermore, the fifth column offered the president grounds to accuse his critics of treason. Roosevelt warned in a fireside chat five days later that the Nazi threat to America's national security was "not a matter of military weapons alone." He claimed to "know of new methods of attack. The Trojan Horse. The Fifth Column that betray a nation unprepared for treachery. Spies, saboteurs and traitors are the actors in this new strategy."[76] While New Deal isolationists like Wheeler and Republican isolationists like Nye would continue to charge that Roosevelt violated the spirit of neutrality until the attack on Pearl Harbor in December 1941, Roosevelt spent the interim challenging their loyalty.

FDR's education campaign against isolationists emphasized the threat of fifth columns, in part, to justify how he expanded the FBI. Beyond expansive jurisdiction, the president gave the bureau a $10 million emergency supplemental appropriation in the spring of 1940 while many unexplained fires disrupted industry.[77] The president and his surrogates wrongly blamed this mysterious trend on sabotage. In a June 1940 press conference, for example, a reporter linked the "increased appropriations for the Federal Bureau of Investigation" to Roosevelt's "speeches and other speeches of other people in the American government about the dangers of foreign elements." He asked if the president and "members of the Government are not partly responsible" for the emergence of a "great scare," and asked if the "fifth column activities actually do exist among us." Roosevelt retorted that they did "very definitely" exist and suggested that there were "forty or fifty factories in this country where somebody in the factory has attempted to destroy the tools in those factories." He pledged that these were "perfectly known cases" of the "fifth column," a claim Hoover retracted fifteen months later.[78] With the support of Congress and the president behind him, Hoover launched a wartime information campaign that would change U.S. culture to make room for a repressive law-enforcement apparatus that mimicked the work of A. Mitchell Palmer and the Gestapo, and ultimately unraveled the New Deal after Roosevelt's death.

FRAMING THE FIFTH COLUMN

FDR's embrace of the fifth-column metaphor lent support to arguments that critics of his administration were subversive. Because Hoover was his adviser, FDR's rhetorical presidency offered the director authority to discredit his own adversaries as subversives. Accordingly, he expanded upon a framework that privileged "crime" prevention over criminal prosecution, defining crimes as transgressions against Anglo-American culture. With America's enemies and the administration's critics framed in realistic terms, power was prioritized over procedure in federal law enforcement. Hoover used the fifth column to warrant the administration's new emphasis on counterespionage. He wrote in a syndicated July 1940 article, for example, that success in the battle "against the growing threat of a Fifth Column in America" could not be "gauged by prosecutions" and that the "real test of successful counterespionage" was in "locating the spy, ascertaining his contacts and methods of communication—and then closing off his sources of communication." This argument for neutralization rather than prosecution appropriately fit public knowledge of the Rumrich spy case and meshed with the administration's warnings against industrial sabotage. For example, Hoover concluded that "espionage and sabotage" went "hand in hand" because "where you find one, you will find the other" in "every phase of a nation's industrial, commercial, and social life."[79] The fifth column, therefore, helped the administration communicate the new frame that it set for the DOJ—a frame that privileged surveillance and control over civil liberties and procedural authority, thus signaling a decline of Wickersham's influence.

The narrative frame was heavily informed by cinematic representations of war. *Confessions of a Nazi Spy* helped popularize archetypal characters that the director would continually reference in his official discourse. Keith Booker explains that the "three central Nazi figures, the fanatic intellectual, the evil sadist, and the gullible dupe, established most of the central stereotypes of Nazis that would reappear in the numerous anti-Nazi films of the 1940s."[80] The FBI helped make some of these movies, like MGM's *Joe Smith, American* (1942), Twentieth Century Fox's *They Came to Blow Up America* (1943), and Twentieth Century Fox's *The House on 92nd Street* (1945), the first film about atomic warfare.[81] The image of the dupe was not new, but evolved from gangster films that portrayed police and prison reformers as dangerously naive. Hoover stretched the character types in ways that aligned his critics between these three identities. The frame cast New Dealers like Wheeler, Norris, and Marcantonio as fanatic intellectuals who sought to dupe loyal Americans to advance a sadistic scheme against the police and impose a new racial order.

Not surprisingly, Hoover used the fifth column in ways that had less to do with foreign policy than with critiques of the FBI's handling of internal security. In May 1940, for example, he told the New York Federation of Women's Clubs that the "Communist charge that there is the slightest desire in the FBI for an Ogpu or a Gestapo is nothing but blustering ballyhoo designed to cover their own 'Trojan Horse' activities. The Communists hope that with the FBI shackled, they can proceed without interferences as they go their boring, undermining way to overthrow our Government." Hoover enveloped the feud with Norris inside the realist frame and argued that his critics sought to "breakdown true law enforcement in every part of America under the guise of protection of alleged civil liberties so that they may, in turn, destroy the very things that they pretend to revere." In this script, the feud with Norris was not over alternative institutional frameworks, between tensions of civil liberties and national security, but between loyalty to America and intellectual heresy against patriotism. The director concluded that "hypocritical 'front' organizations" engaged in "subversive activities" traded the "intellectual freedom" of the "true principles of Americanism" for "intellectual debauchery, which is as rotten and untenable as the filth from which it springs."[82] These remarks came shortly after syndicated columnist Ludwell Denny noted that Hoover had seemingly placed "Senator Norris, dean of American liberals and leader of the current FBI criticisms," and the Supreme Court in the "class of subversive enemies of the republic" because they opposed wiretapping.[83] The fifth column, therefore, helped Hoover discredit civil-liberties objections in Congress and the Court against his preferred frame for surveillance and control.

Moreover, the director identified the fifth column in the legislative branch as those politicians who attempted to control law enforcement. Hoover told Father Flanagan's Boys' Town in June 1941, for example, that "corrupt politicians" had reached "high" into "governmental bodies" and legislatures to seize control of "law enforcement agencies" to promote "subversive isms," a term that certainly included Walter Lippmann's "gradual collectivism"[84] The director accentuated Roosevelt's observation that democracy was susceptible to foreign infiltration and intrigue—an idea reinforced by Hoover to Roosevelt. He suggested at Drake University in June 1940 that the "Communist and the Bundsman" relied upon "'Fifth Column' methods" to burrow "deeper and deeper into our system of democracy" where they could obstruct the "national necessity" of "preparedness."[85] Specifically, he claimed that the fifth column had penetrated government, in part, to dismantle his agency through diminishing its reputation. He insisted before the IACP in September 1940, for example, that "persons" in "high places," whom he described as the "high-handed political dictator of the upper world," worked with a "Fifth Column" of "Communists" to launch a "smear campaign" against the FBI and "wreck public confidence in its mission."[86] Hoover thus aligned democracy's alleged vulnerability with legislative leaders who challenged his power and his rhetorical framings of the bureau's wartime activities.

Members of Congress from across the aisle, New Deal Democrats and Southern Democrats, isolationists and interventionists, offered their rhetorical support to the FBI's campaign against the fifth column. Opposite them stood a minority of New Dealers who challenged FDR's embrace of J. Edgar Hoover and the institutional framework of law enforcement that he represented in language and practice. Norris supported FDR's push for intervention. Wheeler and Marcantonio opposed it. But all three supported the president's domestic agenda, which advanced the civil rights of some minority groups. Opposing Hoover was politically dangerous. Norris would lose reelection in 1943 after serving for thirty years in the Senate. Wheeler would also lose in 1947 after serving for twenty-six years. Marcantonio would leave Congress in 1951, at the apex of the Second Red Scare. The anti–New Deal perspective that was planted during the war on crime began to visibly sprout in the wartime era before it reached full bloom in the early years of the Cold War. And, it was somewhat nurtured by New Dealers like Representatives Leavy, Weiss, and Dickstein as well as Senators Ashurst and Green, all Democrats from the North and the West, who attempted to support the administration by reprinting Hoover's speeches. What I examine next is how the president's warnings about fifth columns were transformed into a logic that equated social-democratic cultural changes with internal subversion.

EPISTEMOLOGY UNDER ATTACK

At its core, Hoover defined loyalty in terms of an epistemological row that emerged at the dawn of modernity at the end of the Progressive Era between first- and second-wave reformers, between Protestants and scientists. Although the public persona of the disinterested scientific professional had previously been a mainstay of his narrative structure, Hoover's move toward "Americanism" signified that loyalty was a matter of Christian nationalism. The perspective was grounded in late nineteenth-century religious ideals that were hostile to organized labor and civil rights reformers, and that perceived only sin in modernity. The director used the fifth column to defame New Deal era cultural drift.

Although FDR violated the civil rights of his isolationist critics, he also protected the rights of African Americans and workers in unprecedented ways. He issued Executive Order 8802 in June 1941, which prohibited discrimination in defense industries and established the Fair Employment Practices Committee. FDR was motivated, in part, to preempt A. Philip Randolph's scheduled "March on Washington" and to appease the Committee on Participation of Negroes in the National Defense Program.[87] Hoover, however, used the fifth-column argument to align the burgeoning civil rights movement with the discourse of mass culture in ways that implied New Dealers were Communist revolutionaries. In *Confessions of a Nazi Spy*, for example, Joseph Goebbels explained to an American Nazi propagandist that "our aim must always be to discredit conditions there in the United States." In particular, the German official insisted that "racial and religious hatred must be fostered" and "class hatreds must be encouraged in such a way that labor and the middle classes will become confused and antagonistic. In the ensuing chaos, we will be able to take control."[88] Notions of security, loyalty, and national purity repurposed the practice of segregation and offered Republicans and Southern Democrats a rhetorical tool to frame New Deal Democrats as disloyal and weak on matters of defense. As we have already seen, Hoover morphed the president's education campaign against fifth-column isolationists into another about fifth-column New Dealers who challenged Hoover's repressive police practices. Within this campaign, Hoover raised the specter of race and class insurrection as a wartime threat.

As in the film, Hoover constituted the fifth column in naturalist terms that emphasized visions of fire, flood, pests, and pestilence. He told Drake University, for example, that "war is raging abroad. Its fire and flying embers menace our shores."[89] He told the New York Federation of Women's Clubs in May 1940 that a "flood of vilification has recently been loosed upon all things American by scandal sheets which espouse the cause of foreign 'isms.'"[90] He told the IACP in October 1939 that the "way to cure a plague" was by "quarantine, by ferreting out the carriers of disease and either eradicating them, or placing them where they cannot infect the populace."[91] That same month, he announced before the *New York Herald Tribune* Forum that "foes within our gates, like termites, have sought by every scheming means to inculcate their alien ideas into our social order, fouling our cradle of liberty."[92] Hoover told the National Police Academy the previous month that crime was a "social disease" that must be "treated" like a "cancerous growth," it must be "cut out or burned out of the body politic."[93] Such containment rhetoric from the Progressive Era informed the fifth column in ways that aligned America's wartime enemies with citizens that Hoover identified as cultural adversaries.

From its literary foundation, the American realist tradition had long associated Marxism with disease and portrayed workers as contagion. William Lynn Watson observes that novelists incorporated the language of science and reform politics to neutralize how the working class had become class-conscious and threatened the social order. Writers borrowed language from official government reports that equated crime with "*conceptually* contagious" disease. Their discourse imagined "contagion spreading through the working class and perhaps synonymous with it, a disease that is both a 'moral stagnation of desires' and an actual malady spread through" bodily fluids and "bad smells." In this sense, disease was literal and figurative, both medical and social. Workers were imagined as unclean, drunk, sexually promiscuous, and mentally ill. This framework helped justify political reforms in terms of "socio-medical prophylaxes: barriers and inoculations against figurative contagions of working-class consciousness and revolt, and literal epidemics originating in working-class tenements."[94] Hoover's rhetorical realism, therefore, tapped into an old-line defense against class agitation.

Moreover, his generic conventions incubated a cultural fissure that emerged at the end of the Progressive Era. Randolph S. Bourne outlined a disjuncture between older and younger progressives at the dawn of modernity in an article he titled "This Older Generation" (1915) for the *Atlantic Monthly*. He outlined a break in cultural continuity that happened sometime after the "Victorian era, which in its secret heart this older generation still admires so much," when "all the latent individualism of Christian ethics" had produced a code that "would have spiritually guaranteed forever all moral caste divisions and inequalities of modern society" had not the younger generation rebelled. The younger progressives broke a lineage that traced back to the "rugged old Puritans, who wrestled with the devil and stripped their world of all that might seduce them from the awful service of God." To properly imagine those he spoke about, Bourne placed the older generation in their "typical setting of the small town or city, clustered about the institutions of church and family. If we have any society which can be called 'America,' it is this society. Its psychology is American psychology; its soul is America's soul" and belonged to the "comfortable or fairly comfortable American middle class." Bourne detested the code for its hypocrisy, and referred to its adherents as "parasite[s]." Rather than support the revolutionary ideas of "social democracy" or "social justice" in order to "remove the barriers of caste and race and economic inequality," the code instead favored "social service" as a means of "getting all the luxury of the virtues of goodness, while conserving all the advantages of being in a vicious society." The code reduced Protestantism to exhortations for those actions that would "least disturb the normal routine of modern middle-class life: common honesty in business life, faithfulness to duty, ambition in business and profession, filial obligation, the use of talents, and always and everywhere simple human kindness and love."[95] It was this code that Director Hoover made the test of loyal citizenship in the name of Americanism.

The fissure between older and younger progressives was caused by a change in value structures. Reformers, David B. Danbom observes, were split in "two separate but related groups—secular thinkers who yearned for a more Christian world, and religious thinkers [who] fashioned a more worldly Christianity." Scientists offered alternative hypotheses to orthodox doctrines that helped explain and solve problems related to industrialization, urbanization, and immigration.[96] The Progressive Era became increasingly detached from Christian orthodoxy as time moved forward. Influential liberal reformers questioned whether science was a better reform apparatus than religion. By the early teens, Christian reformers opened the door for a second generation of reformers who broke from Victorian culture and helped transition the nation into modernity. This epistemological move of artists, scientists, and political reformers associated progress with communalism rather than rational individualism, which abandoned Enlightenment belief in gradual social change.[97] Scientific progressives "wanted to modernize values *and* alter reality," Danbom notes, whereas the Christian progressives who first welcomed their arrival only tried to "make reality conform to traditional values." Scientific progressives dramatically departed from Protestant orthodoxy when they further reduced the primacy of the individual in the world. They emphasized society rather than its individual members and encouraged statist solutions. They highlighted the hypocrisy of the Victorian value of individualism—the contradiction that "while those who sin against individuals, by mugging, robbing, murdering them, face severe penalties, those who sin against society, by robbing consumers and taxpayers or poisoning the air and water, often receive social approval." This critique of Victorian culture offered a rationale to regulate business, a radical idea that was previously perceived to infringe upon the individualism of capitalists, and which neoliberals would later detest.[98] Hoover lent them valuable assistance when he identified scientific reformers as Communists, though he had previously aligned himself with them after the Palmer Raids and the Teapot Dome scandal. The campaign against the fifth column helped him reframe his duty to America and his role within government.

Much like Palmer, who warned that American institutions of law and order were threatened—marriage, home, church, and school—Hoover equated Victorian institutions and values with the purpose of national security, especially church and segregation.[99] The director warned the DAR in April 1940, for example, that "newly-allied deconstructionists stand for the complete overthrow of all American institutions. They plan for the destruction of all religion." He elaborated that these "scoundrels" disrespected the "sanctity of the American home" and that they "dream of the day when every American school shall become their own training ground." After Southern Democrats broke from the New Deal, Hoover suggested that "agitators have worked among farmers, particularly sharecroppers, painting rosy pictures of the day when skies shall be red with the flames of destruction, and that which has belonged to others shall change hands—simply for the taking." He warned that these "defamers of American traditions" planned for the "infiltration of agitators and destructionists into youth-serving organizations."[100] If Hoover's language left any doubt about which institutions were under assault, Representative Walter Ploeser (R-MO) clarified the matter in April 1941 when he cited a speech delivered by Assistant Director Nichols about "schools for saboteurs." He used FBI discourse to evidence a bulletin from the Alabama Council of Democratic Clubs that defended "our voting laws, segregation of the races, and our southern traditions."[101] The charge of atheism and disrespect for American traditions and institutions had long characterized those charges made by older progressives. Bourne paraphrased how the older generation begrudged "agnostic professors" and "remorseless scientists," whom they called mere "sensation-mongers" that "unsettle the faith of our youth" for the cause of "social justice" and "unveil great masses of political and social corruption."[102] Hoover's public campaign against fifth columns, therefore, directed the authority of the presidency against the New Deal and the challenge to traditional institutions that it posed.

The director's rhetorical realism superimposed anxieties about racial mixing over the stresses of foreign sabotage and espionage, and made intrigue a metaphor for challenges to Anglo-American culture. He linked the war to sexual norms and emphasized the homestead as a place that should teach Victorian orthodoxy, but was compromised by faraway fathers in combat and working mothers outside the home. Charles argues that "juvenile delinquency" in FBI discourse was code for civil rights agitation, interracial romance, and sex crime wherein African Americans were described as sexually driven and incapable of self-restraint. In this frame, social purity advocates identified critics of segregation as obscene for how they condoned interracial romance, and they labeled modern art with sexual messages obscene for how it allegedly tempted the uncontrollable desires of black men.[103]

In the wartime era, anticommunist and social purity discourse fused into a common campaign against modernism. Claire A. Culleton observes that both discourses were "couched in the language of the 'crusade,'" drew on the fifth-column metaphor, and traced corrupting forces to foreign lands that allegedly sought to destabilize America.[104] Hoover used the frame to direct containment culture against public intellectuals who challenged sex, class, and race structures. He linked their challenges to alien doctrines, warning the graduates of Notre Dame University in May 1942, for example, that fifth columnists preached a "foreign 'ism'" from "some pulpits, some lecture halls, some radios, some presses and even on some screens."[105] Culleton argues that more than any other art form, Hoover was most anxious about modern literature and how it informed other artistic venues that challenged Victorian sensibilities. The FBI interfered with the work and lives of artists like Langston Hughes, Ralph Ellison, John Steinbeck, Ernest Hemingway, Theodore Dreiser, Edna St. Vincent Millay, and James Baldwin. In their FBI files, she notes, they were "described as manufacturing fifth, vulgarity, and/or anti-American sentiment, and Hoover feared that through their filth, they could win their bewildered audiences to communism, socialism, or some other form of the Red menace."[106] With renewed focus on Afro-modernism and the architects of the Harlem Renaissance, William J. Maxwell adds, the FBI reinstated Palmer's surveillance of black writers by the start of World War II—writers who offered "bitter-comic commentary on the FBI's practical alliance with Jim Crow."[107] The fifth-column idea, therefore, offered Hoover a means to critique challenges to the racial order and cultural drift in religion, academics, and popular culture, all as matters of national security.

Rhetorical realism was adept at conflating fears of foreign intrigue with fears of social realignments. During the war on crime, Hoover's discourse emphasized the invasion, creep, or spread of new ideas that threatened the Victorian home space, linking ideologies of reform with homosexuality and tying both to sex crime. It was only a small move, therefore, to tweak the Cooper-Collier formula to discuss the civil rights movement with sexualized language that emphasized issues of hygiene, miscegenation, reproduction, and biological degeneration. Hoover warned the National Fifty Years in Business Club in May 1939, for example, that the "birthrights of freeborn American citizens" had been stolen by "politicians" who "prostituted and corrupted" their profession. In the "modern age," he argued, the "traditional virtues of our heritage" had been "assailed by fly-by-night schemes and theories. Since the dawn of time adherence to certain rules of conduct has been fundamental. Laws of morality cannot be violated with impunity and neither can the laws of nature or of man." He elaborated that "violation of the fundamental principles of sanitation and hygiene ultimately means incarceration by ostracism by reason of ill health." Mimicking Walter Lippmann's neoliberal concern that the New Deal violated core principles, the director drew an analogy between economic experimentation and how it challenged issues of race and labor. He suggested in catastrophic terms that "violation of the laws of economics means virtual bondage. The infraction of the laws of morality, if not forfeiting health, will surely mar character and decency" akin to "nature's catastrophes." He therefore called on law enforcement to protect the "national blood stream" from an "alien spirit," because "America cannot exist half American and half alien."[108] Highlighting notions of race-mixing, he added in his October 1939 speech before the *New York Herald Tribune* Forum that the "present task of law enforcement—the battle against alien-minded mongrels and against crime—is of the same kind and type."[109] It was thus important, Hoover concluded in a syndicated July 1940 article, to keep America's "main line of defense impregnable."[110] The rhetoric of hygiene that characterized how Victorians described the Anglophile home space was thus mimicked to reaffirm the values of racial purity, class distinction, and capitalism.

Hoover's emphasis on race purity was continuous with Lombroso's criminal anthropology, and used innuendo to racialize the New Deal with calls for state-imposed restraint over minority groups. He professed the credo that Bourne assigned to the older generation of progressives who disdained notions of social democracy with its emphasis on social justice. By addressing the laws of nature or of man, Hoover spoke to the epistemological divide between reformers who advanced modernity and brought about a shift in value structures from rational individualism to communalism. This transformation stirred Palmer to declare that America's institutions of law and order were under attack during the First Red Scare. Hoover, therefore, returned to this theme in the wartime era and set the stage for the Second Red Scare and how the Cold War would be waged on the home front.

A WAR OF RACE, LABOR, AND RELIGION

The rise of scientific progressivism was marked, in part, by its embrace of Marxism and a platform that sometimes embraced tolerance of some minority groups. Although the rhetoric of science had offered Hoover a public persona to mask his ideological work in the 1920s and afterward, he rebelled against the platform in the wartime era and became more visibly ideological. He particularly rebuked the value of tolerance when it empowered groups and voices that used tolerance in ways that limited his own culture work. Still, his authority was grounded in FDR's presidency, which constrained how much he could deride cultural changes that the president empowered. Rather than attack newcomers to the mainstream more generally, he limited from where in public life they could come. Specifically, Hoover only welcomed conservative members of previously excluded groups and so divided Catholics and Jews between their more conservative and liberal elements, and aligned the latter with Communism. The legerdemain helped the FBI endow itself with sacredness. In January 1939, Nichols advised Hoover that he should invite clergy to celebrate invocations and benedictions at FBI graduations to build prestige for the bureau, and argued that such was appropriate because the "cause of the FBI and the graduates is as Holy as that assumed by members of the Clergy."[111] This vision for law enforcement would help erode separations between church and state.

The move to invoke religion reshaped and adapted mainstream religion with language that mimicked Christian realism and infused rhetorical realism with an apocalyptic fervor. In the early 1930s, Reinhold Niebuhr promoted a theology that he described as neo-orthodoxy, which was allegedly more "real" than "illusory" cultural pluralism. Larry L. Rasmussen observes that Christian realism attempted to blend Christianity and culture in ways that justified the "need for coercion in the interests of justice" and that placed "issues of power at the center of ethics."[112] Niebuhr was tremendously influential. He held the "ear of politicians" and became "the century's most influential native-born American theologian," argues Martin E. Marty.[113] William D. Dean adds that "Hans Morgenthau called him 'the greatest living political philosopher of America'; George Kennan called Niebuhr 'the father of us all'; and Vice-President Hubert Humphrey said of Niebuhr, 'No American has made a greater contribution to political wisdom and moral responsibility.'"[114] Ultimately, Niebuhr's realism bestowed moral legitimacy upon anticommunism and Communist containment.

Niebuhr criticized liberals for how they emphasized reason and shared too many ideas with Communists. He challenged the idealistic belief that all peoples were capable of rational thought.[115] Accordingly, the theologian posited that "liberal culture was dying" from its rationalistic and "optimistic illusions" in "both the religious and the political."[116] He wrote in 1933 that "political realists" were growing "cynical about moral and religious idealism in politics" because "confused liberals" had overestimated "human nature."[117] He dismissed the potential for achieving intergroup tolerance through "rational capacity."[118] Christian realists rejected liberalism for how it displaced Protestant domination of American culture. Specifically, Niebuhr rejected the tolerance encouraged by liberalism as a compromise of principle. He defined the "final sin" in national life as the spread of atheism, secularism, or other ideologies that did not recognize the primacy of Christianity.[119] He quipped in 1935 that "Democracy, mutual cooperation, the League of Nations, international trade reciprocity" and other idealist commitments were marks of "modern secular liberal culture, to which liberal Christianity is unduly bound." Niebuhr averred that such commitments destroyed the "original tension of Christian morality" through "devitalized and secularized religion."[120] His argument was predicated on the premise that ancient Israel fell because it broke its covenant with God, and so too could the new Israel of American Protestantism collapse in the cosmological wilderness if it broke from God, a threat that the FBI amplified.

By turning to religion, Hoover enhanced the role of the federal government to police public life and limit the advance of multiculturalism. Dianne Kirby observes that the FBI director "sought to smear specific groups and individuals he associated with radicalism, including labor movement activists and Christian leaders advocating for equality and justice for those at the bottom of the socioeconomic scale." Of course, he could not directly attack religion, so he instead worked to reshape the American religious landscape. When the FBI targeted religious groups that backed the New Deal, it divided churches, denominations, and religious communities, especially over issues of race, class, and war. Kirby concludes that by the dawn of the Cold War, he was particularly helped by Catholic Church leaders who supported "widespread acceptance of absolute anticommunism, which favored religion as a way of imposing political, social, and moral conformity."[121] Whereas the FBI worked to make Catholics more aligned with Protestants, it also tried to align Jews with Christianity at a time when Jews were frequently presumed to be Communists, and anticommunism was frequently code for anti-Semitism. Sarah Imhoff observes that "Hoover cast communism as the enemy of religion, by which he meant both Christianity (including Catholicism) and Judaism." He stigmatized Jewish Communists and positioned himself as a defender of Judaism. By his logic, "Jews who allied themselves with communism might claim to be Jews, but by adopting its ideology they could only 'claim' a Jewish origin, because they were no longer true Jews."[122] By dissociating "real" from "fake" or "true" from "false," Hoover's FBI fragmented Protestantism, Catholicism, and Judaism.

Hoover's interest in religion was motivated, in part, by New Deal interventions into issues of race. In its effort to build a more unified war effort, the Office of War Information launched a campaign that denounced racial hatred as un-American. The federal government took steps to redraw notions of race in ways that recast all people of European descent as white. Eric L. Goldstein observes that the "Roosevelt administration believed that domestic stability would best be achieved by consolidating immigrants into the 'white' population and by reestablishing the clear division between blacks and whites" that had become ambiguous with the arrival of Catholic and Jewish immigrant groups that were classified as not-white.[123] Hoover ultimately limited who could be assimilated into mainstream public life.

Christian realism offered a helpful backdrop for the FBI to scrutinize organized religion and turn conservative religious bodies against their more liberal counterparts. The Jewish American community was at the forefront of a campaign to promote racial tolerance during the wartime era. The American Jewish Committee (AJC) and B'nai B'rith's Anti-Defamation League (ADL) worked in an intergroup collaborative effort with more liberal Catholic and Protestant councils as well as with labor unions, educational associations, and civil rights agencies to encourage tolerance. Since the American Catholic Church published the *Bishops' Program of Social Reconstruction* (1919), it sponsored Catholic labor unions that sometimes stood with Marxist groups before Joseph Stalin attacked Polish Catholics in 1945. The Bishop's Program was a guide to remodel American politics, society, and economics, and was inspired by Pope Leo XIII's *Rerum Novarum* (1891), which coined the term "social justice."[124] Stuart Svonkin observes that the intergroup movement launched a large-scale social-scientific public education campaign that depicted "Nazism as atheistic, antidemocratic, and un-American," and "anti-Semitism" as the "opening gambit in a Nazi scheme to 'divide and conquer' the United States."[125]

The program helped popularize the research of anthropologists Franz Boas, Ruth Benedict, and Margaret Mead, who argued against "race" as a category for people.[126] Their work encouraged cultural pluralism and tolerance. Like Christian realists, however, more religious and conservative Jews rejected and broke from the program and more narrowly resisted anti-Semitism. These two different approaches were evident in the AJC and ADL. The former was more secular and argued for broader notions of tolerance and inclusion, while the latter was more religious and worked closely with the FBI to more singularly target the Ku Klux Klan.[127] Hoover's propaganda chief, Assistant Director Nichols, privately praised the leadership of B'nai B'rith in 1942 for how it supported the "Bureau one hundred percent" and did "anything" the FBI requested. He noted that it dismissed its own members who challenged Hoover and severed "all connections with the American Jewish Committee." This triumph was commemorated in Nichols's personnel file.[128] Realism was a helpful tool to accomplish this goal because its epistemology was already on the rise and suggested that unfettered democracy was dangerous or naively idealistic.[129]

The director identified the AJC as a threat to national security. The FBI documented a speech delivered by Boas in April 1940 to the American Committee for Democracy and Intellectual Freedom. In it, the father of American anthropology argued that J. Edgar Hoover and his "Bureau" were "dangerously overstepping the bounds of legality" and "raised problems of the gravest kind for all Americans who believe in the maintenance of orderly and constitutional government." Specifically, Boas charged that the FBI targeted any person "connected with liberal, progressive, labor, and radical movements" for their "cultural activities" with "no stated crime," and thereby identified the burgeoning neoliberal frame that valued market stability over civil liberties.[130]

The move to divide the AJC and the ADL was part of a larger attack on civil rights reformers. In April 1940, for example, the *Daily Worker* reported that CIO president John L. Lewis called for "full and unrestricted rights of citizenship" for the "Negro people" and urged them to "unite with labor for the 'common welfare' of both great groups."[131] The paper also reported in June that Lewis challenged Hoover to recognize that Americans were "being lashed by white-robed riders" and to investigate the "dark night trails of lynching parties."[132] Instead, Roosevelt directed Hoover to investigate the labor leader for his unsupportive views, which Lewis discovered and made public.[133] Moreover, the director warned the

White House in June 1943 that Congressman Vito Marcantonio delivered a speech at the "Negro Freedom Rally" and promoted an "Anti-Poll Tax Bill" after he delivered another "Communist Party" speech that attacked "Jim Crow in the Armed Forces."[134] In July, Hoover reported that the Communist Party sought to unite the "Negro and the Labor Movement," in part, to address "racial problems" in law enforcement.[135] In September, he warned the president that the Communist Party advanced its revolutionary program through a "'boring-from-within' technique" of the civil rights movement. Its "agitational program" allegedly targeted the NAACP, A. Philip Randolph's 1940 "March on Washington" committee, the "Negro press," and the "Negro churches." At other times, Hoover blamed the Axis Powers for disunity that fostered racial agitation among African Americans. Conspiratorial forces allegedly worked to make the black community sympathize with the Japanese because they were also of the "colored race" and therefore also perceived World War II as a "race war."[136]

The FBI used the threat of the fifth column to sow division among the intergroup movement and stall its push for cultural tolerance. Hoover told B'nai B'rith in May 1940, for example, that the "Nation was formed upon the foundation of TOLERANCE," and that the "Republic should stand fast as a sanctuary, where the voices of religious and racial bigotry are absent, where all are dedicated to faith in and service to God and human freedom."[137] Thus, he concluded in a February 1941 speech to the organization that it should stand against the "Godless forces of totalitarianism" that pretended to "aid the less fortunate and the oppressed" in their promotion of "revolutionary activities."[138] He used atheism, therefore, to discredit Marxism and liberalism as well as the broader intergroup collaborative effort for tolerance.

The call to arms was characteristic of the CRS's strategy of innuendo that mimicked Christian realism and underscored the FBI's desire to break apart idealistic partnerships. The FBI used similarly divisive tactics before Catholic audiences. Hoover told Notre Dame University in May 1942, for example, that the "Nazi threat" facing the "American people from within" was compounded by an "insidious injection of several European 'isms'" from the "Fifth Column," which flourished in "the Republic under the false guise of Democracy." He insisted that "Alien foes reached their height of perfidy when they devised programs to endow University Chairs to teach young Americans the glories of a New Order, which more correctly can only be described as a state of Hell."[139] Social-democratic New Deal politics, Hoover charged, was a threat to Protestant culture in the way it had engendered social-justice ideology. In November 1942, he told a group of Protestants that if "more emphasis were placed on the Gospel of Salvation and less on social justice, the latter would become a greater reality."[140] Whereas the former highlighted the individual sinner who lacked self-restraint, the latter highlighted societal sins of the collective. Hoover's distinction, therefore, again highlighted the epistemological disjuncture that emerged with modernity between first- and second-wave reformers as he longed for the past.

The context of war and the chance to be included in the white community pressed some Catholics to abandon previous commitments. Writing about antimodernist perspectives shared between Hoover and the Catholic Jesuit community, Steve Rosswurm observes that their language revealed a move that "narrowed the number and kinds of explanations and solutions considered legitimate for approaching the problem being examined," which placed Pope Leo's goals for social justice beyond the bounds of possibility.[141] Indeed, the community had previously supported organized labor and its civil rights effort. In July 1944, however, the dean of the faculties at the University of San Francisco relayed that he substituted the director's speeches for the customary "spiritual book read at one of the meals each day." The dean further informed Hoover that the FBI had the "best informed man" about Communism who was also the "best analyst of international strategy." Hoover acknowledged this accomplishment in his propaganda chief's personnel file, as well.[142] While the Roosevelt administration reclassified Jews and Catholics as white, the FBI worked to ensure that they abandoned ideologies that helped workers and African Americans, and thereby softened challenges to Victorian traditions and Protestant domination of public life.

By incorporating Christian realism, Hoover infused the epistemology of rhetorical realism with apocalyptic undertones that cross-referenced biblical imagery and social Darwinism.[143] For example, he told the Knights of Columbus in March 1942 that the "world" was "bruised and bleeding because the forces of the anti-Christ" had ascended "over the forces of decency."[144] In Hoover's framework, evil forces could only be balanced by more righteous power. He asserted to St. John's University Law School in June 1942, for example, that the "Axis forces and the pagan evil" could only be met by a "superior force of spiritual development."[145] Notions of force and counterforce were also used to conceptualize intergroup relations. After race riots erupted across the country in the summer of 1943, he directed the IACP in August to use "superior strength" in a clash of "force" against "force" to control any "outbursts" that might pit "race against race, creed against creed."[146] While the intergroup church movement attempted to build racial and religious tolerance to prevent such outbursts, Hoover argued that the root of intergroup hatred was godlessness, which he assigned to outgroups. He suggested to Holy Cross College in June 1944, for example, that the "conflicts between groups in our large cities" were not "truly religious" in nature because they were drawn along "racial" lines and existed between communities where "God" had "not entered."[147] Such appeals to spiritual warfare aligned racial integration with end times, a particularly Southern perspective that looked to Jim Crow to uphold the racial establishment against supposedly godless New Dealers who backed Marxism, thus atheism.

When Assistant Director W. H. D. Lester observed in January 1935 that the CRS made "considerable criticism, directly and by innuendo, of local police departments as well as of the Bureau of Prisons of the Department of Justice," he described a strategy of attack that would be adapted and extended in the wartime era, and used against a wide swath of cultural outsiders who worked toward inclusion and against the grain of Victorian traditions and institutions.[148] In the war on crime, Hoover preferred innuendo because it allowed him to deny the meaning or purpose of discrete texts.[149] When his rhetorical campaign is read as a diffuse text, however, when his speeches, articles, internal memoranda, and correspondence to the White House are read together and in the foreground of FDR's race and labor work, the institutional frame carefully constituted by the CRS becomes clear and legible and suggests why and how it was more obscure to the White House. The strategy saturated the cultural landscape with discourse that imbued audiences with a mythic role and invited them to participate. They were encouraged to draw inferences from religion that lauded premodern cultural traditions—traditions that survived through conventions that sounded merely patriotic but had been repurposed to communicate Anglo-American nationalism.

A Rebirth of the American Way

The FBI director used the Cooper-Collier narrative formula as a backdrop to cast and coordinate his narrative persona, which gendered the nation's problems and solutions. He pulled from the old progressive binary between red-bloods and mollycoddles to envision a "real" American man, and how that character would respond to encroachments of nationalism. Similar to how G. Lowes Dickinson idealized businessmen and soldiers as emblematic of red-blooded Americana, Hoover narrated the war effort with a red-blooded voice that aligned heterosexuality, national loyalty, and the FBI's war work.[150] Steeped in the frontier myth, he narrated intervention as a racialized and sexualized mission to preserve older cultural hierarches that favored rugged individualism, which he aligned with unfettered capitalism in his rhetoric of Americanism. By telling stories with a voice that cast a red-blooded narrative persona upon his character, he helped reaffirm his public persona amid continued whispers about his sexuality.

Hoover encouraged a hard-boiled response to cultural challenges posed by the New Deal. At the end of the war on crime, when the CRS worked to transition toward the wartime frame, Hoover adopted a pattern of discourse that would be extended in *Confessions of a Nazi Spy*. He told the General Federation of Women's Clubs in May 1938 that the "fathers who founded our country evolved certain phases of thought and action that may be called distinctively American," and that

> among these elements of native, distinctive Americanism was a respect for law and order, for orderly processes of government, and for ethical forms of behavior. Obedience to the law of God signified obedience to the established laws of our democracy in those days, and we are sadly in need of a revival of this basic spirit of America.

Therefore, he argued, patriots "must preserve the country's institutions and forms of government" with "rigid Americanism that typifies all that is best in human achievement and human attainment. May we all dedicate ourselves to the suppression of lawlessness and preservation of cherished American traditions and liberty."[151]

Planted in the Progressive Era and popularized, in part, by Theodore Roosevelt, the rhetoric of Americanism was thereafter adapted by reactionaries in the decades that followed. Brian R. McGee observes that the Ku Klux Klan (KKK) campaigned on "Americanism" in the 1920s. Americanism, the Klan asserted, implied that full U.S. citizenship was limited to only those Americans who followed its own logic and reason, and discounted all others who held different beliefs.[152] The KKK used "Americanism" as synecdoche to make the ethnic and religious demographics of the founders essential for American citizenship. In the name of Americanism, the Klan categorized non-Protestant, non-Anglo, and liberal persons and perspectives as genetically and culturally inferior. Jews, Catholics, and African Americans were routinely identified as un-American and alien.[153] Furthermore, Klansmen argued that white liberals betrayed their Anglo-Saxon racial heritage when they defended the rights of foreigners to gather and discuss allegedly foreign ideas—all of which illustrated anti-Americanism to them.[154] McGee concludes that while "we might date the end of progressivism to the time of World War I, the rhetoric of the Progressive Era lingered long after the conclusion of that war, circulating once again in response to racial tension and religious antipathy."[155]

While the Ku Klux Klan kept Americanism current throughout the 1920s, members of Congress circulated such rhetoric in the 1930s. Representative Fish's (R-NY) Special Committee to Investigate Communist Activities in the United States (1930–1931) was formed to examine alleged Soviet conspiracies in the homeland.[156] John William McCormack's (D-MA) and Samuel Dickstein's (D-NY) Special Committee to Investigate Nazi and Other Propaganda (1934–1937) also heavily focused on charges of Soviet activities in America.[157] Dickstein rhetorically backed Hoover by reprinting his speeches, but also secretly worked for the Soviet Union.[158] Still, his committee reported in 1935 that America "must be preserved from communism, fascism, and naziism [*sic*]. The only 'ism' in this country should be 'Americanism.'"[159] Warner Brothers mimicked this language in *Confessions of a Nazi Spy* when a member of the American Legion shouted down an American Nazi propagandist at a public assembly: "We don't want any 'isms' in this country except Americanism!"[160] Furthermore, Dies's Special Committee on Un-American Activities (1938–1944) defined Americanism in a manner that aligned un-Americanism more with Communism than with fascism. Dies wrote in January 1939, for example, that "Americanism" recognized that "fundamental rights" were derived from "God" and included the freedoms of worship and "property rights." According to Dies, the "essence of Americanism" was of "class, religious, and racial tolerance."[161] In his context, racial tolerance implied the toleration of racial inequality by African Americans. Dies strongly supported segregation and sympathized with the KKK.

Hoover transformed the frame popularized by *Confessions of a Nazi Spy* into an expression of Anglo-American nationalism, which once again obscured the motives of New Dealers and bolstered neoliberalism. He declared before the IACP in October 1939, for example, that "America has room for only one ism—Americanism. All other isms are inimical to the best interest of our Nation." He defined "true Americanism" as an "abiding adherence to our Democracy that sprang from the Declaration of Independence and is defined by the Bill of Rights and the Constitution" and "love for our time-honored institutions."[162] Hoover's emphasis on founding documents and traditional institutions reified the racial hierarchy instituted by Article I, Section II of the U.S. Constitution with its mention of "free Persons" and the Three-Fifths Compromise. This language was modified by the Fourteenth Amendment (1868), but the racial hierarchy it had created was preserved in ways far beyond segregation. The practice of peonage extended slavery until 1942, when the DOJ reluctantly began to prosecute Southern farms and corporations that profited from the forced labor of local black people.[163] Rather than sympathize with these enslaved Americans, Hoover was concerned about the rights of white people to own and control black people. The FBI director told the DAR in April 1940, for example, that "these are not bright days for the America which your forefathers fought so valiantly to preserve" because "foreign 'isms' are seeking to engulf Americanism" and advocate the "destruction of civil rights, destruction of happiness, destruction of freedom and the destruction of life." He argued that subversives sought to "exploit the working man, the colored races, the farmer, the renter, and the white collar class." He concluded that the "real test of citizenship is our devotion to the preservation of the American democracy for which our forefathers fought and died, and which we are permitted to enjoy as a blessed heritage" on the "path which has led us to happiness in the past."[164] Hoover's brand of Americanism was thus encoded with notions of Anglo-Saxon racial supremacy that conflated nationalism, patriotism, and unfettered capitalism.

Similar to Theodore Roosevelt, Hoover linked the frontier myth to Americanism and argued for the reinstatement of principles that preceded modernity. He told the American Legion in September 1940, for example, that the "vital test of Americanism is the revival of the pioneer spirit of our ancestors. As a people, we have become soft. Modern science has poured the fruit of its inventions into our laps. Physical effort has been minimized. We have been led to believe that struggle was not an essential part of our environment."[165] The FBI director used the frontier myth to guide how religious minorities adapted to mainstream white culture and emphasized individualism over pluralism or communalism. He told B'nai B'rith in February 1941, for example, that the

> ideal in government which we have achieved in our Union is worth the hunger of the men at Valley Forge. It is worth the aching muscles and blistered hands suffered by the sturdy frontiersmen who shoved westward along unknown trails. What our forebears built for us is worth our working for and struggling to make more perfect. We want peace in which individual enterprise and application of energy will bring a fuller life to our people. To our citizens there can be no peace or fullness of life without the freedom we know so well.[166]

Consistent with Lippmann's neoliberalism, the FBI used appeals to the nation's mythic history to condemn the social-democratic foundations of the New Deal as a foreign threat. Hoover told Rutgers University in May 1943, for example, that graduates should "preserve the America of our forefathers by reviving the teaching of our country's history, uncontaminated by economic and social blundering, and 'ism' inspired experimentation."[167] The director also used the frontier myth to vaguely justify how he affiliated the FBI with Nazi and fascist police systems. Hoover boasted before the FBI Police Academy in July 1939, for example, that its members belonged to a group of "pioneers" who conducted a study of "law-enforcement agencies and police training throughout the world, in order that the best methods of police training might be made available to American law enforcement. That survey extended to practically every country of Europe."[168] Continuous with his idealization of the home space during the war on crime, he cast encroachments of Anglo-American culture as subversion. The director told the *New York Herald Tribune* Forum that like the "days of the early pioneers . . . the home still remains supreme as the basis of our social order. The very forces that attack the home attack the Nation, which is the aggregate of all our homes."[169] The FBI used the frontier myth, therefore, to ground the ideological work of its wartime practices and the containment culture that it insisted upon.

The frontier myth and the rhetoric of Americanism had long been a resource for public men to perform and project heterosexual ethos. Before Theodore Roosevelt became nationally known for his red-blooded adventures into the wilderness, he was jeered for being effeminate. Gail Bederman recounts that daily "newspapers lampooned Roosevelt as the quintessence of effeminacy. They nicknamed him 'weakling,' 'Jane-Dandy,' 'Pumpkin-Lily,' and 'the exquisite Mr. Roosevelt.' They ridiculed his high voice, tight pants, and fancy clothing. Several began referring to him by the name of the well-known homosexual Oscar Wilde." Roosevelt's much publicized trip to the West was, in part, a campaign to remake his public persona and thereby advance his political career.[170] For all his red-blooded talk, behind it stood a man who wanted, in part, to not be seen as homosexual or called out as such.

Similarly, Hoover's rhetoric of Americanism was also a means to reaffirm his sexuality at a time when rumors and even his own relationship with Tolson belied his public performances. Louis Nichols maintained a file that he titled "Director" with a subdivision titled "alleged homosexuality." Athan Theoharis summarizes that the content of this file reveals how "Hoover did not hesitate to use the FBI's resources to suppress such allegations and either to discredit or silence his detractors."[171] For example, an informant relayed to the FBI in 1943 that a Washington, DC, businessman told his dinner party guests, "J. Edgar Hoover was a sexual pervert" and claimed to "have no fear of the F.B.I., inasmuch as he 'was the only one who had positive proof that J. Edgar Hoover is a fairy.'"[172] The report is followed by a memorandum to Tolson that referred to "two instances where scandalous and scurrilous remarks of a vicious nature had been made concerning the Director" in which Hoover again was referred to as a "fairy."[173] These incidents turned into a larger investigation of individuals who were accused of discussing Hoover's sexual orientation in private conversations.[174]

Such gossip posed a threat to Hoover's stature and how he operated the FBI, in part, because his partner was also a high-ranking official for whom he could sometimes not hide his affection. In an October 1943 letter, for example, the director pledged himself to Tolson in terms of ineffable language. When Hoover presented Tolson with a commemorative Ten Year Service Key, he wrote,

> Words are mere man-given symbols for thoughts and feelings, and they are grossly insufficient to express the thoughts in my mind and the feelings in my heart that I have for you. But I did want you to know that I realize and appreciate full well the decided influence you have exerted over the Bureau and its policies during the past fifteen years, which has played a large part in bringing it through this period of tremendous expansion and growth with flying colors. You have devoted yourself to the Bureau, and just as its life has been your life, so is its success your success. No one knows better than I the invaluable assistance you have been to the Bureau and to me personally as its Director. You have indeed been a true friend as well as a loyal associate. I want you to accept this key with my every thought of deepest appreciation, gratitude, and thanks. I hope I will always have you beside me. With kindest personal regards, Sincerely, J. Edgar Hoover.[175]

The hope he articulated in this letter was reified when Tolson was buried adjacent to him at Congressional Cemetery near the Hoover family plot. Andrew Bennett and Nicholas Royle observe that in the prose of love letters, "filial or romantic, straight or queer, love is often associated with what cannot be said, with the inexpressible or ineffable. And, paradoxically, talking about what cannot be said, about the ineffable, about what is 'beyond words,' can prove to be an especially effective way of talking about love."[176] The closeness of their partnership was under intense public scrutiny and threatened Hoover's stature, lest it reveal hypocrisy and the ruse of his public persona.

Like Roosevelt's use of Americanism, the stresses of sexuality and gender in Hoover's private life informed his red-blooded performances. He pronounced before the American Legion in September 1940, for example, that "Americanism is on trial. Its real test lies in the ability of red-blooded Americans to meet and defeat the Fifth Column of destruction."[177] What was implied about red-blooded culture during the war on crime was more explicitly stated in wartime, that a man could prove his sexual identity through Christian militancy. He elaborated on what was meant by "red-blood" in his March 1942 speech to the Knights of

Columbus. Hoover declared that there "must be a reborn consecration to the militant spirit of liberty which is fundamentally American. Red-blooded men rise to action" and answer the "call to arms" when "things American in soul and action have been challenged" with the "rugged discipline and decency of those who fought and died to found America. We should resurrect the plain, strong ideals of our God, our home, and our Country."[178] Similarly, he observed that "red-blooded Americanism, typified by the valorous men of Notre Dame, will not permit our Nation to bow to defeat. True defense of a democracy comes from unity of mind, soul and body. American patriotism is inseparable from religion; is strengthened by fervent religious expressions and devotions, and Americans should be more and more religious" and deploy "righteous wrath with every weapon we can muster."[179] Such messages to a homosocial Catholic institution was significant, Rosswurm observes, because Hoover shared with these antimodernists a continued need to prove manhood through contest.[180] The system of meaning that circulated with Christian militancy and its missives against homosexuality thus offered Hoover a culturally embedded resource to prove his sexual identity and reaffirm his personae.

Since the red-blooded man was the man of action who excelled at war and enjoyed the fight, unmarked by the degeneracy and sinfulness of homosexuality, Hoover's public exhortations for internal defense neatly deflected attention away from his private life. His ability to stoke fear and anger helped him direct suspicions away from his more affectionate standpoint toward Tolson. The FBI director defended and preserved his private life by attacking that of others, offering a rough and tough "American" face to policies that could otherwise be traced to the Gestapo. Ann Chisholm observes that the "credibility of a narrator's account often hinges on the extent to which it unifies its narrator's public and narrative personae," and that the power of such accounts can be enhanced by constructing a mythically significant role for its audience.[181] Hoover's call to action with red-blooded Americanism, therefore, placed him and his audiences in a cosmic battle against atheistic evildoers, pagans, and gays, which protected him where he was most vulnerable.

The Protestant tenor embedded within "Americanism" aligned Hoover with its heteronormative moral code and offered a means to drape his authoritarian vision in democratic terms. He encouraged Christian youth organizations like the Boy Scouts in June 1939 to maintain "traditional virtues that never change" in their "conquest of life" and dedicate themselves to "activities which strengthen character." In so doing, he enumerated Victorian norms and encouraged them to "love your home and your church. Keep yourselves physically strong, mentally pure, and morally straight."[182] Such notions of purity and straightness carried sexual undertones that traced back to Puritan codes. For example, Congressman Louis Ludlow (D-IN) lauded Hoover on the House floor in March 1944 for "finding ways and means of stamping out the evil which is threatening to undermine the purity and strength of our social structure at its juvenile source." He lamented that children are "permitted to grow up 'like Topsy' and to sow all of the wild oats their inclinations lead them to sow. The result is an epidemic of juvenile misdemeanors and sex irregularities without a parallel. One does not have to be pragmatic or puritanical to realize that this is a lethal tendency."[183] This racialized, sexualized mission was proudly cast in authoritarian terms. Hoover concluded before the National Fifty Years in Business Club, for example, that "democracy does not exist in its purest form" when "justice is not real," so America needed a "dictatorship of the people, for the people, and by the people. In the United States we call it Democracy—the dictatorship of the collective conscience of our people. We could just as well call it Justice."[184] The dictatorship of justice, enforced by the FBI in the Department of Justice, was the endgame of Anglo-American nationalism with the revival of Anglo-Saxon racial supremacy.

Although Hoover mimicked Theodore Roosevelt in ways that highlighted Roosevelt's prejudices, he departed from Roosevelt in ways that revealed a much more exclusive orientation. He told the General Federation of Women's Clubs in May 1938, for example, that the "entire problem of punishment and the possible reformation of criminals deserves intensive, realistic study and treatment, free from the Scylla of sentimentalism on one side and the Charybdis of hypercriticism on the other."[185] This language certainly sounded like Roosevelt. In "Latitude and Longitude among Reformers" (1900), for example, he described the "Scylla and Charybdis" between "vain prattlers" of an impractical "ideal" who were different in "mental and moral habit" on the one hand, and the "attitude of deifying mere efficiency, mere success without regard to the moral qualities lying behind it" on the other.[186] Roosevelt frequently used the device in speeches that encouraged moderation between what he identified as dangerous extremes. As president, for example, he told Williams College in 1905 that "it shall not help us if we avoid the Scylla of baseness of motive, only to be wrecked on the Charybdis of wrong-headedness, of feebleness and inefficiency."[187] Unlike Hoover, however, he also used it to indict capitalists and reactionaries who ignored the plight of workers. He told the Main Convention of the Republican Party in March 1918 that "industrial conditions" required the party to "shun equally the bourbon reactionaries who invite disaster by refusing to face and grapple with the needs of the hour, and the sinister demagogues and loose-minded visionaries who preach a red folly that would bring us to even worse disaster. It will not help us in the least to have avoided Scylla if we land on Charybdis."[188] Whereas Roosevelt and Hoover both used the device to ridicule idealists and socialists in gendered terms, Roosevelt balanced warnings against socialism with warnings against unfettered capitalism while Hoover presented capitalism as a solution to socialism. Hoover pressed the ideological spectrum well into a domain that Roosevelt attempted to steer clear of, a toxic neoliberalism that would soon flourish.

Fading American Idealism and the Usurpation of Dissent

In July 1943, the editor of *The Nation* recounted a recent conversation she had had with ranking New Dealers about the work of the FBI and the Special Committee on Un-American Activities, and what they did in the name of security. "They all agreed that the inquisition was aimed at ridding the government service of as many New Dealers and other progressives as possible" with a strong antipathy toward Jews, she wrote. The editor then asked her readers to accept the difficult fact that federal police forces were "more afraid of liberals and progressives, of Socialists and near-Socialists, of Communists and fellow-travelers, than they are of pro-Nazis or native fascists. We must accept the fact that the present Congress, by a big majority, supports this position." Rather than blame Hoover, a foregone conclusion, the editor blamed the crisis on the president and other ranking New Dealers who failed to resist the containment culture that he encouraged, especially Attorney General Francis Biddle (1941–1945). She argued that

> Biddle's fault lies in his acquiescence in equally detestable methods employed by the FBI. He has never dared to challenge the operations of the redoubtable Edgar Hoover. Rather than risk a showdown with an agency which has such tremendous prestige in Congress and the country, he allows Hoover to terrorize the people who are Biddle's natural political friends and allies. Putting the matter bluntly, Biddle has far less guts than his reactionary subordinate. And with a few exceptions . . . the same must be said of the other liberals in government. They let the men of will, the ruthless and unscrupulous men, ride over them and their decent convictions. And so our political practices continue to war with our political faith—and democracy is divided and weakened from top to bottom.[189]

Her analysis of the situation captured the collapse of political idealism and how it ceded to opportunistic anticommunists, how people of decent convictions let the men of will ride over them for lack of courage. But to blame Biddle for such lack of leadership also missed that liberals and idealists spent little time practicing for confrontations with unscrupulous people, hoping to avoid conflict by modeling decency. What they failed to grasp about issues of race and class was that their vision of decency was not shared by people outside their orbit who were pleased by the legacy of slavery and longed for a return to the nation's past. For them, there was beauty in the brutality, and that beauty was at the core of their national identity.

New Dealers were vulnerable to the coercive tactics of anticommunists who translated signifiers of cultural change into evidence of internal subversion to be fought with containment culture. While the Cooper-Collier formula did survive for decades, it was recalculated by Nichols after the war on crime to imagine the FBI as a bulwark against an army of Nazi and Communist guerrillas. However, the fifth column represented more than just spies and saboteurs. The FBI used the metaphor to signify a large underground movement of disloyal Americans from more liberal walks of life who allegedly waited quietly to openly attack and destroy the United States. Containment, therefore, represented a conspiracy against the New Deal coalition and its supporters. Containment was an opportunity for the South to rise again in subtle ways continuous with Nazi fascism.

Hoover's fifth-column conspiracy theory was but one more example of a communication tactic to muddy the waters of debate. When FDR accused isolationists of conspiring with foreign enemies, he opened the door for Hoover to move against the New Deal in broader terms and with the explicit authority of the rhetorical presidency. FDR looked to Hoover to corroborate the wartime reality that he presented, based in part on information supplied to the president by the FBI director. This request leveraged the president to share the power of the Oval Office in unprecedented ways—ways he could not control that the director turned against him. Backed by the president, Hoover and his CRS propagandists attempted to contain the influences of villains who spanned the cultural landscape. Religion, economics, academia, popular culture, news media, and the home space all became battlegrounds for the FBI to patrol. Such reach justified the FBI's monitoring of churches, schools, community centers, and local and national media outlets. More importantly, the reach opened disparate fields of meaning in which the CRS could intervene and thereby begin a process that would ultimately alter the epistemic order of reality. The order Hoover insisted upon during World War II was the order that Attorney General Palmer and Vice President Marshall advanced during the First Red Scare, the order outlined by Bourne that resented the advances of modernity. Hoover returned to the old attempt to reverse the triumph of science over Protestantism as the nation's cultural center.

The strategy was tragic. The very world that Hoover sought to create was one to which he could not belong. He constrained himself, trapped himself, in dreams of a heteronormative past. While he played the role of red-blooded soldier frontstage, whispers continued to suggest that he was a mollycoddle backstage, so much so that Nichols opened a file on Hoover's private life to hunt down the whisperers. But more than just the whispers, Hoover had to reconcile what was ineffable, his forbidden thoughts and feelings for Tolson. The world that Hoover sought to create rejected the language that he could not speak, and Hoover's recourse was to forever pass as one who belonged to the culture he endorsed so that he could lead it, which led him down an increasingly radical, disloyal, if not subversive, path. It was from this world of reconciled contexts that Hoover and Tolson modeled the FBI after authoritarian police systems that signified control and restraint, attitudes that gays or sex perverts were said to lack. The institution that Hoover made synonymous with himself was an idealized version of the superman he strained to model but could never be.

Hoover's doublespeak would soon take the nation to the brink of catastrophe. He was Roosevelt's rogue cop, who used vested unconstitutional powers to counteract the spirit of the New Deal under the guise of helping Roosevelt. After the president's death in April 1945, the director used this power to curb FDR's plans for expanded economic liberties. Hoover's epistemology was greeted by fans of Fredrich Hayek's *The Road to Serfdom* (1944), a work that responded to Lippmann's *Good Society* and constituted the founding text of the Chicago School of neoliberalism. That same month, Hayek's work was reprinted and popularized by FBI collaborators at the *Reader's Digest* in ways that maximized its anticommunist effect.[190] Harry S. Truman's Fair Deal and his domestic security agenda were Hoover's next targets—targets that once again reaffirmed his manhood and his right to be the nation's top cop in a campaign against "pinks." His proofs of sexuality supposedly proved that he knew what loyalty looked like, or at least persuaded the national audience to think so. Anticommunists reacted against the National Labor Relations Act in ways that would formalize a toxic neoliberalism in the Cold War era and beyond; it put the state in the service of corporations and against the plight of workers and racial minorities. This institutional move occurred within the epistemological context that was created by the Cooper-Collier narrative formula, which seemed credible because it was continuous with Hoover's public and narrative personae.

CHAPTER 4

The Masquerade and the Menace, 1946–1953

When President Harry S. Truman delivered the Truman Doctrine speech before Congress on March 12, 1947, he closed his remarks with an ornamental statement that was uncharacteristic of his plain style.[1] He first introduced the problems of "subjugation by armed minorities" and "outside pressures," as well as that of "such subterfuges as political infiltration." He then drew a naturalist analogy to belligerence that highlighted the problem of Communist expansion. "The seeds of totalitarian regimes are nurtured by misery and want," he argued. "They spread and grow in the evil soil of poverty and strife. They reach their full growth when the hope of a people for a better life has died."[2] Rather than limit where the Soviet Union might spread its influence to faraway places, the president pointed inward when he issued Executive Order 9835 on March 22. The order decreed that "the presence within the Government service of any disloyal or subversive person constitutes a threat to our democratic processes," and therefore ordered a loyalty investigation of all current members of, and future applicants to, the executive branch. Among other things, these reviews were to include reference to "Federal Bureau of Investigation files."[3] The president appeared before Congress to help defend Greece and Turkey from Soviet belligerence. The juxtaposition of these two texts, however, led some to mistakenly conclude that the purpose of the speech was to prepare the way for loyalty investigations.[4]

By the time of Truman's delivery, Hoover's rhetorical realism had saturated U.S. public life. It was time for Hoover to launch a wholesale rhetorical assault on the New Deal and the presidency. The FBI director told the House Un-American Activities Committee (HUAC) on March 26 that Communism was a "way of life—an evil and malignant way of life. It reveals a condition akin to disease that spreads like an epidemic; and like an epidemic, a quarantine is necessary to keep it from infecting the nation." Like Truman, Hoover also warned against political infiltration. He advocated the "necessity of alertness in keeping Communists and sympathizers out of government services." He made clear that Communists did not "have a right to government jobs." By authority of the "Hatch Act," Hoover boasted that the FBI had already ensured that a "total of 1,906 individuals are no longer employed in the government." They were removed before they could spread the "virus of Communism" under the "window dressing" of "old age security, houses for veterans, child assistance," and other social-democratic New Deal programs.[5]

Although the New Deal was responsible for the FBI's unprecedented growth, Hoover had fair reason to believe that Truman would be less permissive than FDR. Hoover's disdain for the new president stretched back to Truman's time in the Senate when he worked with Max Lowenthal and Burton K. Wheeler on the Interstate Commerce Committee. In May 1941, Truman began a yearlong probe into the problems of wiretapping, in part, as a violation of the Federal Communications Act (1934), and he even wrote a letter to a Hoover loyalist in the DOJ that requested clarity on Hoover's authority.[6] But Truman and Hoover had more than a professional disagreement between them; they also had Lowenthal. Ted Morgan writes that "Truman's antipathy for the bureau

National Archives and Records Administration.

J. Edgar Hoover testifying before House Committee on Un-American Activities on Communists in the New Deal, wearing wedding ring, March 26, 1947.

was nurtured and reinforced by his friend Max Lowenthal," who "took the line, to which Truman was receptive, that the postwar spy scare had been concocted by his political enemies."[7] Although spies were certainly present, Lowenthal was right to trace the scare to enemies of the New Deal.

In January 1946, credible rumors began to circulate that Truman was going to replace Hoover as FBI director with an analyst from the Budget Bureau who was a former social worker. Congressman Fred Bradley (R-MI) reprinted a *Washington Evening Star* article in the *Congressional Record* that reported on a move to replace the director with "a new man with 'streamlined ideas' as head of the FBI." Hoover's boosters in Congress were quick to label the speculated ouster a Communist conspiracy. Bradley blamed the plan on a "former Assistant Secretary of Agriculture under Henry Wallace" who was "just as pink as Wallace." The congressman charged that the assistant had equated the "right to belong to the Communist Party" with the right to belong to the "Democratic or Republican

Party." He urged Truman to "immediately put an end to these repeated efforts on the part of the Communists, radicals, and left-wing politicians in this country to dispose of Mr. Hoover."[8] Two days later, Bradley connected the story to Hoover's feud with New Dealers over wiretaps in 1940.[9] Karl Mundt (R-SD) wondered aloud if "inner-circle left-wingers" secretly plotted to remove the director.[10] Beyond discourse, members of Congress also lent Hoover material support. In May, the chairman of the House Committee on Appropriations, Clarence Cannon (D-MO), announced that a raise in Hoover's salary was an "answer to those Communists and the Bureau of the Budget who have been after Hoover's scalp for some time. It is the answer to those who want to get rid of Mr. Hoover. The House today is affirmatively telling them where we stand so far as this great American is concerned."[11] Republicans and Southern Democrats called for a showdown with the president over the future of the FBI, a department that would systematically remove New Dealers from the federal workforce under the guise of spy hunting.

Moreover, the FBI and the anti–New Dealers in Congress used Truman's rhetorical realism to curb the New Deal more broadly. Months before he delivered the Truman Doctrine address, the president pledged to continue FDR's "economic bill of rights" and to expand programs for health, housing, education, employment, and catastrophic protection.[12] While he advocated more social programs, Truman simultaneously cut FBI appropriations from $44 million in 1945 to $35 million in 1947.[13] After the presidential rhetoric of March 1947, however, Hoover and Congress leveraged Truman to reverse the flow of resources and redirected appropriations to national security.

Truman witnessed the ground of his presidency shift beneath his feet at a time when the New Deal drowned in a hostile sea of accusations against social-democratic reformers and their motives. The FBI director told HUAC in his March 1947 speech that Moscow had inserted lines, scenes, and sequences into films that conveyed the "Communist lesson" and had worked to censor "anti-Communist lessons." The Kremlin supposedly accomplished this message campaign by ordering American Communists to infiltrate labor unions and the arts.[14] The alleged purpose of the propaganda and infiltration strategies was to exploit workers and African Americans in a Communist uprising. Hoover quoted Vladimir Lenin to argue that the ultimate objective was revolution, "by exerting pressure from without as a political movement . . . 'the economic strike develops into a political strike and the latter develops into insurrection'" to "overthrow the American way of life" and for the "overthrow of our government."[15] Hoover's appearance before HUAC was a provocative program launch for an apparatus built between the FBI and Congress wherein the bureau would secretly and illegally pass material to the committee, which would then hold public hearings to discredit and disempower those who were indicted, a system that disproportionately targeted Jews.[16] The program was unconstitutional because it signified a serious infringement on the separation of powers. Ellen Schrecker observes that from "Harvard to Hollywood, employers in every sector of American society fired the men and women" subpoenaed, adding that the "repercussions were greatest where Communists had been most active: labor, civil rights, international affairs, and culture." Universal health care was blocked, welfare agencies were slashed, college and university teachers were fired, and schools were coerced to teach content that aligned with Hoover's epistemology, and barred from teaching about Marxism, where issues of race and class coalesced. Perhaps most visibly, the Hollywood Ten were blacklisted, and screenwriters like Dalton Trumbo were forced underground.[17] The FBI created a context hospitable to neoliberalisms and hostile to social democracy. Whereas the conflict between Hoover and Truman escalated with rumors of the director's ouster from the FBI, it ended with New Dealers terminated and their speech chilled. In this time, the FBI's appropriations rebounded to $91 million for fiscal year 1952 alone.[18] Hoover, therefore, ultimately prevailed at institutionalizing his vision for internal security.

The Truman Doctrine speech sits in a key place in the canon of realist texts because it announced a tough new direction in foreign-policy planning after the war. The address crystallized a divergent paradigm from what Truman had first pledged. It activated a rhetorical framework that conceptualized the nation-state as the primary unit of action in world politics, and the commander-in-chief as the state's centralized authority figure. The speech lent authority to a philosophy that suggested nation-states naturally exist in a condition of anarchy and are forced to define their foreign-policy objectives in terms of a more singular national interest that can be achieved by tough diplomatic and military power. Such singularity benefits the dominant groups that control the nation's strategic resources, because the needs of the dominant groups are viewed as the needs of the nation, and hence pair with neoliberalisms.[19]

The FBI's work to amplify the presence and authority of Hoover's conspiracy rhetoric shifted the epistemology of public life from one that embraced social democracy to another that imagined the American experience as a Victorian dystopia that required containment culture. The shift grounded a new worldview from which Cold War philosophy emerged—namely, political realism and neoliberalism. This philosophy spread, in part, from how Hoover's public persona narrated public life. The anticommunist showdown with Truman suggested that either Republicans, Southern Democrats, and the FBI director had betrayed the presidency, or the executive branch was breached by an army of guerrillas that anticommunists sought to forestall. Both scenarios comprised casts of supporting characters with distinct sets of motivations. Anticommunists were either patriots or subversive nationalists. New Dealers were either optimistic about the human condition or traitors. Public life would either be structured by commitments to cooperation or the FBI's brand of toxic individualism. The animus between Truman and Hoover was either over disloyalty to the presidency or a president who was dangerously naive. These two realities invited two distinct audiences, one duped by Communists to support the New Deal and foreign aggressors, or another duped by years of FBI propaganda to support tyranny at home. Whereas FDR empowered Hoover to corroborate the reality that Hoover suggested and the president presented, Hoover used the power of the rhetorical presidency to displace the reality presented by Truman. To tell his story, Hoover identified individualism as the defining component of American loyalty and fostered containment culture against members of the intelligentsia who represented Marxist perspectives in government, education, religion, civil rights, labor, and the arts. Under such constraint, the New Deal's Keynesian social-democratic rhetorical frame collapsed and was displaced by a radically different epistemology that reframed the meaning of "democracy" and the institutions that belonged to it. The FBI's move to more fully displace the New Deal with a neoliberal, heteronormative rhetoric of the past trapped Hoover forever in a secretive marriage with Clyde Tolson, an arrangement that made both increasingly paranoid about exposure, which they reconciled with endless warnings that Communists were everywhere and out to discredit them. America's Cold War nightmare was thus invented inside of Hoover's hypocritical closet, and would define his remaining tenure as FBI director for decades to come.

Conspiracy!

The early Cold War era was marked by a series of high-profile espionage cases. John Earl Haynes and Harvey Klehr summarize that in the late 1940s and early 1950s, newspapers "repeatedly trumpeted the exposure of yet another nest of Communist spies or saboteurs who had infiltrated American laboratories or labor unions or government agencies." Many Americans worried that traitors had "burrowed into their institutions and had to be exposed or removed. The issue of Soviet espionage became a U.S. obsession, and domestic security dominated public discourse." The executive branch worked to root out disloyal employees. The courts rebalanced the First Amendment to strengthen how national security could be further institutionalized. Trade unions and other parts of the New Deal coalition removed and expelled Communists from their ranks. In the fall of 1945, the FBI documented evidence of espionage in the State Department. The discovery was followed by the spectacular spy cases of Alger Hiss (1948–1950) and Julius and Ethel Rosenberg (1950–1953), which revealed that some members of the New Deal government were motivated to help the Soviet Union out of "personal rejection of capitalism and the American social order."[20] While these spies did not seek the hostile overthrow of America, as the FBI had long claimed, their actions did justify concerns about Soviet espionage in America. If the Truman Doctrine and the loyalty program offered credibility to Hoover's many conspiracy theories, spy cases made his warnings "real."

Before HUAC commenced its national spectacles, the House Committee on Appropriations gathered in May 1946 to debate the merits of a supplemental appropriation for the investigative committee. The debate foreshadowed the paranoia that would soon characterize how the Cold War was experienced at home, steeped in the FBI's rhetorical realism. Mundt quoted heavily from the director's wartime speeches and concluded with a line from a constituent: "'The best time to cure a snake bite is before it happens.' I believe this is good advice for Congress to follow today."[21] The purpose of the meeting and the analogy was directed at an alleged Communist conspiracy in America. John Rankin (D-MS) announced that "this committee is going after those un-American elements, in the House or elsewhere, who are attempting to undermine and destroy this government."[22] Daniel Reed (R-NY) expanded on the scope of threat and added that "radical communistic organizations" were working surreptitiously to "overthrow the Government."[23] William Colmer (D-MS) argued that there was "no question about the subversive influences being at work in this country. It is a known fact that many Communists have worked themselves into key positions in our Government" and into the "various armed services which are maintained for the defense of our country."[24] Similarly, Carl Andersen (R-MN) warned of the "infiltration of communistic activity in our schools and colleges under the slogan of academic freedom. . . . You will find it everywhere, in schools, churches, labor organizations, political parties, in well-meaning social organizations and, above all, in the very core of our Government."[25]

Concerns about foreign affairs and the international scene, however, did not drive the conversation about why HUAC was needed. Rather, it was concerns about Anglo-American nationalist dominance at home. Hatton Sumners (D-TX) summarized that proponents of HUAC proposed to "have some committee of this House, vigilant and on the firing line, and watching what these people are doing in this country, and disclosing their discoveries to the people of this democracy, who are its government" and thereby promoted the "Anglo-Saxon sort of government."[26] His emphases mimicked those of the KKK in the 1920s. The Klan had long argued that white supremacy was requisite for American democracy to function, and suggested that the whiteness of the nation's founders was responsible for the nation's democratic institutions. Brian R. McGee observes that the "white, and more specifically, the Anglo-Saxon racial identity of Washington, Jefferson, Hamilton, and Madison was held up as evidence of white supremacy where democratic institutions were concerned."[27] Coded as it was, Sumners complaint was against New Dealers who were meddling with the Southern establishment. He was a longtime supporter of the Klan, segregation, and lynching. Rankin elaborated upon this theme when he warned of Communist "booklets advocating a 'Negro Soviet' for the Southern States" that would strike against the "white women of the South" and deliver the "same fate as is now being meted out to the helpless Christian women of Poland," that Communists "raped more innocent women, murdered more innocent men, plundered more helpless individuals, and robbed more homes than has ever been done before."[28]

Sumners and Rankin failed to mention the FBI's role in their project. For the three decades that followed, the FBI would secretly supply the committee with files, staff, witnesses, names, and charges. Curt Gentry summarizes that the "FBI not only gave HUAC the names of those persons it wanted called; it provided lists of questions to be asked, on the basis of accusations in FBI files. Even the files themselves were not sacrosanct: their contents selectively leaked to the committee."[29] Schrecker argues that the FBI was the "bureaucratic heart of the McCarthy era. It designed and ran much of the machinery of political repression, shaping the loyalty programs, criminal prosecutions, and undercover operations that pushed the communist issue to the center of American politics during the early years of the Cold War."[30] Kenneth O'Reilly catalogs that by the summer of 1948, the FBI frequently leaked material to Senator Homer Ferguson (R-MI), chairman of the Investigations Subcommittee of the Committee on Expenditures in the Executive Departments, as well as to Representatives Richard Nixon (R-CA) and Mundt of HUAC, before the FBI leaked files to Senator Joseph McCarthy (R-WI) and his aide Roy Cohn, all to publicly shame the accused and discredit their ideological bent.[31]

The spectacle of congressional hearings, moreover, lent a rhetorical context to Hoover's discourse that seemed to independently verify the credibility of his conspiracy theories. Indeed, conspiracy weighed heavily on Hoover's mind. He had long warned that Communist fifth columnists conspired against the republic, and he would amplify that charge under Truman with strategic help from Rankin, Mundt, Nixon, McCarthy, Cohn, and others. However, he also remembered the fallout that sank Attorney General A. Mitchell Palmer when no evidence of revolution materialized in 1920. Hoover substituted the need for material evidence for the spectacle of spy hearings, predicated on the strategic silence of congressmen about the illegal file-sharing program. Shevaun E. Watson observes that conspiracy "is a crime of illicit speech and dangerous persuasion aimed to orchestrate unlawful acts. The leader of a conspiracy may enjoin participants to silence about the scheme, but the crime itself is one of speech."[32] Hoover's crime was how he enjoined Republicans and Southern Democrats with his illegal supply of information, a system that required silence about cooperation in the midst of congressional hearings to create the needed rhetorical effect, what Charles Morris calls the fourth persona.[33]

The FBI director needed to maintain a public persona that lent his reality credibility. Just as he worked to deflect attention from his gender identity, Hoover worked tirelessly to "pass" as loyal to the commander-in-chief and deflect attention from his side deals with HUAC. As previously discussed, Hoover passed for straight during the war on crime and World War II by pretending to be a red-blooded moral crusader, quick to impugn the sexuality of social reformers. I argue below that the same strategy was in play when he warned of disloyalty in the executive branch. Hoover secured his own political stature on the backs of people he cast as traitors, people allegedly with secret plots that he and Congress had the expertise to identify by way of their investigative clairvoyance, their ability to see what was hidden to the untrained eye. What he said about others, therefore, is key to interpreting his own tactics.

When the president used naturalist imagery in the Truman Doctrine address to describe Soviet intrigue, he accessed a world that the Crime Records Section (CRS) had spent many years cultivating, from stories about the underworld of organized crime with links to prison reformers, to stories of Nazi and Communist fifth columnists with hidden links to isolationists and police critics. Operating from within this world, Hoover used his position as FBI director to take the mantle of clairvoyance and cast his opponents as Communist dupes or traitors. With lessons learned from Palmer, Hoover understood the necessity of appearing nonpartisan and ideologically disinterested. Accordingly, he triangulated his arguments between a rhetoric of science that communicated personal neutrality, and innuendo that linked New Dealers to the Kremlin. The FBI director's innuendos were enthymemes to be decoded with HUAC hearings and Hollywood film projects that provided the suppressed premises. These were sites of discourse that overtly accused social reformers of treason.

Hoover's performance depended on members of HUAC to say what he could not lest he appear biased, which sealed their fates. Troubling for Hoover, Republicans did not need to appear neutral and sometimes revealed too much about the file-sharing program. Hoover, I argue, spoke simultaneously from multiple positions to multiple audiences: as a professional clairvoyant to other professionals on HUAC with whom he colluded, as a professional clairvoyant to accused infiltrators who knew better but were discredited, and as a professional clairvoyant to mass audiences who were allegedly duped by the New Deal as a Communist front. Such multiplicity helped produce a philosophy that was grounded in Hoover's ideological work using a careful balance of personae for the director to appear more credible than Truman. Ann Chisholm underscores that first-person narratives can "encourage and enhance audience identification and participation" and can also "augment the persuasive power of the roles they construct for their audiences" by making mythic appeals to the national identity and patriotism.[34] Hoover's narratives and personae modeled audience participation and taught Americans to accept that the nation was engulfed by a Communist conspiracy and that it had been duped by the New Deal. This lesson had been the central theme of the Cooper-Collier formula since the war on crime. Hoover feared gay clairvoyants who saw through his passing performance at the start of the New Deal. He then mimicked their agency during the Cold War as an investigative clairvoyant to shield himself from criticism and to attack adversaries. Both types of clairvoyance were grounded in gender and sexuality. He first gendered the FBI with red-blooded culture, in part, to rebut gossip about his sexuality; then he reinscribed red-blooded culture in the Cold War when he accused infiltrators of violating traditional Anglo-American norms.

Rhetorical Realism and FBI Dominance of Public Culture

Hoover's stories of intrigue were made compelling, in part, by his deft rhetorical ability to conflate "Soviet" with "Communist" so that character logic did not permit a subject to be a loyal American Communist, or sympathetic to loyal American Communists. This narrative resource was compounded by the rhetorical-institutional work of the CRS, which continued to amplify Hoover's presence and credibility on Communist intrigue. Even more so than before, Congress played an important role in elevating Hoover's authority to heights above that of even the president in national security and offered the FBI as an alternative to Truman's leadership while still authoritatively backing the president in the public eye.

The postwar era was a time of flux for FBI propaganda. Content quickly moved from uncertainty about the future role of law enforcement in public life to support for hardcore anticommunist policies and practices in government. In 1946, no member of Congress reprinted a current speech from Hoover. Between 1947 and 1953, however, the anticommunist consensus took hold through another vast propaganda operation. Representatives John Rankin (D-MS), George Schwabe (R-OK), Arthur Klein (D-NY), Fred Crawford (R-MI), George Wilson (D-OK), Joseph Bryson (D-SC), Lawrence Smith (R-WI), John Wood (D-GA), and Everett Dirksen (R-IL) added speeches and articles to the *Congressional Record*, as did Senator Kenneth McKellar (D-TN), one of which was also reprinted in *Vital Speeches of the Day*.[35] In particular, the speeches addressed the American Legion, HUAC, and the Grand Lodge of Freemasons.[36] Moreover, they added articles from *American Magazine*, *Newsweek*, *New York Herald Tribune*, *New York Times Magazine*, *Lookout Magazine*, *Parade Magazine*, and *U.S. News and World Report*, the latter of which reprinted Hoover's speech to the Freemasons and more.[37]

Additionally, members of Congress registered their support for Hoover in ways that dwarfed their earlier work and in patterns that highlighted the FBI's heavy support from Republicans in the North and Democrats in the South. Between 1946 and 1952, at least twenty-nine representatives from both parties and across regions registered their support for Hoover on the House floor, and no representative said otherwise.[38] In that same time frame, at least eight senators from both parties and across regions, along with Vice President Alben Barkley (D-KY), registered their support for Hoover on the Senate floor, and no senator said otherwise.[39] Congressmen lauded Hoover for his many years of service and for how the FBI handled the Hiss case. They also defended him against criticisms lobbed by Max Lowenthal in *The Federal Bureau of Investigation* (1950), and floated his name for the 1952 Republican Party nomination. Wiley even commended Hoover's work with Hollywood on Columbia Pictures' *Walk East on Beacon* (1952).[40] Members of Congress traded this support for information on their opponents as well as for information on the personal lives of friends and family.[41]

Within the context of the era, Hoover retained the support of some Democrats aligned with the New Deal, in part, because the FBI was widely seen as the civically responsible alternative to HUAC, which was more overtly hostile to Truman. This image was projected in FBI film collaborations like Universal Pictures's *Ride the Pink Horse* (1947), Columbia Pictures's *Walk a Crooked Mile* (1948), Twentieth Century Fox's *Street with No Name* (1948), Republic Pictures's *Federal Agents vs. Underworld, Inc.* (1949), Twentieth Century Fox's *Mister 880* (1950), King Brothers Productions's *Southside 1-1000* (1950), Jedgar Productions's *FBI Girl* (1951), Republic Pictures's *Government Agents vs. The Phantom Legion* (1951), Warner Brothers's *I Was a Communist for the FBI* (1951), and *Walk East on Beacon.*[42] In these films, pacifists and teachers frequently played the role of dupes to Communist agents.[43] The character types popularized in *Confessions of a Nazi Spy*—the intellectual, sadist, and dupe—were recast in terms of the new international context.[44] FBI discourse, its bipartisan support in Congress, and its Hollywood collaborations all reinforced the image of a disinterested and scientifically professional organization pitted against complicit or criminally naive New Dealers, which invited Americans of all stripes to support the bureau.

Hoover's discourse helped transition the epistemology of public life from New Deal social democracy to Cold War containment culture with conspiracy rhetoric that cast reformers as Communist operatives who advanced a violent revolution along racialized lines. FBI rhetoric had extensive implications for how U.S. institutions were organized and operated. If the New Deal were a front, then its members, their philosophy, and their practices were all suspect. Not only did the FBI delegitimize Keynesianism, its discourse opened spaces for a distinctly different mode of economic thought: neoliberalism in the name of Americanism. Of course, rhetorical realism was less about economic theory than public philosophy. Work by Friedrich Hayek was manipulated and exploited to maximize a liberal-scientific backdrop that also shunned the New Deal, a move that repopulated and reorganized the American intelligentsia and the institutions they scripted, a move that traded a democratic, bottom-up model of authority for a top-down system of control that was planned in FBI headquarters and executed by Congress.

A CALL TO CLAIRVOYANCE

Rumors of Hoover's ouster in January 1946 presented a now-or-never moment in the director's longtime feud with New Dealers. President

Truman attempted to constrain the FBI and even communicated a basic distrust of Hoover when he took the presidency. Bureau of the Budget director Harold Smith wrote in a September 1945 diary entry that Truman "thought the FBI should be cut back as soon as possible to at least the prewar level; that he proposed to confine the FBI to the United States; and that he had in mind a quite different plan for intelligence."[45] This came after Smith recorded in May that the "President" did "not want to set up a gestapo." Smith observed that Truman did not approve of some of the FBI's work.[46] He recorded in July that Truman questioned if "having the FBI in South America" compromised FDR's idealistic "good neighbor relations."[47] It was in this context that Truman planned to oust Hoover and cut his annual budget by $9 million. Whereas Truman and Hoover loathed each other in private, Hoover hid his contempt in public and worked to pass as loyal to the president.

As head of the anticommunist apparatus, it was Hoover's role to model the balance between disinterested professionalism and realist critique. Morris notes that during the war on crime, Hoover was menaced by a "silent, savvy but discreet audience" of gay clairvoyants and passers who collaborated in "making duplicitous utterances appear legitimate before an audience of [heterosexual] dupes." This double audience required triangulation to "invite complicity from a dupe who ultimately aids in constructing the passer's *subversive enthymeme* (and his own deception), all the while evoking the fourth persona as a stealth partner who quietly affirms and colludes by acknowledging the pass."[48] Hoover was no stranger to conspiratorial rhetoric. He was a sexual conspirator most of his life with Tolson, and he used the three positions—passer, clairvoyant, and dupe—to invent political conspiracies. As we have seen, he imposed the role of the passer first upon prison reformers, who he said had infiltrated from the underworld. He later cast the role upon isolationists, labor organizers, and civil rights advocates, and then upon New Dealers more generally in the Cold War, while he claimed to be a clairvoyant who saw through their various conspiracies to make dupes of the citizenry. Gender and politics intersected where he dissociated red-bloods from mollycoddles. He used his own station as a red-blooded clairvoyant to detect political infiltrators who were effete and cunning, and always seeking new ways to deceive the nation. Hoover conspired with Southern Democrats to betray party leaders and pass as loyal to the president in the public eye to enhance the credibility of their politics.

Like before, Hoover balanced his warnings against a public persona that bespoke neutrality, independence, and professionalism. In February 1946, Attorney General Tom Clark formally denied a request from Congress for access to FBI files and wrote that he and Hoover agreed that the DOJ and FBI must preserve the "steadfast policy that the files of the Bureau should be maintained in confidential status."[49] Accordingly, when Hoover appeared before HUAC in March 1947, he opened his remarks by claiming that the "FBI is essentially an investigative agency. It is our duty to get the facts. We do not establish policies—that is the responsibility of higher authority. We do not make decisions as to prosecutions—that is the responsibility of the attorney general, his assistants, and the various United States attorneys." Document security, he reminded his audience, was at the core of their feigned neutrality—precisely the regulations he broke and for which he could be censured. He pledged that "our chief responsibility is the duty to obtain information and to protect confidence. Thus, when a citizen furnishes information on a confidential basis, his confidence must be respected. In any intelligence operation, security of information is of primary concern."[50] This frame of neutrality was necessary in a situation shared differently by Republicans who spoke much more candidly about the anticommunist apparatus. For example, Chairman Thomas (R-NJ) assured Nixon (R-CA) at HUAC hearings in July 1948 that the

> closest relationship exists between this committee and the FBI. I can't say as much as between this committee and the attorney general's office, but the closest relationship exists between this committee and the FBI. I think there is a very good understanding between us. It is something, however, that we cannot talk too much about. I am quite certain that if they felt that they could give us anything, without endangering their

> own position, or in any way endangering their sources of information, they would be glad to cooperate.[51]

His statement was foolish because the director was technically under the supervision of the attorney general, but acknowledged a rift in practice. Hoover's sustained emphasis on objectivity and neutrality, therefore, was an important counterpoint to members of Congress who threatened the requisite silence for their conspiracy against the president.

The apparatus was built upon language that disingenuously promised neutrality. When the House Committee on Appropriations gathered in May 1946 to fund HUAC, Mundt assured skeptics that the committee would be guided by the "scientific and impartial" Brookings Institution. He elaborated that there was no need for worries about bias or partisanship because

> The criterion followed by our committee in its approach to the many problems before it is not the viewpoint of its chairman, the gentleman from Georgia, John Wood [D]. It is not the viewpoint of the gentleman from Mississippi, John Rankin [D]. Nor is it that of the gentleman from Arizona, John Murdoch [D], or any of the six other members of the committee. Neither the Democratic sextet nor the Republican trio writes the tune and directs the steps taken by this committee. It is a nine-man committee, in which each member has equal rights, equal influence, and equal opportunity to exercise his judgment. It neither follows the traditional procedures of the Dies committee, which preceded it, nor the ethereal elucidations of such a wobbly liberal as Henry Agard Wallace.[52]

In this pledge of fairness, Mundt did not share that the committee would function, in part, to selectively leak FBI files and thereby discredit New Dealers.

The foolish candor of Thomas exemplified the peril of Hoover's collaborative effort and the necessity to appear neutral. Assistant press secretary Eben A. Ayers observed in an August 1948 diary entry that

Truman refused as a "matter of principle" to "give the Congress or legislative branch, confidential material from the executive departments." He noted in the same entry that the president did not trust Hoover's loyalty. Specifically, he recorded that the "President said that the trouble" with Hoover was that he was "concerned with his own future." Truman suggested that the "election in November" made it impossible to trust him not to reveal "secret and confidential information in the executive department files."[53] By then, Thomas was instructed by the Republican National Committee to hold spy hearings to influence the 1948 presidential election.[54] Fears of domestic Communists had become so piqued that Hoover's disloyalty to Truman became a nonpolitical afterthought. The attorney general angrily wrote to an FBI official in July 1948 that "any S.O.B. that gives Congressman Mundt any information gets his ass kicked out of this building. . . . I want you to get the word around that anyone giving information to the Committee is out—O-U-T."[55] Syndicated columnist Drew Pearson revealed the FBI/DOJ rift in January 1949 on his radio program. According to an FBI memo, Pearson told his listeners that there was to be a "showdown between the Attorney General and the FBI" because its employees were acting insubordinately.[56] Assistant Director Nichols relayed that Pearson's suggestion that the bureau had "violated regulations" had "something to do" with the FBI's "relations with the Un-American Activities Committee and went back before the election."[57] Nichols advised Tolson that the bureau should treat the "leak of information from the Department to Drew Pearson" delicately because the FBI might otherwise play into the "Department's hands."[58] With support from Congress and with stories of espionage abounding, Clark's threat and Truman's authority over the FBI were relatively unenforceable.

While such a rift would normally justify the removal of a department head, the rhetorical context set by the FBI about infiltrators helped reframe any move against the bureau as evidence of behind-the-scenes machinations, an argument that Congressman Bradley floated in January 1946. The act of passing always suggests frontstage and backstage activity. Jack Babuscio observes that passing-for-straight is akin to theater, "playing a role: pretending to be something that one is not; or, to shift the motive somewhat, to camouflage [orientation] by withholding facts . . . which might lead others to the correct conclusion about sexual orientation." The art of passing attempts to alter reality by playing roles to create and sustain appearances. Babuscio adds that passing is an "acting art: to pass is to be 'on stage,' to impersonate heterosexual citizenry, to pretend to be a 'real' (i.e., non-gay) man or woman."[59] Here, an analogy emerged between the hidden world of Hoover's personal life and his conspiracy theory against New Dealers. He wrote in the June 1947 issue of *Newsweek* that there were

> two levels in the Communist organization. One level is "above ground" and its espousers are out in the open. They employ high-sounding, deceitful phrases, and pin the label "Red-baiter," "reactionary," or "Hitlerite" on all who reject their doctrines. Anyone who opposes the Soviet Union is a "Fascist," "imperialist" or "monopoly capitalist." The Communist brigades of swindlers and confidence men extol democracy, but when they do they are speaking of Communism and not the American brand of democracy. They conceal their real designs by attaching themselves to progressive causes, to the cause of labor, social security and education.

He contrasted this space with the "Communist underground," which was "composed of the disciplined brigades of Communist conspirators who drop their dialectical double talk behind locked doors. There the dangers of Communism become real," where they plot a "revolution intended to overthrow our democratic government and substitute a Soviet of the United States."[60] Like his own gendered performances, this scenic mapping required a multiplicity of positions where language and practice were incongruous and benign frontstage, but aligned in subversive ways backstage where persona was "real" and motives were legible. Like other political realists, he asked the nation to read idealistic discourse for ulterior motivations, making him persuasive even to the very audiences he attacked.[61]

The elaborate set design positioned anticommunists at center stage of national politics and moved New Dealers offstage. By projecting what was "real" and what was not, Hoover's position became real and New Dealers like Wallace were cast as either naive or subversive, which symbolically annihilated the old left position. The FBI emphasized the covert strategy of doublespeak to triangulate a double audience and remap public life. Babuscio notes that passing produces a "heightened awareness and appreciation for disguise, impersonation, and projection of personality."[62] Similarly, Hoover reported to HUAC that the "deceptiveness of Communist 'double talk' fulfills the useful propaganda technique of confusion," a strategy that he attributed to Vladimir Lenin's "Aesopian language."[63] Such discourse was a literary system of coded language that allowed authors and readers to interact in ways that duped potential censors.[64] Consistent with his pattern of reframing arguments, denial, and accusing critics of what he might be accused of himself, this system of code words was the FBI's own strategy to realign the meaning of U.S. democracy with what it meant to Southerners. He elaborated that "Communists use it today to mislead the public. The use of the term 'democracy' by the Communists, we have learned to our sorrow, does not have the meaning to them that it does to us. To them it means communism and totalitarianism and our understanding of the term is regarded by them as imperialistic and Fascist."[65] From his experience of passing-for-straight, Hoover impersonated liberals and projected a personality upon his adversaries that forced audiences to decide between him or his critics. FBI discourse invited complicity from people in disbelief to participate in a subversive enthymeme (and their own deception) and to see him as a clairvoyant in their midst who had long seen through the Communist conspiracy.

Hoover's remarks to HUAC realized the warnings made by New Dealers in May 1946. Emanuel Celler (D-NY) identified what Hatton Sumners called the "Anglo-Saxon form of government" as a "type of totalitarianism" that "demands that the opinions of the people conform to his opinion." He further warned that if John Rankin "could deny freedom of press and speech to a Communist, the door is open to deny such freedom to an anti-poll-tax advocate and then to opponents of TVA [Tennessee Valley Authority], and finally to all who voice opposition to the gentleman from Mississippi."[66] Klein, another New York Democrat, predicted that the committee would "become a forum for the dissemination of racial and religious theories," and that it would ignore "fascistic groups" like the Ku Klux Klan, as the Dies Committee had done before.[67] The meaning of "democracy" depended on ideological position. Nationalists equated democracy with the racialized historical-cultural system that ordered society while New Dealers privileged notions of legitimacy and the practices it justified. The FBI's axis of "democracy" divided Americans between loyal and disloyal, real and unreal, and encouraged them to gravitate toward nationalism.

Moreover, Hoover worked to normalize his clairvoyant stature and grounded his leadership in Truman's rhetorical presidency. In a November 1947 interview with the *New York Herald Tribune*, for example, the director shared that the "FBI has been assigned the task of conducting investigations under the loyalty program. Its task is clearly defined by the President's Executive order, and it has no administrative choice as to what it will do or not do." And, he disingenuously reassured readers that FBI agents did not inquire whether federal employees read "liberal or other publications, nor do they tap telephones, as has been rumored."[68] Hoover's appeal to institutional routine concealed the FBI's ideological project. When Truman issued Executive Order 9835 under pressure from HUAC, he reluctantly established the Federal Employee Loyalty Program (FELP).[69] He advised the Loyalty Review Board to limit the role of the FBI to prevent witch-hunting.[70] The FBI, however, engaged in an unfriendly competition with the Civil Service Commission over jurisdiction for loyalty investigations. Douglas M. Charles adds that Hoover frequently leaked information about suspected gays who worked for the commission to get them fired.[71] The information implied they were biologically degenerate and thus likely criminals, and certainly belonged to a backstage underworld. George Elsey, assistant to Clark Clifford, who was the special counsel to the president, noted in May 1947 that Truman felt "very strongly anti-FBI and sides positively" with the Civil

Service commissioners. He added that Truman wanted to "be sure to hold" the "F.B.I. down" because he feared an American "Gestapo."[72] Clifford wrote weeks later to the president that a Hoover loyalist in the DOJ was making "mountains out of molehills" in his successful attempt to make the FBI "fully responsible for all investigations in every case in which there is a suspicion of disloyalty in an applicant for Federal employment." Truman wrote in the margin of this memo that "J. Edgar will in all probability get this backward looking Congress to give him what he wants. It's dangerous."[73] Despite Truman's antipathy, therefore, Hoover invoked his rhetorical presidency and the institutionality that linked their offices to project an image of ideological disinterest and mask his illegal police techniques.

Truman capitulated and acknowledged the persuasiveness of Hoover's strategy. One of the director's assistants confirmed in July 1949 that Hoover had by then successfully consolidated his rhetorical power in the federal government. The assistant relayed a private conversation between Truman and one of his advisers about the emergent police structure. He wrote that the "President had made up his mind to let the Director go," but the adviser encouraged Truman to "face certain facts, namely the Director is tremendously popular throughout the country and that if the President did anything which would cause the Director to leave, it would reflect adversely on the elections in 1950 and 1952." Truman admitted that he knew "this was so" and decided not to act.[74] In short, Hoover's passing rhetoric evolved, over time, into a wholesale language that shifted the hermeneutics of daily life from the New Deal social-democratic order into the apocalyptic world of rhetorical realism.

The anticommunist mantle held by clairvoyants allegedly allowed them to see through the deceitful performances of passers, and also gave them access to hidden worlds unknown to dupes, places where passers shared their desires and meanings more openly without the cover of doublespeak. Hoover knew this type of space well and counted Tolson's official and personnel file as one of them.[75] Hoover was secretive and kept this space hidden. He made a career of straddling worlds and confidently spoke as an expert who could see deceitful motivations in people who crept in from the underworld, from secret backstage positions. And from this multidimensional position, Hoover argued, he could regulate those who sought to infiltrate American culture and tear asunder the racialized historical-cultural system.

RED FASCISM: AN ATTACK FROM WITHIN

The FBI used the Truman Doctrine speech as context to ground Hoover's conspiracy theory against New Dealers and realized an epistemology that traded Keynesianism for neoliberalism. After the president warned of "such subterfuges as political infiltration" in March, Truman inartfully elaborated in May that there was not "any difference in totalitarian states. I don't care what you call them—you call them Nazi, Communist or Fascist, or Franco, or anything else—they are all alike."[76] His analogy emphasized that both systems were totalitarian by highlighting their coercive tactics. The analogy helped give rise to the Munich analogy, which was described in the period as "red fascism." William H. Chamberlin summarized in a January 1935 *New York Times* article that there existed a "distinct analogy, in cause and in method, between Stalin's method of meeting a political crisis and the method which Hitler employed."[77] He elaborated in a September article for the *Atlantic Monthly* that "Bolshevism" was "rapidly shedding its international revolutionary skin and evolving into something that might reasonably be called Red Fascism" while Germany was going "through a reverse process" and coined the term.[78] Les K. Adler and Thomas G. Paterson observe that the analogy reemerged in the early postwar era and was used by Americans who "deliberately articulated distorted similarities between Nazi and Communist ideologies, German and Soviet foreign policies, authoritarian controls and trade practices, and Hitler and Stalin." They conclude that the "popular analogy was a potent and pervasive notion that significantly shaped American perception of world events in the cold war."[79] Lynn Boyd Hinds and Theodore Otto Windt Jr. add that the analogy merged divergent sets of motives, ideas, and goals into a more singular concept of totalitarianism.[80]

Moreover, the red fascism analogy was continuous with nascent neoliberal theory, which compared the New Deal to totalitarianism. Writing about FDR, for example, Lippman observed in *The Good Society* that Americans had never before been "tempted to regard the primitive tyrannies in Russia, Italy, or Germany as the beginnings of a better life for mankind."[81] Similarly, in April 1945, the month of Roosevelt's untimely death, *Reader's Digest* reprinted from Hayek's *The Road to Serfdom* (1944) that

> By the time Hitler came to power, liberalism was dead in Germany. And it was socialism that killed it. To many who have watched the transition from socialism to fascism at close quarters the connection between the two systems has become increasingly obvious, but in the democracies the majority of people still believe that socialism and freedom can be combined.[82]

The FBI did not write either *Good Society* or *Road to Serfdom*, but the FBI's allies certainly helped popularized and frame the latter in ways that advanced Hoover's brand of anticommunism. Angus Burgin observes that most readers of Hayek's work had "encountered the text through a version that was substantially different from Hayek's own. The condensation published by the *Reader's Digest* was less an abridgment than a re-creation," authored by anticommunists who owned and edited the magazine.[83] The condensed version was strongly reworked by the magazine's editor and publisher, DeWitt Wallace, who Hoover observed in 1952 had been "very friendly and helpful to the FBI" over the course of "many years."[84] Burgin concludes that Hayek was used as a "symbolic figure, appropriated to serve as a public relations tool and source of intellectual legitimation for critics of the New Deal."[85] Indeed, Representative Max Schwabe (R-MO) reprinted the *Reader's Digest* article in the *Congressional Record* in October 1945.[86] While the red fascism analogy had always been a means to relate fascism with Communism, therefore, it also circulated in ways that linked those totalitarian systems with the New Deal and encouraged an alternative, toxic epistemology that reimagined the many intellectual domains in which the FBI intervened.

Hoover played a central role in how the analogy was repurposed after the war. Congressman Henderson Lanham (D-GA), for example, compared the Truman Doctrine to "fighting the spread of 'Red Fascism'" in May 1947, a term he said was "used first, I believe, by J. Edgar Hoover, Director of the FBI."[87] Hoover linked the analogy to the Truman Doctrine address when he appeared before HUAC and noted that the "mad march of Red Fascism" accelerated after "President Truman called for aid to Greece and Turkey" just two weeks earlier.[88] Hoover adopted the analogy early and first used it in his September 1946 speech to the American Legion, when he warned that "American Communists have made their deepest inroads upon our national life" and that the organization could "defeat the Red Brand of Fascism by raising their voices on behalf of Democracy and by exposure and denunciation of every force which weakens America."[89] In October, days before the midterm elections, the *Brooklyn Eagle* printed that the "Republican Speaker's Bureau" regarded Hoover as its "best unpaid spellbinder" because no one better "dramatized" the "issue of the Red menace more vividly," and that if the "sudden pre-election shift" signified the "death of the New Deal," then Hoover was among its "assassins."[90] By the time of Truman's delivery six months later, the domestic context had been set in such ways that he extended his rhetorical presidency to subversives who sought to undermine the social-democratic order.

It is commonplace to trace the Truman Doctrine speech's lineage to George F. Kennan's Long Telegram of February 22, 1946. Robert Ivie attributes Truman's imagery of disease, in part, to Kennan's text and notes that metaphors of "disease, strategically embedded in the design of the speech, converged with existing images of fire and flood to construct a sense of epidemic and impending disaster," images that helped construct "red fascism."[91] As I have already shown, the FBI played an integral role in stockpiling such anticommunist imagery since the late 1930s. Moreover, the Long Telegram also ran parallel to an institutional lineage that was kept hidden from the White House. On February 27, 1946, FBI officials set in motion what would become the anticommunist apparatus. They laid plans for "educational material" to be "released through available channels" like HUAC to develop an "informed public opinion" about the "basically Russian nature of the Communist Party in this country." Learning from Attorney General Palmer's experience, their goal was to circumvent a "flood of propaganda from Leftists and so-called Liberal sources" in the "event of extensive arrests of Communists." Specifically, the FBI sought to establish that the CPUSA was the "most reactionary, intolerant and bigoted force in existence." This message was supposed to undermine the support of Communism "from 'Liberal' sources and from its connections in labor unions" as well as from "persons prominent in religious circles."[92] The Long Telegram moved the White House and the FBI in a similar direction, but to different ends.

Kennan's message helped solidify a strategy to discredit the FBI's critics. The plan formalized as the Responsibilities Program in February 1951, wherein the FBI expanded its file-sharing program to then include governors, civic officials, police departments, prominent Republicans, and at least twelve different congressional committees.[93] Together, they removed and replaced state employees as well as teachers at the elementary, high school, and college levels in public and private institutions.[94] In April 1951, Tolson celebrated that members of local governments could then safely "remove public school teachers based on information furnished by the FBI" without fear that such purges "could be twisted by the Communist Party and its sympathizers into an endeavor by the FBI to control the thinking in the education field." His confidence stemmed from the fact that the "public" was then "educated to the dangers of Communism and that public opinion" would then "back up the dissemination of such information by the FBI."[95] The shift from dupes to clairvoyants was complete. Audiences participated in Hoover's stories as they had been directed. More than a hundred college teachers were blacklisted by this operation.[96]

What the FBI called "Communism," however, was gradual cultural change and the advancement of modernity, especially in regard to issues of class and labor. The *New Republic* charged in December 1947 that Hoover was a "politically and ideologically unsophisticated cop" who sought to enforce his vision of "Americanism" through collecting "anti-labor, anti-Roosevelt, anti-Russian pap" from wealthy and conservative citizens.[97] Hoover's epistemological work to exploit the presidency was evident to his critics. The magazine lamented in May 1948 that his perception that "all liberals are radicals, that all radicals are Communists, that all Communists are bomb throwers and should be deported or jailed—has taken root." The writer elaborated that anticommunist support for the Truman Doctrine had transformed into rejection of all that was not "orthodox and generally accepted," and noted that this "subtle change in thought" had taken place throughout the country.[98] Former Interior secretary Harold Ickes (1933–1946) added in a July 1949 article for the magazine that the FBI's definition of "improprieties" had "not been regarded as such since the Victorian age."[99] This insight set the director squarely at odds with the New Deal and Truman's Fair Deal. The *Yale Law Journal* agreed in February 1949 and observed that the "readiness by the chief of the FBI to identify (what are to him) unorthodox views with Communist views throws a revealing light upon the atmosphere in which the FBI operates. We cite it as a further sign of the direction in which that agency is moving."[100] Former Federal Communications Commissioner Clifford R. Durr (1941–1948) described Hoover's epistemology in a 1949 article for the *Chicago Law Review*. Continuous with the FBI's appeals to the past, neoliberal and otherwise, Durr wrote that they tended to "force all political, economic, and social thinking into orthodox patterns" and created an "atmosphere hostile to reason, an atmosphere in which" the nation could be "dangerously misled into rejecting information of vital importance solely because it appears to conflict with accepted beliefs of what is so."[101] The Loyalty Program and its mission to contain Americans outside of the Anglo-nationalist fold grew in this atmosphere and became a project to restaff public and private institutions with personnel who shared Hoover's ideological proclivities.

The FBI argued that infiltrators permeated public life, which coded how marginal groups were read as Communists by Anglo-American nationalists. In either case, their presence signified the collapse of cultural bulwarks against "degeneracy," a Victorian term that referred to criminality, homosexuality, cross-dressing, misogyny, and modern art.[102] Whereas genetic theories of criminality became taboo after the Holocaust, its naturalist language continued to circulate in rhetorical realism.[103] The FBI used Progressive Era reform rhetoric to project how an invisible world of indecency had crashed upon American public life and eroded its cultural infrastructure. The director told the American Legion, for example, that to "allow America to become infected with the malignant growth of Communism or to be infested by crime is a breach of our trust to those who gave their lives for American principles." It was thus important to "defend our Constitution and our way of life against the virulent poison of Communist ideology" so that "basic freedoms and spiritual ideas" would not be "destroyed from within." The problem was widespread, Hoover argued, because "American Communists with their 'boring from within' strategy" had projected "propaganda" into "practically every phase of our national life" in a campaign "supported by dishonor, deceit, tyranny, and a deliberate policy of falsehood."[104] In his world of doublespeak, double audiences, and inverted roles, Hoover characterized New Dealers in terms of his own propaganda strategizing.

COLD WAR CONTAINMENT CULTURE

The Munich analogy helped the FBI expand upon patterns that it introduced in the wartime era to indict the multicultural value of tolerance, which the bureau constituted as a Trojan horse. Jutta Weldes explains that the metaphor implies that "reform movements are not, in fact, indigenous movements" or "spontaneous indigenous responses to structures of oppression." Instead, the "Trojan horse metaphor" constructs reform movements as "weapons wielded by an external, alien enemy secretly and deceitfully to infiltrate the Western Hemisphere."[105] Hoover used the metaphor to attack political idealism. He wrote in the August 1950 issue of *U.S. News and World Report*, for example, that the

> Communist Party is today a Trojan horse of disloyalty, coiled like a serpent in the very heart of America. It may mouth sweet words of

> peace, democracy, equality, and flourish gay slogans of international solidarity and brotherhood of men, but its body and feet are from the Russian bear. Wherever the Trojan horse feet of Communist fifth columns have walked, the indelible footprints of Russian imperialism remain behind.[106]

In the legend of Troy, Greek soldiers deceptively offered a wooden horse to the Trojans as a sign of truce. A battalion of soldiers hid inside of the presumed gift. These infiltrators sacked the city after the statue was brought within the city's walls. The FBI related the value of tolerance to the naiveté of Troy. Hoover told the American Legion, for example, that in "our vaunted tolerance for all peoples the Communists have found our 'Achilles' heel."[107] He therefore used the metaphor to cast aspersions upon the motives of New Dealers who encouraged tolerance, which had profound implications for the social-democratic order.

The anticommunist attack on tolerance opened spaces for new modes of economic theory. An international body of scholars gathered at the 1938 Colloque Walter Lippmann in Paris to discuss his *Good Society*. Through Hayek's organizing, attendees regrouped nine years later to inaugurate the Mont Pelerin Society, just two weeks after Hoover addressed HUAC. Rob Van Horn and Philip Mirowski observe that the society and the Chicago School were joint ventures. The former was registered as a nonprofit corporation with offices located at the University of Chicago, which helped Hayek and his colleagues expand the society's areas of expertise "well outside any notional boundaries of disciplinary economics in the 1940s as a technical subject. Law, religion, history, and scientific philosophy would be as relevant as economics in the search for a rejuvenated liberal creed."[108] The Mont Pelerin Society aligned "neoliberalism" with Victorian visions of political liberalism and the neoclassical economics that emerged in the late nineteenth century. Like the FBI, the society wrote in its founding document that "freedom of thought and expression" were "threatened by the spread of creeds which, claiming the privilege of tolerance when in the position of a minority, seek only to establish a position of power in which they can suppress and obliterate all views but their own." Also like the FBI, the group blamed epistemology that destabilized moral absolutism, academic theories that questioned the rule of law, and fading belief in capitalism.[109] As with Victorian culture, neoliberalisms were marked by unqualified support of self-reliance and self-restraint. David Harvey notes, for example, that they attributed "individual success or failure" to "entrepreneurial virtues or personal failings (such as not investing significantly enough in one's own human capital through education) rather than being attributed to any systemic property (such as class exclusion usually attributed to capitalism)."[110] Neoliberalisms and Hoover's Cold War realism were thus realized within, and benefited from, the epistemological contexts of each other.

Like the early neoliberal theorists, the FBI argued that infiltrators exploited cultural tolerance across disparate communities of meaning to dupe Americans, so emphasized security rather than equality. Hoover told HUAC that Communists recruited "apparently well-meaning but thoroughly duped persons" and called on New Dealers to expose the charade. He argued that the "honest liberal and progressive should be alert" to Communist motives and wordplay because the "Communists' most effective foes can be real liberals and progressives who understand their devious machinations." An interconnected network of liberal discursive practices would have to change, Hoover argued, to accept how nationalists defined "democracy." He warned,

> I do fear for the liberal and progressive who has been hoodwinked and duped into joining hands with the Communists. I confess a real apprehension so long as Communists are able to secure ministers of the gospel to promote their evil work and espouse a cause that is alien to the religion of Christ and Judaism. I do fear so long as school boards and parents tolerate conditions whereby Communists and fellow travelers, under the guise of academic freedom, can teach our youth a way of life that will eventually destroy the sanctity of the home, that undermines faith in God, that causes them to scorn respect for constituted authority and sabotage our revered Constitution. I do fear so long as American

> labor groups are infiltrated, dominated or saturated with the virus of communism. I do fear the palliation and weasel-worded gesture against communism indulged in by some of our labor leaders who should know better but who have become pawns in the hands of sinister but astute manipulations for the Communist cause.[111]

Because Communists had allegedly infiltrated liberal sectors of public life, loyal Americans were expected to see people outside the bounds of nationalism as dangerously suspicious. If they did not, they too were dangerously suspicious for playing the role of dupe. Clairvoyant, therefore, was the only plausible identity left available for loyal Americans, which relocated "liberals" into the realist camp of neoliberalism and destroyed the old left position.

The Trojan-horse metaphor helped Hoover map out where and how infiltrators abused American tolerances, and thereby mapped domains for the FBI to secure. In a striking example of his pattern of reframing arguments, denial, and accusing critics, he warned Congress of "people who infiltrate and corrupt various spheres of American life," spies and saboteurs who "have been able to penetrate and infiltrate many respectable and reputable public opinion mediums." The director elaborated that the Communist Party "departed from depending on the printed word as a medium of propaganda and has taken to the air. Its members and sympathizers have not only infiltrated the airwaves but they are now persistently seeking radio channels." In particular, he claimed that the "American Communists launched a furtive attack on Hollywood in 1935, by the issuance of a directive calling for a concentration in Hollywood. The orders called for action on two fronts. (1) An effort to infiltrate the labor unions; (2) infiltrate the so called intellectual and creative fields."[112] His warnings about clandestine Soviet war tactics, therefore, justified and normalized his culture-war tactics, which would become the basis of his Counterintelligence Program (COINTELPRO). Kristen Hoerl and Erin Ortiz identify the program as a system to "deliver anonymous messages to members of targeted organizations, public officials, and local communities in which organizations were active" through hidden organizing and pseudonymous communication. The program enabled the FBI to subvert democratic processes.[113] Of course, this perspective depends on what counts as "democracy."

The focus on Hollywood was a move to control and align mass culture with the FBI's containment strategies. The bureau began to investigate filmmakers during the war, Seth Rosenfeld observes, to "determine the extent of Communist penetration of film industry unions, and to identify Communist activities by screenwriters, actors, directors, executives, and, as one FBI report put it, 'the so-called intellectuals in general.'"[114] According to Ronald Reagan, former president of the Screen Actors Guild, the FBI relayed to him in the fall of 1946 that the "party was attempting not only to gain control of the Hollywood work force but striving to influence the content of movies through the work of several prominent film writers and actors who were party members or party sympathizers."[115] By then, Reagan had already worked as an FBI informant and helped disrupt the Hollywood Independent Citizens Committee of the Arts, Sciences, and Professions; the American Veterans Committee; and the Conference of Studio Unions.[116] With information collected from Reagan and leaked to HUAC, the committee would blacklist prominent screenwriters like Dalton Trumbo the following year as Reagan rose to become president of the guild.[117] Craig R. Smith describes Reagan's embrace of anticommunism at this moment as one of transformation from FDR Democrat to conservative Republican.[118] The position of loyal American Communists like Trumbo, and New Dealers in general, was reframed by fears that all Communists attempted to pass as loyal Americans by duping others about their motives. The identity of New Dealers eroded, leaving only room for Southern Democrats and Republicans in national politics as many former New Dealers moved from dupes to Cold War liberal clairvoyants, whose economic worldview was forced to embrace a toxic neoliberalism.

Accordingly, Hoover worked to eclipse representations of class and race in public life. For example, in their criticism of RKO's *It's a Wonderful Life* (1946), a film on which Trumbo worked, FBI reviewers observed that Mr. Potter "represented a rather obvious attempt to discredit bankers" and that the "picture deliberately maligned the upper class attempting to show that people who had money were mean and despicable characters." Regarding George Bailey, the reviewers argued that a "subtle attempt was made to magnify the problems of the so-called 'common man' in society." The film's writers were identified as highly suspicious because they were "observed eating lunch daily with such Communists as Lester Cole, screen writer." Moreover, writing about RKO's *Crossfire* (1947), reviewers noted that the "picture is a good example of placing over-emphasis on the racial problem." Similarly, they summarized that Universal Pictures's *Another Part of the Forrest* (1948) "deals with the reconstruction period in the South and portrays the Southern aristocracy as a degenerate and ignorant class. . . . The only characters that are decent are the negroes and the insane mother."[119] Consistently, agents identified films that pressed against Anglo-American nationalism as likely Soviet propaganda on the premise that American Communists were tools of the Kremlin and certainly not loyal to America. Such logic limited the nation's ideals to that of Anglo-American nationalism and thereby excluded people who, by their genetics or ideology, fell outside the boundaries set by nationalists.

Counterpoised against these films, *Walk East on Beacon* (1952) illustrated Hoover's preferred cinematic style. The film was presented in a semidocumentary format and opened with a paratext:

> This is a drama of real life, adapted from the recorded experiences of the Federal Bureau of Investigation. Of the FBI's many responsibilities, none is more urgent than its duty to protect the people of the United States from a worldwide conspiracy which seeks through subversion to destroy established governments everywhere. Fighting in the frontlines of the FBI offensive against the forces of treason are alert and highly trained special agents. Their strategy is based on the utmost tactical use of the scientific techniques of crime detection. But, nothing is more essential to the success of the Bureau's operations against all criminals than the support of responsible and alert Americans.

The film presented the FBI as a scientifically disinterested fact-finding agency and teased the relationship between Communist passers, dupes, and clairvoyants. In the final narration, audiences were reminded that "none knows better than John Edgar Hoover and the men of the FBI that there are others in secret alliance with communism and that they can only be exposed with the help of citizens."[120] Such films encouraged audience participation and taught rhetorical realism wherein criticism of the American social order represented disloyalty and cast the citizenry as a team of loyal informants in everyday life.

The anticommunist apparatus guided how films were produced. In 1947, Ronald Reagan's Motion Picture Alliance for the Preservation of American Ideals published the *Screen Guide for Americans*, written by Ayn Rand, another founding member of the alliance.[121] These neoliberals instructed producers, "Don't Smear the Free Enterprise System: Don't pretend that Americanism and the Free Enterprise System are two different things. They are inseparable, like body and soul. The basic principle of inalienably individual rights, which is Americanism, can be translated into practical reality only in the form of the economic system of Free Enterprise." Filmmakers were warned not to "attack individual rights, individual freedom, private action, private initiative, and private property," or to "smear" industrialists, wealth, the profit motive, success, independent men, or American political institutions. The Motion Picture Alliance also warned filmmakers not to glorify or celebrate failure, depravity, the common man, or communalism.[122] It was, therefore, through mass culture that nationalists marketed their public philosophy.

The fantasy that the FBI projected masked the interest of segregationists behind concerns that infiltrators sought to teach dialectical materialism and ultimately atheism. Hoover told the Freemasons in May 1950, for example, that "traitorous Communists, constantly gnawing away like termites," practiced their "double-dealing, double-minded, double-tongued and double-faced tactics on all fronts of our American life, whether it be in politics, in labor, in the press, in radio, in motion pictures, in the schools or even in some of our churches." The endgame, he argued, was to inculcate "Marxist-Leninist philosophy" by infusing "idea by idea, thought by thought, attitude by attitude, the dialectics of materialism and secularism." He concluded that "atheistic materialism is their idol; the destruction of the God of our Fathers their goal."[123] In his study of the anticommunist drive against philosophy professors who taught dialectical materialism, John McCumber observes that American philosophical idealism had all but vanished from the academy by the early years of the Cold War. This branch of thought was rooted in Protestant religiosity and ran parallel to literary and political idealisms. It placed God at the center of the universe as a guiding force in human affairs and valorized the white, Christian, male individual. The general collapse of faith in the invisible hand of the Protestant God over the American economy traced back to the stock-market crash of Black Tuesday. The collapse opened a space for philosophers to argue that the absence of divine intervention necessitated purposeful human coordination over public affairs, a perspective that elevated New Dealers, social activists, and marginalized groups. McCumber argues that the Cold War drive against atheism provided ideological cover for a move that ultimately sought to attack unnamed targets like socialists, Jews, African Americans, gays, and feminists.[124] Such arguments for Christianity flanked liberal Christians and masked unstated arguments for unfettered capitalism, anti-Semitism, segregation, homophobia, and patriarchy.

Not surprisingly, many proponents of social democracy experienced Hoover's containment culture in terms of thought control. Eleanor Roosevelt wrote in a March 1947 *Washington Daily News* article that the Loyalty Program would make it "possible to declare" any group "subversive" that opposed the "thinking of certain powerful groups."[125] The *Washington Post* printed in November that the program could destroy America's "heritage of free thought" and that the FBI had become a "thought police."[126] Durr sarcastically observed in a January 1948 speech to the American Political Science Association that the administration had attempted "to safeguard our liberties by giving our secret police the power of surveillance over the speech, writings, affiliations, and even the social life of our citizens."[127] He wrote to Truman in June 1949 and again in January 1950, and complained that "FBI employees" exhibited "intellectual limitations" that were manifest in their "investigations of the social, economic and political views and associations of private citizens."

Such thought-policing, Durr charged, occurred in "almost complete secrecy and obscurity." He suggested that Hoover used this power to investigate "Americans suspected of no criminal activity," which marked a "dangerous tendency toward a police state." Accordingly, the lawyer called upon the "executive branch of government" to examine the extent to which the FBI had become a "dangerous political secret police."[128] A contributor to the *Washington Post* announced to the American Association of University Professors in March 1951 that Hoover's "inquisition" had "permeated our schools and our institutions of higher learning" as well as "State governments" and "professional associations and even into private industry" as a form of "thought control" that was predicated on "political belief and affiliation."[129] Indeed, the shape and nature of the FBI had drifted far from what Raymond Moley reported in 1934, an organization that he said showed "no danger of autocracy" as long as its increased power was matched by "increased citizen participation in public affairs."[130]

Thought-policing and brainwashing narrowed how and where citizens could participate in public life, making room for a tyrant and his collaborators whose rhetoric drew from similar foundations as the Nazi government. Wendy Brown concludes that neoliberalism and twentieth-century fascism converged where they valorized a national economic project for a "greater good into which all are integrated, but from which most must not expect personal benefit." They also converged where the collective purposes requisite for popular sovereignty were devalued, like politics, publics, intellectuals, and educated citizenship, leaving only economy and national security as matters of collective action.[131] When Truman warned of infiltrators, instituted loyalty checks, and equated totalitarian systems, he substantiated Hoover's propaganda against the New Deal. As an official representative of the president, the FBI director mapped out the places and spaces Truman had allegedly sent the bureau in its hunt for Soviet guerrillas. These spaces were strategic for the director because they offered him control over the mediums of mass culture and information. From this position, he presented the nation with a new reality.

Americanism in Cold War Reality: Rhetoric and Philosophy

The new reality operated in stark contrast to the world presented by Truman. In his Third Annual Message of January 1948, the president announced that the nation sought "answers which will embody the moral and spiritual elements of tolerance, unselfishness, and brotherhood upon which true freedom and opportunity must rest. . . . Religious freedom, free speech, and freedom of thought are cherished realities in our land." He continued to say that "any denial of human rights is a denial of the basic beliefs of democracy and our regard for the worth of each individual." Therefore, he concluded, it was troubling that "some are denied equal protection under laws. Whether discrimination is based on race, or creed, or color, or land of origin, it is utterly contrary to American ideals of democracy." He reassured his audience, however, that the "recent report of the President's Committee on Civil Rights points the way for corrective action by the Federal Government and by State and local governments."[132] Issued in October 1947, the report focused on the "limitations on civil rights in our southern states. To a great extent this reflects reality; many of the most sensational and serious violations of civil rights have taken place in the South." The committee recommended the "elimination of segregation, based on race, color, creed, or national origin, from American life," anti-lynching and anti-peonage legislation, the "enactment of a federal Fair Employment Practice Act prohibiting all forms of discrimination in private employment," and correctives for discriminatory practices in government employment, education, housing, health care, and public services.[133] The committee even recommended using the FBI to enforce some of its proposals. Hoover's vision, to the contrary, used such proposals to suggest that the federal government had been infiltrated by Communists.

Rather than a federal system that organized public life at local levels to address inequality and build tolerance for others, anticommunists favored the rights of Anglo-Americans to decide how they should treat others. When the House Committee on Appropriations approved funding for HUAC in May 1946, Southern Democrats laid out a view of American philosophy that would soon become the only protected perspective. Sumners told his audience that the Anglo-Saxon system of "democracy" was an "association of private people engaged in a common enterprise of governing themselves. It is diametrically opposed to a totalitarian government, a government which operates from the top downward." He emphasized that a "totalitarian government operates from the top down, and that is the sort of thing that many people seem busy to be trying to establish in this country, a government dominant, a people regimented, controlled, dependent." To the contrary, he argued that "democracy" had "always been away from centralized power and totalitarianism, the direction in which these subversive elements would move us." He concluded that, rather than the president's plans, the "way to spread democracy is to demonstrate its vitality, its superiority, as the sort of government under which people can have liberty, opportunity, and happiness, where the individual citizenship speaks the voice of government."[134]

Sumners's language was continuous with Hayek's work. The *Reader's Digest*, for example, reprinted that social-democratic planning "leads to dictatorship because dictatorship is the most effective instrument of coercion and, as such, essential if central planning on a large scale is to be possible." Rather than support the New Deal, Hayek implored his readers to return to the

> virtues which are held less and less in esteem in Britain and America . . . precisely those on which Anglo-Saxons justly prided themselves and in which they were generally recognized to excel. These virtues were independence and self-reliance, individual initiative and local responsibility, the successful reliance on voluntary activity, noninterference with one's neighbor and tolerance of the different, and a healthy suspicion of power and authority.[135]

Indeed, Hayek's work lent Republicans and Southern Democrats a liberal rationale to support the FBI's coercive tactics.

Rhetorically, the FBI relied on Anglo-American nationalism and neoliberalism to substitute New Deal social democracy for realism. He told HUAC in his March 1947 appearance, for example, that an "easy test to establish the real character" of an organization was to question whether it denounced "American and British foreign policy" or if it espoused the "cause of Americanism or the cause of Soviet Russia." He reassured the committee that the "best antidote to communism is vigorous, intelligent, old-fashioned Americanism with eternal vigilance."[136] Similarly, the director told the American Legion in September 1946 that those who "stand for the American way of life must arise and defeat Red Fascism in America by focusing upon it the spotlight of public opinion and by building up barriers of common decency through which it cannot penetrate."[137] His containment discourse suggested that social reformers had ulterior motives behind what they publicly stated, both of which could be equitably judged by nationalists. Hoover wrote in the June 1947 issue of *Newsweek*, for example, that the "first step in the fight to preserve the American way of life is the exposure of the true aims of Communism and then a contrast of them with our American way of life." From there, he argued, the "American people will do the rest—quarantine them from effectively weakening our country."[138] By dissociating what was "American" from what was not, Hoover aligned New Dealers with foreign enemies, and normalized and deflected attention from the FBI's own secret and illegal programs.

With the bureau staffed by agents who enforced Hoover's ideology, he elected them as ideal for determining who was loyal to the American nation. He explained in the April 1950 issue of the *New York Times Magazine*, for example, that the "typical F.B.I. man" was a "typical American. He is just as anxious to see to it that American principles are preserved, either in F.B.I. investigative activity or in any other phase of daily life, as he is to continue to enjoy the freedom incident to democratic living."[139] Hoover specified that the FBI would be intolerant of people and ideas that diverged from his vision. He told the Freemasons in May 1950, for example, that "America's tolerance is predicated upon the premise of equality and justice for all, a tolerance which must be merited, cherished, and constantly practiced. When a minority group, by abusing tolerance, attempts to destroy the fabric of democracy, it forfeits its right to the Nation's tolerance. Tolerance toward tyranny is absurd"—a perspective shared by Hayek and other neoliberal thinkers.[140] The rhetoric of Americanism, therefore, justified militant practices of cultural purification and identified minority rights as irrational.

Moreover, the FBI justified the use of force against minority groups because they did not comport with reason. Hoover told the American Legion in September 1946, for example, that the American Communist Party was "not truly a political party," for if it "were a political party its adherents could be appealed to by reason. Instead, it is a system of intrigue, actuated by fanaticism. It knows no rules of decency."[141] While public and private employees from all sectors of public life were blacklisted for their support of the New Deal, the director argued why their philosophy justified their ouster. He wrote in the August 1950 issue of *U.S. News and World Report*, for example, that the "'philosophical Communist' who advocates Marxism-Leninism might just as well be working as an agent of a foreign power because he is aiding its cause. He is, in fact, however, being 'played for a sucker' by the Communists, who consider him a 'dupe,' a person not to be trusted but only to be used and then discarded."[142] With such disregard for liberals, whom he aligned with Marxists and dupes, the director laid grounds for COINTELPRO to be normalized in political culture.

At its foundation, rhetorical realism was grounded in the FBI's move to dissociate the real from the unreal. He wrote in *U.S. News and World Report*, for example, that Communists worked "behind the masquerade of hypocrisy. For this reason, America must be vigilant to recognize Communism for what it actually is—a malicious evil which would destroy this nation." The FBI played an essential role in protecting the nation, Hoover argued, in investigating backstage and looking behind the masquerade of Trojan horses. He wrote that a "Communist is not always easy to identify. He is trained in deceit and uses cleverly camouflaged movements to conceal his real purposes." Monitoring was necessary because the enemy used secrecy to dupe the citizenry. He concluded that if "every American faced the reality of what the fulfillment of the Communist objectives would mean to him—he would be inspired to work harder to protect and preserve the individual liberty and freedom which is part and parcel of our American way of life."[143] The CPUSA and its defenders in the Democratic Party were discredited by the ideological axis that redefined what "democracy" meant. The director argued in *Newsweek*, for example, that there was "sentiment that a Communist has as much right to a government job as a Democrat or a Republican because the Communists claim to be a political party. In reality, they are a part of an international criminal conspiracy."[144] What Communists secretly planned backstage, he argued, was to strip Americans of their subjectivity. Hoover told the Freemasons that the "end result of this alien 'redblooding' of thousands of men and women, is to create a 'Communist man'—a creature intellectually sterile, spiritually void and oblivious to the realities of life," what he described as a "robot—thoughtless, lifeless and senseless."[145] The personae of dupe, clairvoyant, and passer did more than push New Dealers out of government or into anticommunism; they also projected a new political reality to contextualize world events and the human nature that animated them.

The new realities of international relations and economics were steeped in the frontier myth. Peter Josef Mühlbaur observes that frontier imagery presents neoliberal arguments in libertarian draping. The "boundlessness of a frontier is a comfortable prerequisite of libertarian models," which advance neoliberalisms. Accordingly, "libertarian ideology uses—in one form or another—a conception of the frontier, of the space that still can be conquered—and thus finds itself in a specifically American tradition."[146] The context of the myth had long been set in a racialized historiography that equated the spread of white English-speaking peoples with the spread of democracy, Christianity, and civilization.[147] In the Progressive Era, reformers sometimes defined national loyalty as racial loyalty, which they vaguely identified in terms of Teutonic or Anglo-Saxon bloodlines.[148] David W. Southern observes that public intellectuals professed a deterministic sense of history in which "Anglo-Saxons were destined to dominate the globe."[149] Theodore Roosevelt, for example, professed "linguistically based theories of Aryanism and Teutonism" that suggested Americans composed a master race when he defined rugged individualism as an American trait, observes Richard Slotkin.[150] At the core of the frontier myth, "the meaning and direction of America—perhaps of western history as a whole—is found in the metaphoric representation of history as an extended Indian war," which cast villains in terms of savages, and heroes in terms of entrepreneurial individualists.[151] Accordingly, Hoover wrote in a February 1949 article for *Redbook* that the "zeal of early Christians stamped out paganism in Rome and conquered the savage gods of the northern barbarians. That same zeal could convert godless Communism. It is up to the churches of America to recapture the militant spirit of Paul and to fulfill the magnificent prophesy of John," who foretold of the apocalypse in Revelation. Hoover quoted from John 8:32, "And ye shall know the truth, and the truth shall make you free," which was soon after etched into the lobby wall of the Central Intelligence Agency.[152] A new frontier had been announced, one with familiar roles, identities, and purposes.

The FBI and its supporters in Congress and the press shared the historiography and located such toxic individualism at the nation's ideological core in ways that intervened in U.S. religious culture. Sumners traced America's cultural history to "Germanic political ancestors," to the Angles, Saxons, and Jutes who brought it to England in the fifth and sixth centuries. New Dealers (i.e., Jews), he argued, conversely "came from countries where for centuries and centuries the government has operated from the top downward," which suggested that their genetic differences explained their ideological disagreement.[153] Similarly, Hayek observed in the *Reader's Digest* that "Individualism, in contrast to socialism and all other forms of totalitarianism, is based on the respect of Christianity for the individual man and the belief that it is desirable that men should be free to develop their own individual gifts and bents."[154] Continuous with Sumner and Hayek, Hoover wrote in *Newsweek*: "We should never forget that Communism begins with the group; democracy and Christianity begin with the individual."[155] He also made individualism the centerpiece of his August 1951 article for *Lookout Magazine*: "A Good Christian Is a Good Citizen." He wrote that laws were necessary to ensure that the "welfare of one individual would not be endangered by the actions of others. This is the reason we have laws. They are the rules in which we govern ourselves. . . . The type of government we have depends in a large measure on the type of society we have."[156] Hoover's emphasis on individualism helped to fragment mainstream Protestantism. Diana Kirby observes that he exploited a fissure between more liberal Christians who supported the New Deal and more conservative Christians who heretofore constituted a religious fringe, and thereby helped prepare the way for the rise of the religious right years later.[157] Together, the FBI and the Christian right realigned capitalism with Christianity by equating collectivism with materialism and atheism.[158] The bureau thus helped reshape the American religious landscape and made it a tool to remap relationships between the individual and society, and society and government, a project that also animated the purpose of nationalists and justified COINTELPRO and the Cold War world it helped make.

The emphasis on individualism synced with the rise of rational choice theory in the academy, which epistemologically underpinned political realism and neoliberalism.[159] Lawrence Freedman summarizes that behavioralism emerged as a value-free approach to social and political theory at a time when "'social science' smacked too much of a 'socialist science' or social reform. The individualistic assumptions behind this approach fit naturally with theories of markets and democracy and challenged Marxist notions of class struggle." Ultimately, behavioralism "encouraged the view that liberal individualism was rational and collectivism was irrational," and that "individuals made their own choices in order to maximize their utilities" in terms of "economic rewards and the acquisition of power."[160] McCumber concurs, arguing that where "Marxism claimed that history and society were shaped by large-scale social forces," rational choice theory "directed attention to market and voting behavior, where the only thing that ever happened was that individuals made free choices in order to maximize their utility. Where Marxism demanded subordination of individual aspirations to the common good," rational choice theory suggested "there is no such thing as a 'common good' (except as a preference of individuals)." McCumber, therefore, identifies rational choice theory as Cold War philosophy. He traces how neoliberalism crept into universities in the early 1950s when college teachers of the social sciences were removed by the FBI for what they taught, and their positions were replaced by a different class of applicants who dismissed and displaced Marxist perspectives.[161] The FBI forcibly changed the American intelligentsia and the institutional order that its collective voice scripted and legitimated. Hoover's bureau traded a bottom-up model of democratic institutional control that emanated from culture, for a top-down model that manipulated culture to seize control of U.S. institutions and ultimately imposed a radically different vision of democracy that was steeped in eugenics.

Cold War epistemology had profound consequences for relationships between the citizenry and government. Ned O'Gorman observes that neoliberalism was conceived in response to European and American political culture of the 1930s and 1940s, against police and fascist states as well as against the liberal state. Neoliberalism reconstructed liberalism to make law, the police, and public policy the servants of market forces, which pressed into education, medicine, and social welfare. He concludes that neoliberalism was a social philosophy with a "particular vision of society organized around the liberation of the human spirit before the centralized and concentrated idols of the age."[162] The mid-century philosophy repudiated Keynesian welfare-state economics with pre-Keynesian visions of rational individualism, and extended rational choice theory to many institutions and social actions. Brown notes that neoliberalism eroded those institutions, venues, and values that could not or would not comply. The philosophy constructed individuals as rational entrepreneurial actors, whose value was measured in terms of the Victorian ideal of self-reliance. This value made the individual fully responsible for the consequences of her or his actions, regardless of constraints placed on those actions by various modes of inequality.[163] The social-democratic philosophy of New Dealers who celebrated the ideal of cooperation or communalism receded.

When Max Lowenthal appeared before HUAC in September 1950, his testimony highlighted the problem that anticommunism and neoliberalism posed to people who subscribed to a theory of democracy that emphasized rights rather than race. He was represented by Burton K. Wheeler, who lost his primary election in 1946 to a challenger who lost the Senate election to a Republican. Like Reagan, Nixon had become a key FBI collaborator and moved in and out of the chamber with former FBI agent Representative Harold H. Velde (R-IL) as Wheeler and Lowenthal responded to the committee. Former FBI agent and HUAC staffer Louis Russell asked a litany of questions about Lowenthal's associates, most of whom were Hollywood personnel, their lawyers, or otherwise considered suspicious for their associations. Lowenthal warned the committee that if it continued to "attach the theory of guilt by association to the lawyer who is willing to accept such a retainer, I think we are undermining one of the most wonderful principles of our jurisprudence. . . . If you keep up this process of making charges, there isn't a corporation in the United States that won't be charged with being communistic or anti-American." He continued, "If you keep up this process, there will be no American who will be known as an American."[164] The signifiers of "American" and "un-American" changed under the feet of New Dealers like him.

Unfortunately for Lowenthal, one major exception to his contact list was how he knew Alger Hiss. They were friends. They both worked on the Wickersham Commission. New Dealers praised his work. When Hiss applied for a position with Senator George L. Radcliffe (D-MD) in 1935, for example, a recommender recounted that Hiss "stood high in the regard of his associates" at the Agricultural Adjustment Administration, and his "departure was noticed with great regret by his superiors, including Secretary [Henry] Wallace."[165] Hiss had become toxic to the New Deal. His toxicity spread to his defenders, and Lowenthal was mistaken about his innocence. Security experts in the CIA, FBI, and Congress knew Lowenthal was wrong because of the classified Venona project, which would not be made public for another four decades.[166] Lowenthal was called to testify in court after Hiss was convicted of perjury. Lowenthal called the case a miscarriage of justice and qualified that from "what I read I gathered the basic issue was one of credibility, as between Mr. Chambers and Mr. Hiss. I do not know Mr. Chambers, but have known Mr. Hiss. My opinion of him is that he would not lie."[167] The more Lowenthal defended Hiss, the more he implicated himself as a collaborator. Lowenthal's reputation was so impugned by 1953 that even espionage ringleader Nathan Gregory Silvermaster would plead the fifth to avoid discussing how he knew the lawyer.[168] It was in this context that Lowenthal published *The Federal Bureau of Investigation* (1950), a book that documented Hoover's breaches of law and ethics, but received scant, if not hostile, attention.[169]

Public Opinion, Propaganda, and the Rhetorical Presidency

Nixon attended Hoover's speech to HUAC in March 1947. He was a committee member and would soon become an FBI surrogate. He played a key role in prosecuting Hiss, and impugning Lowenthal by proxy.[170] After Hoover concluded his remarks, Nixon asserted that "a considerable amount of opposition" had arisen to the president's recent order about "Communists in the Government service." He suggested that criticisms of the Loyalty Program were based "on the grounds that proper safeguards for persons who are accused of being disloyal are not set up in the order." Nixon reminded Hoover that the FBI had a "great deal to do with furnishing the information," which critics opposed because the accused then did not "have the opportunity to be confronted with the witnesses against him" and did "not have the right to a jury trial." Hoover responded that the information program was a "matter affecting the security of the country. Obviously we would not . . . disclose the identity of a confidant . . . because it would prevent usefulness in the future, and might endanger his life." However, these concerns were not worthy of consideration anyway, Hoover suggested, because they had been raised only to "force a disclosure of sources of information by elements that are particularly un-American who still may be in the Government service." Hoover added that he suspected that such "shouts and screams" were from that "source particularly."[171]

Hoover's speech to the committee invoked Truman's rhetorical presidency and situated his doctrine in a context that helped Hoover model a persona for Republicans and Southern Democrats to mimic, which concealed their anti–New Deal agenda behind concerns for national security. Not surprisingly, Republicans praised the FBI director for his speech. Chairman Thomas (R-NJ) clumsily identified Hoover's statement as a "continuation of an era of cooperation between the Federal Bureau of Investigation and the Un-American Activities Committee of the House of Representatives." John McDowell (R-PA) added to the record that he "wanted to compliment this great American public servant for a very substantial contribution to good government." Karl Mundt (R-SD) immediately regarded the speech as the "most masterful and conclusive statement of [Hoover's] career" and insisted that it was then time for "so-called liberal and progressive forces" to "take vigorous and active steps to expose and defeat the activities of Communists, and not simply to damn Communism with faint praise." What might have sounded unusual were the laudatory comments offered by Democrats to an FBI director who had aligned the New Deal with subversion. J. Hardin Peterson (D-FL) agreed "with what [his] colleagues said about the fine presentation." He added that he had known of Hoover's "fine work of this kind for a number of years" and spoke for HUAC when he said, "We are quite proud of the work you have done." Herbert C. Bonner (D-NC) agreed in gendered terms and told Hoover that he was "very proud of your record. I admire you personally as a man, and I appreciate the great service you have rendered and are rendering this country."[172] For these Democrats, Southern politics superseded party loyalty and even democratic legitimacy, and the rhetoric of Anglo-American nationalism provided a means to cast their motives in terms of the identity that Hoover coordinated between his professional stature as a public servant and his narrative authority as a doomsayer.

Truman's and Hoover's discourse combined in ways that legitimized the concerns of nationalists through illegitimate rhetorical processes. Truman warned of "such subterfuges as political infiltration" on March 12, and then nine days later he ordered the FBI to investigate the loyalty of federal employees. The boundaries of nationalism and national security were blurred and fell upon the racialized and gendered lines of Americanism. Many liberals moved to support Hoover because they presumed that he was aligned with Truman. In a nationally broadcast speech, Hoover essentially told the president's opponents in Congress that labor and civil rights advocacy was a Communist plot that should be ignored and discredited. Truman's rhetorical power was co-opted. He was not the only one frustrated to have his language misconstrued. Representative Walter Judd (R-MN) reprinted a May 1945 article from the *Minneapolis Tribune*, "Reception Given 'Road to Serfdom' Surprises Author," one month after it appeared in *Reader's Digest.* Hayek warned his readers:

> My main concern is now that I find far too many people talking about what I am represented to have said rather than about the argument that I have actually used. I certainly do not wish to be held responsible for all the interpretations of my views. If those who want to use part of my argument for special pleading are allowed to get away with it, this is not my fault. . . . If an argument is true, it does not cease to be so by being used in the service of particular interest: this will always happen, and has always happened to the true philosophy of freedom.

Still, Hayek admitted that his language was significant because it sought to redraw "boundaries between legitimate and illegitimate government activities."[173] His defense was naive. Like Truman, he was unprepared for how technological developments in mass communication had changed dynamics of discourse and democracy.

Amid the FBI director's rhetorical coup, fear of Communist subversion overcame objections to his illegal methods. Nixon could "express complete confidence" in Hoover's work on behalf of the House of Representatives in June 1949 after court documents revealed some of his illegal programs.[174] The next month, Representative Gerald Ford (R-MI) introduced an amendment to raise Hoover's salary, observing: "We need the best personnel obtainable to ensure the protection of our citizens. Mr. Hoover's record for the past 25 years is unassailable. The monetary reward proposed by my amendment, after long years of faithful and devoted service, is small compensation for his invaluable contribution."[175] That year, Nixon and Ford founded the Republican Party's covert Chowder and Marching Club, a hidden party mechanism that strategized political environments at local and national levels.[176] Moreover, Senator Lyndon B. Johnson (D-TX) recounted to the FBI that he reassured one of his constituents in February 1950 that Hoover would not "encounter any loss of confidence either from the general public or the Congress," regardless of what critics like Lowenthal might say about him.[177] The apparatus cemented his premier status in American political culture. McCarthy made this evident when he sycophantically gushed in a July 1952 letter to the director that the FBI stood as a monument to "J. Edgar Hoover" and that this would "always be."[178] His aide, Roy Cohn, helped make this so when he administrated the J. Edgar Hoover Foundation with Louis Nichols and Joseph Kennedy, and later advised Republican presidents Ronald Reagan and Donald J. Trump, and their campaign strategist Roger Stone.[179] Public-opinion polling was on Hoover's side. Gallup recorded in January 1950 that 82 percent of respondents felt that Hoover had "done a good job as head of the F.B.I.," and only 2 percent said otherwise.[180] Hoover's discourse thus fostered a political climate that was more receptive to an expanded and militarized FBI in peacetime. Adler and Paterson credit the "Red-fascist image" for how it helped reshape the rationale of U.S. policy planners when "possibilities for accommodation" with the Soviet Union were still tangible in 1945–1946.[181] FBI discourse locked the course of history in more decisive ways that made such accommodation impossible.

The director led a nationalist movement that mimicked the rhetorical framework of the Nazis. Kenneth Burke observed in "The Rhetoric of Hitler's Battle" (1939) that the dictator offered a "trinity of government" that interlocked "*popularity* of the leader, *force* to back the popularity, and popularity and force maintained together long enough to become backed by a *tradition*."[182] He further noted that "Hitler appeals" to his audiences "by relying upon a bastardization of fundamentally religious patterns of thought." He suggested that religion did not require a "fascist state," but that religion could be misused to create one. Hitler offered his followers an opportunity for symbolic rebirth.

> The projective device of the scapegoat, coupled with the Hitlerite doctrine of inborn racial superiority, provides its followers with a "positive" view of life. They can again get the feel of *moving forward*, towards a *goal* (a promissory feature of which Hitler makes much). In Hitler, as the group's prophet, such rebirth involved a symbolic change of lineage. Here, above all else, we see Hitler giving a malign twist to a benign aspect of Christian thought. For whereas the Pope, in the familistic pattern of thought basic to the Church, stated that the Hebrew prophets were the *spiritual ancestors* of Christianity, Hitler uses this same mode of thinking in reverse. He renounces this "ancestry" in a "materialistic" way by voting himself and the members of his lodge a different "blood stream" from that of the Jews.

Burke concluded that "politicians of his kind" were also in America and that such "corruptors of religion" constituted a "major menace to the world" because they gave the "profound patterns of religious thought a crude and sinister distortion."[183] Such was used to replace American social democracy with institutional discourse that empowered COINTELPRO. The ideology celebrated force and violence as forms of political expression. The rhetoric of Americanism borrowed from, and operated as, a rhetoric of fascism to perform cultural purification.

Conclusion

The rhetorical legacy of J. Edgar Hoover is best measured by his vast influence over domestic politics, rather than the heights of his own expansive institutional power. After Harry S. Truman left office in January 1953, Hoover went on to serve under Presidents Dwight Eisenhower, John F. Kennedy, Lyndon B. Johnson, and Richard Nixon, a feat that required the father of the Great Society to issue an executive order that exempted Hoover from the mandatory federal retirement age of seventy in 1964.[1] He set a rhetorical landscape that constrained these presidencies in different ways and to the advantage of the Republican Party in his lifetime and thereafter. Nixon borrowed language from FDR's isolationist critics on the America First Committee when he campaigned to "Make America First Again" in 1968, which Ronald Reagan adapted to "Make America Great Again" in 1980, and Donald Trump repeated in 2016 before he campaigned to "Keep America Great" in 2020. When Trump accepted the Republican

National Archives and Records Administration.

President Dwight D. Eisenhower pins the National Security Medal on J. Edgar Hoover, with Vice President Richard M. Nixon and others gathered around, May 27, 1955.

Party's nomination, he pledged to "put America First. Americanism, not globalism, will be our credo."[2] Nixon clarified that their language was grounded in the FBI's notions of law and order when he elaborated that he sought to "make America first again in respect to order and justice under law" at an October 1968 campaign event.[3]

Critics have already noted a pattern of codes embedded within the rhetoric of Americanism, which continued to recirculate Hoover's worldview after his death. Walter R. Fisher observes that Reagan's pledge to "Make America Great Again" was linked to how the president presented himself as a romantic figure through the frontier myth, as the "quintessential hero of the West—the town marshal," a symbol of law and order. Fisher argues that Reagan's discourse was romantic in that it promised to restore nineteenth-century laissez-faire ideology. He superimposed elements of American thought and action from a mythic past onto the present to fantasize about the future. Fisher identifies this rhetorical system as Reagan's "conception of Americanism." He elaborates that like Hoover, Reagan used code words like "family" for the nuclear family, "work" for no welfare, "neighborhood" for no integration, "peace" for deterrence and manifest destiny, and "freedom" for the free enterprise system.[4] Reagan's discourse was fostered by Hoover throughout the course of decades. Years after he informed on Dalton Trumbo and the Hollywood Ten, Reagan collaborated with the FBI again when he was governor of California (1967–1975), before Hoover's death in 1972. Together, they strategized to discredit student and faculty protesters who complained of political censorship on university campuses, protesters whose speech they both identified as being subversive.[5] The coded rhetoric of Americanism continued to circulate for decades thereafter. Trump tweeted in May 2015, "I was proud to be one of Ronald Reagan's earliest supporters. Like Reagan, it's time to Make America Great Again!"[6] The Americanism of Nixon, Reagan, and Trump highlights a system of meaning that was invented by the FBI to unsettle the New Deal, a system that manipulated the Americanism of Theodore Roosevelt and remained a hallmark of Republican Party discourse in its defense of capitalism and culture.

Indeed, what critics have written about Reagan's Americanism informs the broader language system and offers a means to more holistically read the FBI's New Deal discourse in terms of (1) how it unified Hoover's public and narrative personae with the frontier myth and rhetorical realism, (2) how the FBI invented a heterosexual persona to ground Hoover's rhetoric of Americanism, (3) how Hoover used notions of Americanism to simultaneously signify loyalty to the presidency and realign the FBI with Roosevelt's and then Truman's opponents, (4) how the FBI exploited nascent neoliberal discourse to confound the grounds of objections to the New Deal, and (5) how the FBI helped substitute institutional frames of governance in law enforcement and public life more generally.

The Rhetorical Presidency and Americanism

J. Edgar Hoover's power was ultimately grounded in how he used discourse to intersect the institutional and rhetorical presidencies. Whereas the former offered the pretense of legal authority, the latter extended the symbolic authority of the executive to his own office. Though he was hostile to the New Deal's social-democratic underpinnings, his meteoric rise was linked to how the program expanded the federal government in the overlapping contexts of FDR's and Truman's domestic and international agendas. These three tensions—between the rhetorical and institutional presidencies, between Hoover's disdain for the New Deal and how it expanded the FBI, and between its domestic and international agendas—offered a dynamic field of action for Hoover's rhetorical agency wherein he played the tensions against each other and against the presidents he allegedly served. The product of his invention was a new institutional frame that he identified as "Americanism," a term that nodded back to the Progressive Era and the culture championed by Theodore Roosevelt. This strategy offered him a legacy to mimic and a perception of continuity for Republicans to push forward, despite Hoover's disregard for Roosevelt's emphasis on moderation.

From its conceptual inception, scholars of the rhetorical presidency have counted surrogacy as a symbolic strategy, but have otherwise not explored how the chain of command empowered a bench of appointed officeholders to consolidate or undermine the president's authority.[7] This move departed from the framers' vision for executive leadership and their suspicion of popular appeals to the citizenry. Moreover, the rise of the FBI exemplifies how FDR changed the institutional and rhetorical presidencies. Will Irwin observed in *Propaganda and the News* (1936) that the "number of publicity agents for Federal departments grew constantly during fifteen years until in this, the administration of Franklin D. Roosevelt, the director, adviser or producer of publicity seems indispensable to even the smallest alphabetical bureau."[8] Some of Roosevelt's contemporaries were uncomfortable with this growth of the institution. For example, James L. McCamy wrote in *Government Publicity: Its Practice in Federal Administration* (1939) that a whole class of unelected leaders in the federal bureaucracy would use mass media to erode constitutional checks on their authority.[9] Walter Lippmann astutely warned in *The Good Society* that "people longed for kings who were philosophers. And so the men who wished to be kings declared that they were philosophers. All the things lacking in the actual world were projected upon the imaginary state that men so desperately desired."[10] Certainly, these charges applied to Hoover. He exploited FDR's transformation of the presidency when he aligned executive leadership with the spectacle of sensational crime busts, informed and shaded the president's perceptions of threat, corroborated the president's public statements in a manner that advanced his own political interests, and offered his own leadership as an alternative to the president's. These moves were made possible by the network of laws, statutes, executive orders, and customs that institutionally networked their offices, which blurred important differences between them in the public imagination. James W. Ceaser, Glen E. Thurow, Jeffrey Tulis, and Joseph M. Bessette warn that an "institutionalized speechwriting staff" in the White House "may bring to presidential speeches interests of its own that conflict with presidential policy" or include "remarks in speeches at the expense of presidential coherence."[11] Compounding this problem further, the FBI's moves illustrate how appointed officeholders could use their institutional links to betray the White House. By expanding the bureaucracy, FDR opened up a host of unprecedented and unexplored rhetorical problems.

Studying the FBI's influence over the New Deal illustrates, in part, Parry-Giles's interest in more expanded notions of the rhetorical presidency that account for covert "discourse controlled by the executive branch" and disseminated by surrogates as secondary orality.[12] By looking at the spaces between the Oval Office and federal departments, scholars can account for the expansive federal workforce that exists to serve the president. These permanent employees are managed by officials who have the cultural right to invoke the name of the president to perform their duties. This right illustrates an intersection of the two presidencies and how the New Deal expanded both. *Time* magazine probed this intersection in 1975 when it noted that Hoover's ability to acquire and keep tyrannical "power raises disturbing questions not merely about the role of a national police in a democracy, but also about the political system that tolerated him for so long."[13] That system is one that witnessed a collapse of checks and balances when a trusted surrogate used his institutional stature to turn the presidency against itself with a wholesale domestic propaganda campaign. Accounting for the presidency's institutional and rhetorical growth invites scholars to question how presidential authority is symbolically shared through institutional linkages, with whom it is shared, and how it may be used. Such questions emphasize rhetorical and archival histories of the federal bureaucracy as well as the rhetorical biographies of its employees. The system merits exploration because, as FBI discourse illustrates, appointees have historically constrained the presidency.

Past critiques of anticommunist speakers have already charted the rhetorical landscape of Americanism that Hoover left to his collaborators who became presidents. Writing about public and narrative personae in Reagan's 1988 Republican National Convention speech, Ann Chisholm observes that "Reagan's role as narrator both personalized and mythologized him. Using mythic referents, Reagan associated his personal public persona with his narrative persona as citizen, creating the illusion that an intimate relationship existed between him and the American people." What made him appear credible, she argues, was his ability to narrate in a voice and style that unified his public persona with his narrative persona. His identity as a citizen in public life pulled from the literary realism of Mark Twain's *The Adventures of Huckleberry Finn* (1885), which he made continuous with "sentiments of true Americanism." His "narrative portrayed him not only as a president who had a close personal relationship with the American people but also as a president who understood and championed the people." This public identity was illusory, Chisholm argues, because Reagan was more secluded and stage-managed than his predecessors. What voters knew of Reagan, in part, came purposefully prepackaged from professional packagers. Combined, the personae constituted Reagan's ethos, a man motivated to act by "his love for America and its people."[14] Americanism was a system of meaning available to crafty speakers who could perform red-blooded masculinity to project credibility. The FBI, therefore, crafted an epistemology that empowered a culture rife with contradictions that would outlive the Cold War and span until at least the Trump administration.

FDR could expand the institutional and rhetorical presidencies as he did, in part, because of changes in mass communication technologies—changes that Hoover exploited with domestic propaganda in ways that helped unify his public and narrative personae and ultimately enhanced his credibility above that of even the president. James J. Kimble identifies a "rough consensus which suggests that propaganda generally possesses three contextual characteristics: institutionality, mass distribution, and multiple iterations."[15] With help from strategists like Clyde Tolson, Louis Nichols, Courtney Riley Cooper, and Rex Collier, not to mention the nameless staff writers of the Crime Records Section (CRS), Hoover orchestrated a campaign that spanned almost four decades, undoubtedly the longest in U.S. history, which made him the nation's premier propagandist. While Tolson, Nichols, and the CRS were instrumental mechanics who networked with Congress and mass media, Cooper and Collier shaped the rhetorical form that Hoover invented for his office in 1925 when he became director, what historians identify as a narrative formula that unified "all aspects of the FBI's operations into one coherent image."[16] The image emerged where biographical content about Hoover intersected the types of narratives he delivered, both of which were grounded in rhetorical realism and how it invoked the frontier myth. His public persona as Christian proselytizer, crime fighter, spy chaser, and scientific expert placed him comfortably within the realm of the red-bloods, men known to be straight because they enjoyed battle. Such character logic belonged to literary naturalism and the realistic reality it conveyed. CRS writers used the same logic and conventions when they drafted the many speeches that Hoover delivered to depict the world in which the FBI operated—speeches that were as much about his heroism as they were about public safety. Unification between his public and narrative personae was the product of a propaganda program that carefully followed the Cooper-Collier formula and adapted it to wartime situations.

Historians like Douglas M. Charles, Matthew Cecil, and Steve Rosswurm dismiss the subject of Hoover's sexual orientation as unimportant to evaluate his cultural significance, and prefer to identify him as "homosocial."[17] Charles states their position succinctly in *Hoover's War on Gays: Exposing the FBI's "Sex Deviates" Program* (2015) with a chapter titled "Was J. Edgar Hoover Gay? Does It Matter?" He answers, "We simply do not—and, indeed, cannot know—what Hoover's sexual preference (whether gay, straight, bisexual, or repressed) was and whether it played any discernible role in what he and his FBI did," and warns against drawing "theoretical conclusions using gossip as historical evidence over Hoover's sexuality."[18] These historians reduce the significance of the question to the fodder of homophobic gossip, and dismiss the preponderance of evidence as inconclusive because, they argue, it is impossible to know Hoover's and Tolson's sexual desires or activities. This burden of proof is unreasonable because it conflates sexual orientation with sexual activity, requires documentation of what was intentionally not documented by security experts, and discounts other expressions of romantic love, like lifelong monogamous intimate companionship, a level of burden not expected in discussions about heterosexual partnerships. Of course, the historians also do not account for Hoover's 1943 love letter to Tolson, which does not fit the homosocial mold, likely because the letter was not available to them. Furthermore, Hoover's sexual orientation does matter because it intersected issues of gender in ways that were quite relevant to Hoover and those who wrote and later recalculated the Cooper-Collier formula. Hoover's public persona was invented, in part, to rebut whispers that he was gay, and it was in response to such concerns that he was re-gendered as a red-blood. Hoover would thereafter use the gendered formula to unite Southern Democrats with Republicans, and cast public life as a dystopic conspiracy, rich with anxieties about who might be watching and for what purposes, where "real" men were compelled to prove their toughness (and straightness) with public acts of bravado. And, it was this vision of conspiracy that empowered the rise of

COINTELPRO and Cold War containment culture. The rhetorical trajectory of Hoover's conspiracy theories was informed by his own gender panic and experience with passing-for-straight, as well as his desire to communicate "toughness" to prove himself straight, and toughness was the attitude that the Truman Doctrine communicated, making these texts continuous with each other. Accordingly, Hoover's sexual orientation and the gender panic that accompanied it is rife with implications for the rise of rhetorical realism, the political realism it encouraged, and the undemocratic policies and practices that realism executed, including the betrayal of the U.S. presidency—arguably the most culturally significant, documented political conspiracy in U.S. history, a wholesale domestic propaganda program that brainwashed Americans and remade their politics.

From this backdrop, Hoover's rhetorical agency is legible. Though he despised the social-democratic foundations of the New Deal, he positioned himself near the center of New Deal politics to protect his job and ultimately expand the FBI. He wove together shared historical circumstances addressed by FDR that were symbolic of his own leadership with rhetoric from popular culture to perform a character type that was persuasive at the dawn of the war on crime when he needed to rebut rumors that he was gay. That this performance paid such dividends was a bonus to a move that was more immediately about keeping his job at a time when it was most imperiled by critics who sympathized with the National Commission on Law Observance and Enforcement. He offered a vision for the FBI as a scientifically administered national police force that could safely protect the nation from brutes with technology. Utilizing realist gender norms, his leadership of such an organization was a means to prove his heterosexuality as a gangbuster, an identity that had the requisite credibility to defame his rivals. Of course, such an organization never existed and was always far more ideologically inclined than reported. Similarly, he wove anxieties about Nazi espionage stirred by FDR with the rhetoric of film noir to repackage himself as a spy hunter, another allegedly heterosexual identity that protected his public stature and offered even more credibility to discredit his ideological critics.

Moreover, he was, in part, responsible for what would become the Cold War at home. He made the Truman Doctrine address continuous with a panic incited by Congress about Communist guerrillas in the New Deal to once again preserve his job, and he ultimately removed New Dealers from the federal workforce to drastically expand his own power. His agency, therefore, was that of a tailor who sewed different threads of discourse together in ways that presented himself as most appropriately qualified, or most appropriately gendered, to respond to what he presented as real. His power was thus grounded in large measure by his presentation of self, fit for the reality he conveyed.

He effectively persuaded audiences to see him as straight, even while fostering a gay relationship with his second-in-command. His public and narrative personae lent credibility to each other, and the combined product, over time, made his rhetoric more credible than Truman's not only on matters of national security but also on the animating force of the New Deal more generally. Hoover's effort to pass-for-straight was read by audiences as proof of authenticity in other domains of culture, as a man who understood what "America" meant and what it meant to be an "American." Certainly, the answer to these questions was complicated, but he reduced them to Americanism, which suggested that heterosexuality, whiteness, pugnacity, competitiveness, and individualism were foundational to the national identity. These traits, Hoover argued, were at the core of trustworthy or credible ideology. The proof of this argument rested in the persona of power that he projected. While New Dealers attempted to balance idealism in domestic and international politics, Hoover's rhetoric and reputation as a trusted adviser to the president pointed elsewhere. Fallout abroad hollowed idealism at home.

Audiences were pressed to decide between the believability of the president or of the FBI director, and the director won the skirmish because he made himself appear credible even to New Dealers who did not share Hoover's reactionary politics but nonetheless trusted him. As his successors in the Republican Party would later mimic, Hoover's performance illustrated that the rhetoric of Americanism required heterosexual spokesmen, and heterosexuality evidenced the credibility of hard-line politics. Straightness, toughness, capitalism, power, and good government were linked together and mutually reinforced each other. This formula required external antagonists, which the CRS made of Hoover's adversaries: prison reformers, New Dealers, sex offenders, Nazis, Communists, and people who did not fit these labels but were successfully assigned them nonetheless. The antithetical relationship that Hoover drew between himself and his adversaries persuaded national audiences to adhere to a new epistemology that resisted Keynesian social democracy and its support of race and labor reforms. Through his gendered performance, Hoover successfully asked audiences to see themselves in him and he in them. This request was made possible by the way he unified Americanism in culture and politics to communicate political realism.

The rhetoric of Americanism was key to the CRS's propaganda strategy and masked its nationalist work behind patriotism. Anatol Lieven observes that patriotism is a "desire to defend one's country as it actually is; whereas nationalism is a devotion to an ideal, abstract, unrealized notion of one's country, often coupled with a belief in some wider national mission to humanity."[19] The rhetoric of Americanism spanned a spectrum between these two motives and blurred the distinction between them. Accordingly, it was a helpful resource to simultaneously signify loyalty to the presidency and realign the FBI with Roosevelt's and Truman's opponents. Such rhetoric helped create a double audience. While New Dealers heard doublespeak that seemed appropriate for wartime by national security experts, their visible and invisible adversaries identified language that targeted the New Deal as a foreign conspiracy. Moreover, Americans who turned to the FBI for cultural leadership could more clearly decode the suppressed premises of his innuendos because these audiences came equipped to participate as he intended, with cultural knowledge that placed his discourse in the tradition of Anglo-American nationalism. The CRS's reliance on innuendo helped it mask its disloyalty—disloyalty that was further masked behind Hoover's public persona as a scientific and disinterested expert of law enforcement. Of course, Kimble's juncture of message and mechanics highlights an institutional feature that also masked disloyalty. The CRS's tireless promotion within Congress to have its discourse reprinted helped create an illusion of consensus, the appearance that New Dealers uniformly counted Hoover as one of their own. The combined effect of message and mechanics helped Hoover become too influential under FDR to be curbed by Truman, even though Truman had long distrusted him.

Hoover's institutional work, coupled with the rhetoric of Americanism, substantiated a reality that departed from the New Deal and underpinned a vision of public life that equated liberty with deregulation, which had implications for the civil rights movement and organized labor. The FBI's brand of Americanism was hard-line anticommunist, and the rhetoric of Americanism was also a rhetoric of anticommunism. At its center was a fear of foreign interlopers who used multiculturalism to mask foreign loyalties. New Deal race and labor reforms like the National Labor Relations Act were used to signify Marxist or social-justice epistemologies that privileged "foreign" ideology. The rhetoric of Americanism transformed public life in ways that changed relationships between the citizen, society, and government. Blacklists dissipated an intellectual class of workers who sympathized with social-justice activism and replaced them with an alternative class that had anticommunist bona fides. The intelligentsia was particularly targeted for their support of government intervention into issues of race and labor. Instead, the FBI and the anticommunist apparatus supported an antithetical reality that privileged rational individualism. The role of the government was much different in this reality, relegated to the service of corporate interests and agendas that reaffirmed Victorian cultural hierarchies, especially those rooted in the Protestant virtue of self-reliance. In this epistemological context, Keynesian social democracy ceded to neoliberalism, and Henry Clay's system for unfettered capitalism was once again identified as "American" in nature.

The rhetoric of Americanism helped the FBI substitute institutional frames of governance in law enforcement and public life more generally. The FBI director reinvented himself as a scientific reformer in the image of Berkeley police chief August Vollmer after Attorney General Harlan

F. Stone ordered him to dismantle the General Intelligence Division in the wake of the Palmer Raids and the Teapot Dome scandal. The persona was welcomed by reformers who aligned with the Wickersham Commission, which chided nationalists who advanced the "easy theory that our social difficulties are not to be charged to our own mistakes and failures" but to "nationals of other countries."[20] The image of the disinterested scientific professional placed Hoover within a prestigious group of academic reformers who invented a model of professionalism that rebuffed a history of xenophobic excesses within law enforcement.

The FBI's scientific rhetoric helped Hoover appear to be a New Dealer, or at least sympathetic to the New Deal, which moved him into FDR's orbit and made him a presidential surrogate. By using the language of the New Deal, he infiltrated its spaces and repackaged Americanism as a language of loyalty with the backing of the president and Congress. FDR mistakenly accepted Hoover's support to promote the New Deal during the war on crime and to secretly monitor American Communists and Nazis. In this capacity, Roosevelt broke from the juridical frame privileged by Wickersham and prized control over procedure as war approached. Subtly, the rhetoric of Americanism began to point toward a different frame altogether, one that turned against FDR's rhetorical presidency. Hoover popularized the frame under FDR in wartime, and he forced it upon Truman at a time when his job was once again imperiled. As with his gender work during the war on crime, the move paid dividends and incited a red scare. Whereas Roosevelt had the stature to rein in the rogue cop he empowered, Truman was made to appear disconnected from the reality of internal subversion after he warned of Soviet belligerence in the Truman Doctrine speech. With institutional support from the CRS, and with the authority of the rhetorical presidency behind him, Hoover presented himself as America's most realistic defender of national security and civil liberties, between idealists in the Truman administration and reactionaries in Congress. From this position, the FBI invented an alternative reality that made his frame the only realistic option for the nation. Of course, what counted as "real" belonged to the realm of myth, was centuries old, and was far more familiar to the FBI's audiences than the academic experimentation of New Dealers. Hoover's Americanisms pointed backward to attitudes and practices heralded by progressives as patriotic, and was welcomed by economic theorists, Southern Democrats, and Republicans who all wanted to push back against New Deal social and economic interventionism, to restore America to something it was mythically once before.

Realism, Epistemology, and Institutions

In all, Hoover's success and institutional work was predicated on his agency. With profound artistry, he, with the help of a cast of accomplices, combined language, mass-media technology, and professional norms of police administration into a coherent paradigm legible to diverse audiences that would eventually be identified as realism. Writing about literary realism, Mack Smith observes that realistic texts are made in a process that "displays several possible worlds implicitly to claim verisimilitude for a privileged one, continuous with the text's own mimetic norms, by showing its superiority over other false possible worlds that are textually represented as discontinuous with the text's mimesis."[21] Accordingly, Hoover offered cream-puff criminologists, fifth columnists, and red fascists as characters who belonged to false or unreal worlds, all of whom he gendered as gay and effete—an identity that Jack Babuscio qualifies as not "real" in the eyes of the heterosexual citizenry.[22] Smith adds that realistic texts are those that suggest transcendent truths that are continuous with "some ontological, ethical, or epistemological standard that exists by consensual agreement in the stories we create about the 'actual' world." Neoliberalism, literary realism and naturalism, criminal anthropology, Christian realism, Christian and scientific progressivisms, scientific administration, true-crime pulps, urban-crime and semidocumentary film noir all offered texts for Hoover to mimic as FBI director, a role that made him responsible for drawing conclusions about public life and what was "real" therein. He used the texts to separate what was real and pure from what needed to be contained.

Moreover, his agency was evident in his ability to narrate daily life in terms of world events. Smith observes that the life cycle of a linguistic paradigm resembles that of a scientific paradigm in that a "revolutionary, innovative model becomes traditional once its representations are fully incorporated within a cultural lexicon of realistic conventions," which he describes as frozen metaphoric constructions of experience that create an illusion of correspondence between the textual world and everyday life.[23] Hoover held his post across an arc of history rich with historical events to exploit. He had the agony of racial hatred, World War I, the Great Depression, World War II, the Holocaust, and the atom bomb available in the minds of audiences to use as evidence for the world he presented. Such pain corresponded to his metaphoric constructions and diverged from the idealism of Newman F. Baker, Sanford Bates, Max Lowenthal, George Wickersham, Henry Wallace, Harry S. Truman, and others. FDR had the stature to stand between these divergent worlds and could balance them to push the New Deal forward. He was a credible witness for charity who inspired a generation of reformers. With his death, however, went the requisite ethos necessary to rein in Hoover's demagoguery. In FDR's absence, American epistemology transformed in perverse ways into a nightmare that cast the hopes of New Dealers as a conspiracy to extinguish liberty. The FBI's realism was legible to mass audiences because the world, indeed, seemed to be on the brink of collapse as evidenced by the arms race and spy trials—trials that he secretly orchestrated to make his presentation of reality "real."

The image of a world in collapse refracted the collapse of a social world that Hoover sought to rebuild. He was loyal to FDR until the National Labor Relations Act was passed in 1935, which represented a significant challenge to American racial and class hierarchies. The law was used by organized labor to assail Jim Crow and the Southern establishment, a move that was intensified by the Justice Department's attack on peonage. Segregation and racialized inequality more generally were threatened, which destabilized the cultural world into which Hoover was socialized. His discourse suggested that, to him, the racialized class structure was what made America exceptional. Without it, the America that he knew would be no more. The anxiety of this prospect was evident in his Cold War discourse, which almost fostered a self-fulfilling prophecy. As Les K. Adler and Thomas G. Paterson observe, the rhetoric of red fascism played a large role in reshaping perceptions of the world between 1945 and 1946 while Truman remained reticent about world events when possibilities for accommodation were still tangible.[24] FBI propaganda superimposed the stresses that faced the South onto the nation and elevated hard-line anticommunism. The worldview suggested that the United States faced a future akin to what the South suffered in the Civil War, which rallied national support for Southern interests—namely, defeating the civil rights movement and undermining organized labor—a task that united Southern Democrats and Republicans, and replaced New Dealers with neoliberals. This plan risked America's national security and would take it to the brink of nuclear war with the Soviet Union. Hoover insisted that an army of Russian fifth columnists had already infiltrated America by the time Joseph McCarthy warned of Communists in the State Department, which certainly informed the Cold War vision of defense planners who perceived the Soviet Union to be responsible for the spread of Communism to places like Vietnam and Southeast Asia.

Hoover's propaganda illustrates a linguistic strategy to remake the FBI and the world in which it operated, to epistemologically remake public life in ways that reinscribed the values of the Progressive Era. My earlier institutional critique demonstrated that "competitive frames fight for control over the writing or re-writing of institutions. Ultimately, the language used by representatives to describe people and prescribe practices inform how material arrangements are perceived according" to the social positions of institutional leaders to resist or maintain cultural hierarchies.[25] Alarmingly, Hoover used his authority as the FBI director to control how reality was represented across art, philosophy, politics, economics, religion, and the social sciences. Such frames are, in part, epistemological and work to animate institutions in ways that correspond to what is constituted as real. The FBI used these frames to map social spaces to be contained, and to enforce strict boundaries of acceptable speech and thought. These moves were an affront to democracy because they infused Friedrich Hayek's interest in reframing "boundaries between legitimate and illegitimate government activities" with white supremacy, and thereby invented a neoliberalism that Hayek would not recognize as his own, yet was still attributed to him.[26] Although institutions are communally written, Hoover manipulated, exploited, and controlled the community of writers who scripted the FBI with laws, directives, and executive orders. He traded the scripts written by the Wickersham Commission for others based in popular culture. This locus of power undermined the democratic principle of informed consent. Hoover and his accomplices remade political realism and neoliberalism into a more singular ideology that distrusted democracy and the leveling power of the ballot box.

Writing in response to the Committee on Public Information, Walter Lippmann forewarned in *Liberty and the News* (1920) that the foundations of liberal democracy were imperiled by the rise of mass communication technologies, which allowed for the "manufacture of what is usually called consent."[27] Hoover fully realized the potential of Lippmann's warnings and stocked the public imagination with language that the citizenry relied upon to evaluate his leadership. He even transformed Lippmann's warnings against the bureau in ways that advanced the system of tyranny that Lippmann sought to prevent. This power was unique to Hoover's position, a public servant trusted to keep the nation informed of the threats that it faced, the power to philosophize about the human condition, and the power to coerce wide-scale policies across institutions in response to what he presented. The *New York Times* was correct to surmise in 1969 that the FBI director "wielded more power longer than any man in American history."[28] Historians are also right to press against the notion that his power rested in his ability to blackmail presidents and others, that his power was in the files that he kept on his critics. He could only be a blackmailer because he was first a propagandist who gained the trust of liberals and conservatives in order to collect sensitive information—a trust that extended from how he manipulated their perceptions of his role as a heroic protector of the nation's security. His strategizing raises troubling questions about how the citizen, society, and government are related; about the effectiveness of checks and balances; about the very meaning of democracy. With all that is known about J. Edgar Hoover today, the prophesy of Joseph McCarthy remains true. Hoover's name remains on FBI headquarters as a monument to what he created, surviving at least thirteen congressional attempts to redesignate the building at 935 Pennsylvania Avenue.[29]

Notes

Preface

1. Ronald H. Carpenter, "Postscript: A Disciplinary History of Rhetorical History: Retrospect and Prospect," in *Doing Rhetorical History: Concepts and Cases*, ed. Kathleen J. Turner (Tuscaloosa: University of Alabama Press, 1998), 222.
2. Davis W. Houck, "On or About June 1988," *Rhetoric & Public Affairs* 9, no. 1 (2006): 136.
3. James J. Kimble, "Whither Propaganda? Agonism and 'The Engineering of Consent,'" *Quarterly Journal of Speech* 91, no. 2 (2005): 215.
4. Leroy G. Dorsey and Rachel M. Harlow, "'We Want Americans Pure and Simple': Theodore Roosevelt and the Myth of Americanism," *Rhetoric & Public Affairs* 6, no. 1 (2003): 62.
5. Richard Slotkin, *The Fatal Environment: The Myth of the Frontier in the Age of Industrialization, 1800-1890* (Norman: University of Oklahoma Press, 1985), 23–24; Richard Slotkin, *Gunfighter Nation: The Myth of the Frontier in*

Twentieth-Century America (Norman: University of Oklahoma Press, 1992), 5–6.

Introduction

1. Harry S. Truman, "Recommendation for Assistance to Greece and Turkey," March 12, 1947: 4–5, Harry S. Truman Library [hereafter HSTL].
2. Representative Thomas, remarks on J. Edgar Hoover's address to HUAC on March 26, 1947, 80th Cong., 1st sess., March 27, 1947: A1333.
3. Tom Wicker, "What Have They Done since They Shot Dillinger?," *New York Times Magazine*, December 28, 1969: 6.
4. "The Truth about Hoover," *Time* magazine, December 22, 1975: 14.
5. Curt Gentry, *J. Edgar Hoover: The Man and the Secrets* (New York: W.W. Norton, 1991), 57.
6. Richard Gid Powers, *G-Men: Hoover's FBI in American Popular Culture* (Carbondale: Southern Illinois University Press, 1983), 112.
7. Richard Gid Powers, *Secrecy and Power: The Life of J. Edgar Hoover* (New York: Free Press, 1987), 113, 129.
8. Matthew Cecil, *Branding Hoover's FBI: How the Boss's PR Men Sold the Bureau to America* (Lawrence: University Press of Kansas, 2016), 31.
9. Powers, *Secrecy and Power*, 152, 308, 211, 311–14.
10. Kenneth O'Reilly, "The Roosevelt Administration and Black America: Federal Surveillance Policy and Civil Rights during the New Deal and World War II," *Phylon* 48, no. 1 (1987): 15.
11. Leroy G. Dorsey, *We Are All Americans, Pure and Simple: Theodore Roosevelt and the Myth of Americanism* (Tuscaloosa: University of Alabama Press, 2007), 18, 43.
12. Joseph M. Valenzano III and Erika Engstrom, "Cowboys, Angels, and Demons: American Exceptionalism and the Frontier Myth in the CW's *Supernatural*," *Communication Quarterly* 62, no. 5 (2014): 557.
13. Richard Slotkin, *Gunfighter Nation: The Myth of the Frontier in Twentieth-Century America* (Norman: University of Oklahoma Press, 1992), 39–48, 53–54.
14. Richard Slotkin, "Nostalgia and Progress: Theodore Roosevelt's Myth of the Frontier," *American Quarterly* 33, no. 5 (Winter 1981): 633.

15. Gary R. Thompson, *Reading the American Novel, 1865-1914* (Malden, MA: Wiley-Blackwell, 2012), 55, 63.
16. June Howard, *Form and History in American Literary Naturalism* (Chapel Hill: University of North Carolina Press, 1985), 38, 50, 133–35.
17. Donna M. Campbell, *Resisting Regionalism: Gender and Naturalism in American Fiction, 1885-1915* (Athens: Ohio University Press, 1997), 4.
18. Bert Bender, "Nature and Naturalism," in *The Oxford Handbook of Literary Naturalism*, ed. Keith Newlin (New York: Oxford University Press, 2011), 52–54.
19. Joseph R. Roach, "Darwin's Passion: The Language of Expression on Nature's Stage," *Discourse* 13, no. 1 (Fall/Winter 1990–1991): 43.
20. Mike Hawkins, *Social Darwinism in European and American Thought, 1860-1945: Nature as Model and Nature as Threat* (New York: Cambridge University Press, 1997), 34.
21. Robert M. Crunden, *A Brief History of American Culture* (New York: Paragon House, 1994), 131–32.
22. Slotkin, *Gunfighter Nation*, 157.
23. Campbell, *Resisting Regionalism*, 75–78; Amy Kaplan, *The Social Construction of American Realism* (Chicago: University of Chicago Press, 1988), 45.
24. Thompson, *Reading the American Novel, 1865-1914*, 63; Steven Beller, "Degeneration," in *Antisemitism: A Historical Encyclopedia of Prejudice and Persecution*, vol. 1, ed. Richard S. Levy (Santa Barbara, CA: ABC-CLIO, 2005), 167–68; Thomas F. Gossett, *Race: The History of an Idea in America* (Oxford: Oxford University Press, 1965), 198–99.
25. Frank Norris, "An Opening for Novelists: Great Opportunities for Fiction Writers in San Francisco," *The Wave* (May 22, 1897), in *The Apprenticeship Writings of Frank Norris: 1896-1898*, ed. Joseph R. McElrath Jr. and Douglas K. Burgess (Philadelphia: American Philosophical Society, 1996), 273–74.
26. David B. Danbom, *"The World of Hope": Progressives and the Struggle for an Ethical Public Life* (Philadelphia: Temple University Press, 1987), 6–9.
27. Charles C. Walcutt, *American Literary Naturalism: A Divided Stream* (Minneapolis: University of Minnesota Press, 1956), 20, 90.
28. David Leverenz, *Paternalism Incorporated: Fables of American Fatherhood,*

1865-1940 (Ithaca, NY: Cornell University Press, 2003), 21.

29. Phillip J. Barrish, *The Cambridge Introduction to American Literary Realism* (Cambridge: Cambridge University Press, 2011), 131; Herbert F. Tucker, *A New Companion to Victorian Literature and Culture* (Malden, MA: Wiley-Blackwell, 2014), 133–34.
30. Gail Bederman, *Manliness and Civilization: A Cultural History of Gender and Race in the United States, 1880-1917* (Chicago: University of Chicago Press, 1996), 14.
31. Ellery Sedgwick, *A History of the "Atlantic Monthly," 1857-1909: Yankee Humanism at High Tide* (Amherst: University of Massachusetts Press, 1994), 11–12.
32. Walcutt, *American Literary Naturalism*, 93.
33. Bederman, *Manliness and Civilization*, 17–18.
34. Walcutt, *American Literary Naturalism*, 20–21, 95, 141, 147.
35. Barrish, *The Cambridge Introduction to American Literary Realism*, 44.
36. Slotkin, *Gunfighter Nation*, 244–52.
37. Ibid., 259–65.
38. Ira Katznelson, *Fear Itself: The New Deal and the Origins of Our Time* (New York: Liveright Publishing, 2013), 4–7.
39. Athan G. Theoharis, "A Brief History of the FBI's Role and Powers," in *The FBI: A Comprehensive Reference Guide*, ed. Athan G. Theoharis (Phoenix: Oryx Press, 1999), 4.
40. Powers, *Secrecy and Power*, 289.
41. Katznelson, *Fear Itself*, 163, 271–77.
42. O'Reilly, "The Roosevelt Administration and Black America," 15.
43. Kenneth O'Reilly, "The Roosevelt Administration and Legislative-Executive Conflict: The FBI vs. The Dies Committee," *Congress and the Presidency* 10, no. 1 (Spring 1983): 80–81.
44. Walter Lippmann, *An Inquiry into the Principles of the Good Society* (Boston: Little, Brown and Co., 1937); Friedrich August Hayek, *The Road to Serfdom* (Chicago: University of Chicago Press, 1944).
45. Inderpal Grewal, *Transnational America: Feminisms, Diasporas, Neoliberalisms* (Durham, NC: Duke University Press, 2005), 19.
46. Dieter Plehwe, "Introduction," in *The Road from Mont Pèlerin: The Making of the Neoliberal Thought Collective*, ed. Philip Mirowski and Dieter Plehwe

(Cambridge, MA: Harvard University Press, 2009), 8.

47. Rob Van Horn and Philip Mirowski, "The Rise of the Chicago School of Economics and the Birth of Neoliberalism," in Mirowski and Plehwe, *The Road from Mont Pèlerin: The Making of the Neoliberal Thought Collective*, 158–59.
48. Angus Burgin, *The Great Persuasion: Reinventing Free Markets since the Depression* (Cambridge, MA: Harvard University Press, 2012), 117–20.
49. O'Reilly, "The Roosevelt Administration and Black America," 20.
50. O'Reilly, "The Roosevelt Administration and Legislative-Executive Conflict," 90.
51. Lawrence E. Gelfand, *The Inquiry: American Preparations for Peace, 1917-1919* (New Haven, CT: Yale University Press, 1963), 38–39, 51.
52. Denna Frank Fleming, *The United States and World Organization, 1920-1933* (New York: Columbia University Press, 1938), 235; Harold Josephson, *James T. Shotwell and the Rise of Internationalism in America* (Rutherford, NJ: Fairleigh Dickinson University Press, 1975), 90; James T. Shotwell, *The Autobiography of James T. Shotwell* (New York: Bobbs-Merrill Co., 1961), 127.
53. Trevor Taylor, "Utopianism," in *International Relations: British and American Perspectives*, ed. Steve Smith (Oxford: British International Studies Association, 1985), 93–95; Michael Joseph Smith, *Realist Thought from Weber to Kissinger* (Baton Rouge: Louisiana State University, 1986), 57–58.
54. John A. Vasquez, *The Power of Power Politics: A Critique* (New Brunswick, NJ: Rutgers University Press, 1983), 14.
55. John Herz, *Political Realism and Political Idealism* (Chicago: University of Chicago Press, 1951), 162, 37, 32.
56. Woodrow Wilson, "An Address to a Joint Session of Congress: January 8, 1918," in *The Papers of Woodrow Wilson*, vol. 45, *November 11, 1917–January 15, 1918*, ed. Arthur S. Link (Princeton, NJ: Princeton University Press, 1984), 536–38.
57. Edward Hallett Carr, *The Twenty Years' Crisis, 1919-1939: An Introduction to the Study of International Relations* (London: Macmillan, 1939), 11, 13, 14.
58. Robert O. Keohane, "Realism, Neorealism, and the Study of World Politics," in *Neorealism and Its Critics*, ed. Robert O. Keohane (New York: Columbia University Press, 1986), 7.
59. Reinhold Niebuhr, *The Nature and Destiny of Man*, vol. 1, *Human Nature* (New

York: Charles Scribner's Sons, 1941), 178–260; Reinhold Niebuhr, *The Children of Light and the Children of Darkness* (New York: Charles Scribner's Sons, 1944).

60. Reinhold Niebuhr, "American Power and World Responsibility," *Christianity and Crisis* 3, no. 5 (April 5, 1943): 4.
61. Ronald H. Stone, *Reinhold Niebuhr: Prophet to Politicians* (New York: Abingdon Press, 1972), 177.
62. Hans J. Morgenthau, "Another 'Great Debate': The National Interest of the United States," *American Political Science Review* 46, no. 4 (December 1952): 972–73, 975.
63. Robert Hariman and Francis A. Beer, "What Would Be Prudent? Forms of Reasoning in World Politics," *Rhetoric & Public Affairs* 1, no. 3 (1998): 299–300.
64. Hayek, *The Road to Serfdom*, 186–87.
65. David Harvey, *A Brief History of Neoliberalism* (Oxford: Oxford University Press, 2005), 2, 21–22, 66.
66. Wendy Brown, *Undoing the Demos: Neoliberalism's Stealth Revolution* (New York: Zone Books, 2015), 219.
67. Paul A. Chilton, *Security Metaphors: Cold War Discourse from Containment to Common House* (New York: Peter Lang, 1996), 197; Timothy Barney, "Richard Edes Harrison and the Cartographic Perspective of Modern Internationalism," *Rhetoric & Public Affairs* 15, no. 3 (2012): 402–3.
68. Steven Belletto and Daniel Grausam, *American Literature and Culture in an Age of Cold War: A Critical Reassessment* (Iowa City: University of Iowa Press, 2012), 5.
69. Elaine Tyler May, *Homeward Bound: American Families in the Cold War Era* (New York: Basic Books, 2008), 8–13.
70. William J. Maxwell uses the term literary "blackface" to describe a process of "ventriloquized blackness" in which members of the FBI posed as black writers with their use of Africanist accents and characters when they anonymously wrote to black readers. Maxwell, *F.B. Eyes: How J. Edgar Hoover's Ghostreaders Framed African American Literature* (Princeton, NJ: Princeton University Press, 2015), 4.
71. Alan Nadel, *Containment Culture: American Narratives, Postmodernism, and the*

Atomic Age (Durham, NC: Duke University Press, 1995), 6–8; Robert L. Ivie, "Cold War Motives and Rhetorical Metaphor: A Framework of Criticism," in *Cold War Rhetoric: Strategy, Metaphor, and Ideology*, ed. Martin J. Medhurst, Robert L. Ivie, Philip Wander, and Robert L. Scott (East Lansing: Michigan State University Press, 1997), 76.

72. Pam Morris, *Realism* (New York: Routledge, 2003), 136.
73. Cecil, *Branding Hoover's FBI*, 15, 25.
74. Matthew Cecil, *Hoover's FBI and the Fourth Estate: The Campaign to Control the Press and the Bureau's Image* (Lawrence: University Press of Kansas, 2014), 11.
75. Claire Bond Potter, *War on Crime: Bandits, G-men, and the Politics of Mass Culture* (New Brunswick, NJ: Rutgers University Press, 1998), 1–2.
76. Mike Forrest Keen, *Stalking the Sociological Imagination: J. Edgar Hoover's Surveillance of American Sociology* (Westport, CT: Greenwood Press, 1999), 3.
77. Fred Jerome, *The Einstein File: The FBI's Secret War against the World's Most Famous Scientist* (Montreal: Baraka Books, 2018), 28, 30.
78. Steve Rosswurm, *The FBI and the Catholic Church, 1935–1962* (Amherst: University of Massachusetts Press, 2009), 2, 12.
79. Sylvester A. Johnson and Steven Weitzman, "'True Faith and Allegiance'—Religion and the FBI," in *The FBI and Religion: Faith and National Security before and after 9/11*, ed. Sylvester A. Johnson and Steven Weitzman (Oakland: University of California Press, 2017), 8.
80. John Sbardellati, *J. Edgar Hoover Goes to the Movies: The FBI and the Origins of Hollywood's Cold War* (Ithaca, NY: Cornell University Press, 2012), 2–3.
81. Claire A. Culleton, *Joyce and the G-Men* (New York: Palgrave Macmillan, 2004), 1.
82. Maxwell, *F.B. Eyes*, 5.
83. William Beverly, *On the Lam: Narratives of Flight in J. Edgar Hoover's America* (Jackson: University Press of Mississippi, 2003), xii.
84. Hartut Behr, "'Common Sense,' Thomas Reid and Realist Epistemology in Hans J. Morgenthau," *International Politics* 50, no. 6 (2013): 757–58.
85. Denise M. Bostdorff, *Proclaiming the Truman Doctrine: The Cold War Call to Arms* (College Station: Texas A&M University Press, 2008), 36–37, 134, 60.
86. Martin J. Medhurst, "Truman's Rhetorical Reticence, 1945–1947: An

Interpretive Essay," *Quarterly Journal of Speech* 74 (1988): 64, 67.

87. Bostdorff, *Proclaiming the Truman Doctrine*, 128; Robert Ivie, "Fire, Flood, and Red Fever: Motivating Metaphors of Global Emergency in the Truman Doctrine Speech," *Presidential Studies Quarterly* 29 (1999): 571.
88. Paul A. Chilton, "The Meaning of Security," in *Post-Realism: The Rhetorical Turn in International Relations*, ed. Francis A. Beer and Robert Hariman (East Lansing: Michigan State University Press, 1996), 197–98, 208.
89. Chilton, *Security Metaphors*, 197, 133–34, 153.
90. Stephen M. Underhill, "Prisoner of Context: The Truman Doctrine Speech and J. Edgar Hoover's Rhetorical Realism," *Rhetoric & Public Affairs* 20, no. 3 (2017): 453–88.
91. Stephen M. Underhill, "J. Edgar Hoover's Domestic Propaganda: Narrating the Spectacle of the Karpis Arrest," *Western Journal of Communication* 76 (2012): 453.
92. Charles E. Morris III, "Pink Herring and the Fourth Persona: J. Edgar Hoover's Sex Crime Panic," *Quarterly Journal of Speech* 88, no. 2 (2002): 230.
93. Claire Bond Potter, "Queer Hoover: Sex, Lies, and Political History," *Journal of the History of Sexuality* 15, no. 3 (2006): 365.
94. Nancy Chodorow, *The Reproduction of Mothering: Psychoanalysis and the Sociology of Gender* (Berkeley: University of California Press, 1978), 9.
95. Jessica R. Pliley, *Policing Sexuality: The Mann Act and the Making of the FBI* (Cambridge, MA: Harvard University Press, 2014), 8.
96. Lynn Boyd Hinds and Theodore Otto Windt Jr., *The Cold War as Rhetoric: The Beginnings, 1945–1950* (New York: Praeger, 1991), 38–39, 48.
97. Shawn J. Parry-Giles, *The Rhetorical Presidency, Propaganda, and the Cold War, 1945–1955* (Westport, CT: Praeger, 2002), xx, xviii, 185.
98. William D. Harpine, *From the Front Porch to the Front Page: McKinley and Bryan in the 1896 Presidential Campaign* (College Station: Texas A&M University Press, 2005), 3.
99. Richard J. Ellis, "Introduction," in *Speaking to the People: The Rhetorical Presidency in Historical Perspective*, ed. Richard J. Ellis (Amherst: University of Massachusetts Press, 1998), 1.
100. Thomas Hollihan, "Propagandizing in the Interest of War: A Rhetorical

Study on the Committee on Public Information," *Southern Speech Communication Journal* 49, no. 3 (1984): 250.

101. James J. Kimble, "Whither Propaganda? Agonism and 'The Engineering of Consent,'" *Quarterly Journal of Speech* 91, no. 2 (2005): 210.

102. On April 13, 1917, President Wilson signed Executive Order 2594, which established the CPI based on the exact recommendations made by the secretaries of state, war, and navy. The committee was "charged with encouraging and then consolidating the revolution of opinion which changed the United States from anti-militaristic democracy to an organized war machine." James R. Mock and Cedric Larson, *Words That Won the War* (Princeton, NJ: Princeton University Press, 1939), 51, 14.

103. Walter Lippmann, *Liberty and the News* (Princeton, NJ: Princeton University Press, 1920), 36–37.

104. William H. Irwin, *Propaganda and the News* (New York: Whittlesey, 1936), 202. For a detailed summary of Irwin's and Suydam's work in the CPI, see Mock and Larson, *Words That Won the War.*

105. James L. McCamy, *Government Publicity: Its Practice in Federal Administration* (Chicago: University of Chicago Press, 1939), 252–53.

106. Parry-Giles, *The Rhetorical Presidency, Propaganda, and the Cold War, 1945-1955*, xx, xviii, 185.

107. Karlyn Kohrs Campbell, "Agency: Promiscuous and Protean," *Communication and Critical/Cultural Studies* 2, no. 1 (March 2005): 1–8.

108. Louis A. Montrose, "Professing the Renaissance: The Poetics and Politics of Culture," in *The New Historicism*, ed. H. Aram Veeser (New York: Routledge, 1989), 16.

109. Jack Babuscio, "The Cinema of Camp (*aka* Camp and the Gay Sensibility)," in *Camp: Queer Aesthetics and the Performing Subject*, ed. Fabio Cleto (Ann Arbor: University of Michigan Press, 2002), 122–24.

110. James S. Baumlin, "Introduction," in *Ethos: New Essays in Rhetorical and Critical Theory,* ed. James S. Baumlin and Tita French Baumlin (Dallas: Southern Methodist University Press, 1994), xiii.

111. C. Jan Swearingen, "Ethos: Imitation, Impersonation, and Voice," in Baumlin and Baumlin, *Ethos: New Essays in Rhetorical and Critical Theory*, 115–18.

112. Neil Postman, *Amusing Ourselves to Death: Public Discourse in the Age of Show Business* (New York: Penguin Books, 2006), 17–18.
113. Bonnie J. Dow, "Feminism and Public Address Research: Television News and the Constitution of Women's Liberation," in *The Handbook of Rhetoric and Public Affairs*, ed. Shawn J. Parry-Giles and J. Michael Hogan (Malden, MA: Wiley-Blackwell, 2010), 353.
114. John Louis Lucaites and Celeste Condit, "Re-Constructing Narrative Theory: A Functional Perspective," *Journal of Communication* (Autumn 1985): 102.
115. Ann Chisholm, "Conventional Narrative as Rhetorical Strategy: Ronald Reagan's 'Address to the 1988 Republican National Convention,'" in *Critiques of Contemporary Rhetoric*, 2nd ed., ed. Karlyn Kohrs Campbell and Thomas R. Burkholder (New York: Wadsworth, 1997), 281.
116. Underhill, "J. Edgar Hoover's Domestic Propaganda," 452.
117. Kimble, "Whither Propaganda?," 203, 207, 209, 212.
118. Stephen M. Underhill, "Urban Jungle, Ferguson: Rhetorical Homology and Institutional Critique," *Quarterly Journal of Speech* 102, no. 4 (2016): 401.
119. John W. Meyer and Brian Rowan, "Institutionalized Organizations: Formal Structure as Myth and Ceremony," *American Journal of Sociology* 83, no. 2 (September 1977): 340–41, 345.
120. Pushkala Prasad, "The Protestant Ethic and the Myths of the Frontier: Cultural Imprints, Organizational Structuring, and Workplace Diversity," in *Managing the Organizational Melting Pot*, ed. Pushkala Prasad, Albert J. Mills, Michael Elmes, and Anshuman Prasad (Thousand Oaks, CA: Sage Publications, 1997), 137, 139.

Chapter 1. The Life and Times of J. Edgar Hoover, 1895–1932

1. "Palmer Pledges 'War on Radicals,'" *New York Times*, January 1, 1920: 17.
2. A. Mitchell Palmer, "The Case against the 'Reds,'" *Forum* 63 (1920): 173.
3. "Quick Deportation of Reds Is Likely," *New York Times*, January 27, 1920: 1.
4. Thomas R. Marshall, "Americanism," in *Trestle Board Magazine*, ed. Benjamin Franklin Bledsoe (March 1920; reprint 2010): 36.
5. Kenneth D. Ackerman, *Young J. Edgar* (New York: Carroll and Graf, 2007), 44.

6. Thomas W. Gregory to J. E. H. Hoover, July 20, 1917, Record Group 60, Entry 312, A1, vol. 127: 256, National Archives and Records Administration, College Park [hereafter NARA-CP]; Sam J. Graham to John Edgar Hoover, July 20, 1917, Record Group 60, Entry 312, A1, vol. 127: 256–57, NARA-CP.
7. Ackerman, *Young J. Edgar*, 58. See the following file for more on the War Emergency Division: Record Group 60, Entry 112-B, A1, Boxes 2818 through 2824, File 190470.
8. Frank Burke to T. Dec. Ruth, July 25, 1919, Record Group 165, Entry 68, NM-84, Box 4057, File PF 26737, NARA-CP.
9. The GID was originally named the "Radical Division." Its name was changed in 1920. A. Mitchell Palmer to J. Edgar Hoover, July 1, 1919, Record Group 60, Entry 312, vol. 134: 678, NARA-CP; Homer S. Cummings and Carl McFarland, *Federal Justice: Chapters in the History of Justice and the Federal Executive* (1937; New York: Da Capo Press, 1970), 429n.
10. House of Representatives, *Annual Report of the Attorney General, 1920: Bureau of Investigation, General Intelligence*, 66th Cong., 3d sess., 1920: 173.
11. Regit Schmidt, *Red Scare: FBI and the Origins of Anticommunism in the United States* (Copenhagen: Museum of Tusculanum Press, 2000), 25.
12. Interchurch World Movement, *Report on the Steel Strike of 1919* (1920; New York: Da Capo Press, 1971); Federal Trade Commission, *Utility Corporations: Efforts by Associations and Agencies of Electric and Gas Utilities to Influence Public Opinion*, 70th Cong., 1st sess., Senate Document 92, part 71-A (Washington, DC: U.S. Government Printing Office, 1934); George Seldes, *Lords of the Press* (New York: J. Messner, 1938).
13. Schmidt, *Red Scare*, 26.
14. Richard Gid Powers, *Not without Honor* (New York: Free Press, 1995), 22.
15. Albert Fried, *Communism in America: A History in Documents* (New York: Columbia University Press, 1997), 2.
16. "391 Alien Reds Now under Arrest," *New York Times*, November 11, 1919: 1; "Tons of 'Red' Papers Bare Anarchists Plot," *Washington Post*, January 4, 1920: 1.
17. "Raids Ordered by Palmer," *New York Times*, November 14, 1919: 1; "'Ark'

with 300 Reds Sails Early Today for Unnamed Port," *New York Times*, December 21, 1919: 1.

18. Andrew Simpson, "Schooling J. Edgar: The Shaping of Hoover's Legal Philosophy at The George Washington University," *Intelligencer: Journal of U.S. Intelligence Studies* (Fall 2009): 44.
19. Steve Rosswurm, *The FBI and the Catholic Church, 1935–1962* (Amherst: University of Massachusetts Press, 2009), 26.
20. J. Edgar Hoover, September 11, 1910, "Hoover Original Diary: 1910," National Law Enforcement Museum, Washington, DC.
21. Fletcher Knebel, "J. Edgar Hoover: The Cop and the Man," *Look* magazine, May 31, 1955: 33.
22. "District of Columbia Reorganized," *American Issue*, December 1908: 7.
23. Andrew Wilson, "District of Columbia," *Proceedings of the Fifteenth National Convention of the Anti-Saloon League of America: Twenty Year Jubilee Convention, November 10–13, 1913*, 282.
24. "Americanize Aliens," *American Issue*, April 1, 1916: 14.
25. U.S. Constitution, Eighteenth Amendment, January 16, 1919.
26. Volstead Act, October 27, 1919, 41 Stat. 306; Ruth C. Engs, *The Progressive Era's Health Reform Movement: A Historical Dictionary* (Westport, CT: Praeger, 2003), 346.
27. Claire Bond Potter, *War on Crime: Bandits, G-Men, and the Politics of Mass Culture* (New Brunswick, NJ: Rutgers University Press, 1998), 34.
28. "Lawyers Denounce Raids on Radicals," *New York Times*, May 28, 1920: 6; National Popular Government League, *To the American People: Report upon the Illegal Practices of the Department of Justice* (Washington, DC: National Popular Government League, 1920).
29. Ronald Kessler, *The Bureau: The Secret History of the FBI* (New York: St. Martin's Press, 2003), 82–83.
30. Known as the Committee of Twelve, this group of esteemed legal minds included Zechariah Chaffee Jr., professor of law at Harvard Law School; Felix Frankfurter, professor of law at Harvard Law School; Roscoe Pound, dean of Harvard Law School; Alfred S. Niles, former judge and professor of law at Maryland University Law School; Ernst Freund, professor of law at University of Chicago Law School; Tyrrel Williams,

dean of Washington University Law School in St. Louis; Francis Fisher Kane, former United States attorney from Philadelphia; R. G. Brown, attorney from Memphis, Tennessee; Swinburne Hale, attorney from New York City; Jackson H. Ralston, attorney from Washington, DC; David Wallerstein, attorney from Philadelphia; and Frank P. Walsh, attorney from New York and Kansas City.

31. National Popular Government League, *To the American People*, 4–5.
32. William J. Maxwell, *F.B. Eyes: How J. Edgar Hoover's Ghostreaders Framed African American Literature* (Princeton, NJ: Princeton University Press, 2015), 52–53, 58.
33. "Judge Knox's Order Frees 9 Radicals; Sixty-five More on Ellis Island Will Be Released on Bail Today; Officials Fear Results by Refusing to Answer Questions They Can Escape Deportation, Government Representative Says," *New York Times*, January 16, 1920: 3; "Halts Deportation of Alleged 'Reds'; Boston Federal Judge Denounces Arrests without Warrant and Grants Writs for Thirteen," *New York Times*, April 23, 1920: 14; "Louis Post Defends Rulings on Aliens," *New York Times*, May 9, 1920: 12.
34. House Committee on Rules, *Attorney General A. Mitchell Palmer on Charges Made against Department of Justice by Louis F. Post and Others*, part 1, 66th Cong., 2d sess., June 1, 1920; Senate Judiciary Committee, *Charges of Illegal Practices of the Department of Justice*, 66th Cong., 3d sess., March 3, 1921.
35. "'Critics Are Liars,' Palmer Declares," *Washington Post*, May 18, 1920: 5; "Calls Post Factor in Revolution Plan," *New York Times*, June 2, 1920: 4; "Palmer Criticizes Critics," *New York Times*, June 3, 1920: 7; "Retract Charges Demands Palmer," *New York Times*, June 5, 1920: 27.
36. Powers, *Not without Honor*, 31.
37. Ibid., 2, 69–91.
38. Blair Coan, *The Red Web* (Chicago: Northwest Publishing, 1925).
39. R. M. Whitney, *Reds in America* (New York: Beckwith Press, 1924), 17.
40. Athan G. Theoharis, *The FBI and American Democracy: A Brief Critical History* (Lawrence: University Press of Kansas, 2004), 31.
41. Harry M. Daugherty to All Officers and Employes [*sic*], October 1, 1922, Record Group 60, Entry 121-A, A1, Box 41, Circular 1348, NARA–CP.

42. Harland F. Stone to All United States Attorneys, United States Marshals, and Officers of the Bureau of Investigation, June 11, 1924, Record Group 60, Entry 121-A, A1, Box 41, Circular 1521, NARA–CP.
43. John G. Sargent to the Department of Justice, March 20, 1925, Record Group 60, Entry 121-A, A1, Box 41, Circular 1601, NARA–CP. This order was in line with previous rules on press relations; see George Wickersham to Heads of Departments and Bureau Chiefs, undated, Record Group 60, Entry 325, A1, Box 1, Circular 77, NARA–CP.
44. John G. Sargent to All Officers and Employees of the Department of Justice, September 1, 1926, Record Group 60, Entry 121-A, A1, Box 42, Circular 1748, NARA–CP.
45. Harland F. Stone to J. Edgar Hoover, May 10, 1924, Record Group 60, Entry 312, A1, vol. 148: 962, NARA–CP; Harland F. Stone to J. Edgar Hoover, December 10, 1924, Record Group 60, Entry 312, A1, vol. 150: 651, NARA–CP.
46. Sanford J. Ungar, *FBI: An Uncensored Look behind the Walls* (Boston: Little, Brown and Co., 1976), 48–49.
47. Record Group 65, Entry 37-A, A1, "Classification 61 (Treason)—Index to Headquarters Case Files, 1921–1936," NARA–CP.
48. Committee on Efficiency Ratings to Solicitor General, May 18, 1922, Record Group 60, Entry 121-A, A1, Box 40, Circular 1299, NARA–CP.
49. Daugherty to Officers of the Department of Justice, August 3, 1922, Record Group 60, Entry 121-A, A1, Box 41, Order 1330, NARA–CP.
50. Rush L. Holland to Officials of the Department of Justice, July 5, 1923, Record Group 60, Entry 121-A, A1, Box 40, Circular 1436, NARA–CP; George E. Strong to All U.S. Officials in the Department in Washington and in the Field Service, April 30, 1924, Record Group 60, Entry 121-A, A1, Box 41, Circular 1509, NARA–CP.
51. James Q. Wilson, *The Investigators: Managing FBI and Narcotics Agents* (New York: Basic Books, 1978), 173, 29–30, 96–98; Richard Gid Powers, *Secrecy and Power: The Life of J. Edgar Hoover* (New York: Free Press, 1987), 383; Walter Pincus, "The Bureau's Budget: A Source of Power," in *Investigating the FBI*, ed. Pat Watters and Stephen Gillers (New York: Doubleday and Co., 1973), 67; Joseph L. Schott, *No Left Turns* (New York: Praeger

Publishing, 1975), 10–12.

52. Judith A. Merkle, *Management and Ideology: The Legacy of the International Scientific Management Movement* (Berkeley: University of California Press, 1980), 67–68, 269.
53. Philip P. Purpura, *Criminal Justice: An Introduction* (Boston: Butterworth-Heinemann, 1997), 122–23.
54. *Annual Report of the Attorney General of the United States for the Fiscal Year 1934: Testimony of J. Edgar Hoover* (Washington, DC: U.S. Government Printing Office, 1934), 128.
55. *Annual Report of the Attorney General of the United States for the Fiscal Year 1932: Testimony of J. Edgar Hoover* (Washington, DC: U.S. Government Printing Office, 1932), 104; *Annual Report of the Attorney General of the United States for the Fiscal Year 1934: Testimony of J. Edgar Hoover* (Washington, DC: U.S. Government Printing Office, 1934), 125; *Annual Report of the Attorney General of the United States for the Fiscal Year 1935: Testimony of J. Edgar Hoover* (Washington, DC: U.S. Government Printing Office, 1935), 135; Oliver McKee Washington, "Laboratory for Crime," *New York Times*, July 8, 1934: XX18; Homer S. Cummings and Carl McFarland, "Progress toward a Modern Administration of Criminal Justice in the United States," *American Bar Association Journal* 22, no. 5 (1936): 348.
56. J. Edgar Hoover, "Detection and Apprehension," August 30, 1934 (American Bar Association): 7, Record Group 65, Entry 51, Box 6, NARA-CP.
57. J. Edgar Hoover, "Police Science: Organized Protection against Organized Predatory Crimes, Bankruptcy Frauds," *Journal of Criminal Law and Criminology* 23, no. 6 (April 1933): 1074.
58. J. Edgar Hoover, "Physical Science in the Crime Detection Laboratory," *Review of Scientific Instruments* 9 (November 1938): 335.
59. Hoover, "Police Science," 1074.
60. Walter Lippmann, *An Inquiry into the Principles of the Good Society* (Boston: Little, Brown and Co., 1937), 23.
61. Powers, *Secrecy and Power*, 157–58.
62. Matthew Cecil, *Branding Hoover's FBI: How the Boss's PR Men Sold the Bureau to America* (Lawrence: University Press of Kansas, 2016), 11.

63. Powers, *Secrecy and Power*, 170–72.
64. Matthew Cecil, *Hoover's FBI and the Fourth Estate: The Campaign to Control the Press and the Bureau's Image* (Lawrence: University Press of Kansas, 2014), 70.
65. Michael Newton, *The FBI Encyclopedia* (Jefferson, NC: McFarland, 2012), 247.
66. Cecil, *Branding Hoover's FBI*, 27.
67. Memorandum for J. Edgar Hoover, May 15, 1937, File 67-HQ-39021, Sec. 2, Record Group 65, Entry 13, Box 1, NARA–CP.
68. Memorandum from R. E. Joseph to Clyde Tolson, December 5, 1935, File 67–9524, Sec. 1, Record Group 65, Entry 13, Box 1, NARA–CP.
69. Memorandum from Louis Nichols to J. Edgar Hoover, April 13, 1936, File 67–9524, Sec. 1, Record Group 65, Entry 13, Box 1, NARA–CP.
70. Richard Gid Powers, *G-Men: Hoover's FBI in American Popular Culture* (Carbondale: Southern Illinois University Press, 1983), 111.
71. Matthew Cecil, "Friends of the Bureau: Personal Correspondence and the Cultivation of Journalist-Adjuncts by J. Edgar Hoover's FBI," *Journalism & Mass Communication Quarterly* 88 (2011): 278.
72. Powers, *G-Men: Hoover's FBI in American Popular Culture*, 314 n. 34.
73. J. Edgar Hoover, "32nd Annual Conference," July 14, 1925 (International Association of Chiefs of Police): 1–2, 8, Record Group 65, Entry 51, Box 6, NARA–CP.
74. Newton, *The FBI Encyclopedia*, 79.
75. *Law Enforcement Bulletin*, 1932–1939, Record Group 65, Entry 4: UD-09D, Box 1, NARA–CP; Powers, *Secrecy and Power*, 157.
76. *Annual Report of the Attorney General of the United States for the Fiscal Year 1936: Testimony of J. Edgar Hoover* (Washington, DC: U.S. Government Printing Office, 1936), 126.
77. For example, M. L. Ramsay, "U.S. to Pattern Kidnap Unit on Scotland Yard," *Washington Herald*, July 27, 1933, Group 65, Entry 49, Box 3, NARA–CP; Henry Suydam, "How Kidnappers Are Caught," *Forum*, April 1, 1934, Group 65, Entry 49, Box 4, NARA–CP; "Hoover Flays Shysters as Crime Aids," *New York Daily Mirror*, July 11, 1935, Group 65, Entry 49, Box 12, NARA–CP; "Edgar Hoover Flays Police Politics,"

Washington Times, October 19, 1935, Group 65, Entry 49, Box 14, NARA–CP. For more on the "sex-pervert" campaign, see Charles E. Morris III, "Pink Herring and the Fourth Persona: J. Edgar Hoover's Sex Crime Panic," *Quarterly Journal of Speech* 88, no. 2 (2002): 228–44.

78. *Annual Report of the Attorney General of the United States for the Fiscal Year 1937: Testimony of J. Edgar Hoover* (Washington, DC: U.S. Government Printing Office, 1937), 135.
79. To view recipients, see finding aid for Record Group 65, Classification 94 (Research Matters), in Room 2000 at NARA–CP. This finding aid indexes CRS contacts.
80. J. Edgar Hoover to R. G. Conover, January 14, 1938, Record Group 60, Entry 140, Box 9, File 7: The FBI, NARA–CP.
81. William C. Sullivan and Bill Brown, *The Bureau: My Thirty Years in Hoover's FBI* (New York: W.W. Norton and Co., 1979), 83.
82. Powers, *G-Men: Hoover's FBI in American Popular Culture*, 140–42; FBI File 62–37036 (*The War on Crime* comic strip correspondence), FBI, Records Management Division, Winchester, VA [hereafter cited as FBI–VA].
83. Natalie Robins, *Alien Ink: The FBI's War on Freedom of Expression* (New York: William Morrow, 1992), 108.
84. Cecil, *Branding Hoover's FBI*, 30–31.
85. Palmer, "The Case against the 'Reds,'" 173.
86. Theodore Roosevelt, "What 'Americanism' Means," *Forum* (April 1894): 198, 200–201.
87. Churchill Williams, "Red Blood in Fiction," *World's Work* 6, no. 1 (May 1903): 3694, 3700.
88. James Lane Allen, "Two Principles in Recent American Fiction," *Atlantic Monthly*, October 1897: 436–37.
89. Donna M. Campbell, *Resisting Regionalism: Gender and Naturalism in American Fiction, 1885-1915* (Athens: Ohio University Press, 1997), 60.
90. June Howard, *Form and History in American Literary Naturalism* (Chapel Hill: University of North Carolina Press, 1985), ix–x, 12, 131.
91. Campbell, *Resisting Regionalism*, 199; James R. Giles, "The Grotesque City, the City of Excess, and the City of Exile," in *The Oxford Handbook of American Literary Naturalism*, ed. Keith Newlin (Oxford: Oxford University

Press, 2011), 327.

92. David W. Southern, *The Progressive Era and Race: Reaction and Reform, 1900–1917* (Wheeling, IL: Harlan Davidson, 2005), 45.
93. J. Michael Hogan, "Introduction," in *Rhetoric and Reform in the Progressive Era*, ed. J. Michael Hogan (East Lansing: Michigan State University Press, 2003), xiii.
94. Richard L. Watson Jr., *The Development of National Power: The United States, 1900–1919* (Boston: Houghton Mifflin, 1976), 84.
95. Leroy G. Dorsey, "Preaching Morality in Modern America," in *Rhetoric and Reform in the Progressive Era*, ed. J. Michael Hogan (East Lansing: Michigan State University Press, 2003), 50–51.
96. Robin E. Jensen, *Dirty Words: The Rhetoric of Public Sex Education, 1870–1924* (Urbana: University of Illinois Press, 2010), xvii.
97. Dorsey, "Preaching Morality in Modern America," 49.
98. *An Act in Amendment to the Various Acts Relative to Immigration and the Importation of Aliens under Contract or Agreement to Perform Labor* (Immigration Act of 1891), 51st Cong., 2d sess., 26 stat 1084, March 3, 1891; *An Act to Regulate the Immigration of Aliens into the United States* (Anarchist Act of 1903), 57th Cong., 2d sess., 32 stat 1213, sec. 38, March 3, 1903; *White Slave Traffic Act* (Mann Act), Public Law 12, 61st Cong., 3d sess., June 25, 1910: 825; *Harrison Narcotics Tax Act*, Public Law No. 223, 63d Cong., 2d sess., December 17, 1914.
99. Immigration Act of 1891, 26 stat 1084; John Higham, *Strangers in the Land* (New York: Atheneum, 1968), 99–100.
100. William Preston, *Aliens and Dissenters: Federal Suppression of Radicals* (New York: Harper and Row, 1963), 66.
101. Gaines M. Foster, *Moral Reconstruction: Christian Lobbyists and the Federal Legislation of Morality, 1865–1920* (Chapel Hill: University of North Carolina Press, 2002), 143.
102. Edward Huntington Williams, "Negro Cocaine 'Fiends' Are a New Southern Menace: Murder and Insanity Increasing among Lower Class Blacks Because They Have Taken to 'Sniffing' since Deprived of Whisky by Prohibition," *New York Times*, February 8, 1914: SM12.
103. Foster, *Moral Reconstruction*, 2, 4, 7, 23, 73–76, 143–46.

104. Howard, *Form and History in American Literary Naturalism*, 138–39.
105. Donald Pizer, *The Novels of Frank Norris* (New York: Haskell House Publishers, 1966), 56–63.
106. Gina M. Rossetti, "Things Fall Apart: Degeneration and Atavism in American Literary Naturalism," in Newlin, *The Oxford Handbook of American Literary Naturalism*, 173–75.
107. Henry M. Boies, *Prisoners and Paupers: A Study of the Abnormal Increase of Criminals, and the Public Burden of Pauperism in the United States; the Causes and Remedies* (New York: G.P. Putnam's Sons, 1893), 184, 293.
108. Wiley Feinstein, *The Civilization of the Holocaust in Italy: Poets, Artists, Saints, Anti-Semites* (Madison, NJ: Fairleigh Dickinson University Press, 2003), 162; Steven Beller, "Degeneration," in *Antisemitism: A Historical Encyclopedia of Prejudice and Persecution*, vol. 1, ed. Richard S. Levy (Santa Barbara, CA: ABC-CLIO, 2005), 167–68.
109. Fredric Jameson, *The Political Unconscious: Narrative as a Socially Symbolic Act* (Ithaca, NY: Cornell University Press, 1981), 24, 27–28, 53, 189, 202.
110. Melissa Stein, "'Nature Is the Author of Such Restriction': Science, Ethnological Medicine, and Jim Crow," in *The Folly of Jim Crow: Rethinking the Segregated South*, ed. Stephanie Cole and Natalie J. Ring (College Station: Texas A&M University Press, 2012), 125, 133–36, 139–42.
111. Kirt H. Wilson, *The Reconstruction Desegregation Debate: The Politics of Equality and the Rhetoric of Place* (East Lansing: Michigan State University Press, 2002), 12, 186–87.
112. Celeste Michelle Condit and John Louis Lucaites, *Crafting Equality: America's Anglo-African Word* (Chicago: University of Chicago Press, 1993), 132–33.
113. Howard, *Form and History in American Literary Naturalism*, 134.
114. Quentin Skrabec Jr., *William McKinley: Apostle of Protectionism* (New York: Algora, 2008), 27, 30.
115. Alexander Hamilton, "Report on Manufacturers," in *On the Wealth of Nations*, ed. Ian S. Ross (Bristol, UK: Thoemmes Press, 1998), 241, 237.
116. Rogers M. Smith, *Civic Ideals: Conflicting Visions of Citizenship in U.S. History* (New Haven, CT: Yale University Press, 1997), 290.
117. William McKinley, "Inaugural Address" of March 4, 1897, in *A Compilation*

of the Messages and Papers of the Presidents (New York: Bureau of National Literature, 1917), 6238–39.

118. Theodore Roosevelt, *The Strenuous Life* (New York: Century, 1901), 1, 6, 7.
119. Marilyn Lake and Henry Reynolds, *Drawing the Global Colour Line: White Men's Countries and the International Challenge of Racial Equality* (Cambridge: Cambridge University Press, 2008), 9.
120. Roosevelt, *The Strenuous Life*, 18.
121. Theodore Roosevelt, *American Ideals* (New York: G.P. Putnam's Sons, 1897), 24–25, 29–31; John F. McClymer, "The Federal Government and the Americanization Movement, 1915–24," *Prologue* 10, no. 1 (Spring 1978): 25.
122. Woodrow Wilson, "A Flag Day Address," June 14, 1917, in *The Papers of Woodrow Wilson*, vol. 42 (Princeton, NJ: Princeton University Press, 1983), 498–99.
123. McClymer, "The Federal Government and the Americanization Movement," 26, 32, 29.
124. Ibid., 23–24, 26–29, 35, 37.

Chapter 2. The War on Crime, 1933–1938

1. *G-Men*, Warner Brothers and The Vitaphone Corp., 1935.
2. *Scarface*, The Caddo Company, 1932.
3. "Federal Officer to Take Custody of Fred Hunter; Gangster 'Yellow Rat,' Says Hoover," *Times-Picayune*, May 3, 1936, Record Group 65, Entry 49, Box 22, National Archives and Records Administration, College Park [hereafter cited as NARA–CP]; "Karpis Quit 'Like Rat,' Says Chief of G-Men," *(Pittsburgh) Sun-Telegraph*, May 3, 1936, Record Group 65, Entry 49, Box 22, NARA–CP; "'Respectable' Citizens Who Shield 'Rats' the Real Public Enemies," *Milwaukee Journal*, May 28, 1936, Record Group 65, Entry 49, Box 25, NARA–CP.
4. Herbert Hoover, "State of the Union," December 3, 1929, in *Public Papers of the Presidents of the United States: Herbert Hoover*, vol. 1, comp. National Archives and Records Service General (Washington, DC: U.S. Government Printing Office, 1974), 295.
5. National Commission on Law Observance and Enforcement, *Report on*

Crime and the Foreign Born (Washington, DC: U.S. Government Printing Office, 1931), 416.

6. National Commission on Law Observance and Enforcement, *Report on the Enforcement of the Deportation Laws of the United States* (Washington, DC: U.S. Government Printing Office, 1931), 3, 7; National Commission on Law Observance and Enforcement, *Report on Police* (Washington, DC: U.S. Government Printing Office, 1931), 1, 5–6; National Commission on Law Observance and Enforcement, *Report on Lawlessness in Law Enforcement* (Washington, DC: U.S. Government Printing Office, 1931), 3–4.
7. Herbert Hoover, "State of the Union," December 3, 1929: 295.
8. Bureau of the Budget, *Service of the Fiscal Year Ending June 30, 1934* (Washington, DC: U.S. Government Printing Office, 1933), 391, 414, 498.
9. Justin Miller to Clarence E. Martin, September 11, 1933, Record Group 60, Entry 139, Box 1, File: American Bar Association, NARA–CP.
10. *An Act to Amend an Act Providing for the Parole of United States Prisoners*, Public Law 202, 71st Cong., 2d sess., May 13, 1930, 272; *An Act to Authorize the Public Health Service to Provide Medical Service in the Federal Prisons*, Public Law 203, 71st Cong., 2d sess., May 13, 1930: 273; *An Act to Establish Two United States Narcotic Farms for the Confinement and Treatment of Persons Addicted to the Use of Habit-Forming Narcotic Drugs Who Have Been Convicted of Offenses against the United States, and for Other Purposes*, Public Law 672, 70th Cong., 2d sess., January 19, 1929: 1085; *An Act Establishing Two Institutions for the Confinement of United States Prisoners*, Public Law 270, 71st Cong., 2d sess., May 27, 1930: 388; *An Act to Amend an Act to Establish a Hospital for Defective Delinquents*, Public Law 201, 71st Cong., 2d sess., May 13, 1930: 270; *An Act to Provide for the Diversification of Employment of Federal Prisoners, for their Training and Schooling in Trades and Occupations, and for Other Purposes*, Public Law 271, 71st Cong., 2d sess., May 13, 1930: 272; *An Act to Amend the Act of March 4, 1925, Chap. 521, and for Other Purposes*, Public Law 310, 71st Cong., 2d sess., June 6, 1930: 503.
11. National Commission on Law Observance and Enforcement, *Report on Penal Institutions, Probation, and Parole* (Washington, DC: U.S. Government Printing Office, 1931), 146.

12. Charles E. Morris III, "Pink Herring and the Fourth Persona: J. Edgar Hoover's Sex Crime Panic," *Quarterly Journal of Speech* 88, no. 2 (2002): 228, 233, 235.
13. Ray Tucker, "Hist! Who's That?," *Collier's*, August 19, 1933: 15, 49.
14. "Sleuth School," *Time* magazine, August 5, 1935: 12.
15. Jack Alexander, "Profiles: The Director II," *New Yorker*, October 2, 1937: 21.
16. Morris, "Pink Herring and the Fourth Persona," 235.
17. Max Nordau, *Degeneration* (New York: D. Appleton, 1892), 539.
18. Homer S. Cummings, "The Department of Justice and the New Deal," June 11, 1933 (radio address): 6, Record Group 60, Entry 132, Box 2, File: Speeches, NARA–CP.
19. "Crime War Real, Asserts Cummings," *New York Times*, September 12, 1933: 3.
20. Stephen M. Underhill, "J. Edgar Hoover's Domestic Propaganda: Narrating the Spectacle of the Karpis Arrest," *Western Journal of Communication* 76, no. 4 (2012): 453.
21. Morris, "Pink Herring and the Fourth Persona," 229.
22. Franklin D. Roosevelt, "Inaugural Address," March 4, 1933, in *The Public Papers and Addresses of Franklin D. Roosevelt*, vol. 2 (New York: Random House, 1938), 15.
23. Joseph B. Keenan, "Uncle Sam Presses His New War on Crime: Joseph B. Keenan, Who Heads the Government's Nation-Wide Drive against Racketeers and Kidnappers, Tells of the Federal Aims, the Need for New Laws, and the Forming of a Sound Plan for Widening the Campaign to Relieve Gang-Ridden Communities," *New York Times*, August 20, 1933: 1.
24. Homer S. Cummings, "Lessons of the Crime Conference," December 13, 1934, in *Proceedings of the Attorney General's Conference on Crime, Held December 10 to December 13, 1935* (Washington, DC: U.S. Government Printing Office, 1935), 458.
25. Homer S. Cummings, "Modern Tendencies and the Law," *American Bar Association Journal* 19, no. 10 (1933): 578, 577.
26. Raymond Moley to Franklin Roosevelt, "Department of Justice," May 19, 1934: 5, 7, 18–19, FDR Library, Box 190, Printed Materials.

27. Underhill, "J. Edgar Hoover's Domestic Propaganda," 451.
28. Cecil, *Branding Hoover's FBI*, 21.
29. Jeffrey K. Tulis, *The Rhetorical Presidency* (Princeton, NJ: Princeton University Press, 1987), 7–8, 17–18.
30. Richard Gid Powers, *G-Men: Hoover's FBI in American Popular Culture* (Carbondale: Southern Illinois University Press, 1983), 9.
31. "Battle Rages to Close Down G-Man Bureau," *Washington Herald*, October 8, 1935, Record Group 65, Entry 49, Box 14, NARA–CP.
32. J. Edgar Hoover, "Abolish Parole Abuses," *Forum* (August 1938): 71–73.
33. Morris, "Pink Herring and the Fourth Persona," 228, 230–31, 238, 241.
34. Matthew Cecil, *Hoover's FBI and the Fourth Estate: The Campaign to Control the Press and the Bureau's Image* (Lawrence: University Press of Kansas, 2014), 25.
35. Newman F. Baker, "J. Edgar Hoover," *Journal of Criminal Law and Criminology* 28, no. 5 (1938): 627–29.
36. Donald Pizer, *American Naturalism and the Jews: Garland, Norris, Dreiser, Wharton, and Cather* (Urbana: University of Illinois Press, 2008), 17–18; Nordau, *Degeneration*, 539.
37. Courtney Ryley Cooper to J. Edgar Hoover, October 31, 1933, FBI File 94-3-4-20, Sec. 1, Record Group 65, Entry UD-09D 8, Box 105, NARA–CP.
38. Douglas M. Charles, *Hoover's War on Gays: Exposing the FBI's "Sex Deviates" Program* (Lawrence: University Press of Kansas, 2015), 33, 110, 116.
39. Ibid., 271.
40. Powers, *G-Men*, 108, 113.
41. Courtney Ryley Cooper to J. Edgar Hoover, September 19, 1934, FBI File 94-3-4-20, Sec. 2, Record Group 65, Entry UD-09D 8, Box 105, NARA–CP.
42. J. Edgar Hoover to Courtney Ryley Cooper, October 11, 1934, FBI File 94-3-4-20, Sec. 2, Record Group 65, Entry UD-09D 8, Box 105, NARA–CP.
43. Roger Dooley, *From Scarface to Scarlett: American Films in the 1930s* (New York: Harcourt Brace Jovanovich, 1981), 311–16.
44. Courtney Ryley Cooper to J. Edgar Hoover, October 31, 1933, FBI File

94-3-4-20, Sec. 1, Record Group 65, Entry UD-09D 8, Box 105, NARA–CP.

45. Dooley, *From Scarface to Scarlett: American Films in the 1930s*, 317.
46. "Palmer Pledges 'War on Radicals,'" *New York Times*, January 1, 1920: 17.
47. Morris, "Pink Herring and the Fourth Persona," 233–34.
48. G. Lowes Dickinson, *Appearances* (New York: Doubleday, Page and Co., 1914), 180–84.
49. Kevin P. Murphy, *Political Manhood: Red Bloods, Mollycoddles, and the Politics of Progressive Era Reform* (New York: Columbia University Press, 2008), 4, 14, 17.
50. Fred L. Crawford, 75th Cong., 3d sess., March 1, 1938: 2642–43.
51. Underhill, "J. Edgar Hoover's Domestic Propaganda," 452.
52. Franklin D. Roosevelt, "Address to the Conference on Crime Called by the Attorney General of the United States, December 10, 1934," in *The Public Papers and Addresses of Franklin D. Roosevelt*, vol. 3 (New York: Random House, 1938), 492–93.
53. Franklin D. Roosevelt, "Statement on Signing Bill to Help the Federal Government Wage War on Crime and Gangsters, May 18, 1934," in ibid., 242–44.
54. Representative Connery, remarks on Hoover's rhetorical style, 75th Cong., 3d sess., March 24, 1938: 1171–72.
55. Baker, "J. Edgar Hoover," 627–28.
56. Connery, remarks on Hoover's rhetorical style, 1171–72.
57. Underhill, "J. Edgar Hoover's Domestic Propaganda," 451; Morris, "Pink Herring and the Fourth Persona," 236.
58. W. H. D. Lester to Clyde Tolson, January 10, 1935, FBI File 94-3-4-20, Sec. 4, Record Group 65, Entry UD-09D 8, Box 106, NARA–CP.
59. J. Edgar Hoover to Courtney Ryley Cooper, November 7, 1933, FBI File 94-3-4-20, Sec. 1, Record Group 65, Entry UD-09D 8, Box 105, NARA–CP.
60. Connery, remarks on Hoover's rhetorical style, 75th Cong., 3d sess., 1172.
61. *An Act to Reorganize the Administration of Federal Prisons; to Authorize the Attorney General to Contract for the Care of United States Prisoners; to Establish Federal Jails, and for Other Purposes*, Public Law 218, Sec. 1, 2, 4, 71st Cong., 2d sess., May

14, 1930: 325–26.

62. *Annual Report of the Attorney General of the United States for the Fiscal Year 1933: Testimony of Sanford Bates* (Washington, DC: U.S. Government Printing Office, 1934), 113–14.
63. L. H. Robbins, "New Prison Ideals in a New-Type Prison," *New York Times*, January 15, 1933: SM8.
64. Connery, remarks on Hoover's rhetorical style, 75th Cong., 3d sess., 1171.
65. House Committee on Appropriations, *Department of Justice Appropriation Bill for 1936: Testimony of Sanford Bates (Dir, Bur of Prisons)*, 74th Cong., 2d sess., 241.
66. Sanford Bates, "The Prison: A Complex Problem," *New York Times*, February 4, 1934: SM1.
67. Ann Chisholm, "Conventional Narrative as Rhetorical Strategy: Ronald Reagan's 'Address to the 1988 Republican National Convention,'" in *Critiques of Contemporary Rhetoric*, 2nd ed., ed. Karlyn Kohrs Campbell and Thomas R. Burkholder (New York: Wadsworth, 1997), 280.
68. Richard Gid Powers, "The FBI in American Popular Culture," in *The FBI: A Comprehensive Reference Guide*, edited by Athan G. Theoharis (Phoenix: Oryx Press, 1999), 272–83.
69. Bob Herzberg, *The FBI and the Movies: A History of the Bureau on Screen and Behind the Scenes in Hollywood* (Jefferson, NC: McFarland, 2007), 47.
70. Powers, "The FBI in American Popular Culture," 272–83.
71. Thomas Shatz, *Hollywood Genres: Formulas, Filmmaking, and the Studio System* (New York: McGraw-Hill, 1981), 16, 31, 85, 87.
72. The term "hard-boiled" refers to a narrative style common to pulp fiction and film noir that portrays crime and violent punishment in an unsentimental manner.
73. Cecil, *Hoover's FBI and the Fourth Estate*, 42.
74. Phillips H. Lord to J. Edgar Hoover, June 10, 1935, Record Group 60, Entry 132, Box 61, File: Lord (Seth Parker), NARA–CP.
75. Baker, "J. Edgar Hoover," 628.
76. Powers, "The FBI in American Popular Culture," 277.
77. Michael Denning, *Mechanic Accents: Dime Novels and Working-Class Culture in America* (New York, Verso, 1987), 205–7; Wilbur R. Miller, "From Old Cap

to Nick Carter; Or, Images of Crime and Criminal Justice in American Dime Novel Detective Stories," in *Crime and Culture*, ed. Amy Gilman Srebnick and Rene Levy (Burlington, VT: Ashgate Publishing, 2005), 203; Powers, *G-Men*, 77.

78. Miller, "From Old Cap to Nick Carter," 202, 204.
79. Representative Wearin, 75th Cong., 1st. sess., March 23, 1937: 2653.
80. Courtney Ryley Cooper, "J. Edgar Hoover Has Formed Nucleus of Powerful Federal Police Force," *Kansas City Star*, August 7, 1933, Record Group 65, Entry 49, Box 3, NARA-CP.
81. "Hoover: The One Who Is in the Department of Justice," *Newsweek*, August 12, 1933, Record Group 65, Entry 49, Box 3, NARA-CP.
82. Era Connolly, "Uncle Sam's 400,'" *New York Herald Tribune*, February 4, 1934, Record Group 65, Entry 49, Box 4, NARA-CP.
83. J. Edgar Hoover, *Persons in Hiding* (Boston: Little, Brown and Co., 1938), viii, ix.
84. Ron Goulart, *The Dime Detectives* (New York: Mysterious Press, 1988), 9.
85. George Orwell, "Boys' Weeklies," in *The Collected Essays, Journalism and Letters of George Orwell*, vol. 1, ed. Sonia Orwell and Ian Angus (New York: Harcourt, Brace and World, 1968), 476.
86. Ibid., 476.
87. Goulart, *The Dime Detectives*, 8.
88. Miller, "From Old Cap to Nick Carter," 209.
89. Representative McCormack, remarks in support of J. Edgar Hoover, 74th Cong., 2d sess., June 15, 1936: 9461.
90. Representative Zioncheck, remarks in dissent of J. Edgar Hoover, 74th Cong., 2d sess., April 20, 1936: 5733–34.
91. McCormack, remarks in support of J. Edgar Hoover, 9462.
92. Senator Ashurst, remarks in support of J. Edgar Hoover, 74th Cong., 2d sess., May 12, 1936: 7093.
93. McCormack, remarks in support of J. Edgar Hoover, 9462.
94. Representative Jenckes, remarks in support of J. Edgar Hoover, 75th Cong., 1st sess., March 22, 1937: 2588–89.
95. Representative Crawford, remarks in support of J. Edgar Hoover, 75th Cong., 3d sess., May 3, 1938: 6186.

96. Athan G. Theoharis, "A Brief History of the FBI's Role and Powers," in Theoharis, *The FBI: A Comprehensive Reference Guide*, 4.
97. Cecil, *Hoover's FBI and the Fourth Estate*, 48.
98. Representative Connery, remarks on J. Edgar Hoover's address to the New York Chamber of Commerce on February 7, 1935, 74th Cong., 1st sess., February 14, 1935: 1945–47; Representative Connery, remarks on J. Edgar Hoover's address to the International Association of Chiefs of Police on July 9, 1935, 74th Cong., 1st sess., July 17, 1935: 11346–48; Representative Conner, remarks on J. Edgar Hoover's address to the Peace Officers Association of Oklahoma on January 13, 1936, 74th Cong., 2d sess., January 23, 1936: 965–67; Representative McMillan, remarks on J. Edgar Hoover's address to the Round Table Forum of the *New York Herald Tribune* on March 11, 1936, 74th Cong., 2d sess., March 19, 1936: 4033–35; Representative Duffy, remarks on J. Edgar Hoover's address to the Daughters of the American Revolution on April 23, 1936, 74th Cong., 2d sess., April 30, 1936: 6418–20; Representative Patman, remarks on J. Edgar Hoover's address to the Boys' Club of America on May 20, 1936, 74th Cong., 2d sess., May 26, 1936: 7960–63; Representative Connery, remarks on J. Edgar Hoover's address to the American Newspaper Publishers Association on April 22, 1937, 75th Cong., 1st sess., April 29, 1937: A1023–25; Representative Randolph, remarks on J. Edgar Hoover's address to the Association of Life Insurance Presidents on December 3, 1937, 75th Cong., 2d sess., December 6, 1937: A311–13; Representative Crawford, remarks on J. Edgar Hoover's address to the National Police Academy on April 2, 1938, 75th Cong., 3d sess., April 4, 1938: A1308–10; Representative Jenckes, remarks on J. Edgar Hoover's address to the General Federation of Women's Clubs on May 17, 1938, 75th Cong., 3d sess., May 19, 1938: A2059–62; Representative McAdoo, remarks on J. Edgar Hoover's address to Oklahoma Baptist University on May 23, 1938, 75th Cong., 3d sess., May 26, 1938: A2167–70.
99. See the following articles by J. Edgar Hoover: "Modern Problems of Law Enforcement," *Vital Speeches of the Day* 1, July 21, 1935: 682–87; "Local Law Enforcement in Relation to National Crime," *Dicta* 13, no. 139 (1935–1936): 141–50; "The Influence of Crime on the American Home," *Vital*

Speeches of the Day 2, March 23, 1936: 390–95; "Politics and Crime," *New York Times*, April 26, 1936: E8; "Education against Crime," *Vital Speeches of the Day* 3, December 1, 1936: 109–14; "The Role of the Press in the War on Crime," *The Quill* 25, no. 5 (May 1937): 12–15; "Combatting Lawlessness," *Vital Speeches of the Day* 4, February 15, 1938: 269–73.

100. Duffy, remarks on Hoover's address to DAR, 6420.
101. Patman, remarks on Hoover's address to the Boys' Club of America, 7962.
102. Randolph, remarks on Hoover's address to the Association of Life Insurance Presidents, A312.
103. Frank Norris, "A Case for Lombroso," in *The Apprenticeship Writings of Frank Norris*, vol. 2, *1897-1898* (Philadelphia: American Philosophical Society, 1996), 128–30.
104. Donald Pizer, *Novels of Frank Norris* (New York: Haskell House, 1973), 62.
105. Cesare Lombroso, *Criminal Man*, trans. Mary Gibson, Nicole Hahn Rafter, and Mark Seymour (Durham, NC: Duke University Press, 2006), 91, 134–35, 222, 277, 348; Gina Lombroso, *Criminal Man, According to the Classification of Cesare Lombroso* (Montclair, NJ: Patterson Smith, 1972), 135–36.
106. Murphy, *Political Manhood*, 181, 183–84.
107. Theodore Roosevelt, "How Not to Help Our Poor Brother," in *The Works of Theodore Roosevelt: American Ideals: Administration-Civil Service* (New York: G.P. Putnam's Sons, 1897), 243.
108. Patman, remarks on Hoover's address to the Boys' Club of America, 7961.
109. Duffy, remarks on Hoover's address to DAR, 6418.
110. Murphy, *Political Manhood*, 172–73.
111. Connery, remarks on Hoover's address to the IACP, 11346.
112. A. Mitchell Palmer, "The Case against the 'Reds,'" *Forum* 63 (1920): 173.
113. Conner, remarks on Hoover's address to the Peace Officers Association of Oklahoma, 965–67.
114. David B. Danbom, *"The World of Hope": Progressives and the Struggle for an Ethical Public Life* (Philadelphia: Temple University Press, 1987), 3–6, 8, 17, 28.

115. Nancy Tome, "The Private Side of Public Health: Sanitary Science, Domestic Hygiene, and Germ Theory, 1870–1900," in *Sickness and Health in America*, ed. Judith Walzer Leavitt and Ronald L. Numbers (Madison: University of Wisconsin Press, 1997), 507.
116. Walter Lippmann, *An Inquiry into the Principles of the Good Society* (Boston: Little, Brown and Co., 1937), 5–6, 40, 110, 241, 330.
117. Dieter Plehwe, "Introduction," in *The Road from Mont Pèlerin: The Making of the Neoliberal Thought Collective*, ed. Philip Mirowski and Dieter Plehwe (Cambridge, MA: Harvard University Press, 2009), 13.
118. Angus Burgin, *The Great Persuasion: Reinventing Free Markets since the Depression* (Cambridge, MA: Harvard University Press, 2012), 55.
119. Duffy, remarks on Hoover's address to DAR, 6420.
120. Jenckes, remarks on Hoover's address to the General Federation of Women's Clubs, A2060, A2062.
121. Connery, remarks on Hoover's address to the ANPA, A1023–24.
122. William Beverly, *On the Lam: Narratives of Flight in J. Edgar Hoover's America* (Jackson: University Press of Mississippi, 2003), 68, 71.
123. "Bad Man at Large," *Time* magazine, May 7, 1934: 20.
124. McMillan, remarks on Hoover's address to the *New York Herald Tribune* Forum, 4034.
125. Richard Slotkin, *Regeneration through Violence: The Mythology of the American Frontier, 1600–1860* (Norman: University of Oklahoma Press, 1973), 6.
126. Crawford, remarks on Hoover's address to the National Police Academy, A1309.
127. McAdoo, remarks on Hoover's address to Oklahoma Baptist University, A2167–68.
128. Ibid., A2169.
129. Connery, remarks on Hoover's address to the New York Chamber of Commerce, 1947.
130. Connery, remarks on Hoover's address to the IACP, 111347.
131. McAdoo, remarks on Hoover's address to Oklahoma Baptist University, A2167.
132. E. A. Tamm to J. Edgar Hoover, March 8, 1935, FBI File 94-3-4-20, Sec. 6, Record Group 65, Entry UD-09D 8, Box 106, NARA–CP.

133. J. Edgar Hoover to William Stanley, March 9, 1935, FBI File 94-3-4-20, Sec. 6, Record Group 65, Entry UD-09D 8, Box 106, NARA–CP; Courtney Ryley Cooper to J. Edgar Hoover, September 5, 1935, FBI File 94-3-4-20, Sec. 6, Record Group 65, Entry UD-09D 8, Box 106, NARA–CP.
134. Sanford Bates to Homer Cummings, May 16, 1936, Record Group 60, Entry 132, Box 3, File "Prisons."
135. Sanford Bates to Courtney Ryley Cooper, March 15, 1935, FBI File 94-3-4-20, Sec. 6, Record Group 65, Entry UD-09D 8, Box 106, NARA–CP.
136. Cecil, *Hoover's FBI and the Fourth Estate*, 231.
137. Order 3019, August 28, 1937, Record Group 60, Entry 132, Box 26, File: Departmental Publications, NARA–CP. This order repeated almost verbatim the preceding orders on press matters issued March 1925, March 1933, and September 1933.
138. "G-Men See Era of Gangsters Gone," *Washington Star*, August 15, 1938, Group 65, Entry 49, Box 62, NARA–CP.
139. *Survey by Gallup Organization, January 22–January 27, 1939*, from the iPOLL Databank, Roper Center for Public Opinion Research, University of Connecticut, https://ropercenter.cornell.edu.
140. Powers, *G-Men*, 92.
141. Ibid., 108.

Chapter 3. Fighting the Fifth Column, 1939–1945

1. Francis MacDonnell, *Insidious Foes: The Axis Fifth Column and the American Home Front* (New York: Oxford University Press, 1995), 63–68.
2. Raymond J. Batvinis, *The Origins of FBI Counterintelligence* (Lawrence: University Press of Kansas, 2007), 11–14.
3. "More Spy Ring Arrests Expected Momentarily by F.B.I. Agents," *Washington Post*, February 27, 1938: 1.
4. *Confessions of a Nazi Spy*, Warner Brothers, 1939.
5. Richard W. Steele, "Franklin D. Roosevelt and His Foreign Policy Critics," *Political Science Quarterly* 94, no. 1 (Spring 1979): 19–20.
6. MacDonnell, *Insidious Foes*, 137.
7. Albert Fried, *FDR and His Enemies* (New York: St. Martin's Press, 1999),

10–11, 163–65.

8. MacDonnell, *Insidious Foes*, 139.
9. The dilemma of political factions had long troubled American presidents. George Washington, for example, warned in his Farewell Address of September 17, 1796, that "different parties" might "serve to organize faction" and ultimately "subvert the power of the people" by exploiting "the regular deliberation and action of the constituted authorities." Such "unprincipled men," he foreshadowed, could "usurp for themselves the reins of government, destroying afterwards the very engines which have lifted them to unjust dominion." In *A Compilation of the Messages and Papers of the Presidents* (New York: Bureau of National Literature, 1917), 209–10.
10. J. Edgar Hoover, "Soldiers—In Peacetime," September 19, 1938 (American Legion): 14–15, Record Group 60, Entry 132, Box 12, National Archives, College Park [hereafter NARA-CP].
11. Pioneered by Theodore Roosevelt Jr. in 1919, the American Legion was founded in response to fears that organized labor was controlled by Bolshevik revolutionaries amid the red scare. The Legion's National Americanism Commission was founded in 1924 and charged to teach American nationalism. "Federal Officials Linked to 'Reds' at Dies Inquiry: Sifting Charges of Un-Americanism," *Christian Science Monitor*, August 17, 1938: 1; Richard Seelye Jones, *A History of the American Legion* (New York: Bobbs-Merrill Co., 1946), 23–26; Roscoe Baker, *The American Legion and American Foreign Policy* (New York: Bookman Associates, 1954), 32.
12. Ira Katznelson, *Fear Itself: The New Deal and the Origins of Our Time* (New York: Liveright Publishing, 2013), 265–72, 329; Kenneth O'Reilly, "The Roosevelt Administration and Legislative-Executive Conflict: The FBI vs. The Dies Committee," *Congress and the Presidency* 10 (Spring 1983): 80–81; Kenneth O'Reilly, "The Roosevelt Administration and Black America: Federal Surveillance Policy and Civil Rights during the New Deal and World War II," *Phylon* 48, no. 1 (1987): 15; Robert L. Zangrando, "The NAACP and a Federal Antilynching Bill, 1934–1940," *Journal of Negro History* 50 (1965): 110–17.
13. Batvinis, *The Origins of FBI Counterintelligence*, 196, 67–68.

14. Kenneth O'Reilly, "A New Deal for the FBI: The Roosevelt Administration, Crime Control, and National Security," *Journal of American History* 69, no. 3 (December 1982): 639, 656.
15. Frank J. Donner, *The Age of Surveillance: The Aims and Methods of America's Political Intelligence System* (New York: Alfred A. Knopf, 1980), 7.
16. Athan G. Theoharis, "A Brief History of the FBI's Role and Powers," in *The FBI: A Comprehensive Reference Guide*, ed. Athan G. Theoharis (Phoenix: Oryx Press, 1999), 4.
17. O'Reilly, "A New Deal for the FBI," 646, 648, 639, 656.
18. Douglas M. Charles, *J. Edgar Hoover and the Anti-Interventionists: FBI Political Surveillance and the Rise of the Domestic Security State, 1939–1945* (Columbus: Ohio State University Press, 2007), 62–63, 68, 79–81; J. Edgar Hoover to Edwin Watson, March 19, 1941, Personal and Confidential Letter, Official File 10-B, Franklin Delano Roosevelt Library [hereafter FDRL].
19. David Harvey, *A Brief History of Neoliberalism* (Oxford: Oxford University Press, 2005), 77.
20. J. Edgar Hoover, "Present Status of Espionage and Counterespionage Operations of the Federal Bureau of Investigation," October 24, 1940: 7, 2, FBI Reports–Numerical Series no. 408, Official File 10-B, FDRL.
21. Harvey, *A Brief History of Neoliberalism*, 28.
22. Charles, *J. Edgar Hoover and the Anti-Interventionists*, 32–33, 35.
23. "U. S.-British Ship Deal Is Assailed and Commended: Varying Views Voiced by Congress Members," *Chicago Daily Tribune*, September 4, 1940: 6.
24. Harold B. Hinton, "Wheeler Asserts Aid Bill Seeks War and Dictatorship," *New York Times*, March 1, 1941: 1.
25. "Wheeler Committee Joins Demand for Probe of FBI," *Great Falls Tribune*, March 13, 1940, Record Group 65, Entry 49, Box 75, NARA–CP.
26. Richard Lowitt, *George W. Norris: The Triumph of a Progressive, 1933-1944* (Chicago: University of Illinois Press, 1978), 261, 321.
27. Senator Norris, remarks on J. Edgar Hoover and civil liberties, 76th Cong., 3d sess., February 26, 1940: 1981–82; "American Ogpu," *New Republic*, February 19, 1940: 230.
28. "Mr. Jackson and the FBI," *New Republic*, April 8, 1940, Record Group 65, Entry 49, Box 76, NARA–CP.

29. "Mine Workers Accuse G-men of Nazi Tactics," *(Birmingham, AL) Southern News Almanac*, May 16, 1940, Record Group 65, Entry 49, Box 77, NARA-CP.
30. "FBI Doped Prisoners to Get Confessions, Robinson Charges," *(Helena, MT) People's Voice*, May 29, 1940, Record Group 65, Entry 49, Box 77, NARA-CP.
31. Senator Bridges, remarks on criticisms of J. Edgar Hoover, 76th Cong., 3d sess., April 26, 1940: 5062, 5064; Senator Norris, remarks on J. Edgar Hoover and civil liberties, 76th Cong., 3d sess., April 25, 1940: 4988.
32. Marcantonio's politics most clearly represented the type of challenge to Victorian Protestantism that Hoover campaigned against. The son of an Italian immigrant, he was Catholic and sympathized with the Socialist Party, the Communist Party of the United States of America (CPUSA), and labor unions. Thaddeus Russell argues that he was "one of the greatest champions of black civil rights" in the 1930s and 1940s because of how he "sponsored several civil rights bills, led the congressional fight against the discriminatory poll tax in southern states, and worked to make lynching a federal crime." In foreign policy, he followed the Communist Party line by supporting isolationism until the Nazi-Soviet non-aggression pact was broken when Germany invaded the Soviet Union in June 1941. He then supported intervention. Russell, *A Renegade History of the United States* (New York: Free Press, 2010), 188; Representative Marcantonio, remarks on J. Edgar Hoover and civil liberties, 76th Cong., 3d sess., January 11, 1940: 292.
33. Memorandum for the Director, May 5, 1940, *The Louis Nichols Official and Confidential File and the Clyde Tolson Personal File*, Reel 11, File "Smear Campaign" (Bethesda, MD: University Publications of America, 1990).
34. National Commission on Law Observance and Enforcement, *Report on Police* (Washington, DC: U.S. Government Printing Office, 1931), 1, 5–6; National Commission on Law Observance and Enforcement, *Report on Lawlessness in Law Enforcement* (Washington, DC: U.S. Government Printing Office, 1931), 3–4.
35. William L. Marbury to George L. Radcliffe, July 30, 1935, Box 1, William Marbury Outgoing Correspondence, 1934–1977, Maryland Historical

Society, Baltimore.

36. Memorandum for the Director, December 6, 1940, "Smear Campaign, Part 2," *The Louis Nichols Official and Confidential File and the Clyde Tolson Personal File*, Reel 11; Memorandum for the Director, December 30, 1940, in ibid.; Memorandum for the Director, February 13, 1942, in ibid.; Hearings before the House Committee on Un-American Activities, *Hearings regarding Communism in the United States Government*, part 2, *Testimony of Max Lowenthal, September 15, 1950* (Washington, DC: U.S. Government Printing Office, 1950), 2960.
37. Max Lowenthal, *The Federal Bureau of Investigation* (New York: Harcourt Brace Jovanovich, 1950); Max Lowenthal, "Notes on J. Edgar Hoover's Responsibility for Palmer Raids, circa 1940," in *Max Lowenthal Papers, 1855–1975*, described by Susan Hoffman (Minneapolis: University of Minnesota Archives, 2011), Box 10, folder 31.
38. Max Lowenthal, "Alexander Holtzoff and Mary Beard, March–April 1940, Correspondence regarding J. Edgar Hoover," in *Max Lowenthal Papers, 1855–1975*, Box 11, folder 5; Senator Norris, remarks on J. Edgar Hoover's role in the Palmer raids, 77th Cong., 1st sess., May 23, 1941: A2466; Lowenthal, *The Federal Bureau of Investigation*); William W. Turner, *Hoover's FBI: The Men and the Myth* (Los Angeles: Sherbourne Press, 1970).
39. Senator Norris, remarks on J. Edgar Hoover and civil liberties, 76th Cong., 3d sess., May 7, 1940: 5645, 5664.
40. The ICPC was predecessor to the International Police (Interpol). Hoover to the Attorney General, May 13, 1935, FBI File 62-20747, Interpol Part 1: 3, https://vault.fbi.gov/Interpol; Hoover to Divisions One and Four, December 4, 1941, FBI File 94-1-2061, Interpol Part 5: 97, 2016, https://vault.fbi.gov/Interpol.
41. To All Members of the International Criminal Police Commission, August 26, 1940, FBI File 94-1-2061, Interpol Part 5: 86, https://vault.fbi.gov/Interpol; Edouard Calic, *Reinhard Heydrich: The Chilling Story of the Man Who Masterminded the Nazi Death Camps*, trans. Lowell Bair (New York: Morrow, 1985); Mario R. Dederichs, *Heydrich: The Face of Evil* (Barnsley, UK: Greenhill Books, 2006), 117.
42. R. C. Hendon to Louis B. Nichols, May 10, 1941, FBI File 65-35798, Sec.

1, Record Group 65, Entry 136 P, Box 1, NARA-CP.

43. "Diplomats and Police Chiefs Honor Italians," *Washington Star*, September 24, 1934, Record Group 65, Entry 49, Box 5, NARA-CP; "Medal Presented to Mr. Hoover by Premier Mussolini's Touring University Students on their Visit to Washington," September 24, 1934, Record Group 65, Entry 49, Box 5, NARA-CP.
44. Al Belmont to Mr. Glavin, February 17, 1939, FBI File 94-1-2061, Interpol Part 4: 58, https://vault.fbi.gov/Interpol.
45. Memorandum from the Permanent Reporter of the ICPC, January 19, 1939, FBI File 94-1-2061, Interpol Part 4: 68, https://vault.fbi.gov/Interpol.
46. For example, J. W. H. Drane Lester, "Modern Trends in Criminology in the United States of America," June 7–10, 1937 (International Criminal Police Commission), Record Group 60, Entry 132, Box 12, File: "Mr. Hoover's Speeches," NARA-CP.
47. Charles Patterson, *Eternal Treblinka: Our Treatment of Animals and the Holocaust* (New York: Lantern Books, 2002), 46; Randall L. Bytwerk, *Julius Streicher: Nazi Editor of the Notorious Anti-Semitic Newspaper* Der Stürmer (New York: Cooper Square Press, 2001), 35, 168, 181.
48. Fritz Lenz, "The Inheritance of Intellectual Gifts," in *Human Heredity*, by Erwin Baur, Eugen Fisher, and Fritz Lenz, trans. Eden Paul and Cedar Paul (New York: Macmillan, 1931), 681.
49. Edwin Black, *War Against the Weak: Eugenics and America's Campaign to Create a Master Race* (New York: Four Walls Eight Windows, 2003), 271–76.
50. Cesare Lombroso wrote, for example, that abolitionism in the United States had failed to create racial equality because of innate racial inferiority among the "degenerate races." Accordingly, he discouraged "uniform civil, penal, and political code" because they only "provoke continual discontent," and encouraged, instead, that the "sovereignty" of dark colored peoples be substituted for a system that diminished "dependence, contacts, and dissensions" to prevent "rebellions" and "insurrections." *Crime, Its Causes and Remedies* (Boston: Little, Brown, and Company, 1911), 223, 325–26, 447; Wiley Feinstein, *The Civilization of the Holocaust in Italy: Poets, Artists, Saints, Anti-Semites* (Madison, NJ: Fairleigh

Dickinson University Press, 2003), 162; Steven Beller, "Degeneration," in *Antisemitism: A Historical Encyclopedia of Prejudice and Persecution*, vol. 1, ed. Richard S. Levy (Santa Barbara, CA: ABC-CLIO, 2005), 167–68.

51. J. F. Buckley to Mr. Tracy, November 22, 1941, The Vault, File: Interpol Part 5: 95, https://vault.fbi.gov/Interpol.
52. J. Edgar Hoover to Clyde Tolson, March 28, 1939, The Vault, File: Interpol Part 4: 96, https://vault.fbi.gov/Interpol.
53. Matthew Cecil, *Hoover's FBI and the Fourth Estate: The Campaign to Control the Press and the Bureau's Image* (Lawrence: University Press of Kansas, 2014), 73–74.
54. Charles, *J. Edgar Hoover and the Anti-Interventionists*, 60.
55. Stephen Early to J. Edgar Hoover, February 21, 1941, File 100-4712-18, Federal Bureau of Investigation, Winchester, Virginia [hereafter FBI–VA].
56. Charles, *J. Edgar Hoover and the Anti-Interventionists*, 68.
57. J. Edgar Hoover to Edwin Watson, February 13, 1942: 7, Personal and Confidential Letter, Official File 10-B, FDRL; R. B. Hood to J. Edgar Hoover, February 8, 1941, 100-4712-7X, FBI–VA; J. Edgar Hoover to the Attorney General, 100-4712-14, FBI–VA; Blind Memorandum, March 3, 1941, 100-4712-17X, FBI–VA.
58. J. Edgar Hoover to Edwin M. Watson, March 19, 1941, FBI Reports–Numerical Series, no. 690, Official File 10-B, FDRL. This report was also sent to the attorney general: Attorney General, March 19, 1941, File 100-4712-20, FBI–VA.
59. Chicago Field Office to Headquarters, May 26, 1942, File 100-4712-384, p. 3, FBI–VA.
60. Charles, *J. Edgar Hoover and the Anti-Interventionists*, 52, 44–45, 49, 87, 53, 103, 106.
61. Whereas Daniel Reed (R-NY), Fred Hartley Jr. (R-NJ), Fred Crawford (R-MI) voted against Lend-Lease, Charles Leavy (D-WA), Joseph O'Brien (R-NY), Samuel Dickstein (D-NY), Samuel Weiss (D-PA), Martin Dies (D-TX), and Charles Plumley (R-VT) supported the program.
62. J. Edgar Hoover, "Problems of Law Enforcement," *Vital Speeches of the Day*,

December 15, 1939: 54–57; J. Edgar Hoover, "The Test of Citizenship," *Vital Speeches of the Day*, May 1, 1940: 440–43.

63. Representative Dickstein, remarks on J. Edgar Hoover's address to the United States Junior Chamber of Commerce on June 21, 1939, 76th Cong., 1st sess., June 27, 1939: A2898–900; Senator Barkley, remarks on J. Edgar Hoover's address to the International Association of Chiefs of Police on October 10, 1939, 76th Cong., 2d. sess., October 11, 1939: A248–50; Representative Grant, remarks on J. Edgar Hoover's address to the FBI National Police Academy on September 30, 1939, 76th Cong., 2d. sess., October 2, 1939: A113–14; Representative Hartley, remarks on J. Edgar Hoover's address to the Daughters of the American Revolution on April 18, 1940, 76th Cong., 3d sess., April 18, 1940: A2229–31; Representative O'Brien, remarks on J. Edgar Hoover's address to the Daughters of the American Revolution on April 18, 1940, 76th Cong., 3d sess., April 22, 1940: A2281–83; Representative O'Brien, remarks on J. Edgar Hoover's address to the New York Federation of Women's Clubs on May 3, 1940, 76th Cong., 3d sess., May 8, 1940: A2800–802; Representative O'Brien, remarks on J. Edgar Hoover's address to the Federal-State Conference on Law Enforcement Problems of National Defense on August 5, 1940, 76th Cong., 3d sess., August 7, 1940: A4849–52; Representative O'Brien, remarks on J. Edgar Hoover's address to the International Association of Chiefs of Police on September 9, 1940, 76th Cong., 3d sess., September 13, 1940: A5691–93; Representative O'Brien, remarks on J. Edgar Hoover's address to the American Legion on September 23, 1940, 76th Cong., 3d sess., September 25, 1940: A5895–96; Representative O'Brien, remarks on J. Edgar Hoover's address to Drake University on June 3, 1940, 76th Cong., 3d sess., June 5, 1940: A3584–85; Senator Ashurst, remarks on J. Edgar Hoover's address to the New York Federation of Women's Clubs on May 3, 1940, 76th Cong., 3d sess., May 6, 1940: A2694–95; Representative Weiss, remarks on J. Edgar Hoover's address to B'nai B'rith on February 21–28, 1941, 77th Cong., 1st sess., February 24, 1941: A821–22; Senator Green, remarks on J. Edgar Hoover's address to the National Police Academy on March 29, 1941, 77th Cong., 1st sess., April 3, 1941: A1598–99; Representative O'Brien,

remarks on J. Edgar Hoover's address to Rutgers University on May 23, 1943, 78th Cong., 1st sess., May 25, 1943: A2590–91; Representative O'Brien, remarks on J. Edgar Hoover's address to the Daughters of the American Revolution on April 17, 1944, 78th Cong., 2d sess., April 19, 1944: A1884–86; Representative Crawford, remarks on J. Edgar Hoover's address to the National Police Academy circa May 1944, 78th Cong., 2d sess., May 2, 1944: A2095–96; Representative Plumley, remarks on J. Edgar Hoover's address to the International Association of Chiefs of Police on December 10, 1945, 79th Cong., 1st sess., December 17, 1945: 12218–20; Senator Wiley, remarks on J. Edgar Hoover's address to the International Association of Chiefs of Police on December 10, 1945, 79th Cong., 1st sess., December 11, 1945: A5410–15.

64. Senator Reynolds, remarks on J. Edgar Hoover's article in the *New York Herald Tribune* on July 14, 1940, 76th Cong., 3d sess., July 22, 1940: A4498–99; J. Edgar Hoover, "Is There a Spy Menace?," *Atlanta Constitution*, July 14, 1940: B2; J. Edgar Hoover, "Is There a Spy Menace?," *Los Angeles Times*, July 14, 1940: J2; J. Edgar Hoover "Is There a Spy Menace?," *Baltimore Sun*, July 14, 1940: TM2; Representative Crawford, remarks on J. Edgar Hoover's article in *Signs of the Times* in September 1940, 76th Cong., 3d sess., September 4, 1940: A5461; Representative Dies, remarks on J. Edgar Hoover's article in the *Washington Post* on August 4, 1941, 77th Cong., 1st sess., August 4, 1941: A3753; J. Edgar Hoover, "Big Scare," *American Magazine*, August 1941: 24–25, 66–67.
65. See the following by J. Edgar Hoover: Remarks to B'nai B'rith on May 12, 1940, Record Group 65, Entry 51, Box 2; remarks at Boys' Town, Record Group 65, Entry 51, Box 2, NARA–CP; remarks to the Knights of Columbus, March 22, 1942, Record Group 65, Entry 51, Box 2, NARA–CP; remarks to Notre Dame University, May 10, 1942: 2, Record Group 65, Entry 51, Box 2, NARA–CP; remarks to St. John's University, June 11, 1942, Record Group 65, Entry 51, Box 2, NARA–CP; remarks to the Holland Society of New York, November 19, 1942: 4, Record Group 65, Entry 51, Box 2, NARA–CP; remarks to the IACP, August 9, 1943, Record Group 65, Entry 51, Box 2, NARA–CP; remarks to Holy Cross College, June 29, 1944, Record Group 65, Entry 51, Box 2, NARA–CP.

66. Representative O'Brien, remarks on FBI publicity, 76th Cong., 3d sess., May 9, 1940: 5835; For an example of speeches written for congressmen, see Representative Randolph, remarks on FBI Appropriations, 76th Cong., 1st sess., March 22, 1939: 3110; Representative Crawford, remarks on FBI Appropriations, 76th Cong., 1st sess., March 22, 1939: 3125. The CRS tactic of writing speeches for members of Congress is also documented by historians like Theoharis, "A Brief History of the FBI's Role and Powers," 34.
67. Representative O'Brien, remarks on FBI publicity, 76th Cong., 3d sess., May 9, 1940: 5835.
68. Senator Reynolds, remarks on FBI publicity, 76th Cong., 3d sess., March 19, 1940: 2877.
69. Robert H. Jackson, March 18, 1940, press release, Box 21, File 129, RG 65, Entry 14 (UD-05D), NARA-CP.
70. Max Lowenthal, "Senate Line-up in the FBI Battle," undated, in *Max Lowenthal Papers*, Box 10, folder 69: 2–3; Senator Wiley, remarks in defense of J. Edgar Hoover, 76th Cong., 3d sess., April 11, 1940: 6560.
71. *Confessions of a Nazi Spy*, Warner Brothers, 1939.
72. William P. Carney, "Madrid Rounds Up Suspected Rebels; 2,000 Are Seized in Homes as Result of Mola's Boast of Aid from within the Capital," *New York Times*, October 16, 1936: 2.
73. Exod. 10:10–18; *Confessions of a Nazi Spy*.
74. Franklin D. Roosevelt, "Appropriations for National Defense," May 16, 1940, in *The Public Papers and Addresses of Franklin D. Roosevelt*, vol. 1940, *War—and Aid to the Democracies* (New York: Macmillan Co., 1941), 198.
75. Franklin D. Roosevelt to Robert H. Jackson, May 21, 1940, Box 17, File 91, RG 65, Entry 14 (UD-05D), NARA-CP.
76. Franklin D. Roosevelt, "Fireside Chat on National Defense," May 26, 1940, in *The Public Papers and Addresses of Franklin D. Roosevelt*, vol. 1940: 238.
77. Steele, *Free Speech in the Good War*, 87–88.
78. Franklin D. Roosevelt, Press Conference 649-A, June 5, 1940, in *Complete Presidential Press Conferences of Franklin D. Roosevelt*, vol. 15 (New York: Da Capo Press, 1972), 484.
79. Reynolds, remarks on Hoover's article in the *New York Herald Tribune*,

A4498.

80. M. Keith Booker, *Film and the American Left: A Research Guide* (Westport, CT: Greenwood Press, 1999), 69.
81. Richard Gid Powers, "The FBI in American Popular Culture," in Theoharis, *The FBI: A Comprehensive Reference Guide*, 272–83.
82. Ashurst, remarks on Hoover's address to the New York Federation of Women's Clubs: A2694.
83. Ludwell Denny, "Would Hoover Be Implying That Norris and Wheeler May Be Foreign Saboteurs?," *(Fort Wayne, IN) News Sentinel*, April 19, 1940, Record Group 65, Entry 49, Box 76, NARA-CP.
84. J. Edgar Hoover, "The Challenge to Youth," June 1, 1941 (Boys' Town): 5, Record Group 65, Entry 51, Box 2, NARA-CP.
85. J. Edgar Hoover, "An Adventure in Public Service," June 3, 1940 (Drake University): 2–4, Record Group 65, Entry 51, Box 2, NARA-CP.
86. J. Edgar Hoover, "The Present Task of Law Enforcement," September 9, 1940 (International Association of Chiefs of Police): 2, Record Group 65, Entry 51, Box 2, NARA-CP.
87. Robert A. Hill, *The FBI's RACON: Racial Conditions in the United States during World War II* (Boston: Northeastern University Press, 1995), 4–5, 31, 406–14, 419.
88. *Confessions of a Nazi Spy*.
89. O'Brien, remarks on Hoover's address to Drake University, A3584.
90. Ashurst, remarks on Hoover's address to the New York Federation of Women's Clubs, A2694.
91. Barkley, remarks on Hoover's address to the IACP, A250.
92. O'Brien, remarks on Hoover's address to the *New York Herald Tribune* Forum, A499.
93. Representative Grant, remarks on Hoover's address to the National Police Academy, A114.
94. William Lynn Watson, "'The Facts Which Go to Form This Fiction': Elizabeth Stuart Phelps's *The Silent Partner* and the Massachusetts Bureau of Labor Statistics Reports," *College Literature* 29, no. 4 (Fall 2002): 16–19.
95. Randolph Bourne, "This Older Generation," *Atlantic Monthly*, September 1915: 385–89.

96. David B. Danbom, *"The World of Hope": Progressives and the Struggle for an Ethical Public Life* (Philadelphia: Temple University Press, 1987), 44, 59, 65.
97. Filipe Carreira da Silva, *Mead and Modernity: Science, Selfhood, and Democratic Politics* (Lanham, MD: Lexington Books, 2008), 14.
98. Danbom, *The World of Hope*, 114–18.
99. A. Mitchell Palmer, "The Case against the 'Reds,'" *Forum* 63 (1920): 173.
100. Representative Hartley, remarks on Hoover's address to DAR, A2230.
101. Representative Ploeser, remarks on Communists in the civil rights movement, 77th Cong., 1st sess., April 15, 1941: 3127–28.
102. Bourne, "This Older Generation," 386.
103. Douglas M. Charles, *The FBI's Obscene File: J. Edgar Hoover and the Bureau's Crusade against Smut* (Lawrence: University Press of Kansas, 2012), 29–31.
104. Claire A. Culleton, *Joyce and the G-Men* (New York: Palgrave Macmillan, 2004), 178.
105. Hoover, remarks to Notre Dame University, May 10, 1942: 2.
106. Culleton, *Joyce and the G-Men*, 173, 175, 185–86.
107. William J. Maxwell, *F.B. Eyes: How J. Edgar Hoover's Ghostreaders Framed African American Literature* (Princeton, NJ: Princeton University Press, 2015), 234–35.
108. O'Brien, remarks on Hoover's address to the National Fifty Years in Business Club, A2140–42.
109. O'Brien, remarks on Hoover's address to the *New York Herald Tribune* Forum, A499.
110. Reynolds, remarks on Hoover's article in the *New York Herald Tribune*, A4499.
111. Louis B. Nichols to J. Edgar Hoover, January 16, 1939, File 67-HQ-39021, Sec. 2, Record Group 65, Entry 13, Box 1, NARA–CP.
112. Larry L. Rasmussen, "Introduction: A Few Facets of Niebuhr's Thought," in *Reinhold Niebuhr: Theologian of Public Life*, ed. Larry L. Rasmussen (Minneapolis: First Fortress Press, 1991), 22–23.
113. Martin E. Marty, *Modern American Religion*, vol. 2, *The Noise of Conflict, 1919-1941* (Chicago: University of Chicago Press, 1986), 321.
114. William D. Dean, "Niebuhr and Negative Theology," in *Reinhold Niebuhr Revisited: Engagements with an American Original*, ed. Daniel F. Rice and Martin

E. Marty (Grand Rapids, MI: Wm. B. Eerdmans Publishing, 2009), 107.

115. Reinhold Niebuhr, "Zeal without Knowledge," in *Beyond Tragedy* (New York: Charles Scribner's Sons, 1937), 235.

116. Reinhold Niebuhr, "Editor, *The Christian Century*," *Christian Century*, March 15, 1933: 363.

117. Reinhold Niebuhr, "After Capitalism, What?," *World Tomorrow*, March 1, 1933: 204–5.

118. Reinhold Niebuhr, *Moral Man and Immoral Society: A Study in Ethics and Politics* (New York: Scribner's, 1932), 3.

119. Reinhold Niebuhr, *The Nature and Destiny of Man*, vol. 1, *Human Nature* (New York: Charles Scribner's Sons, 1941), 219. This volume reprinted ideas he originally delivered at the Gifford Lectures in April 1939.

120. Reinhold Niebuhr, *An Interpretation of Christian Ethics* (New York: Harper & Brothers, 1935), 10.

121. Dianne Kirby, "J. Edgar Hoover, the FBI, and the Religious Cold War," in *The FBI and Religion: Faith and National Security before and after 9/11*, ed. Sylvester A. Johnson and Steven Weitzman (Oakland: University of California Press, 2017), 68, 70, 74.

122. Sarah Imhoff, "Hoover's Judeo-Christians: Jews, Religion, and Communism in the Cold War," in Johnson and Weitzman, *The FBI and Religion: Faith and National Security before and after 9/11*, 124–25, 130, 132.

123. Eric L. Goldstein, *The Price of Whiteness: Jews, Race, and American Identity* (Princeton, NJ: Princeton University Press, 2006), 191–92.

124. James Paul Old, "Social Justice," *Encyclopedia of American Religion and Politics*, ed. Paul A. Djupe and Laura R. Olson (New York: Facts on File, 2003), 73, 82, 420–21.

125. Stuart Svonkin, *Jews against Prejudice: American Jews and the Fight for Civil Liberties* (New York: Columbia University Press, 1997), 1–2, 15, 24.

126. Ibid., 62–63.

127. Jonathan Jeremy Goldberg, *Jewish Power: Inside the American Jewish Establishment* (Reading, MA: Addison-Wesley, 1996), 104; Eli N. Evans, *The Provincials: A Personal History of Jews in the South* (New York: Free Press Paperbacks, 1997), 220.

128. Louis Nichols to Clyde Tolson, November 26, 1942: 1–2, File 67-39021,

Sec. 2, Record Group 65, Entry 13, Box 1, NARA–CP.

129. Robert Hariman and Francis A. Beer, "What Would Be Prudent? Forms of Reasoning in World Politics," *Rhetoric & Public Affairs* 1, no. 3 (1998): 300.
130. P. E. Foxworth to J. Edgar Hoover, April 16, 1940, "Smear Campaign, Part 1," *The Louis Nichols Official and Confidential File and the Clyde Tolson Personal File*, Reel 11.
131. "Lewis Demands Full Negro Rights; Lashes Warmakers, Denounces FBI," *Daily Worker*, April 27, 1940, Record Group 65, Entry 49, Box 77, NARA–CP.
132. "Body of Negro Leader Found in River Bears Witness against FDR's Stab-in-the-Back of Anti-Lynch Bill," *Daily Worker*, June 27, 1940, Record Group 65, Entry 49, Box 77, NARA–CP.
133. Gentry, *J. Edgar Hoover*, 237–38.
134. J. Edgar Hoover to General Edwin M. Watson, June 11, 1943, Federal Bureau of Investigation, Report# 2235, President Roosevelt's Papers, Official File 10-B, Box 18, Justice Department, FDRL.
135. J. Edgar Hoover to Harry Hopkins, July 1, 1943, Federal Bureau of Investigation, Report# 2354A, President Roosevelt's Papers, Official File 10-B, Box 18, Justice Department, FDRL.
136. Robert A. Hill explains that with 155 African American newspapers in the United States, the black press was one of the "most effective and important forces attracting the attention of the colored race." The *Pittsburgh Courier*, for example, promoted civil rights as a key attribute of America's war effort. It organized the Committee on Participation of Negroes in the National Defense Program, which worked in conjunction with the March on Washington movement. Hill maintains that the CPNNDP effectively "forced President Roosevelt to issue his famous Executive Order 8802 banning discrimination in defense industries and establishing the Fair Employment Practices Committee." In Hill, *The FBI's RACON*, 4–5, 31, 406–14, 419, 622.
137. Hoover's remarks to B'nai B'rith on May 12, 1940: 1.
138. Representative Weiss, remarks on address to B'nai B'rith, A821–22.
139. Hoover, remarks to Notre Dame University, 3.

140. New Netherland was a seventeenth-century Dutch colonial province that stretched from the Delmarva Peninsula to Cape Cod. It was relinquished to the British Crown under the Treaty of Westminster, which ended the Third Anglo-Dutch War; Hoover, remarks to the Holland Society of New York, November 19, 1942: 4.
141. Steve Rosswurm, *The FBI and the Catholic Church, 1935-1962* (Amherst: University of Massachusetts Press, 2009), 21.
142. Raymond T. Feely, SJ to J. Edgar Hoover, July 5, 1944, File 67-39021, Sec. 2, Record Group 65, Entry 13, Box 1, NARA–CP.
143. Robert M. Crunden, *A Brief History of American Culture* (New York: Paragon House, 1994), 131–32; Mike Hawkins, *Social Darwinism in European and American Thought, 1860–1945: Nature as Model and Nature as Threat* (New York: Cambridge University Press, 1997), 34.
144. Hoover, remarks to the Knights of Columbus, March 22, 1942: 3.
145. Hoover, remarks to St. John's University, June 11, 1942: 1.
146. Hoover, remarks to the IACP, August 9, 1943: 3.
147. Hoover, remarks at Holy Cross College, June 29, 1944: 5.
148. W. H. D. Lester to Clyde Tolson, January 10, 1935, FBI File 94-3-4-20, Sec. 4, Record Group 65, Entry UD-09D 8, Box 106, NARA–CP.
149. J. Edgar Hoover to Courtney Ryley Cooper, November 7, 1933, FBI File 94-3-4-20, Sec. 1, Record Group 65, Entry UD-09D 8, Box 105, NARA–CP.
150. G. Lowes Dickinson, *Appearances* (New York: Doubleday, Page & Co., 1914), 180–84.
151. Representative Jenkes, remarks on J. Edgar Hoover's address to the General Federation of Women's Clubs on May 17, 1938, 75th Cong., 3d sess., May 19, 1938: A2059.
152. Brian R. McGee, "Rehabilitating Emotion: The Troublesome Case of the Ku Klux Klan," *Argumentation and Advocacy* 34 (Spring 1998): 183, 179.
153. Brian R. McGee, "Speaking about the Other: W. E. B. Du Bois Responds to the Klan," *Southern Communication Journal* 63, no. 3 (1998): 211.
154. Brian R. McGee, "Rehabilitating Emotion," 178.
155. Brian R. McGee, "Rhetoric and Race in the Progressive Era," in *Rhetoric and Reform in the Progressive Era*, ed. J. Michael Hogan (East Lansing:

Michigan State University Press, 2003), 332.

156. Special Committee to Investigate Communist Activities in the United States, *Investigation of Communist Propaganda*, H.R. 2290, 71st Cong., 3d sess., January 17, 1931; Powers, *Not without Honor*, 90.
157. Special Committee to Investigate Nazi and Other Propaganda, *Investigation of Nazi and Other Propaganda*, H.R. 153, 74th Cong., 1st sess., February 15, 1935: 23.
158. Allan Weinstein and Alexander Vassiliev, *The Haunted Wood* (New York: Modern Library, 2000), 141.
159. Special Committee to Investigate Nazi and Other Propaganda, *Investigation of Nazi and Other Propaganda*, 23.
160. *Confessions of a Nazi Spy*.
161. Special Committee on Un-American Activities, *Investigation of Un-American Activities and Propaganda*, H.R. 2, 76th Cong., 1st Sess., January 3, 1939, 10.
162. Barkley, remarks on Hoover's address to the IACP, A248.
163. Article I, Section II, U.S. Constitution; Douglas A. Blackmon, *Slavery by Another Name: The Re-Enslavement of Black Americans from the Civil War to World War II* (New York: Anchor Books, 2009), 378–82.
164. Hartley, remarks on Hoover's address to DAR, A2229.
165. O'Brien, remarks on Hoover's address to the American Legion, 5896.
166. Weiss, remarks on Hoover's address to B'nai B'rith, A822.
167. O'Brien, remarks on Hoover's address to Rutgers University, A2591.
168. Leavy, remarks on Hoover's address to the National Police Academy, A3301.
169. O'Brien, remarks on Hoover's address to the *New York Herald Tribune* Forum, A499.
170. Gail Bederman, *Manliness and Civilization: A Cultural History of Gender and Race in the United States, 1880-1917* (Chicago: University of Chicago Press, 1996), 170–71.
171. Athan G. Theoharis, "Director folder," *The Louis Nichols Official and Confidential File and the Clyde Tolson Personal File*, Reel 4, frame 0525.
172. Attention Clyde Tolson, January 19, 1944, "Director folder."
173. Attention Clyde Tolson, January 21, 1944, "Director folder."
174. Nichols to [redacted], February 5, 1944, "Director folder."

175. Hoover to Tolson, October 21, 1943, Box 1, File 67-9524-289, Sec. 2, Record Group 65, Entry 13, NARA–CP.
176. Andrew Bennett and Nicholas Royle, *An Introduction to Literature, Criticism and Theory*, 5th ed. (New York: Routledge, 2016), 239.
177. O'Brien, remarks on Hoover's address to the American Legion, 5896.
178. Hoover, remarks to the Knights of Columbus, March 22, 1942: 3.
179. Hoover, remarks to Notre Dame University, May 10, 1942: 2.
180. Rosswurm, *The FBI and the Catholic Church, 1935–1962*, 12.
181. Ann Chisholm, "Conventional Narrative as Rhetorical Strategy: Ronald Reagan's 'Address to the 1988 Republican National Convention,'" in *Critiques of Contemporary Rhetoric*, 2nd ed., ed. Karlyn Kohrs Campbell and Thomas R. Burkholder (New York: Wadsworth, 1997), 279.
182. O'Brien, remarks on Hoover's address at the Boy Scout Day Celebration, A3080.
183. Representative Ludlow, remarks on juvenile delinquency, 78th Cong., 2d sess., March 8, 1944: 2361.
184. O'Brien, remarks on Hoover's address to the National Fifty Years in Business Club, A2142.
185. Jenkes, remarks on Hoover's address to the General Federation of Women's Clubs, A2061.
186. Theodore Roosevelt, "Latitude and Longitude among Reformers," *Century*, June 1900, in *The Strenuous Life: Essays and Addresses* (Mineola, NY: Dover Publications, 2009), 21.
187. Theodore Roosevelt, remarks at Williams College, June 22, 1905, *A Compilation of the Messages and Speeches of Theodore Roosevelt, 1901–1905*, ed. Alfred Henry Lewis (Washington, DC: Bureau of National Literature and Art, 1906), 647.
188. Theodore Roosevelt, remarks to the Main Convention of the Republican Party, March 1918," in *Newer Roosevelt Messages: Speeches, Letters and Magazine Articles*, ed. Eugene Thwing (New York: Current Publishing Co., 1919), 920.
189. Freda Kirchwey, "End the Inquisition!," *The Nation*, July 31, 1943: 117.
190. Friedrich August Hayek, *The Road to Serfdom* (Chicago: University of Chicago Press, 1944); Friedrich A. Hayek, "The Road to Serfdom,"

Reader's Digest, April 1945: 1–20; Angus Burgin, *The Great Persuasion: Reinventing Free Markets since the Depression* (Cambridge, MA: Harvard University Press, 2012), 88–89.

Chapter 4. The Masquerade and the Menace, 1946–1953

1. Robert L. Ivie, "Literalizing the Metaphor of Soviet Savagery: President Truman's Plain Style," *Southern Speech Communication Journal* 51 (1986): 91–105.
2. Harry S. Truman, "Special Message to Congress on Greece and Turkey: The Truman Doctrine, March 12, 1947," in *Public Papers of the Presidents of the United States: Harry S. Truman, January 1 to December 31, 1947* (Washington, DC: U.S. Government Printing Office, 1963), 178–80.
3. Executive Order 9835, *Prescribing Procedures for the Administration of an Employees Loyalty Program in the Executive Branch of the Government* (Washington, DC: U.S. Government Printing Office, 1947 (1947 CIS microfiche EO 9818–9855), 9835.
4. Martin J. Medhurst, "Truman's Rhetorical Reticence, 1945–1947: An Interpretive Essay," *Quarterly Journal of Speech* 74 (1988): 67.
5. J. Edgar Hoover, "Testimony of J. Edgar Hoover, Director, Federal Bureau of Investigation," March 26, 1947, in *Hearings before the Committee on Un-American Activities, House of Representatives*, 80th Cong., 1st sess., 36–37, 40–41, 43.
6. Harry S. Truman to Alexander Holtzoff, May 2, 1941, in *Max Lowenthal Papers, 1855-1975*, described by Susan Hoffman (Minneapolis: University of Minnesota Archives, 2011), Box 7, folder 4.
7. Ted Morgan, *Reds: McCarthyism in Twentieth-Century America* (New York: Random House, 2004), 323.
8. Representative Bradley, remarks on J. Edgar Hoover's rumored ouster, 79th Cong., 2d sess., January 21, 1946: 165.
9. Ibid., January 23, 1946: 307.
10. Representative Mundt, remarks on J. Edgar Hoover's rumored ouster, 79th Cong., 2d sess., January 23, 1946: 308.
11. Representative Cannon, remarks on FBI appropriations, 79th Cong., 2d sess., May 3, 1946: 4409.

12. Harry S. Truman, "Special Message to the Congress Presenting a 21-Point Program for the Reconversion Period," September 6, 1945, in *Public Papers of the Presidents of the United States: Harry S. Truman* (Washington, DC: U.S. Government Printing Office, 1961), 279–80.
13. Athan G. Theoharis, "A Brief History of the FBI's Role and Powers," in *The FBI: A Comprehensive Reference Guide*, ed. Athan G. Theoharis (Phoenix: Oryx Press, 1999), 4.
14. Hoover, "Statement of J. Edgar Hoover, Director, Federal Bureau of Investigation," March 26, 1947: 39, 43.
15. Ibid., 38, 40, 43.
16. Sarah Imhoff, "Hoover's Judeo-Christians: Jews, Religion, and Communism in the Cold War," in *The FBI and Religion: Faith and National Security before and after 9/11*, ed. Sylvester A. Johnson and Steven Weitzman (Oakland: University of California Press, 2017), 126.
17. Ellen Schrecker, *Many Are the Crimes: McCarthyism in America* (Boston: Little, Brown and Co., 1998), 327–30, 370, 404–7.
18. Theoharis, "A Brief History of the FBI's Role and Powers," 4.
19. Francis A. Beer and Robert Hariman, "Realism and Rhetoric in International Relations," in *Post-Realism: The Rhetorical Turn in International Relations*, ed. Francis A. Beer and Robert Hariman (East Lansing: Michigan State University Press, 1996), 4, 6, 9.
20. John Earl Haynes and Harvey Klehr, *Early Cold War Spies: The Espionage Trials That Shaped American Politics* (New York: Cambridge University Press, 2006), 1–4.
21. Representative Mundt, remarks on Committee on Un-American Activities, 79th Cong., 2d sess., May 17, 1946: 5218–20.
22. Representative Rankin, remarks on Committee on Un-American Activities, 79th Cong., 2d sess., May 17, 1946: 5216.
23. Representative Reed, remarks on Committee on Un-American Activities, 79th Cong., 2d sess., May 17, 1946: 5210.
24. Representative Colmer, remarks on Committee on Un-American Activities, 79th Cong., 2d sess., May 17, 1946: 5214.
25. Representative Anderson, remarks on Committee on Un-American Activities, 79th Cong., 2d sess., May 17, 1946: 5215.

26. Representative Sumners, remarks on Committee on Un-American Activities, 79th Cong., 2d sess., May 17, 1946: 5211.
27. Brian R. McGee, "Rhetoric and Race in the Progressive Era: Imperialism, Reform, and the Ku Klux Klan," in *Rhetoric and Reform in the Progressive Era*, ed. J. Michael Hogan (East Lansing: Michigan State University Press, 2003), 328.
28. Rankin, remarks on Committee on Un-American Activities, 5223–24.
29. Curt Gentry, *J. Edgar Hoover: The Man and the Secrets* (New York: Norton, 1991), 354.
30. Schrecker, *Many Are the Crimes*, 203.
31. Kenneth O'Reilly, *Hoover and the Un-Americans* (Philadelphia: Temple University Press, 1983), 106–9, 126–27.
32. Shevaun E. Watson, "Trying Silence: The Case of Denmark Vesey and the History of African American Rhetoric," in *Silence and Listening as Rhetorical Arts*, ed. Cheryl Glenn and Krista Ratcliffe (Carbondale: Southern Illinois University Press, 2011), 82–83.
33. Charles E. Morris III, "Pink Herring and the Fourth Persona: J. Edgar Hoover's Sex Crime Panic," *Quarterly Journal of Speech* 88, no. 2 (2002): 229.
34. Ann Chisholm, "Conventional Narrative as Rhetorical Strategy: Ronald Reagan's 'Address to the 1988 Republican National Convention,'" in *Critiques of Contemporary Rhetoric*, 2nd ed., ed. Karlyn Kohrs Campbell and Thomas R. Burkholder (New York: Wadsworth, 1997), 280.
35. J. Edgar Hoover, "Our 'Achilles' Heel," *Vital Speeches of the Day* 13, October 15, 1946: 10.
36. Representative Rankin, remarks on J. Edgar Hoover's address to the American Legion on September 30, 1946, 80th Cong., 1st sess., January 7, 1947: A27–28; Senator McKellar, remarks on J. Edgar Hoover's address to HUAC on March 26, 1947, 80th Cong., 1st sess., March 27, 1947: 2689–92; Representative Thomas, remarks on J. Edgar Hoover's address to HUAC on March 26, 1947, 80th Cong., 1st sess., March 27, 1947: A1330–33; Representative Bryson, remarks on J. Edgar Hoover's address to the Grand Lodge of Freemasons on May 2, 1950, 80th Cong., 1st sess., June 12, 1950: A4358–59.

37. Representative Schwabe, remarks on J. Edgar Hoover's February 1947 article for the *American Magazine*, "Red Fascism in the United States Today," 80th Cong., 1st sess., February 13, 1947: A536–38; Representative Klein, remarks on J. Edgar Hoover's June 9, 1947, article for *Newsweek*, "How to Fight Communism," 80th Cong., 1st sess., June 12, 1947: A2811; Representative Crawford, remarks on J. Edgar Hoover's November 1947 interview with the *New York Herald Tribune*, 80th Cong., 1st sess., November 20, 1947: A4286–88; Representative Crawford, remarks on J. Edgar Hoover's November 1947 interview with the *New York Herald Tribune*, 80th Cong., 1st sess., November 24, 1947: A4352–53; Representative Wilson, remarks on J. Edgar Hoover's April 1947 article for the *New York Times Magazine*, "Hoover Answers 10 Questions on the FBI," 80th Cong., 1st sess., May 6, 1950: A3331–33; Representative Schwabe, remarks on J. Edgar Hoover's August 12, 1951, article for *Lookout Magazine*, "A Good Christian Is a Good Citizen," 80th Cong., 1st sess., August 20, 1951: A5268–69; Representative Dirksen, remarks on J. Edgar Hoover's May 11, 1950, article for *Parade Magazine*, "Could Your Child Become a Red?," 80th Cong., 1st sess., May 19, 1952: A3035; Representative Wood, remarks on J. Edgar Hoover's August article for *U.S. News and World Report*, "How Communists Operate," 80th Cong., 1st sess., August 30, 1950: A6237–38; Representative Smith, remarks on J. Edgar Hoover's May article for *U.S. News and World Report*, "Fifty-Five Thousand Communists," 80th Cong., 1st sess., May 10, 1950: A3495–96.
38. Representative Scrivner (R-KA), remarks commending J. Edgar Hoover, 79th Cong., 2d sess., March 28, 1946: A1741; Representative Boykin (D-AL), remarks commending J. Edgar Hoover, 79th Cong., 2d sess., April 5, 1946: A1943; Representative Ludlow (D-IN), remarks commending J. Edgar Hoover, 79th Cong., 2d sess., April 17, 1946: A2223; Representative Reed (R-NY), remarks commending J. Edgar Hoover, 79th Cong., 2d sess., July 15, 1946: A4117; Representative Rabaut (D-MI), remarks commending J. Edgar Hoover, 79th Cong., 2d sess., June 28, 1946: A3806; Representative Mundt (R-SD), remarks commending J. Edgar Hoover, 79th Cong., 2d sess., July 18, 1946: 9391; Representative Woodruff (R-MI), remarks commending J. Edgar

Hoover, 80th Cong., 1st. sess., May 20, 1947: A3806; Representative Hoffman (R-MI), remarks commending J. Edgar Hoover, 80th Cong., 2d sess., January 13, 1948: 121; Representative Fisher (D-TX), remarks commending J. Edgar Hoover, 80th Cong., 2d sess., February 16, 1948: A872; Representative Michener (R-MI), remarks commending J. Edgar Hoover, 80th Cong., 2d sess., May 25, 1948: 6441; Representative Martin (R-MA), remarks commending J. Edgar Hoover, 81st Cong., 1st sess., May 10, 1949: 5975; Representative Walter (D-PA), remarks commending J. Edgar Hoover, 81st Cong., 1st sess., May 10, 1949: 5975; Representative Rogers (R-MA), remarks commending J. Edgar Hoover, 81st Cong., 1st sess., May 19, 1949: A3006; Representative Velde (R-IL), remarks commending J. Edgar Hoover, 81st Cong., 1st sess., June 21, 1949: 8080; Representative Dwight Rogers (D-FL), remarks commending J. Edgar Hoover, 81st Cong., 1st sess., July 8, 1949: 9164; Representative Murray (D-TN), remarks commending J. Edgar Hoover, 81st Cong., 1st sess., July 8, 1949: 9164; Representative Ford (R-MI), remarks commending J. Edgar Hoover, 81st Cong., 1st sess., July 8, 1949: 9164; Representative Hall (R-NY), remarks commending J. Edgar Hoover, 81st Cong., 2d sess., February 13, 1950: 1768; Representative Jennings (R-TN), remarks commending J. Edgar Hoover, 81st Cong., 2d sess., March 4, 1950: A1661; Representative Morrison (D-LA), remarks commending J. Edgar Hoover, 81st Cong., 2d sess., June 8, 1950: A4322; Representative Rankin (D-MS), remarks commending J. Edgar Hoover, 81st Cong., 2d sess., July 10, 1950: A4974; Representative Wolverton (R-NJ), remarks commending J. Edgar Hoover, 81st Cong., 2d sess., July 12, 1950: A5071; Representative Cellar (D-NY), remarks commending J. Edgar Hoover, 81st Cong., 2d sess., November 27, 1950: A7351; Representative Jensen (R-IA), remarks commending J. Edgar Hoover, 81st Cong., 2d sess., November 30, 1950: A7371; Representative Hart (D-NJ), remarks commending J. Edgar Hoover, 81st Cong., 2d sess., December 15, 1950: A7735; Representative Cannon (D-MO), remarks commending J. Edgar Hoover, 82d Cong., 1st sess., March 22, 1951: 2895; Representative Shafer (R-MI), remarks commending J. Edgar Hoover, 82d Cong., 1st sess., July 19, 1951: 8484; Representative Bakewell (R-MO), remarks commending J. Edgar Hoover, 82d Cong., 2d sess., January 16, 1952: A198; Representative Clemente (R-MO), remarks commending J. Edgar Hoover, 82d Cong., 2d sess., May 20, 1952: A3104.

39. Senator Ferguson (R-MI), remarks commending J. Edgar Hoover, 80th Cong., 1st sess., May 21, 1947: 5564; Vice President Alben Barkley (D-KY), remarks commending J. Edgar Hoover, 81st Cong., 1st sess., May 10, 1949: 5934; Senator McCarthy (R-WI), remarks commending J. Edgar Hoover, 81st Cong., 1st sess., May 10, 1949: 5941; Senator McMahon (D-CT), remarks commending J. Edgar Hoover, 81st Cong., 1st sess., May 11, 1949: 6008; Senator Thomas (D-OK), remarks commending J. Edgar Hoover, 81st Cong., 1st sess., May 10, 1949: 5934; Senator Baldwin (R-CT), remarks commending J. Edgar Hoover, 81st Cong., 1st sess., May 10, 1949: 5941; Senator Bridges (R-CT), remarks commending J. Edgar Hoover, 81st Cong., 1st sess., May 10, 1949: 5942; Senator Wiley (R-WI), remarks commending J. Edgar Hoover, 81st Cong., 2d sess., January 23, 1950: 765; Senator O'Conor (D-MD), remarks commending J. Edgar Hoover, 82d Cong., 2d sess., May 14, 1952: 5141.
40. Senator Wiley, remarks commending J. Edgar Hoover, 81st Cong., 2d sess., April 23, 1952: A2486.
41. William C. Sullivan with Bill Brown, *The Bureau: My Thirty Years in Hoover's FBI* (New York: W.W. Norton, 1979), 88.
42. Richard Gid Powers, "The FBI in American Popular Culture," in *The FBI: A Comprehensive Reference Guide*, ed. Athan G. Theoharis (Phoenix: Oryx Press, 1999), 272–83.
43. Wesley Alan Britton, *Onscreen and Undercover: The Ultimate Book of Movie Espionage* (Westport, CT: Praeger, 2006), 85.
44. Peter Roffman and Jim Purdy, "HUAC and the End of an Era," in *Hollywood's America: Twentieth-Century America through Film*, ed. Steven Mintz and Randy W. Roberts (Malden, MA: Wiley-Blackwell, 2010), 184.
45. Harold D. Smith diary entry, September 5, 1945: 1, Box 1, Harry S. Truman Presidential Library, Independence, Missouri [hereafter HSTL].
46. Harold D. Smith diary entry, May 11, 1945: 1–2, Box 1, HSTL.
47. Harold D. Smith diary entry, July 6, 1945: 1, Box 1, HSTL.

48. Morris, "Pink Herring and the Fourth Persona," 241.
49. Representative Byrnes, remarks on FBI files, 80th Cong., 1st sess., April 7, 1947: A1540.
50. Thomas, remarks on J. Edgar Hoover's address to HUAC, A1330.
51. Hearings before the House Committee on Un-American Activities, *Hearings regarding Communist Espionage in the United States Government: Testimony of Elizabeth Bentley, July 31, 1948* (Washington, DC: U.S. Government Printing Office, 1948), 561.
52. Mundt, remarks on Committee on Un-American Activities, 5217.
53. Eben A. Ayers diary entry, August 31, 1948, Eben A. Ayers Papers, Box 20, HSTL.
54. Gentry, *J. Edgar Hoover: The Man and the Secrets*, 358.
55. Kenneth O'Reilly, *Hoover and the Un-Americans*, 109.
56. Louis Nichols to Clyde Tolson, January 17, 1949, in *The Louis Nichols Official and Confidential File and the Clyde Tolson Personal File*, Reel 10, "Pearson, Drew" (Bethesda, MD: University Publications of America, 1990).
57. Louis Nichols to Clyde Tolson, January 24, 1949, in *The Louis Nichols Official and Confidential File and the Clyde Tolson Personal File*, Reel 10.
58. Louis Nichols to Clyde Tolson, January 26, 1949, in *The Louis Nichols Official and Confidential File and the Clyde Tolson Personal File*, Reel 10.
59. Jack Babuscio, "The Cinema of Camp (*aka* Camp and the Gay Sensibility)," in *Camp: Queer Aesthetics and the Performing Subject*, ed. Fabio Cleto (Ann Arbor: University of Michigan Press, 2002), 122–23.
60. J. Edgar Hoover, "How to Fight Communism," *Newsweek*, June 9, 1947: 30.
61. Robert Hariman and Francis A. Beer, "What Would Be Prudent? Forms of Reasoning in World Politics," *Rhetoric & Public Affairs* 1, no. 3 (1998): 229.
62. Babuscio, "The Cinema of Camp (*aka* Camp and the Gay Sensibility)," 124.
63. Thomas, remarks on J. Edgar Hoover's address to HUAC, A1332.
64. Lev Loseff, *On the Beneficence of Censorship: Aesopian Language in Modern Russian Language*, trans. Lane Bobko (Munich: Sagner, 1984), x.
65. Thomas, remarks on J. Edgar Hoover's address to HUAC, A1332.

66. Representative Celler, remarks on Committee on Un-American Activities, 79th Cong., 2d sess., May 17, 1946: 5213.
67. Representative Klein, remarks on Committee on Un-American Activities, 79th Cong., 2d sess., May 17, 1946: 5213–14.
68. Crawford, remarks on Hoover's November 1947 interview with the *New York Herald Tribune*, A4286.
69. Executive Order 9835, *Prescribing Procedures for the Administration of an Employees Loyalty Program in the Executive Branch of the Government* (Washington, DC: U.S. Government Printing Office, 1947 (1947 CIS microfiche EO 9818–9855).
70. Michael J. Hogan, *A Cross of Iron: Harry S. Truman and the Origins of the National Security State, 1945-1954* (Cambridge: Cambridge University Press, 1998), 255.
71. Douglas M. Charles, *Hoover's War on Gays: Exposing the FBI's "Sex Deviates" Program* (Lawrence: University Press of Kansas, 2015), 44.
72. George Elsey, May 2, 1947, Elsey Papers, Box 69, File: Internal Security, FELP Executive Order 9835, HSTL.
73. Clark Clifford to Harry S. Truman, May 23, 1947, Box 69, File: Internal Security, FELP Executive Order 9835, HSTL.
74. Louis Nichols to Clyde Tolson, July 13, 1949, in *The Louis Nichols Official and Confidential File and the Clyde Tolson Personal File*, Reel 4, "Director: Political Support."
75. Hoover to Tolson, October 21, 1943, Box 1, File 67-9524-289, Sec. 2, Record Group 65, Entry 13, NARA–CP.
76. Harry S. Truman, "The President's Special Conference with the Association of Radio News Analysts, May 13, 1947," *Public Papers of the Presidents of the United States: Harry S. Truman, January 1 to December 31, 1947* (Washington, DC: U.S. Government Printing Office, 1963), 238.
77. William H. Chamberlin, "Behind the Events in Russia: Is a New Opposition Arising?," *New York Times*, January 6, 1935: 10.
78. William H. Chamberlin, "Russia and Germany—Parallels and Contrasts," *Atlantic Monthly*, September 1935: 367–68.
79. Les K. Adler and Thomas G. Paterson, "Red Fascism: The Merger of Nazi Germany and Soviet Russia in the American Image of

Totalitarianism, 1930's–1950's," *American Historical Review* 75, no. 4 (1970): 1046; Ernest G. Bormann, John F. Cragan, and Donald C. Shields, "An Expansion of the Rhetorical Vision Component of the Symbolic Convergence Theory: The Cold War Paradigm Case," *Communication Monographs* 63 (1996): 6.

80. Lynn Boyd Hinds and Theodore Otto Windt Jr., *The Cold War as Rhetoric: The Beginnings, 1945–1950* (New York: Praeger, 1991), 50–51.
81. Walter Lippmann, *An Inquiry into the Principles of the Good Society* (Boston: Little, Brown and Co., 1937), 238.
82. Friedrich A. Hayek, "The Road to Serfdom," *Reader's Digest*, April 1945: 4.
83. Angus Burgin, *The Great Persuasion: Reinventing Free Markets since the Depression* (Cambridge, MA: Harvard University Press, 2012), 90.
84. J. Edgar Hoover to Roland L'Allier, September 17, 1952, FBI File 62-97956-1. For more on the FBI's storied relationship with the *Reader's Digest*, see also Matthew Cecil, "Friends of the Bureau: Personal Correspondence and the Cultivation of Journalist-Adjuncts by J. Edgar Hoover's FBI," *Journalism & Mass Communication Quarterly* 88 (2011): 274.
85. Burgin, *The Great Persuasion*, 90.
86. Representative Max Schwabe (R-MO), speaking on "Road to Serfdom," October 2, 1945, 79th Cong., 1st sess., *Appendix to the Congressional Record*, A4122.
87. Representative Lanham, speaking on Aid to Greece and Turkey, May 6, 1947, 80th Cong., 1st sess., *Appendix to the Congressional Record*, A2197.
88. Thomas, remarks on Hoover's address to HUAC, A1331.
89. Rankin, remarks on Hoover's address to the American Legion, A28.
90. Ray Tucker, "Ray Tucker's Letter," *Brooklyn Eagle*, October 22, 1946, Record Group 65, Entry 49, Box 94, NARA–CP.
91. Robert Ivie, "Fire, Flood, and Red Fever: Motivating Metaphors of Global Emergency in the Truman Doctrine Speech," *Presidential Studies Quarterly* 29 (1999): 570.
92. D. Milton Ladd to J. Edgar Hoover, February 27, 1946, Senate Select Committee to Study Governmental Operation, *Supplementary Detailed Staff Reports on Intelligence Activities and the Rights of Americans*, book 3 (Washington, DC: U.S. Government Printing Office, 1976), 429–30.

93. Those congressional committees included the Joint Committee on Atomic Energy, Senate Appropriations Committee, Senate Armed Services Committee, Preparedness Subcommittee to the Armed Services Committee, Senate Judiciary Committee, House Judiciary Committee, Senate Committee on Labor and Public Welfare, Subcommittee on Labor Management Relations of the Senate Committee on Labor and Public Welfare, Senate Foreign Relations Committee, Senate Subcommittee on Internal Security, House Committee on Un-American Activities, and Senate Permanent Investigations Committee. Athan G. Theoharis, "The FBI and the American Legion Contact Program, 1940–1966," *Political Science Quarterly* 100, no. 2 (1985): 284–85.
94. Theoharis, "A Brief History of the FBI's Role and Powers," 29–30.
95. Clyde Tolson to J. Edgar Hoover, April 30, 1951, in *Federal Bureau of Investigation Confidential Files: McCarthy Era Blacklisting of School Teachers, College Professors, and Other Public Employees,* "The FBI Responsibilities Program File," ed. Kenneth O'Reilly (Bethesda, MD: University Publications of America, 1989), Reel 1, frame 645–46.
96. Schrecker, *Many Are the Crimes*, 404.
97. Jan Housbrouck, "J. Edgar Hoover's Gossip Mill," *New Republic*, December 15, 1947: 20.
98. Daniel S. Gillmor, "Guilt by Gossip," *New Republic*, May 31, 1948: 16.
99. Harold L. Ickes, "Hysteria in the Justice Department," *New Republic*, July 4, 1949: 14.
100. Thomas I. Emerson and David M. Helfeld, "A Comment on the Article 'Loyalty among Government Employees': Reply by the Authors," *Yale Law Journal* 58, no. 3 (February 1949): 143.
101. Clifford J. Durr, "The Loyalty Order's Challenge to the Constitution," *University of Chicago Law Review* 16, no. 2 (1949): 301.
102. Max Nordau, *Degeneration* (New York: D. Appleton, 1892), 539; Donald Pizer, *American Naturalism and the Jews: Garland, Norris, Dreiser, Wharton, and Cather* (Urbana: University of Illinois Press, 2008), 18.
103. Simon A. Cole and Michael C. Campbell, "From Subhumans to Superhumans: Criminals in the Evolutionary Hierarchy, or What Became of Lombroso's Atavistic Criminals?," in *The Cesare Lombroso*

Handbook, ed. Paul Knepper and Per Jørgen Ystehede (New York: Routledge, 2013), 147, 149.

104. Rankin, remarks on Hoover's address to the American Legion, A28.
105. Jutta Weldes, *Constructing National Interests: The United States and the Cuban Missile Crisis* (Minneapolis: University of Minnesota Press, 1999), 140.
106. Wood, remarks on Hoover's article in *U.S. News and World Report*, A6238.
107. Rankin, remarks on Hoover's address to the American Legion, A28.
108. Rob Van Horn and Philip Mirowski, "The Rise of the Chicago School of Economics and the Birth of Neoliberalism," *The Road from Mont Pèlerin: The Making of the Neoliberal Thought Collective*, ed. Philip Mirowski and Dieter Plehwe (Cambridge, MA: Harvard University Press, 2009), 159.
109. Mont Pelerin Society, "Statement of Aims," April 8, 1947, https://www.montpelerin.org/statement-of-aims.
110. David Harvey, *A Brief History of Neoliberalism* (Oxford: Oxford University Press, 2005), 20–21, 65–66.
111. Thomas, remarks on Hoover's address to HUAC, A1333.
112. Ibid., A1332.
113. Kristen Hoerl and Erin Ortiz, "Organizational Secrecy and the FBI's COINTELPRO–Black Nationalist Hate Groups Program, 1967–1971," *Management Communication Quarterly* 29, no. 4 (2015): 597, 611.
114. Seth Rosenfeld, *Subversives: The FBI's War on Student Radicals, and Reagan's Rise to Power* (New York: Farrar, Straus and Giroux, 2012), 119–20.
115. Ronald Reagan, *An American Life* (New York: Simon and Schuster, 1990), 111.
116. Rosenfeld, *Subversives*, 126.
117. Ibid., 120, 129–33.
118. Craig R. Smith, "Ronald Reagan's Rhetorical Re-Invention of Conservatism," *Quarterly Journal of Speech* 103 (2017): 39.
119. John Sbardellati, *J. Edgar Hoover Goes to the Movies: The FBI and the Origins of Hollywood's Cold War* (Ithaca, NY: Cornell University Press, 2012), 1–2, 197–98, 200, 201.
120. *Walk East on Beacon*, Columbia Pictures, 1952.
121. Sbardellati, *J. Edgar Hoover Goes to the Movies*, 92–93; Rosenfeld, *Subversives*, 562; Stephanie Fuller, *The US-Mexico Border in American Cold War Film:*

Romance, Revolution, and Regulation (New York: Palgrave Macmillan, 2015), 79.

122. Motion Picture Alliance for the Preservation of American Ideals, *Screen Guide for Americans* (Beverly Hills, CA: Motion Picture Alliance for the Preservation of American Ideals, 1947), 2, https://archive.lib.msu.edu/DMC/AmRad/screenguideamericans.pdf.
123. Bryson, remarks on Hoover's address to the Freemasons, A4358.
124. John McCumber, *The Philosophy Scare: The Politics of Reason in the Early Cold War* (Chicago: University of Chicago Press, 2016), 19, 48–51.
125. Eleanor Roosevelt, "We Must Preserve Individual's Right to Be Different," *Washington Daily News*, March 29, 1947, Record Group 65, Entry 49, Box 96, NARA-CP.
126. Marquis Childs, "Washington Calling: Freedom of Conscience," *Washington Post*, November 18, 1947: 10.
127. "Durr Scores Truman Loyalty Program: Says Anti-Red Tactics Are Communistic in Themselves," *Broadcasting*, January 5, 1948, Record Group 65, Entry 49, Box 99, NARA-CP.
128. Clifford J. Durr to Harry S. Truman, June 20, 1949, and January 19, 1950, President's Official File, Loyalty Program, Box 102, HSTL.
129. Alan Barth was a civil liberties advocate, author, and editorial writer at the *Washington Post.* "The Loyalty of Free Men" (March 16–17, 1951), reprinted in the *Bulletin of the American Association of University Professors* 37, no. 1 (Spring 1951): 9–10.
130. Raymond Moley to Franklin Roosevelt, "Department of Justice," May 19, 1934: 5, 7, 18–19, Box 190, Printed Materials, FDR Library.
131. Wendy Brown, *Undoing the Demos: Neoliberalism's Stealth Revolution* (New York: Zone Books, 2015), 219.
132. Harry S. Truman, "Annual Message to the Congress on the State of the Union," January 7, 1948, *Public Papers of the Presidents of the United States: Harry S. Truman, January 1 to December 31, 1948* (Washington, DC: U.S. Government Printing Office, 1964), 2–3.
133. President's Committee on Civil Rights, *To Secure These Rights* (New York: Simon and Schuster, 1947), x, 116, 100, 166–67.
134. Sumners, remarks on Committee on Un-American Activities, 5211.

135. Schwabe, speaking on "Road to Serfdom," A4123.
136. Thomas, remarks on Hoover's address to HUAC, A1333.
137. Rankin, remarks on Hoover's address to the American Legion, A28.
138. Hoover, "How to Fight Communism," 32.
139. Wilson, remarks on Hoover's article for the *New York Times Magazine*, A3333.
140. Bryson, remarks on Hoover's address to the Freemasons, A4358.
141. Rankin, remarks on Hoover's address to the American Legion, A27.
142. Wood, remarks on Hoover's article in *U.S. News and World Report*, 6237–38.
143. Ibid., 6239.
144. Hoover, "How to Fight Communism," 31.
145. Bryson, remarks on Hoover's address to the Freemasons, A4359.
146. Dieter Plehwe, Bernhard Walpen, and Gisela Newnhöffer, *Neoliberal Hegemony: A Global Critique* (New York: Routledge, 2006), 158.
147. Richard Slotkin, "Nostalgia and Progress: Theodore Roosevelt's Myth of the Frontier," *American Quarterly* 33, no. 5 (Winter 1981): 621.
148. David B. Danbom, *"The World of Hope": Progressives and the Struggle for an Ethical Public Life* (Philadelphia: Temple University Press, 1987), 119–20.
149. David W. Southern, *The Progressive Era and Race: Reaction and Reform, 1900-1917* (Wheeling, IL: Harlan Davidson, 2005), 37.
150. Richard Slotkin, *Gunfighter Nation: The Myth of the Frontier in Twentieth-Century America* (Norman: University of Oklahoma Press, 1992), 43.
151. Richard Slotkin, *The Fatal Environment: The Myth of the Frontier in the Age of Industrialization, 1800–1890* (Norman: University of Oklahoma Press, 1985), 531.
152. J. Edgar Hoover, "God or Chaos?," *Redbook* magazine, February 1949: 64.
153. Sumners, remarks on Committee on Un-American Activities, 5211.
154. Schwabe, speaking on "Road to Serfdom," A4122.
155. Hoover, "How to Fight Communism," 32.
156. Schwabe, remarks on Hoover's August 1951 article for *Lookout Magazine*, A5269.
157. Dianne Kirby, "J. Edgar Hoover, the FBI, and the Religious Cold War," in *The FBI and Religion: Faith and National Security before and after 9/11*, ed. Sylvester A. Johnson and Steven Weitzman (Oakland: University of

California Press, 2017), 75.

158. Michael J. McVicar, "Apostles of Deceit: Ecumenism, Fundamentalism, Surveillance, and the Contested Loyalties of Protestant Clergy during the Cold War," in Johnson and Weitzman, *The FBI and Religion: Faith and National Security before and after 9/11*, 93, 97.
159. Yosef Lapid, "The Third Debate: On the Prospects of International Theory in a Post-Positivist Era," *International Studies Quarterly* 33, no. 3 (1989): 236–37.
160. Lawrence Freedman, *Strategy: A History* (New York: Oxford University Press, 2013), 576–80.
161. McCumber, *The Philosophy Scare*, 74–75.
162. Ned O'Gorman, *The Iconoclastic Imagination: Image, Catastrophe, and Economy in America from the Kennedy Assassination to September 11* (Chicago: University of Chicago Press, 2015), 10–12.
163. Wendy Brown, "Neoliberalism and the End of Liberal Democracy," *Theory & Event* 7, no. 1 (2003): 1–5.
164. Hearings before the House Committee on Un-American Activities, *Hearings regarding Communism in the United States Government*, part 2, *Testimony of Max Lowenthal, September 15, 1950* (Washington, DC: U.S. Government Printing Office, 1950), 2975, 2981.
165. William L. Marbury to George L. Radcliffe, July 30, 1935, Box 1, William Marbury Outgoing Correspondence, 1934–1977, Maryland Historical Society.
166. John Earl Haynes and Harvey Klehr, *Venona: Decoding Soviet Espionage in America* (New Haven, CT: Yale University Press, 1999), 167.
167. Max Lowenthal, "Friday, June 13, 1952, 9 p.m.": 5–6, in *Max Lowenthal Papers, 1855-1975*, described by Susan Hoffman (Minneapolis: University of Minnesota Archives, 2011), Box 11, folder 22.
168. Victor Laskey to Max Lowenthal, May 27, 1953, in *Max Lowenthal Papers*, Box 11, folder 14.
169. Matthew Cecil, *Hoover's FBI and the Fourth Estate: The Campaign to Control the Press and the Bureau's Image* (Lawrence: University Press of Kansas, 2014), 201, 230.
170. Kenneth O'Reilly, "The FBI and the Origins of McCarthyism," *Historian*

45, no. 3 (1983): 379.

171. Hoover, "Testimony of J. Edgar Hoover, Director, Federal Bureau of Investigation," March 26, 1947: 15–16.
172. Ibid., 13, 14, 18.
173. Representative Walter H. Judd (R-MN), speaking on Hayek's disavowal, May 16, 1945, 79th Cong., 1st sess., *Appendix to the Congressional Record*, A2324.
174. Representative Nixon, remarks commending J. Edgar Hoover, 81st Cong., 1st sess., June 22, 1949: 8169.
175. Ford, remarks commending J. Edgar Hoover, 9165.
176. Janet Hook and Natalie Andrews, "There Really Is a Secret Club in Washington Whose Members Run America," *Wall Street Journal*, June 20, 2018.
177. Lyndon B. Johnson to Fred Edwards, February 13, 1950, FBI File 94-41273-261, Record Group 65, Entry 11, Box 346, NARA–CP.
178. Joseph R. McCarthy to J. Edgar Hoover, July 30, 1952, FBI File 94-37708-71X1, Record Group 65, Entry 11, Box 346, NARA–CP.
179. Curt Gentry, *J. Edgar Hoover: The Man and the Secrets* (New York: W.W. Norton, 1991), 365; Nicholas von Hoffman, *Citizen Cohn* (New York: Doubleday, 1988), 333–34; *Get Me Roger Stone*, dir. Dylan Bank, Daniel DiMauro, and Morgan Pehme, Netflix, 2017.
180. *Survey by Gallup Organization, January 28–February 1, 1950*, from the iPOLL Databank, Roper Center for Public Opinion Research, University of Connecticut, https://ropercenter.cornell.edu/.
181. Adler and Paterson, "Red Fascism: The Merger of Nazi Germany and Soviet Russia," 1060, 1063.
182. Adolf Hitler's *Mein Kampf* was originally published in a two-volume series. The first of these was published in 1925 and the second was published in 1926.
183. Kenneth Burke, "The Rhetoric of Hitler's Battle," *Southern Review* 5 (1939): 16, 20–21.

Conclusion

1. Executive Order 11154, *Exemption of J. Edgar Hoover from Compulsory Retirement for Age*, May 8, 1964.
2. "Full Text: Donald Trump 2016 RNC Draft Speech Transcript," *Politico*, July 21, 2016, https://www.politico.com/story/2016/07/full-transcript-donald-trump-nomination-acceptance-speech-at-rnc-225974.
3. Richard M. Nixon, "Buffalo Rally, Buffalo, NY," October 7, 1968, PPS File 208, Box 100, folder: October 7, 1968, Buffalo Rally, Buffalo, NY, p. 9, Richard M. Nixon Presidential Library and Museum.
4. Walter R. Fisher, "Romantic Democracy, Ronald Reagan, and Presidential Heroes," *Western Journal of Speech Communication* 46, no. 3 (1982): 302–3, 305–6.
5. Seth Rosenfeld, *Subversives: The FBI's War on Student Radicals, and Reagan's Rise to Power* (New York: Farrar, Straus and Giroux, 2012), 119–33; Ronald W. Reagan, *An American Life* (New York: Simon and Schuster, 1990), 6, 111, 202.
6. Donald J. Trump, Twitter post, May 12, 2015, 2:09 p.m., https://twitter.com/realdonaldtrump/status/598188263954866176.
7. James W. Ceaser, Glen E. Thurow, Jeffrey K. Tulis, and Joseph M. Bessette, "The Rise of the Rhetorical Presidency," *Presidential Studies Quarterly* 11, no. 2 (1981): 162.
8. William H. Irwin, *Propaganda and the News* (New York: Whittlesey, 1936), 202.
9. James L. McCamy, *Government Publicity: Its Practice in Federal Administration* (Chicago: University of Chicago Press, 1939), 252–53.
10. Walter Lippmann, *An Inquiry into the Principles of the Good Society* (Boston: Little, Brown and Co., 1937), 24.
11. Ceaser et al., "The Rise of the Rhetorical Presidency," 165.
12. Shawn Parry-Giles, *The Rhetorical Presidency, Propaganda, and the Cold War, 1945–1955* (Westport, CT: Praeger, 2002), xviii, xx, 185.
13. "The Truth about Hoover," *Time* magazine, December 22, 1975: 14.
14. Ann Chisholm, "Conventional Narrative as Rhetorical Strategy: Ronald Reagan's 'Address to the 1988 Republican National Convention,'" in *Critiques of Contemporary Rhetoric*, 2nd ed., ed. Karlyn Kohrs Campbell and

Thomas R. Burkholder (New York: Wadsworth, 1997), 283–84.

15. James J. Kimble, "Whither Propaganda? Agonism and 'The Engineering of Consent,'" *Quarterly Journal of Speech* 91, no. 2 (2005): 203.
16. Richard Gid Powers, *G-Men: Hoover's FBI in American Popular Culture* (Carbondale: Southern Illinois University Press, 1983), 108, 113; J. Edgar Hoover, "32nd Annual Conference," July 14, 1925 (International Association of Chiefs of Police). Record Group 65, Entry 51, Box 6, NARA-CP.
17. Douglas M. Charles, *Hoover's War on Gays: Exposing the FBI's "Sex Deviates" Program* (Lawrence: University Press of Kansas, 2015), 1; Matthew Cecil, *Branding Hoover's FBI: How the Boss's PR Men Sold the Bureau to America* (Lawrence: University Press of Kansas, 2016), 19; Steve Rosswurm, *The FBI and the Catholic Church, 1935-1962* (Amherst: University of Massachusetts Press, 2009), 30.
18. Charles, *Hoover's War on Gays*, 9.
19. Anatol Lieven, *America Right or Wrong: An Anatomy of American Nationalism* (Oxford: Oxford University Press, 2012), 8.
20. National Commission on Law Observance and Enforcement, *Report on Crime and the Foreign Born* (Washington, DC: U.S. Government Printing Office, 1931), 416.
21. Mack Smith, *Realism and the Ekphrastic Tradition* (College Station: Penn State University Press, 2008), 19–20.
22. Jack Babuscio, "The Cinema of Camp (*aka* Camp and the Gay Sensibility)," in *Camp: Queer Aesthetics and the Performing Subject*, ed. Fabio Cleto (Ann Arbor: University of Michigan Press, 2002), 122–23.
23. Smith, *Realism and the Ekphrastic Tradition*, 7.
24. Les K. Adler and Thomas G. Paterson, "Red Fascism: The Merger of Nazi Germany and Soviet Russia in the American Image of Totalitarianism, 1930's–1950's," *American Historical Review* 75, no. 4 (1970): 1063.
25. Stephen M. Underhill, "Urban Jungle, Ferguson: Rhetorical Homology and Institutional Critique," *Quarterly Journal of Speech* 102, no. 4 (2016): 412.
26. Representative Walter H. Judd (R-MN), speaking on Hayek's disavowal, May 16, 1945, 79th Cong., 1st sess., *Appendix to the Congressional Record*, A2324.

27. Walter Lippmann, *Liberty and the News* (1920; repr., Princeton, NJ: Princeton University Press, 2008), 36–37.
28. Tom Wicker, "What Have They Done since They Shot Dillinger?," *New York Times Magazine*, December 28, 1969: 6.
29. U.S. Congress, House, Regulatory Integrity Act of 2017, HR 1004, 115th Cong., 1st sess., introduced in House February 13, 2017, https://www.congress.gov/bill/115th-congress/house-bill/1004; U.S. Congress, House, To Redesignate the Federal Building Located at 935 Pennsylvania Avenue Northwest in the District of Columbia as the "Federal Bureau of Investigation Building," HR 3801, 114th Cong., 1st sess., introduced in House October 22, 2015, https://www.congress.gov/bill/114th-congress/house-bill/3801; U.S. Congress, House, To Redesignate the Federal Building Located at 935 Pennsylvania Avenue Northwest in the District of Columbia as the "Frank F. Church Federal Building," HR 4279, 109th Cong., 1st sess., introduced in House November 10, 2005, https://www.congress.gov/bill/109th-congress/house-bill/4279; U.S. Congress, House, To Redesignate the Federal Building Located at 935 Pennsylvania Avenue Northwest in the District of Columbia as the "Federal Bureau of Investigation Building," HR 2333, 109th Cong., 1st sess., introduced in House May 13, 2005, https://www.congress.gov/bill/109th-congress/house-bill/2333; U.S. Congress, House, To Redesignate the Federal Building Located at 935 Pennsylvania Avenue Northwest in the District of Columbia as the "Federal Bureau of Investigation Building," HR 2524, 108th Cong., 1st sess., introduced in House June 19, 2003, https://www.congress.gov/bill/109th-congress/house-bill/4279; U.S. Congress, House, To Redesignate the Federal Building Located at 935 Pennsylvania Avenue Northwest in the District of Columbia as the "Federal Bureau of Investigation Building," HR 5213, 107th Cong., 1st sess., introduced in House July 25, 2002, https://www.congress.gov/bill/107th-congress/house-bill/5213; U.S. Congress, House, To Redesignate the Federal Building Located at 935 Pennsylvania Avenue Northwest in the District of Columbia as the "Frank F. Church Federal Building," HR 1278, 107th Cong., 1st sess., introduced in House March 28, 2001, https://www.congress.

gov/bill/107th-congress/house-bill/1278; U.S. Congress, House, To Redesignate the Federal Building Located at 935 Pennsylvania Avenue, NW, in Washington, DC, as the "Robert F. Kennedy and Martin Luther King, Jr., Federal Building," HR 4243, 106th Cong., 2d sess., introduced in House April 11, 2000, https://www.congress.gov/bill/106th-congress/house-bill/4243; U.S. Congress, House, To Redesignate the Federal Building Located at 935 Pennsylvania Avenue, NW, in Washington, DC, as the "Frank M. Johnson Federal Building," HR 3031, 106th Cong., 1st sess., introduced in House October 6, 1999, https://www.congress.gov/bill/106th-congress/house-bill/3031; U.S. Congress, House, To Redesignate the Federal Building Located at Ninth and Pennsylvania Avenue, N.W., Washington, DC, and Known as the "J. Edgar Hoover Federal Bureau of Investigation Building" as the "Federal Bureau of Investigation Building," HR 3667, 103rd Cong., 1st sess., introduced in House November 22, 1993, https://www.govtrack.us/congress/bills/103/hr3667; U.S Congress, House, To Redesignate the J. Edgar Hoover Federal Bureau of Investigation Building Located at Ninth and Pennsylvania Avenue, N.W., Washington, D.C., as the Federal Bureau of Investigation Building," HR 3181, 103rd Cong., 1st sess., introduced in House September 29, 1993, https://www.congress.gov/bill/103rd-congress/house-bill/3181; U.S. Congress, Senate, A Bill to Redesignate the J. Edgar Hoover Federal Bureau of Investigation Building Located at Ninth and Pennsylvania Avenue, N.W., Washington, D.C., as the Federal Bureau of Investigation Building, S 1489, 103rd Cong., 1st sess., introduced in House September 23, 1993, https://www.congress.gov/bill/103rd-congress/house-bill/3181; U.S. Congress, House, A Bill to Redesignate the Federal Building Known and Designated as the "J. Edgar Hoover F.B.I. Building" as the "F.B.I. Building," HR 5743, 96th Cong., 1st sess., introduced in House October 30, 1979, https://www.congress.gov/bill/96th-congress/house-bill/5743; U.S. Congress, House, A Bill to Change the Name of the J. Edgar Hoover F.B.I. Building, HR 2491, 95th Cong., 1st sess., introduced in House January 26, 1977, https://www.congress.gov/bill/95th-congress/house-bill/2491; U.S. Congress, House, A Bill to Change the Name of the J. Edgar Hoover

F.B.I. Building, HR 10916, 94th Cong., 1st sess., introduced in House December 1, 1975, https://www.congress.gov/bill/94th-congress/house-bill/10916; U.S. Congress, House, A Bill to Designate the Name of the New Federal Building in the District of Columbia Which Is Erected to House the Federal Bureau of Investigation, HR 10918, 94th Cong., 1st sess., introduced in House December 1, 1975, https://www.congress.gov/bill/94th-congress/house-bill/10918.

Bibliography

Ackerman, Kenneth D. *Young J. Edgar.* New York: Carroll and Graf, 2007.

Adler, Les K., and Thomas G. Paterson. "Red Fascism: The Merger of Nazi Germany and Soviet Russia in the American Image of Totalitarianism, 1930's–1950's." *American Historical Review* 75, no. 4 (1970): 1046–64.

Alexander, Jack. "Profiles: The Director II." *New Yorker*, October 2, 1937: 21–26.

Allen, James Lane. "Two Principles in Recent American Fiction." *Atlantic Monthly*, October 1897: 433–41.

"Americanize Aliens." *American Issue*, April 1, 1916: 14.

"American Ogpu." *New Republic*, February 19, 1940: 230.

An Act Establishing Two Institutions for the Confinement of United States Prisoners. Public Law 270. 71st Cong., 2d sess., May 27, 1930.

An Act to Amend an Act Providing for the Parole of United States Prisoners. Public Law 202. 71st Cong., 2d sess., May 13, 1930.

An Act to Amend an Act to Establish a Hospital for Defective Delinquents. Public Law 201. 71st Cong., 2d sess., May 13, 1930.

An Act to Amend the Act of March 4, 1925, Chap. 521, and for Other Purposes. Public Law 310. 71st Cong., 2d sess., June 6, 1930.

An Act to Authorize the Public Health Service to Provide Medical Service in the Federal Prisons. Public Law 203. 71st Cong., 2d sess., May 13, 1930.

An Act to Establish Two United States Narcotic Farms for the Confinement and Treatment of Persons Addicted to the Use of Habit-Forming Narcotic Drugs Who Have Been Convicted of Offenses against the United States, and for Other Purposes. Public Law 672. 70th Cong., 2d sess., January 19, 1929.

An Act to Fix the Date When Sentence of Imprisonment Shall Begin to Run, Providing When the Allowances to a Prisoner of Time for Good Conduct Shall Begin to Run, and Further to Extend the Provisions of the Parole Laws. Public Law 219. 72d Cong., 1st sess., June 29, 1932.

An Act to Prohibit Intoxicating Beverages, and to Regulate the Manufacture, Production, Use and Sale of High-Proof Spirits for Other than Beverage Purposes, and to Insure an Ample Supply of Alcohol and Promote Its Use in Scientific Research and in the Development of Fuel, Dye, and Other Lawful Industries. Public Law 66. 66th Cong., 1st sess., October 28, 1919.

An Act to Provide for the Diversification of Employment of Federal Prisoners, for their Training and Schooling in Trades and Occupations, and for Other Purposes. Public Law 271. 71st Cong., 2d sess., May 13, 1930.

An Act to Reorganize the Administration of Federal Prisons; to Authorize the Attorney General to Contract for the Care of United States Prisoners; to Establish Federal Jails, and for Other Purposes. Public Law 218. Sec. 1, 2, 4. 71st Cong., 2d sess., May 14, 1930.

Annual Report of the Attorney General of the United States for the Fiscal Year 1930: Testimony of Sanford Bates. Washington, DC: U.S. Government Printing Office, 1930.

Annual Report of the Attorney General of the United States for the Fiscal Year 1932: Testimony of J. Edgar Hoover. Washington, DC: U.S. Government Printing Office, 1932.

Annual Report of the Attorney General of the United States for the Fiscal Year 1933: Testimony of Sanford Bates. Washington, DC: U.S. Government Printing Office, 1934.

Annual Report of the Attorney General of the United States for the Fiscal Year 1934: Testimony of J. Edgar Hoover. Washington, DC: U.S. Government Printing Office, 1934.

Annual Report of the Attorney General of the United States for the Fiscal Year 1935: Testimony of J. Edgar Hoover. Washington, DC: U.S. Government Printing Office, 1935.

Annual Report of the Attorney General of the United States for the Fiscal Year 1936: Testimony of J. Edgar Hoover. Washington, DC: U.S. Government Printing Office, 1936.

Annual Report of the Attorney General of the United States for the Fiscal Year 1937: Testimony of J. Edgar Hoover. Washington, DC: U.S. Government Printing Office, 1937.

Annual Report of the Attorney General, 1920: Bureau of Investigation, General Intelligence. 66th Cong., 3d sess., 1920.

"'Ark' with 300 Reds Sails Early Today for Unnamed Port." *New York Times*, December 21, 1919: 1.

Babuscio, Jack. "The Cinema of Camp (*aka* Camp and the Gay Sensibility)." In *Camp: Queer Aesthetics and the Performing Subject*, edited by Fabio Cleto, 117–35. Ann Arbor: University of Michigan Press, 2002.

"Bad Man at Large." *Time* magazine, May 7, 1934: 20.

Baker, Newman F. "J. Edgar Hoover." *Journal of Criminal Law and Criminology* 28, no. 5 (1938): 627–29.

Baker, Roscoe. *The American Legion and American Foreign Policy.* New York: Bookman Associates, 1954.

Barney, Timothy. "Richard Edes Harrison and the Cartographic Perspective of Modern Internationalism." *Rhetoric & Public Affairs* 15, no. 3 (2012): 397–434.

Barrish, Phillip J. *The Cambridge Introduction to American Literary Realism.* Cambridge: Cambridge University Press, 2011.

Barth, Alan. "The Loyalty of Free Men." *Bulletin of the American Association of University Professors* 37, no. 1 (Spring 1951): 9–10.

——. *The Loyalty of Free Men.* New York: Viking Press, 1951.

Bates, Sanford. "How Good Is Parole? A Debate." *Forum* (August 1938): 69–70.

——. *The Juvenile Delinquent in Soviet Russia.* Washington, DC: U.S. Government Printing Office, 1935.

——. "The Parole System Strongly Defended: The Federal Prison Director Replies to Critics Who Have Condemned It." *New York Times*, July 7, 1935: SM5.

——. "The Prison: A Complex Problem." *New York Times*, February 4, 1934: SM1.

———. *Prisons and Beyond.* New York. Macmillan Co., 1936.

"Battle Rages to Close Down G-Man Bureau." *Washington Herald*, October 8, 1935. Record Group 65, Entry 49, Box 14, National Archives and Records Administration, College Park [hereafter NARA–CP].

Batvinis, Raymond J. *The Origins of FBI Counterintelligence.* Lawrence: University Press of Kansas, 2007.

Baumlin, James S. "Introduction." In Baumlin and Baumlin, *Ethos: New Essays in Rhetorical and Critical Theory*, xi–xxxi.

Baumlin, James S., and Tita French Baumlin, eds. *Ethos: New Essays in Rhetorical and Critical Theory*. Dallas: Southern Methodist University Press, 1994.

Bederman, Gail. *Manliness and Civilization: A Cultural History of Gender and Race in the United States, 1880–1917.* Chicago: University of Chicago Press, 1996.

Beer, Francis A., and Robert Hariman, eds. *Post-Realism: The Rhetorical Turn in International Relations.* East Lansing: Michigan State University Press, 1996.

———. "Realism and Rhetoric in International Relations." In Beer and Hariman, *Post-Realism: The Rhetorical Turn in International Relations*, 1–14.

Behr, Hartut. "'Common Sense,' Thomas Reid and Realist Epistemology in Hans J. Morgenthau." *International Politics* 50, no. 6 (2013): 753–67.

Beller, Steven. "Degeneration." In *Antisemitism: A Historical Encyclopedia of Prejudice and Persecution*, vol. 1, edited by Richard S. Levy, 167–68. Santa Barbara, CA: ABC-CLIO, 2005.

Belletto, Steven, and Daniel Grausam. *American Literature and Culture in an Age of Cold War: A Critical Reassessment.* Iowa City: University of Iowa Press, 2012.

Bender, Bert. "Nature and Naturalism." In Newlin, *The Oxford Handbook of Literary Naturalism*, 52–68.

Bennett, Andrew, and Nicholas Royle. *An Introduction to Literature, Criticism and Theory*. 5th ed. New York: Routledge, 2016.

Beverly, William. *On the Lam: Narratives of Flight in J. Edgar Hoover's America.* Jackson: University Press of Mississippi, 2003.

Black, Edwin. *War Against the Weak: Eugenics and America's Campaign to Create a Master Race.* New York: Four Walls Eight Windows, 2003.

Blackmon, Douglas A. *Slavery by Another Name: The Re-Enslavement of Black Americans from the Civil War to World War II.* New York: Anchor Books, 2009.

"Body of Negro Leader Found in River Bears Witness against FDR's

Stab-in-the-Back of Anti-Lynch Bill." *Daily Worker*, June 27, 1940. Record Group 65, Entry 49, Box 77, NARA–CP.

Boies, Henry M. *Prisoners and Paupers: A Study of the Abnormal Increase of Criminals, and the Public Burden of Pauperism in the United States; the Causes and Remedies.* New York: G.P. Putnam's Sons, 1893.

Booker, M. Keith. *Film and the American Left: A Research Guide.* Westport, CT: Greenwood Press, 1999.

Booth, Ken. "Security in Anarchy: Utopian Realism in Theory and Practice." *International Affairs* 67, no. 3 (Fall 1991): 536–39.

Bormann, Ernest G., John F. Cragan, and Donald C. Shields. "An Expansion of the Rhetorical Vision Component of the Symbolic Convergence Theory: The Cold War Paradigm Case." *Communication Monographs* 63 (1996): 1–28.

Bostdorff, Denise M. *Proclaiming the Truman Doctrine: The Cold War Call to Arms.* College Station: Texas A&M University Press, 2008.

Bourne, Randolph. "This Older Generation." *Atlantic Monthly*, September 1915: 385–91.

Britton, Wesley Alan. *Onscreen and Undercover: The Ultimate Book of Movie Espionage.* Westport, CT: Praeger, 2006.

Brown, Wendy. "Neoliberalism and the End of Liberal Democracy." *Theory & Event* 7, no. 1 (2003).

———. *Undoing the Demos: Neoliberalism's Stealth Revolution.* New York: Zone Books, 2015.

Bureau of the Budget. *Service of the Fiscal Year Ending June 30, 1934.* Washington, DC: U.S. Government Printing Office, 1933.

Burgin, Angus. *The Great Persuasion: Reinventing Free Markets since the Depression.* Cambridge, MA: Harvard University Press, 2012.

Burke, Kenneth. "The Rhetoric of Hitler's Battle." *Southern Review* 5 (1939): 1–21.

Bytwerk, Randall L. *Julius Streicher: Nazi Editor of the Notorious Anti-Semitic Newspaper* Der Stürmer. New York: Cooper Square Press, 2001.

Calic, Edouard. *Reinhard Heydrich: The Chilling Story of the Man Who Masterminded the Nazi Death Camps.* Translated by Lowell Bair. New York: Morrow, 1985.

"Calls Post Factor in Revolution Plan." *New York Times*, June 2, 1920: 4.

Campbell, Donna M. *Resisting Regionalism: Gender and Naturalism in American Fiction,*

1885–1915. Athens: Ohio University Press, 1997.

Campbell, Karlyn Kohrs. "Agency: Promiscuous and Protean." *Communication and Critical/Cultural Studies* 2, no. 1 (March 2005): 1–19.

Carney, William P. "Madris Rounds Up Suspected Rebels; 2,000 Are Seized in Homes as Result of Mola's Boast of Aid from within the Capital." *New York Times*, October 16, 1936: 2.

Carpenter, Ronald H. "Postscript: A Disciplinary History of Rhetorical History: Retrospect and Prospect." In *Doing Rhetorical History: Concepts and Cases*, edited by Kathleen J. Turner, 217–31. Tuscaloosa: University of Alabama Press, 1998.

Carr, Edward Hallett. *The Twenty Years' Crisis, 1919–1939: An Introduction to the Study of International Relations.* London: Macmillan, 1939.

Ceaser, James W., Glen E. Thurow, Jeffrey K. Tulis, and Joseph M. Bessette. "The Rise of the Rhetorical Presidency." *Presidential Studies Quarterly* 11, no. 2 (1981): 158–71.

Cecil, Matthew. *Branding Hoover's FBI: How the Boss's PR Men Sold the Bureau to America.* Lawrence: University Press of Kansas, 2016.

———. "Coming on Like Gang Busters: J. Edgar Hoover's FBI and the Battle to Control Radio Portrayals of the Bureau, 1936–1958." *Journalism History* 40 (2015): 252–61.

———. "Friends of the Bureau: Personal Correspondence and the Cultivation of Journalist-Adjuncts by J. Edgar Hoover's FBI." *Journalism & Mass Communication Quarterly* 88 (2011): 267–84.

———. *Hoover's FBI and the Fourth Estate: The Campaign to Control the Press and the Bureau's Image.* Lawrence: University Press of Kansas, 2014.

Chamberlin, William H. "Behind the Events in Russia: Is a New Opposition Arising?" *New York Times*, January 6, 1935: 10.

———. "Russia and Germany—Parallels and Contrasts." *Atlantic Monthly*, September 1935: 359–68.

Charles, Douglas M. *The FBI's Obscene File: J. Edgar Hoover and the Bureau's Crusade against Smut.* Lawrence: University Press of Kansas, 2012.

———. *Hoover's War on Gays: Exposing the FBI's "Sex Deviates" Program.* Lawrence: University Press of Kansas, 2015.

———. *J. Edgar Hoover and the Anti-Interventionists: FBI Political Surveillance and the Rise of the Domestic Security State, 1939–1945.* Columbus: Ohio State University Press, 2007.

Childs, Marquis. "Washington Calling: Freedom of Conscience." *Washington Post*, November 18, 1947: 10.

Chilton, Paul A. "The Meaning of Security." In Beer and Hariman, *Post-Realism: The Rhetorical Turn in International Relations*, 193–216.

——. *Security Metaphors: Cold War Discourse from Containment to Common House.* New York: Peter Lang, 1996.

Chisholm, Ann. "Conventional Narrative as Rhetorical Strategy: Ronald Reagan's 'Address to the 1988 Republican National Convention.'" In *Critiques of Contemporary Rhetoric*, 2nd ed., edited by Karlyn Kohrs Campbell and Thomas R. Burkholder, 278–92. New York: Wadsworth, 1997.

Chodorow, Nancy. *The Reproduction of Mothering: Psychoanalysis and the Sociology of Gender.* Berkeley: University of California Press, 1978.

Coan, Blair. *The Red Web.* Chicago: Northwest Publishing, 1925.

Cole, Simon A., and Michael C. Campbell. "From Subhumans to Superhumans: Criminals in the Evolutionary Hierarchy, or What Became of Lombroso's Atavistic Criminals?" In *The Cesare Lombroso Handbook*, edited by Paul Knepper and Per Jørgen Ystehede, 147–70. New York: Routledge, 2013.

Condit, Celeste Michelle, and John Louis Lucaites. *Crafting Equality: America's Anglo-African Word.* Chicago: University of Chicago Press, 1993.

Confessions of a Nazi Spy. Warner Brothers, 1939.

Cooper, Courtney Ryley. "Getting the Jump on Crime." *American Magazine*, August 1933. Record Group 65, Entry 49, Box 3, NARA-CP.

——. "J. Edgar Hoover Has Formed Nucleus of Powerful Federal Police Force." *Kansas City Star*, August 7, 1933. Record Group 65, Entry 49, Box 3, NARA-CP.

"Crime War Real, Asserts Cummings." *New York Times*, September 12, 1933: 3.

"'Critics Are Liars,' Palmer Declares." *Washington Post*, May 18, 1920: 5.

Crunden, Robert M. *A Brief History of American Culture.* New York: Paragon House, 1994.

Culleton, Claire A. *Joyce and the G-Men.* New York: Palgrave Macmillan, 2004.

Cummings, Homer S. "Lessons of the Crime Conference." December 13, 1934.

In *Proceedings of the Attorney General's Conference on Crime, Held December 10 to December 13, 1935*, 456–61. Washington, DC: U.S. Government Printing Office, 1935.

——. "Modern Tendencies and the Law." *American Bar Association Journal* 19, no. 10 (1933): 574–80.

——. "Progress toward a Modern Administration of Criminal Justice in the United States." *American Bar Association Journal* 22, no. 5 (1936): 345–49.

Cummings, Homer S., and Carl McFarland. "The Department of Justice and the New Deal." June 11, 1933. Record Group 60, Entry 132, Box 2, File: Speeches, NARA-CP.

——. *Federal Justice: Chapters in the History of Justice and the Federal Executive.* New York: Da Capo Press, 1970.

Danbom, David B. *"The World of Hope": Progressives and the Struggle for an Ethical Public Life.* Philadelphia: Temple University Press, 1987.

da Silva, Filipe Carreira. *Mead and Modernity: Science, Selfhood, and Democratic Politics.* Lanham, MD: Lexington Books, 2008.

Dean, William D. "Niebuhr and Negative Theology." In *Reinhold Niebuhr Revisited: Engagements with an American Original*, edited by Daniel F. Rice and Martin E. Marty, 101–14. Grand Rapids: Wm. B. Eerdmans Publishing, 2009.

Dederichs, Mario R. *Heydrich: The Face of Evil.* Barnsley, UK: Greenhill Books, 2006.

Denning, Michael. *Mechanic Accents: Dime Novels and Working-Class Culture in America.* New York: Verso, 1987.

Dickinson, G. Lowes. *Appearances.* New York: Doubleday, Page & Co., 1914.

Dirksen, Everett McK. "Red Fascism: Freedom Is in Jeopardy." *Vital Speeches of the Day* 13, April 1, 1947: 359–61.

"District of Columbia Reorganized." *American Issue*, December 1908: 7.

Donner, Frank J. *The Age of Surveillance: The Aims and Methods of America's Political Intelligence System.* New York: Alfred A. Knopf, 1980.

Dooley, Roger. *From Scarface to Scarlett: American Films in the 1930s.* New York: Harcourt Brace Jovanovich, 1981.

Dorsey, Leroy G. "Preaching Morality in Modern America." In Hogan, *Rhetoric and Reform in the Progressive Era*, 49–84.

———. *We Are All Americans, Pure and Simple: Theodore Roosevelt and the Myth of Americanism.* Tuscaloosa: University of Alabama Press, 2007.

Dorsey, Leroy G., and Rachel M. Harlow. "'We Want Americans Pure and Simple': Theodore Roosevelt and the Myth of Americanism." *Rhetoric & Public Affairs* 6, no. 1 (2003): 55–78.

Dow, Bonnie J. "Feminism and Public Address Research: Television News and the Constitution of Women's Liberation." In *The Handbook of Rhetoric and Public Affairs*, edited by Shawn J. Parry-Giles and J. Michael Hogan, 345–72. Malden, MA: Wiley-Blackwell, 2010.

Durr, Clifford. "The Loyalty Order's Challenge to the Constitution." *University of Chicago Law Review* 16, no. 2 (1949): 298–306.

"Durr Scores Truman Loyalty Program: Says Anti-Red Tactics Are Communistic in Themselves." *Broadcasting*, January 5, 1948. Record Group 65, Entry 49, Box 99, NARA-CP.

Ellis, Richard J. "Introduction." In *Speaking to the People: The Rhetorical Presidency in Historical Perspective*, edited by Richard J. Ellis, 1–11. Amherst: University of Massachusetts Press, 1998.

Emerson, Thomas I., and David M. Helfeld. "A Comment on the Article 'Loyalty among Government Employees': Reply by the Authors." *Yale Law Journal* 58, no. 3 (February 1949): 412–14.

———. "Loyalty among Government Employees." *Yale Law Journal* 58, no. 1 (1948): 1–143.

Engs, Ruth C. *The Progressive Era's Health Reform Movement: A Historical Dictionary.* Westport, CT: Praeger, 2003.

Espionage Act. Public Law 24. 65th Cong., 1st sess., June 15, 1917.

Evans, Eli N. *The Provincials: A Personal History of Jews in the South.* New York: Free Press, 1997.

Executive Order 9806. *Establishing the President's Temporary Commission on Employee Loyalty.* Washington, DC: U.S. Government Printing Office, 1946. 1946 Congressional Information Service [hereafter CIS] microfiche EO 9781–9817.

Executive Order 9808. *Establishing the President's Committee on Civil Rights.* Washington, DC: U.S. Government Printing Office, 1946. 1946 CIS microfiche EO 9781–9817.

Executive Order 9835. *Prescribing Procedures for the Administration of an Employees Loyalty Program in the Executive Branch of the Government.* Washington, DC: U.S. Government Printing Office, 1947. 1947 CIS microfiche EO 9818–9855.

Executive Order 9980. *Regulations Governing Fair Employment Practices within the Federal Establishment.* Washington, DC: U.S. Government Printing Office, 1948. 1948 CIS microfiche EO 9957–9982.

Executive Order 9981. *Establishing the President's Committee on Equality of Treatment and Opportunity in the Armed Services.* Washington, DC: U.S. Government Printing Office, 1948. 1948 CIS microfiche EO 9957–9982.

Executive Order 11154. *Exemption of J. Edgar Hoover from Compulsory Retirement for Age.* May 8, 1964 29 FR 6233, May 12, 1964. .

"FBI Doped Prisoners to Get Confessions, Robinson Charges." *(Helena, MT) People's Voice*, May 29, 1940. Record Group 65, Entry 49, Box 77, NARA-CP.

"Federal Officer to Take Custody of Fred Hunter; Gangster 'Yellow Rat,' Says Hoover," *Times-Picayune*, May 3, 1936, Record Group 65, Entry 49, Box 22, NARA-CP.

"Federal Officials Linked to 'Reds' at Dies Inquiry: Sifting Charges of Un-Americanism." *Christian Science Monitor*, August 17, 1938: 1.

Federal Trade Commission. *Utility Corporations: Efforts by Associations and Agencies of Electric and Gas Utilities to Influence Public Opinion.* 70th Cong., 1st sess., Senate Document 92, part 71-A. Washington, DC: U.S. Government Printing Office, 1934.

Feinstein, Wiley. *The Civilization of the Holocaust in Italy: Poets, Artists, Saints, Anti-Semites.* Madison, NJ: Fairleigh Dickinson University Press, 2003.

Fisher, Walter R. "Romantic Democracy, Ronald Reagan, and Presidential Heroes." *Western Journal of Speech Communication* 46, no. 3 (1982): 299–310.

Fleming, Denna Frank. *The United States and World Organization, 1920-1933.* New York: Columbia University Press, 1938.

Foster, Gaines M. *Moral Reconstruction: Christian Lobbyists and the Federal Legislation of Morality, 1865-1920.* Chapel Hill: University of North Carolina Press, 2002.

Freedman, Lawrence. *Strategy: A History.* New York: Oxford University Press, 2013.

Fried, Albert. *Communism in America: A History in Documents.* New York: Columbia

University Press, 1997.

——. *FDR and His Enemies*. New York: St. Martin's Press, 1999.

"Full Text: Donald Trump 2016 RNC Draft Speech Transcript." *Politico*. July 21, 2016. https://www.politico.com/story/2016/07/full-transcript-donald-trump-nomination-acceptance-speech-at-rnc-225974.

Fuller, Stephanie. *The US-Mexico Border in American Cold War Film: Romance, Revolution, and Regulation*. New York: Palgrave Macmillan, 2015.

Gelfand, Lawrence E. *The Inquiry: American Preparations for Peace, 1917–1919*. New Haven, CT: Yale University Press, 1963.

Gentry, Curt. *J. Edgar Hoover: The Man and the Secrets*. New York: W.W. Norton and Co., 1991.

Get Me Roger Stone. Dir. Dylan Bank, Daniel DiMauro, and Morgan Pehme. Netflix, 2017.

Giles, James R. "The Grotesque City, the City of Excess, and the City of Exile." In Newlin, *The Oxford Handbook of American Literary Naturalism*, 322–38.

Gillmor, Daniel S. "Guilt by Gossip." *New Republic*, May 31, 1948: 13–27.

'G'Men. Warner Brothers and The Vitaphone Corp., 1935.

"G-Men See Era of Gangsters Gone." *Washington Star*, August 15, 1938. Group 65, Entry 49, Box 62, NARA–CP.

Goldberg, Jonathan Jeremy. *Jewish Power: Inside the American Jewish Establishment*. Reading, MA: Addison-Wesley, 1996.

Goldstein, Eric L. *The Price of Whiteness: Jews, Race, and American Identity*. Princeton, NJ: Princeton University Press, 2006.

Goldstein, Judith, and Robert O. Keohane. "Ideas and Foreign Policy: An Analytical Framework." In *Ideas and Foreign Policy: Beliefs, Institutions, and Political Change*, edited by Judith Goldstein and Robert O. Keohane, 17–35. Ithaca, NY: Cornell University Press, 1993.

Gossett, Thomas F. *Race: The History of an Idea in America*. Oxford: Oxford University Press, 1965.

Goulart, Ron. *The Dime Detectives*. New York: Mysterious Press, 1988.

Grewal, Inderpal. *Transnational America: Feminisms, Diasporas, Neoliberalisms*. Durham, NC: Duke University Press, 2005.

Griffith, Robert. "American Politics and the Origins of 'McCarthyism.'" In *The Specter: Original Essays on the Cold War and the Origins of McCarthyism*, edited by Robert Griffith and Athan G. Theoharis, 45–60. New York: New Viewpoints, 1974.

Hack, Richard. *The Secret Life of J. Edgar Hoover.* Beverly Hills, CA: New Millennium Press, 2004.

"Halts Deportation of Alleged 'Reds'; Boston Federal Judge Denounces Arrests without Warrant and Grants Writs for Thirteen." *New York Times*, April 23, 1920: 14.

Hamilton, Alexander. "Report on Manufacturers." In *On the Wealth of Nations*, edited by Ian S. Ross, 230–49. Bristol, UK: Thoemmes Press, 1998.

Hariman, Robert, and Francis A. Beer. "What Would Be Prudent? Forms of Reasoning in World Politics." *Rhetoric & Public Affairs* 1, no. 3 (1998): 299–330.

Harpine, William D. *From the Front Porch to the Front Page: McKinley and Bryan in the 1896 Presidential Campaign.* College Station: Texas A&M University Press, 2005.

Harrison Narcotics Tax Act. Public Law No. 223. 63d Cong. 2d sess., December 17, 1914.

Harvey, David. *A Brief History of Neoliberalism.* Oxford: Oxford University Press, 2005.

Hawkins, Mike. *Social Darwinism in European and American Thought, 1860–1945: Nature as Model and Nature as Threat.* New York: Cambridge University Press, 1997.

Hayek, Friedrich A. "Reception Given 'Road to Serfdom' in United States Surprises Author." *Minneapolis Tribune*, May 13, 1945.

———. "The Road to Serfdom." *Reader's Digest*, April 1945: 1–20.

———. *The Road to Serfdom.* Chicago: University of Chicago Press, 1944.

Haynes, John Earl, and Harvey Klehr. *Early Cold War Spies: The Espionage Trials That Shaped American Politics.* New York: Cambridge University Press, 2006.

———. *In Denial: Historians, Communism and Espionage.* San Francisco: Encounter Books, 2003.

———. *Venona: Decoding Soviet Espionage in America.* New Haven, CT: Yale University Press, 1999.

Hearings before the House Committee on Un-American Activities. *Hearings regarding Communism in the United States Government.* Part 2, *Testimony of Max Lowenthal, September 15, 1950.* Washington, DC: U.S. Government Printing

Office, 1950.

Hechler, Ken. "Truman Laid the Foundation for the Civil Rights Movement." In *The Civil Rights Legacy of Harry S. Truman*, edited by Raymond H. Geselbract, 55–73. Kirkville, MO: Truman University Press, 2007.

Herz, John. *Political Realism and Political Idealism.* Chicago: University of Chicago Press, 1951.

Herzberg, Bob. *The FBI and the Movies: A History of the Bureau on Screen and Behind the Scenes in Hollywood.* Jefferson, NC: McFarland, 2007.

Higham, John. *Strangers in the Land.* New York: Atheneum, 1968.

Hill, Robert A. *The FBI's RACON: Racial Conditions in the United States during World War II.* Boston: Northeastern University Press, 1995.

Hinds, Lynn Boyd, and Theodore Otto Windt Jr. *The Cold War as Rhetoric: The Beginnings, 1945-1950.* New York: Praeger, 1991.

Hinton, Harold B. "Wheeler Asserts Aid Bill Seeks War and Dictatorship." *New York Times*, March 1, 1941: 1.

Hoerl, Kristen, and Erin Ortiz. "Organizational Secrecy and the FBI's COINTELPRO—Black Nationalist Hate Groups Program, 1967–1971." *Management Communication Quarterly* 29, no. 4 (2015): 590–615.

Hogan, J. Michael, ed. *Rhetoric and Reform in the Progressive Era.* East Lansing: Michigan State University Press, 2003.

Hogan, Michael J. *A Cross of Iron: Harry S. Truman and the Origins of the National Security State, 1945-1954.* Cambridge: Cambridge University Press, 1998.

Hollihan, Thomas. "Propagandizing in the Interest of War: A Rhetorical Study on the Committee on Public Information." *Southern Speech Communication Journal* 49, no. 3 (1984): 241–57.

Hook, Janet, and Natalie Andrews. "There Really Is a Secret Club in Washington Whose Members Run America." *Wall Street Journal*, June 20, 2018.

Hoover, Herbert. "State of the Union." December 3, 1929. In *Public Papers of the Presidents of the United States: Herbert Hoover*, vol. 1, compiled by the National Archives and Records Service General, 290–302. Washington, DC: U.S. Government Printing Office, 1974.

Hoover, J. Edgar. "Abolish Parole Abuses." *Forum* (August 1938): 71–73.

——. "Address." February 1941 (B'nai B'rith). Record Group 65, Entry 51,

Box 2, NARA-CP.
——. "Address." September 30, 1939 (FBI National Police Academy). Record Group 65, Entry 51, Box 2, NARA-CP.
——. "An Adventure in Public Service." June 3, 1940 (Drake University). Record Group 65, Entry 51, Box 2, NARA-CP.
——. "An American's Privilege." November 19, 1942 (Holland Society of New York). Record Group 65, Entry 51, Box 2, NARA-CP.
——. "America's Duty to the Future." May 3, 1940 (New York Federation of Women's Clubs). Record Group 65, Entry 51, Box 2, NARA-CP.
——. "Big Scare." *American Magazine*, August 1941: 24–25, 66–67.
——. "The Challenge to Youth." June 1, 1941 (Boys' Town). Record Group 65, Entry 51, Box 2, NARA-CP.
——. "Combatting Lawlessness." *Vital Speeches of the Day* 4, February 15, 1938: 269–73.
——. "Could Your Child Become a Red?" *Parade Magazine*, May 11, 1950. Record Group 65, Entry 51, Box 2, NARA-CP.
——. "Crime and Your Home." May 17, 1938 (Triennial Convention of the General Federation of Women's Clubs). Record Group 60, Entry 132, Box 12, File: "Mr. Hoover's Speeches," NARA-CP.
——. "Detection and Apprehension." August 30, 1934 (American Bar Association). Record Group 65, Entry 51, Box 6, NARA-CP.
——. "Education against Crime." *Vital Speeches of the Day* 3, December 1, 1936: 109–14.
——. "55,000 Communists." *U.S. News & World Report*, May 12, 1950: 60.
——. "Fifty Years of Crime in America." May 20, 1939 (National Fifty Years in Business Club). Record Group 65, Entry 51, Box 2, NARA-CP.
——. "God or Chaos?" *Redbook* magazine, February 1949: 61–64.
——. "A Good Christian Is a Good Citizen." *Lookout* magazine, August 20, 1951. Record Group 65, Entry 51, Box 2, NARA-CP.
——. "A Graduate's Responsibility." June 29, 1944 (Holy Cross College). Record Group 65, Entry 51, Box 2, NARA-CP.
——. "Hoover Answers 10 Questions on the FBI." *New York Times Magazine*, April 16, 1950: SM5.
——. "Hoover Original Diary: 1910." National Law Enforcement Museum,

Washington, DC.

——. "How to Fight Communism." *Newsweek*, June 9, 1947: 30–31.

——. "The Influence of Crime on the American Home." *Vital Speeches of the Day* 2, March 23, 1936: 390–95.

——. "The Internal Defense of America." April 17, 1944 (Daughters of the American Revolution). Record Group 65, Entry 51, Box 2, NARA-CP.

——. "Is There a Spy Menace?" *Atlanta Constitution*, July 14, 1940: B2.

——. "Is There a Spy Menace?" *Baltimore Sun*, July 14, 1940: TM2.

——. "Is There a Spy Menace?" *Los Angeles Times*, July 14, 1940: J2.

——. "Law Enforcement and the Publisher." April 22, 1937 (ANPA). Record Group 65, Entry 51, Box 2, NARA-CP.

——. "Law Enforcement in a Crisis." October 24, 1939 (Annual *New York Herald-Tribune* Forum). Record Group 65, Entry 51, Box 2, NARA-CP.

——. "Local Law Enforcement in Relation to National Crime." *Dicta* 13, no. 139 (1935): 141–50.

——. "Modern Problems of Law Enforcement." July 9, 1935 (IACP). Record Group 65, Entry 51, Box 2, NARA-CP.

——. "Modern Problems of Law Enforcement." *Vital Speeches of the Day* 1, July 29, 1935: 682–87.

——. "A National Ideal." May 12, 1940 (B'nai B'rith). Record Group 65, Entry 51, Box 2, NARA-CP.

——. "A Nation's Call to Duty." June 11, 1942 (St. John's University). Record Group 65, Entry 51, Box 2, NARA-CP.

——. "Our 'Achilles' Heel." *Vital Speeches of the Day* 13, October 15, 1946: 10–13.

——. "Our Future." May 10, 1942 (Notre Dame University). Record Group 65, Entry 51, Box 2, NARA-CP.

——. "Our Nation's Strength." March 22, 1942 (Knights of Columbus). Record Group 65, Entry 51, Box 2, NARA-CP.

——. "Patriotism and the War against Crime." April 23, 1936 (Daughters of the American Revolution). Record Group 65, Entry 51, Box 2, NARA-CP.

——. *Persons in Hiding*. Boston: Little, Brown and Co., 1938.

——. "Physical Science in the Crime Detection Laboratory." *Review of Scientific Instruments* 9 (November 1938): 335–45.

———. "Police Science: Organized Protection against Organized Predatory Crimes, Bankruptcy Frauds." *Journal of Criminal Law and Criminology* 23, no. 6 (April 1933): 1070–84.

———. "Present Status of Espionage and Counterespionage Operations of the Federal Bureau of Investigation." October 24, 1940. FBI Reports–Numerical Series no. 408, Official File 10-B, Franklin Delano Roosevelt Library.

———. "The Present Task of Law Enforcement." September 9, 1940 (International Association of Chiefs of Police). Record Group 65, Entry 51, Box 2, NARA–CP.

———. "Problems of Law Enforcement." October 10, 1939 (International Association of Chiefs of Police). Record Group 65, Entry 51, Box 2, NARA–CP.

———. "Problems of Law Enforcement." *Vital Speeches of the Day* 6, December 15, 1939: 54–57.

———. "Protect America!" August 5, 1940 (Federal-State Conference on Law Enforcement Problems of National Defense). Record Group 65, Entry 51, Box 2, NARA–CP.

———. "Public Duty in Law Enforcement." December 3, 1937 (Association of Life Insurance Presidents). Record Group 65, Entry 51, Box 2, NARA–CP.

———. "The Reconversion of Law Enforcement: Revive Old-Fashioned Discipline and Courage." *Vital Speeches of the Day* 12, February 1, 1946: 253–56.

———. "Red Fascism in the United States Today." *American Magazine*, February 1947: 25–26, 87–90.

———. "Remarks of J. Edgar Hoover, Director, Federal Bureau of Investigation." September 30, 1946 (Annual Convention of the American Legion). Record Group 65, Entry 51, Box 2, NARA–CP.

———. "The Role of the Press in the War on Crime." *The Quill* 25 (May 1937): 12–15.

———. "Soldiers—In Peacetime." September 19, 1938 (American Legion). Record Group 60, Entry 132, Box 12, NARA–CP.

———. "Statement of J. Edgar Hoover, Director, Federal Bureau of

Investigation." March 26, 1947 (House Committee on Un-American Activities). Record Group 65, Entry 51, Box 2, NARA-CP.

——. "The Test of Citizenship." April 18, 1940 (Daughters of the American Revolution). Record Group 65, Entry 51, Box 2, NARA-CP.

——. "The Test of Citizenship." *Vital Speeches of the Day* 6, May 1, 1940: 440–43.

——. "32nd Annual Conference." July 14, 1925 (International Association of Chiefs of Police). Record Group 65, Entry 51, Box 6, NARA-CP.

——. "Your Call to Duty." May 23, 1943 (Rutgers University). Record Group 65, Entry 51, Box 2, NARA-CP.

Horton, Walter Marshall. *Realistic Theology*. New York: Harpers and Brothers, 1934.

Houck, Davis W. "On or About June 1988." *Rhetoric & Public Affairs* 9, no. 1 (2006): 134–41.

Housbrouck, Jan. "J. Edgar Hoover's Gossip Mill." *New Republic*, December 15, 1947: 20.

House Committee on Appropriations. *Department of Justice Appropriation Bill for 1936: Testimony of Sanford Bates (Dir, Bur of Prisons)*. 74th Cong., 2d sess.

House Committee on Rules, *Attorney General A. Mitchell Palmer on Charges Made against Department of Justice by Louis F. Post and Others*. Part 1. 66th Cong., 2d sess., June 1, 1920.

Howard, June. *Form and History in American Literary Naturalism*. Chapel Hill: University of North Carolina Press, 1985.

"How Communists Operate: An Interview with J. Edgar Hoover." *U.S. News & World Report*, August 11, 1950: 30–36.

Ickes, Harold L. "Hysteria in the Justice Department." *New Republic*, July 4, 1949: 14.

Imhoff, Sarah. "Hoover's Judeo-Christians: Jews, Religion, and Communism in the Cold War." In Johnson and Weitzman, *The FBI and Religion: Faith and National Security before and after 9/11*, 121–33.

Immigration Act of 1918 (Alien Act). Public Law 221. 65th Cong., 1st sess., October 16, 1918.

Interchurch World Movement. *Report on the Steel Strike of 1919*. New York: Da Capo Press, 1971.

Irwin, William H. *Propaganda and the News*. New York: Whittlesey, 1936.

Ivie, Robert. "Cold War Motives and Rhetorical Metaphor: A Framework of Criticism." In *Cold War Rhetoric: Strategy, Metaphor, and Ideology*, edited by Martin J. Medhurst, Robert L. Ivie, Philip Wander, and Robert L. Scott, 71–80. East Lansing: Michigan State University Press, 1997.

———. "Fire, Flood, and Red Fever: Motivating Metaphors of Global Emergency in the Truman Doctrine Speech." *Presidential Studies Quarterly* 29 (1999): 570–91.

———. "Literalizing the Metaphor of Soviet Savagery: President Truman's Plain Style." *Southern Speech Communication Journal* 51 (1986): 91–105.

Jameson, Fredric. *The Political Unconscious: Narrative as a Socially Symbolic Act.* Ithaca, NY: Cornell University Press, 1981.

Jensen, Robin E., *Dirty Words: The Rhetoric of Public Sex Education, 1870–1924.* Urbana: University of Illinois Press, 2010.

Jerome, Fred. *The Einstein File: The FBI's Secret War against the World's Most Famous Scientist.* Montreal: Baraka Books, 2018.

Johnson, Sylvester A., and Steven Weitzman, eds. *The FBI and Religion: Faith and National Security before and after 9/11.* Oakland: University of California Press, 2017.

———. "'True Faith and Allegiance'—Religion and the FBI." In Johnson and Weitzman, *The FBI and Religion: Faith and National Security before and after 9/11*, 1–16.

Jones, Richard Seelye. *A History of the American Legion.* New York: Bobbs-Merrill Co., 1946.

Josephson, Harold. *James T. Shotwell and the Rise of Internationalism in America.* Rutherford, NJ: Fairleigh Dickinson University Press, 1975.

"Judge Knox's Order Frees 9 Radicals." *New York Times*, January 16, 1920: 3.

Kaplan, Amy. *The Social Construction of American Realism.* Chicago: University of Chicago Press, 1988.

"Karpis Quit 'Like Rat,' Says Chief of G-Men." *(Pittsburgh) Sun-Telegraph*, May 3, 1936. Record Group 65, Entry 49, Box 22, NARA–CP.

Katznelson, Ira. *Fear Itself: The New Deal and the Origins of Our Time.* New York: Liveright Publishing, 2013.

Keen, Mike Forrest. *Stalking the Sociological Imagination: J. Edgar Hoover's Surveillance of American Sociology.* Westport, CT: Greenwood Press, 1999.

Keenan, Joseph B. "Uncle Sam Presses His New War on Crime." *New York Times*, August 20, 1933: 1.

Kennan, George, to James Byrnes ["Long Telegram"]. February 22, 1946. Elsey Papers, Harry S. Truman Library [hereafter HSTL]. http://www.trumanlibrary.org.

Keohane, Robert O. "Realism, Neorealism, and the Study of World Politics." In *Neorealism and Its Critics*, edited by Robert O. Keohane, 1–23. New York: Columbia University Press, 1986.

Kessler, Ronald. *The Bureau: The Secret History of the FBI*. New York: St. Martin's Press, 2003.

Kimble, James J. "Whither Propaganda? Agonism and 'The Engineering of Consent.'" *Quarterly Journal of Speech* 91, no. 2 (2005): 203–16.

Kirby, Dianne. "J. Edgar Hoover, the FBI, and the Religious Cold War." In Johnson and Weitzman, *The FBI and Religion: Faith and National Security before and after 9/11*, 67–84.

Kirchwey, Freda. "End the Inquisition!" *The Nation*, July 31, 1943: 116–17.

Knebel, Fletcher. "J. Edgar Hoover: The Cop and the Man." *Look* magazine, May 31, 1955: 33.

Lake, Marilyn, and Henry Reynolds. *Drawing the Global Colour Line: White Men's Countries and the International Challenge of Racial Equality*. Cambridge: Cambridge University Press, 2008.

Lapid, Yosef. "The Third Debate: On the Prospects of International Theory in a Post-Positivist Era." *International Studies Quarterly* 33, no. 3 (1989): 235–54.

"Lawyers Denounce Raids on Radicals." *New York Times*, May 28, 1920: 6.

Leab, Daniel J., ed. *Federal Bureau of Investigation Confidential Files: Communist Activity in the Entertainment Industry*. Bethesda, MD: University Publications of America, 1991.

Lenz, Fritz. "The Inheritance of Intellectual Gifts." In *Human Heredity*, by Erwin Baur, Eugen Fisher, and Fritz Lenz, translated by Eden Paul and Cedar Paul, 565–700. New York: Macmillan, 1931.

Lester, J. W. H. Drane. "Modern Trends in Criminology in the United States of America." June 7–10, 1937 (International Criminal Police Commission). Record Group 60, Entry 132, Box 12, File: "Mr. Hoover's Speeches," NARA-CP.

Leverenz, David. *Paternalism Incorporated: Fables of American Fatherhood, 1865–1940.* Ithaca, NY: Cornell University Press, 2003.

"Lewis Demands Full Negro Rights; Lashes Warmakers, Denounces FBI." *Daily Worker*, April 27, 1940. Record Group 65, Entry 49, Box 77, NARA-CP.

Lieven, Anatol. *America Right or Wrong: An Anatomy of American Nationalism.* Oxford: Oxford University Press, 2012.

Lippmann, Walter. *An Inquiry into the Principles of the Good Society.* Boston: Little, Brown and Co., 1937.

———. *Liberty and the News.* 1920; repr., Princeton, NJ: Princeton University Press, 2008.

———. *Public Opinion.* New York: Wicker Harcourt and Brace, 1922.

Lombroso, Cesare. *Crime, Its Causes and Remedies.* Boston: Little, Brown and Co., 1911.

———. *Criminal Man.* Translated by Mary Gibson, Nicole Hahn Rafter, and Mark Seymour. Durham, NC: Duke University Press, 2006.

Lombroso, Gina. *Criminal Man, According to the Classification of Cesare Lombroso.* Montclair, NJ: Patterson Smith, 1972.

Loseff, Lev. *On the Beneficence of Censorship: Aesopian Language in Modern Russian Language.* Translated by Lane Bobko. Munich: Sagner, 1984.

The Louis Nichols Official and Confidential File and the Clyde Tolson Personal File. Reel 11, File: "Smear Campaign." Bethesda, MD: University Publications of America, 1990.

"Louis Post Defends Rulings on Aliens." *New York Times*, May 9, 1920: 12.

Lowenthal, Max. *The Federal Bureau of Investigation.* New York: Harcourt Brace Jovanovich, 1950.

Lowitt, Richard. *George W. Norris: The Triumph of a Progressive, 1933–1944.* Chicago: University of Illinois Press, 1978.

Lucaites, John Louis, and Celeste Condit. "Re-Constructing Narrative Theory: A Functional Perspective." *Journal of Communication* (Autumn 1985): 90–108.

MacDonnell, Francis. *Insidious Foes: The Axis Fifth Column and the American Home Front.* New York: Oxford University Press, 1995.

Maddux, Thomas R. "Red Fascism, Brown Bolshevism: The American Image of Totalitarianism in the 1930s." *The Historian* 40 (1977): 75–93.

Marcantonio, Vito. "Statement." *Congressional Record*, 76th Cong., 3d sess., January 11, 1940.

Marshall, Thomas R. "Americanism." In *Trestle Board Magazine*, edited by Benjamin Franklin Bledsoe (March 1920): 36.

——. "The Creed of a Great Vice-President Believes We Have Finest System of Government Ever Ordained." *Masonic Historiology* 3, no. 27 (1944): 105–7.

Marty, Martin E. *Modern American Religion*. Vol. 2, *The Noise of Conflict, 1919–1941*. Chicago: University of Chicago Press, 1986.

Max Lowenthal Papers, 1855-1975. Described by Susan Hoffman. Minneapolis: University of Minnesota Archives, 2011.

Maxwell, William J. *F.B. Eyes: How J. Edgar Hoover's Ghostreaders Framed African American Literature*. Princeton, NJ: Princeton University Press, 2015.

May, Elaine Tyler. *Homeward Bound: American Families in the Cold War Era*. New York: Basic Books, 2008.

McCamy, James L. *Government Publicity: Its Practice in Federal Administration*. Chicago: University of Chicago Press, 1939.

McClymer, John F. "The Federal Government and the Americanization Movement, 1915–24." *Prologue* 10, no. 1 (Spring 1978): 22–36.

McCumber, John. *The Philosophy Scare: The Politics of Reason in the Early Cold War*. Chicago: University of Chicago Press, 2016.

McGee, Brian R. "Rehabilitating Emotion: The Troublesome Case of the Ku Klux Klan." *Argumentation and Advocacy* 34 (1998): 173–88.

——. "Rhetoric and Race in the Progressive Era: Imperialism, Reform, and the Ku Klux Klan." In Hogan, *Rhetoric and Reform in the Progressive Era*, 311–38.

——. "Speaking about the Other: W. E. B. Du Bois Responds to the Klan." *Southern Communication Journal* 63, no. 3 (1998): 208–19.

McKinley, William. "Inaugural Address" of March 4, 1897. In *A Compilation of the Messages and Papers of the Presidents*, 6227–39. New York: Bureau of National Literature, 1917.

McVicar, Michael J. "Apostles of Deceit: Ecumenism, Fundamentalism, Surveillance, and the Contested Loyalties of Protestant Clergy during the Cold War." In Johnson and Weitzman, *The FBI and Religion: Faith and National Security before and after 9/11*, 85–107.

Medhurst, Martin J. "Truman's Rhetorical Reticence, 1945–1947: An Interpretive Essay." *Quarterly Journal of Speech* 74 (1988): 52–70.

Merkle, Judith A. *Management and Ideology: The Legacy of the International Scientific Management Movement.* Berkeley: University of California Press, 1980.

Meyer, John W., and Brian Rowan. "Institutionalized Organizations: Formal Structure as Myth and Ceremony." *American Journal of Sociology* 83, no. 2 (September 1977): 340–63.

Miller, Wilbur R. "From Old Cap to Nick Carter; Or, Images of Crime and Criminal Justice in American Dime Novel Detective Stories." In *Crime and Culture*, edited by Amy Gilman Srebnick and René Lévy, 196–213. Burlington, VT: Ashgate Publishing, 2005.

"Mine Workers Accuse G-men of Nazi Tactics." *(Birmingham, AL) Southern News Almanac*, May 16, 1940. Record Group 65, Entry 49, Box 77, NARA–CP.

Mirowski, Philip, and Dieter Plehwe, eds. *The Road from Mont Pèlerin: The Making of the Neoliberal Thought Collective*. Cambridge, MA: Harvard University Press, 2009.

Mock, James R., and Cedric Larson. *Words That Won the War*. Princeton, NJ: Princeton University Press, 1939.

Montrose, Louis A. "Professing the Renaissance: The Poetics and Politics of Culture." In *The New Historicism*, edited by H. Aram Veeser, 240–47. New York: Routledge, 1989.

"More Spy Ring Arrests Expected Momentarily by F.B.I. Agents." *Washington Post*, February 27, 1938: 1.

Morgan, Ted. *Reds: McCarthyism in Twentieth-Century America.* New York: Random House, 2004.

Morgenthau, Hans J. "Another 'Great Debate': The National Interest of the United States." *American Political Science Review* 46, no. 4 (December 1952): 970–93.

Morris, Charles E., III. "Pink Herring and the Fourth Persona: J. Edgar Hoover's Sex Crime Panic." *Quarterly Journal of Speech* 88, no. 2 (2002): 228–45.

Morris, Pam. *Realism.* New York: Routledge, 2003.

Motion Picture Alliance for the Preservation of American Ideals. *Screen Guide for Americans*. Beverly Hills, CA: Motion Picture Alliance for the Preservation of American Ideals, 1947. https://archive.lib.msu.edu/DMC/AmRad/screenguideamericans.pdf.

"Mr. Jackson and the FBI." *New Republic*, April 8, 1940: 455–60.

Murphy, Kevin P. *Political Manhood: Red Bloods, Mollycoddles, and the Politics of Progressive Era Reform*. New York: Columbia University Press, 2008.

Nadel, Alan. *Containment Culture: American Narratives, Postmodernism, and the Atomic Age*. Durham, NC: Duke University Press, 1995.

Nardone v. U.S., 302 S. Ct 378 (1937).

Nardone v. U.S., 308 S. Ct 338 (1939).

National Commission on Law Observance and Enforcement. *Report on Crime and the Foreign Born*. Washington, DC: U.S. Government Printing Office, 1931.

———. *Report on Lawlessness in Law Enforcement*. Washington, DC: U.S. Government Printing Office, 1931.

———. *Report on Penal Institutions, Probation, and Parole*. Washington, DC: U.S. Government Printing Office, 1931.

———. *Report on Police*. Washington, DC: U.S. Government Printing Office, 1931.

———. *Report on the Causes of Crime*. Vols. 1 and 2. Washington, DC: U.S. Government Printing Office, 1931.

———. *Report on the Child Offender in the Federal System of Justice*. Washington, DC: U.S. Government Printing Office, 1931.

———. *Report on the Enforcement of the Deportation Laws of the United States*. Washington, DC: U.S. Government Printing Office, 1931.

National Popular Government League. *To the American People: Report upon the Illegal Practices of the Department of Justice*. Washington, DC: National Popular Government League, 1920.

Neutrality Act of 1937. 75th Cong., 1st sess., January 22, 1937.

Newlin, Keith. *The Oxford Handbook of American Literary Naturalism*. Oxford: Oxford University Press, 2011.

Newton, Michael. *The FBI Encyclopedia*. Jefferson, NC: McFarland, 2012.

Niebuhr, Reinhold. "After Capitalism, What?" *World Tomorrow*, March 1, 1933: 204–5.

———. "American Power and World Responsibility." *Christianity and Crisis* 3, no.

5 (April 1943): 3–4.

———. *The Children of Light and the Children of Darkness*. New York: Charles Scribner's Sons, 1944.

———. "Editor, *The Christian Century*." *Christian Century*, March 15, 1933: 363.

———. *An Interpretation of Christian Ethics*. New York: Harper & Brothers, 1935.

———. *Moral Man and Immoral Society: A Study in Ethics and Politics*. New York: Scribner's, 1932.

———. *The Nature and Destiny of Man*. Vol. 1, *Human Nature*. New York: Charles Scribner's Sons, 1941.

———. "Zeal without Knowledge." In *Beyond Tragedy*, 230–45. New York: Charles Scribner's Sons, 1937.

Nixon, Richard M. "Buffalo Rally, Buffalo, NY." October 7, 1968. PPS File 208, Box 100, folder: Oct. 7, 1968, Buffalo Rally, Buffalo, NY, p. 9, Richard M. Nixon Presidential Library and Museum.

Nordau, Max. *Degeneration*. New York: D. Appleton, 1892.

Norris, Frank. "A Case for Lombroso." In *The Apprenticeship Writings of Frank Norris*, vol. 2, *1897-1898*, 128–30. Philadelphia: American Philosophical Society, 1996.

———. "An Opening for Novelists: Great Opportunities for Fiction Writers in San Francisco." *The Wave* (May 22, 1897). In *The Apprenticeship Writings of Frank Norris: 1896-1898*, edited by Joseph R. McElrath Jr. and Douglas K. Burgess, 29–30. Philadelphia: American Philosophical Society, 1996.

Norris, George W. "Statement." *Congressional Record*, 76th Cong. 3d sess., February 26, 1940.

———. "Statement." *Congressional Record*, 76th Cong. 3d sess., May 7, 1940.

O'Gorman, Ned. *The Iconoclastic Imagination: Image, Catastrophe, and Economy in America from the Kennedy Assassination to September 11*. Chicago: University of Chicago Press, 2015.

Old, James Paul. "Social Justice." In *Encyclopedia of American Religion and Politics*, edited by Paul A. Djupe and Laura R. Olson, 420–21. New York: Facts on File, 2003.

O'Reilly, Kenneth. "The FBI and the Origins of McCarthyism." *Historian* 45, no. 3 (1983): 372–93.

———, ed. *Federal Bureau of Investigation Confidential Files: McCarthy Era Blacklisting of School Teachers, College Professors, and Other Public Employees; The FBI Responsibilities Program File and the Dissemination of Information Policy File.* Bethesda, MD: University Publications of America, 1989.

———. *Hoover and the Un-Americans.* Philadelphia: Temple University Press, 1983.

———. "Liberal Values, the Cold War, and American Intellectuals: The Trauma of the Alger Hiss Case." In *Beyond the Hiss Case: The FBI, Congress, and the Cold War*, edited by Athan G. Theoharis, 309–40. Philadelphia: Temple University Press, 1982.

———. "A New Deal for the FBI: The Roosevelt Administration, Crime Control, and National Security." In *Journal of American History* 69, no. 3 (December 1982): 646–66.

———. "The Roosevelt Administration and Black America: Federal Surveillance Policy and Civil Rights during the New Deal and World War II." *Phylon* 48, no. 1 (1987): 12–25.

———. "The Roosevelt Administration and Legislative-Executive Conflict: The FBI vs. The Dies Committee." *Congress and the Presidency* 10, no. 1 (Spring 1983): 79–93.

Orwell, George. "Boys' Weeklies." In *The Collected Essays, Journalism and Letters of George Orwell*, vol. 1, edited by Sonia Orwell and Ian Angus, 475–77. New York: Harcourt, Brace and World, 1968.

Palmer, A. Mitchell. "The Case against the 'Reds.'" *Forum* 63 (1920): 173–85.

"Palmer Criticizes Critics." *New York Times*, June 3, 1920: 7.

"Palmer Pledges 'War on Radicals.'" *New York Times*, January 1, 1920: 17.

Parry-Giles, Shawn. *The Rhetorical Presidency, Propaganda, and the Cold War, 1945-1955.* Westport, CT: Praeger, 2002.

Paterson, Thomas G. *Meeting the Communist Threat.* New York: Oxford University Press, 1988.

Patterson, Charles. *Eternal Treblinka: Our Treatment of Animals and the Holocaust.* New York: Lantern Books, 2002.

Pincus, Walter. "The Bureau's Budget: A Source of Power." In *Investigating the FBI*, edited by Pat Watters and Stephen Gillers, 70–85. New York: Doubleday and Co., 1973.

Pizer, Donald. *American Naturalism and the Jews: Garland, Norris, Dreiser, Wharton, and Cather.* Urbana: University of Illinois Press, 2008.

——. *The Novels of Frank Norris*. New York: Haskell House Publishers, 1973.

Plehwe, Dieter. "Introduction." In Mirowski and Plehwe, *The Road from Mont Pèlerin: The Making of the Neoliberal Thought Collective*, 1–45.

Plehwe, Dieter, Bernhard Walpen, and Gisela Newnhöffer. *Neoliberal Hegemony: A Global Critique*. New York: Routledge, 2006.

Pliley, Jessica R. *Policing Sexuality: The Mann Act and the Making of the FBI*. Cambridge, MA: Harvard University Press, 2014.

Postman, Neil. *Amusing Ourselves to Death: Public Discourse in the Age of Show Business*. New York: Penguin Books, 2006.

Potter, Claire Bond. "Queer Hoover: Sex, Lies, and Political History." *Journal of the History of Sexuality* 15, no. 3 (2006): 355–81.

——. *War on Crime: Bandits, G-Men, and the Politics of Mass Culture*. New Brunswick, NJ: Rutgers University Press, 1998.

Powers, Richard Gid. "The FBI in American Popular Culture." In Theoharis, *The FBI: A Comprehensive Reference Guide*, 261–307.

——. *G-Men: Hoover's FBI in American Popular Culture*. Carbondale: Southern Illinois University Press, 1983.

——. *Not without Honor*. New York: Free Press, 1995.

——. *Secrecy and Power: The Life of J. Edgar Hoover*. New York: Free Press, 1987.

Prasad, Pushkala. "The Protestant Ethic and the Myths of the Frontier: Cultural Imprints, Organizational Structuring, and Workplace Diversity." In *Managing the Organizational Melting Pot*, edited by Pushkala Prasad, Albert J. Mills, Michael Elmes, and Anshuman Prasad, 129–47. Thousand Oaks, CA: Sage Publications, 1997.

"Premier Commands All Madrid Forces; 'Commissioner for War' Named to Control and Harmonize Militia and Army; Gas Service Is Shut Off; City Is Also without Water at Night—Capital Prepares Grimly for Ordeal." *New York Times*, October 17, 1936: 9.

President's Committee on Civil Rights. *To Secure These Rights*. New York: Simon and Schuster, 1947.

Preston, William. *Aliens and Dissenters: Federal Suppression of Radicals*. New York: Harper and Row, 1963.

Purpura, Philip P. *Criminal Justice: An Introduction*. Boston: Butterworth-Heinemann, 1997.

"Quick Deportation of Reds Is Likely." *New York Times*, January 27, 1920: 1.

"Raids Ordered by Palmer." *New York Times*, November 14, 1919: 1.

Rasmussen, Larry L. "Introduction: A Few Facets of Niebuhr's Thought." In *Reinhold Niebuhr: Theologian of Public Life*, edited by Larry L. Rasmussen, 1–23. Minneapolis: First Fortress Press, 1991.

Reagan, Ronald. *An American Life*. New York: Simon and Schuster, 1990.

"'Respectable' Citizens Who Shield 'Rats' the Real Public Enemies." *Milwaukee Journal*, May 28, 1936. Record Group 65, Entry 49, Box 25, NARA-CP.

"Retract Charges Demands Palmer." *New York Times*, June 5, 1920: 27.

Roach, Joseph R. "Darwin's Passion: The Language of Expression on Nature's Stage." *Discourse* 13, no. 1 (Fall/Winter 1990–91): 40–58.

Robbins, L. H. "New Prison Ideals in a New-Type Prison." *New York Times*, January 15, 1933: SM8.

Robins, Natalie. *Alien Ink: The FBI's War on Freedom of Expression*. New York: William Morrow, 1992.

Roffman, Peter, and Jim Purdy. "HUAC and the End of an Era." In *Hollywood's America: Twentieth-Century America through Film*, edited by Steven Mintz and Randy W. Roberts, 211–18. Malden, MA: Wiley-Blackwell, 2010.

Roosevelt, Eleanor. "We Must Preserve Individual's Right to Be Different." *Washington Daily News*, March 29, 1947. Record Group 65, Entry 49, Box 96, NARA-CP.

Roosevelt, Franklin D. "Address to the Conference on Crime Called by the Attorney General of the United States, December 10, 1934." In *The Public Papers and Addresses of Franklin D. Roosevelt*, vol. 3: 492–93. New York: Random House, 1938.

———. "Annual Message to Congress, January 3, 1934." In *The Public Papers and Addresses of Franklin D. Roosevelt*, vol. 3: 10–19. New York: Random House, 1938.

———. "Appropriations for National Defense." May 16, 1940. In *The Public Papers and Addresses of Franklin D. Roosevelt*, vol. 1940, *War—and Aid to the Democracies*, 198. New York: Macmillan Co., 1941.

———. "Fireside Chat on National Defense, May 26, 1940." In *The Public Papers and Addresses of Franklin D. Roosevelt*, vol. 1940: 237–48. New York: Macmillan, 1941.

——. "Inaugural Address, March 4, 1933." In *The Public Papers and Addresses of Franklin D. Roosevelt: The Year of Crisis, 1933*, 13–19. New York: Random House, 1950.

——. "A Letter to a Conference of Law Enforcement Officials on Some Problems of National Defense, July 31, 1940." In *The Public Papers and Addresses of Franklin D. Roosevelt*, vol. 9: 315–16. New York: Macmillan, 1941.

——. "Police Cooperation." January 8, 1943. Record Group 65, Entry 14, Box 15, NARA-CP.

——. Press Conference 649-A, June 5, 1940. In *Complete Presidential Press Conferences of Franklin D. Roosevelt*, vol. 15: 484. New York: Da Capo Press, 1972.

——. "Statement on Signing Bill to Help the Federal Government Wage War on Crime and Gangsters, May 18, 1934." In *The Public Papers and Addresses of Franklin D. Roosevelt*, vol. 3: 242–44. New York: Random House, 1938.

Roosevelt, Theodore. *American Ideals*. New York: G.P. Putnam's Sons, 1897.

——. "Fourth Annual Message to Congress." In *A Compilation of the Messages and Papers of the Presidents*, 6922–24. New York: Bureau of National Literature, 1917.

——. "How Not to Help Our Poor Brother." In *The Works of Theodore Roosevelt: American Ideals: Administration-Civil Service*, 243. New York: G.P. Putnam's Sons, 1897.

——. "Latitude and Longitude among Reformers." *Century*, June 1900. In *The Strenuous Life: Essays and Addresses*, 21. Mineola, NY: Dover Publications, 2009.

——. "Remarks at Williams College, June 22, 1905." *A Compilation of the Messages and Speeches of Theodore Roosevelt, 1901-1905*, edited by Alfred Henry Lewis. Washington, DC: Bureau of National Literature and Art, 1906.

——. "Remarks to Harvard University, June 28, 1905." In *Presidential Addresses and State Papers of Theodore Roosevelt*, vol. 4: 421. New York: Collier, n.d.

——. "Remarks to the Main Convention of the Republican Party, March 1918." In *Newer Roosevelt Messages: Speeches, Letters and Magazine Articles*, edited by Eugene Thwing, 920. New York: Current Publishing Co., 1919.

——. *The Strenuous Life*. New York: Century, 1901.

——. *Theodore Roosevelt: An Autobiography*. New York: Scribner's, 1913.

——. “What ‘Americanism’ Means.” *Forum* (April 1894): 196–206.

Rosenfeld, Seth. *Subversives: The FBI’s War on Student Radicals, and Reagan’s Rise to Power.* New York: Farrar, Straus and Giroux, 2012.

Rosenfeld, Susan. “Biographies.” In Theoharis, *The FBI: A Comprehensive Reference Guide*, 357–400.

——. “Organization and Day-to-Day Activities.” In Theoharis, *The FBI: A Comprehensive Reference Guide*, 309–61.

Rossetti, Gina M. “Things Fall Apart: Degeneration and Atavism in American Literary Naturalism.” In Newlin, *The Oxford Handbook of American Literary Naturalism*, 172–81.

Rosswurm, Steve. *The FBI and the Catholic Church, 1935–1962.* Amherst: University of Massachusetts Press, 2009.

Russell, Thaddeus. *A Renegade History of the United States.* New York: Free Press, 2010.

Sbardellati, John. *J. Edgar Hoover Goes to the Movies: The FBI and the Origins of Hollywood’s Cold War.* Ithaca, NY: Cornell University Press, 2012.

Scarface. The Caddo Company, 1932.

Schmidt, Regit. *Red Scare: FBI and the Origins of Anticommunism in the United States.* Copenhagen: Museum of Tusculanum Press, 2000.

Schott, Joseph L. *No Left Turns.* New York: Praeger Publishing, 1975.

Schrecker, Ellen. *Many Are the Crimes: McCarthyism in America.* Boston: Little, Brown and Co., 1998.

Sedgwick, Ellery. *A History of the “Atlantic Monthly,” 1857–1909: Yankee Humanism at High Tide.* Amherst: University of Massachusetts Press, 1994.

Sedition Act. Public Law 150. 65th Cong., 2d sess., May 16, 1918: 553.

Seldes, George. *Lords of the Press.* New York: J. Messner, 1938.

Senate Judiciary Committee. *Charges of Illegal Practices of the Department of Justice.* 66th Cong., 3d sess., March 3, 1921.

Senate Select Committee to Study Governmental Operation. *Intelligence Activities and the Rights of Americans.* Book 2. Washington, DC: U.S. Government Printing Office, 1976.

——. *Supplementary Detailed Staff Reports on Intelligence Activities and the Rights of Americans.* Book 3. Washington, DC: U.S. Government Printing Office, 1976.

Shatz, Thomas. *Hollywood Genres: Formulas, Filmmaking, and the Studio System.* New York, McGraw-Hill, 1981.

Shotwell, James T. *The Autobiography of James T. Shotwell.* New York: Bobbs-Merrill Co., 1961.

Simpson, Andrew. "Schooling J. Edgar: The Shaping of Hoover's Legal Philosophy at The George Washington University." *Intelligencer: Journal of U.S. Intelligence Studies* (Fall 2009): 39–44.

Skrabec, Quentin, Jr. *William McKinley: Apostle of Protectionism.* New York: Algora, 2008.

"Sleuth School." *Time* magazine, August 5, 1935: 11–13.

Slotkin, Richard. *The Fatal Environment: The Myth of the Frontier in the Age of Industrialization, 1800–1890.* Norman: University of Oklahoma Press, 1985.

——. *Gunfighter Nation: The Myth of the Frontier in Twentieth-Century America.* Norman: University of Oklahoma Press, 1992.

——. "Nostalgia and Progress: Theodore Roosevelt's Myth of the Frontier." *American Quarterly* 33, no. 5 (Winter 1981): 608–37.

——. *Regeneration through Violence: The Mythology of the American Frontier, 1600–1860.* Norman: University of Oklahoma Press, 1973.

Smith, Craig R. "Ronald Reagan's Rhetorical Re-Invention of Conservatism." *Quarterly Journal of Speech* 103 (2017): 33–65.

Smith, Mack. *Realism and the Ekphrastic Tradition.* College Station: Penn State University Press, 2008.

Smith, Michael Joseph. *Realist Thought from Weber to Kissinger.* Baton Rouge: Louisiana State University, 1986.

Smith, Rogers M. *Civic Ideals: Conflicting Visions of Citizenship in U.S. History.* New Haven, CT: Yale University Press, 1997.

Southern, David W. *The Progressive Era and Race: Reaction and Reform, 1900–1917.* Wheeling, IL: Harlan Davidson, 2005.

Special Committee on Un-American Activities. *Investigation of Un-American Activities and Propaganda.* H.R. 2, 76th Cong., 1st sess., January 3, 1939.

Special Committee to Investigate Communist Activities in the United States. *Investigation of Communist Propaganda.* H.R. 2290, 71st, Cong., 3d sess., January 17, 1931.

Special Committee to Investigate Nazi and Other Propaganda. *Investigation of Nazi and Other Propaganda*. H.R. 153, 74th Cong., 1st sess., February 15, 1935.

Southern, David W. *The Progressive Era and Race: Reaction and Reform, 1900–1917.* Wheeling, IL: Harlan Davidson, 2005.

Sproule, J. Michael. *Propaganda and Democracy*. Cambridge: Cambridge University Press, 1997.

Steele, Richard W. "Franklin D. Roosevelt and His Foreign Policy Critics." *Political Science Quarterly* 94, no. 1 (Spring 1979): 1–20.

Stein, Melissa. "'Nature Is the Author of Such Restriction': Science, Ethnological Medicine, and Jim Crow." In *The Folly of Jim Crow: Rethinking the Segregated South*, edited by Stephanie Cole and Natalie J. Ring, 124–49. College Station: Texas A&M University Press, 2012.

Stone, Ronald H. *Reinhold Niebuhr: Prophet to Politicians*. New York: Abingdon Press, 1972.

Sullivan, William C., with Bill Brown. *The Bureau: My Thirty Years in Hoover's FBI.* New York: W.W. Norton and Co., 1979.

Survey by Gallup Organization, May 29–June 4, 1938. iPOLL Databank, Roper Center for Public Opinion Research, University of Connecticut. https://ropercenter.cornell.edu/.

Survey by Gallup Organization, January 22–January 27, 1939. iPOLL Databank, Roper Center for Public Opinion Research, University of Connecticut. https://ropercenter.cornell.edu/.

Survey by Gallup Organization, January 28–February 1, 1950. iPOLL Databank, Roper Center for Public Opinion Research, University of Connecticut. https://ropercenter.cornell.edu/.

Svonkin, Stuart. *Jews against Prejudice: American Jews and the Fight for Civil Liberties.* New York: Columbia University Press, 1997.

Swearingen, C. Jan. "*Ethos:* Imitation, Impersonation, and Voice." In Baumlin and Baumlin, *Ethos: New Essays in Rhetorical and Critical Theory*, 115–48.

Taylor, Trevor. "Utopianism." In *International Relations: British and American Perspectives*, edited by Steve Smith, 93–118. Oxford: British International Studies Association, 1985.

"Text of President Truman's Speech on New Foreign Policy." *New York Times*, March 13, 1947: 2.

Theoharis, Athan G. "A Brief History of the FBI's Role and Powers." In Theoharis, *The FBI: A Comprehensive Reference Guide*, 1–30.

———. *Chasing Spies*. Chicago: Ivan R. Dee, 2002.

———. *A Culture of Secrecy: The Government versus the People's Right to Know*. Lawrence: University Press of Kansas, 1998.

———, ed. *The FBI: A Comprehensive Reference Guide*. Phoenix: Oryx Press, 1999.

———. *The FBI and American Democracy: A Brief Critical History*. Lawrence: University Press of Kansas, 2004.

———. "The FBI and the American Legion Contact Program, 1940–1966." *Political Science Quarterly* 100, no. 2 (1985): 273–85.

———. "The FBI, the Roosevelt Administration, and the 'Subversive' Press." *Journalism History* 19, no. 1 (1993): 1–17.

———. *J. Edgar Hoover, Sex, and Crime*. Chicago: Ivan R. Dee, 1995.

———. *Seeds of Repression: Harry S. Truman and the Origins of McCarthyism*. Chicago: Quadrangle Books, 1971.

———. *Spying on Americans: Political Surveillance from Hoover to the Huston Plan*. Philadelphia: Temple University Press, 1978.

———. *The Truman Presidency: The Origins of the Imperial Presidency and the National Security State*. New York: Earl M. Coleman Enterprises, 1979.

Thompson, Gary R. *Reading the American Novel, 1865–1914*. Malden, MA: Wiley-Blackwell, 2012.

"391 Alien Reds Now under Arrest." *New York Times*, November 11, 1919: 1.

"Tons of 'Red' Papers Bare Anarchists Plot." *Washington Post*, January 4, 1920: 1.

Truman, Harry S. "Annual Message to the Congress on the State of the Union," January 7, 1948. In *Public Papers of the Presidents of the United States: Harry S. Truman, January 1 to December 31, 1948*. Washington, DC: U.S. Government Printing Office, 1964.

———. "The President's News Conference of August 5, 1948." In *Public Papers of the Presidents of the United States: Harry S. Truman, January 1 to December 31, 1948*. Washington, DC: U.S. Government Printing Office, 1966.

———. "The President's Press and Radio Conference." March 30, 1950. David D. Lloyd Files, Box 5, HSTL.

———. "The President's Special Conference with the Association of Radio News Analysts, May 13, 1947." In *Public Papers of the Presidents of the United*

States: Harry S. Truman, January 1 to December 31, 1947. Washington, DC: U.S. Government Printing Office, 1963.

———. "Special Message to Congress on Greece and Turkey: The Truman Doctrine, March 12, 1947." In *Public Papers of the Presidents of the United States: Harry S. Truman, January 1 to December 31, 1947.* Washington, DC: U.S. Government Printing Office, 1963.

———. "Special Message to the Congress Presenting a 21-Point Program for the Reconversion Period, September 6, 1945." In *Public Papers of the Presidents of the United States: Harry S. Truman*, April 12 to December 31, 1945. Washington, DC: U.S. Government Printing Office, 1961.

Tome, Nancy. "The Private Side of Public Health: Sanitary Science, Domestic Hygiene, and Germ Theory, 1870–1900." In *Sickness and Health in America*, edited by Judith Walzer Leavitt and Ronald L. Numbers, 506–28. Madison: University of Wisconsin Press, 1997.

"The Truth about Hoover." *Time* magazine, December 22, 1975: 14.

Tucker, Herbert F. *A New Companion to Victorian Literature and Culture.* Malden, MA: Wiley-Blackwell, 2014.

Tucker, Ray. "Hist! Who's That?" *Collier's*, August 19, 1933: 15, 49.

———. "Ray Tucker's Letter." *Brooklyn Eagle*, October 22, 1946. Record Group 65, Entry 49, Box 94, NARA-CP.

Tulis, Jeffrey K. *The Rhetorical Presidency.* Princeton, NJ: Princeton University Press, 1987.

Turner, William W. *Hoover's FBI: The Men and the Myth.* Los Angeles: Sherbourne Press, 1970.

Underhill, Stephen M. "J. Edgar Hoover's Domestic Propaganda: Narrating the Spectacle of the Karpis Arrest." *Western Journal of Communication* 76, no. 4 (2012): 438–57.

———. "J. Edgar Hoover, Speech before the House Committee on Un-American Activities (26 March 1947)." *Voices of Democracy* 3 (2008): 139–61.

———. "Prisoner of Context: The Truman Doctrine Speech and J. Edgar Hoover's Rhetorical Realism." *Rhetoric & Public Affairs* 20, no. 3 (2017): 453–88.

———. "Urban Jungle, Ferguson: Rhetorical Homology and Institutional Critique." *Quarterly Journal of Speech* 102, no. 4 (2016): 396–417.

Ungar, Sanford J. *FBI: An Uncensored Look behind the Walls*. Boston: Little, Brown and Co., 1976.

"U.S.-British Ship Deal Is Assailed and Commended: Varying Views Voiced by Congress Members." *Chicago Daily Tribune*, September 4, 1940: 6.

U.S. Department of Justice. *FBI, American Legion Contact Program*. Wilmington, DE: Scholarly Resources, 1984.

Valenzano, Joseph M., III, and Erika Engstrom. "Cowboys, Angels, and Demons: American Exceptionalism and the Frontier Myth in the CW's *Supernatural*." *Communication Quarterly* 62, no. 5 (2014): 552–68.

Van Horn, Rob, and Philip Mirowski. "The Rise of the Chicago School of Economics and the Birth of Neoliberalism." In Mirowski and Plehwe, *The Road from Mont Pèlerin: The Making of the Neoliberal Thought Collective*, 139–81.

Vasquez, John A. *The Power of Power Politics: A Critique*. New Brunswick, NJ: Rutgers University Press, 1983.

Volstead Act. October 27, 1919. 41 Stat. 306.

Walcutt, Charles C. *American Literary Naturalism: A Divided Stream*. Minneapolis: University of Minnesota Press, 1956.

Walk East on Beacon. Columbia Pictures, 1952.

Washington, George. "Farewell Address of September 17, 1796." In *A Compilation of the Messages and Papers of the Presidents*, 209–10. New York: Bureau of National Literature, 1917.

Washington, Oliver McKee. "Laboratory for Crime." *New York Times*, July 8, 1934.

Watson, Richard L., Jr. *The Development of National Power: The United States, 1900–1919*. Boston: Houghton Mifflin, 1976.

Watson, Shevaun E. "Trying Silence: The Case of Denmark Vesey and the History of African American Rhetoric." In *Silence and Listening as Rhetorical Arts*, edited by Cheryl Glenn and Krista Ratcliffe. Carbondale: Southern Illinois University Press, 2011.

Watson, William Lynn. "'The Facts Which Go to Form This Fiction': Elizabeth Stuart Phelps's *The Silent Partner* and the Massachusetts Bureau of Labor Statistics Reports." *College Literature* 29, no. 4 (Fall 2002): 6–25.

"Wheeler Committee Joins Demand for Probe of FBI." *Great Falls Tribune*, March 13, 1940. Record Group 65, Entry 49, Box 75, NARA-CP.

Whitney, R. M. *Reds in America.* New York: Beckwith Press, 1924.

Weinstein, Allan, and Alexander Vassiliev. *The Haunted Wood.* New York: Modern Library, 2000.

Weldes, Jutta. *Constructing National Interests: The United States and the Cuban Missile Crisis.* Minneapolis: University of Minnesota Press, 1999.

Whitney, R. M. *Reds in America.* New York: Beckwith Press, 1924.

Wicker, Tom. "Nobody Dares to Pick His Successor." *Life* magazine, April 9, 1971: 45–48.

——. "What Have They Done since They Shot Dillinger?" *New York Times Magazine*, December 28, 1969: 6–10.

Williams, Churchill. "Red Blood in Fiction." *World's Work* 6, no. 1 (1903): 3694–700.

Williams, Edward Huntington. "Negro Cocaine 'Fiends' are a New Southern Menace: Murder and Insanity Increasing among Lower Class Blacks Because They Have Taken to 'Sniffing' since Deprived of Whisky by Prohibition." *New York Times*, February 8, 1914: SM12.

Wilson, Andrew. "District of Columbia." *Proceedings of the Fifteenth National Convention of the Anti-Saloon League of America: Twenty Year Jubilee Convention*, Columbus, Ohio, November 10–13, 1913.

Wilson, James Q. *The Investigators: Managing FBI and Narcotics Agents.* New York: Basic Books, 1978.

Wilson, Kirt H. *The Reconstruction Desegregation Debate: The Politics of Equality and the Rhetoric of Place.* East Lansing: Michigan State University Press, 2002.

Wilson, Woodrow. "An Address to a Joint Session of Congress: January 8, 1918." In *The Papers of Woodrow Wilson*, vol. 45, *November 11, 1917–January 15, 1918*, edited by Arthur S. Link, 536–38. Princeton, NJ: Princeton University Press, 1984.

——. "A Flag Day Address." June 14, 1917. In *The Papers of Woodrow Wilson*, vol. 42: 498–99. Princeton, NJ: Princeton University Press, 1983.

Zangrando, Robert L. "The NAACP and a Federal Antilynching Bill, 1934–1940." *Journal of Negro History* 50 (1965): 106–17.

Index